W9-BLR-629

ESV ERICH
SCHMIDT
VERLAG

GRUNDLAGEN DER ANGLISTIK UND AMERIKANISTIK

Herausgegeben von Rüdiger Ahrens und Edgar W. Schneider

Band 29

Understanding English-German Contrasts

4., neu bearbeitete Auflage

von
Ekkehard König
und
Volker Gast

ERICH SCHMIDT VERLAG

Bibliografische Information der Deutschen Bibliothek
Die Deutsche Bibliothek verzeichnet diese Publikation in der
Deutschen Nationalbibliografie; detaillierte bibliografische Daten
sind im Internet über dnb.ddb.de abrufbar.

Weitere Informationen zu diesem Titel finden Sie im Internet unter
ESV.info/978 3 503 18142 1

ISBN 978 3 503 18142 1

Alle Rechte vorbehalten
© Erich Schmidt Verlag GmbH & Co., Berlin 2018
www.ESV.info

Dieses Papier erfüllt die Frankfurter Forderungen
der Deutschen Bibliothek und der Gesellschaft für das Buch
bezüglich der Alterungsbeständigkeit
und entspricht sowohl den strengen Bestimmungen der US Norm
Ansi/Niso Z 39.48-1992 als auch der ISO-Norm 9706.

Druck und Bindung: Strauss, Mörlenbach

Preface to the fourth edition

While the third edition of this book, published in 2012, represented a considerable extension of the previous editions from 2007 and 2009 (with three additional chapters, Chapter 6 on modals, Chapter 15 on compounding and Chapter 16 on derivation), the present edition differs less from its predecessor as far as matters of content are concerned. We have primarily revised the two 'peripheral' chapters of the book, the introduction (Chapter 1) and the conclusions (Chapter 18). These chapters have been extended with the aim of broadening the perspective a bit and taking some of the more recent work in contrastive (English-German) linguistics into account. The field is thriving and continuously extending in various directions, which we take as evidence for the success of the contrastive approach after its dissociation from the field of language pedagogy (cf. Chapter 1). On a theoretical level, there is some recent work dealing with some of the explanatory questions raised by Hawkins (1986) (cf. Chapter 18). Moreover, we have updated the list of references and the 'Further reading' section of each chapter. For some of the literature used by us new editions have appeared (e.g. Cruttenden 2014, Carr 2015), and there are some entirely new publications that are relevant to our book, e.g. Bauer *et al.* (2013), a handbook of English morphology, Schäfer (2016), a new grammar of German, and Gunkel *et al.* (2017a,b), a grammar of the German noun (phrase) which takes a comparative/European perspective, to name just three of the most comprehensive works.

Many colleagues have helped us to improve this book since the publication of the first edition in 2007. The present editon has primarily benefited from comments sent to us by John Hawkins (Davis) and Julia Schlüter (Bamberg). We are very grateful to them for pointing out some mistakes and inaccuracies that had escaped our attention.

Freiburg/Olomouc, 31.05.2018
Ekkehard König, Volker Gast

Table of Contents

List of Figures

List of Tables

1 Introduction

1.1 The contrastive programme

The programme of 'contrastive linguistics' (or 'contrastive analysis') was formulated from the 1950s onwards with the primary objective of making foreign language teaching more efficient (cf. Fries 1945, Weinreich 1953, Lado 1957, Alatis 1968, Wardhaugh 1970, Nickel 1971, Gradman 1973, Dirven 1976, Fisiak 1981, James 1980, Aarts 1982, among many others). Its basic assumptions can roughly be summarized as follows:

- Second language acquisition differs fundamentally from first language acquisition, especially in those cases where a second language is learned on the basis of the full mastery of the mother tongue.
- Similarities between the first language and the language to be learned will cause no difficulties ('positive transfer'), but differences will, due to 'negative transfer' (or 'interference'). The student's learning task can therefore roughly be defined as the sum of the differences between the two languages.
- A systematic comparison between mother tongue and foreign language to be learned will reveal both similarities and contrasts.
- On the basis of such a comparison it will be possible to predict or even rank learning difficulties and to develop strategies for making foreign language teaching more efficient.

It can hardly be denied that these assumptions have a certain plausibility (cf. also more recent publications such as Kortmann 1996, James 2005, Mair 2005). Especially in pronunciation we can often distinguish native speakers from foreign learners with relative ease. But then, we may acquire a near-native competence in a foreign language if we learn it at an early age and get a sufficient amount of exposure. This is only one of many points in which the basic hypotheses of the 'contrastive programme' were too undifferentiated and too simplistic, so that it came as no surprise that the programme was seriously criticized and challenged before long. Critics of this programme pointed out that it failed to differentiate between various types of second language acquisition (natural vs. mediated, sequential vs. simultaneous, second vs. third language, etc.), that it totally neglected the age factor, that the relations between mother tongue and language to be learned were only one of many factors entering into the learning process (Wienold 1973) and that the major learning problem could simply be ignorance rather than interference (Newmark and Reibel 1968). After some energetic attempts of implementing the contrastive programme the expectations initially invested into it were greatly disappointed and many of its adherents abandoned it in favour of empirical studies of learners' behaviour, i.e. error analysis (Corder 1967) and the study of the 'approximative systems' (Nemser 1971), or the 'interlanguages' (Selinker 1972) built up in the process of foreign language learning. Insofar as they lacked a solid foundation in learning psychology, however, such empirical studies of learners' behaviour also failed to have a major impact on the theory of second language acquisition or the teaching of foreign languages.

There was, moreover, another point in which the contrastive programme as originally formulated failed: it was never put on solid descriptive foundations. While there were some promising beginnings in the 'Contrastive Structure' series published by the University of Chicago Press (e.g. Moulton 1962, Kufner 1962), and in research projects carried out in Stuttgart ('Programm für angewandte kontrastive Sprachwissenschaft'/PAKS), Mannheim, Poznań, Zagreb, Jyväskylä and many other places, the goal of producing comprehensive and detailed comparisons for pairs of languages was never convincingly realized. Neither was the situation substantially improved by the publication of introductory surveys and collective monographs in the 1970s and 1980s (e.g. Burgschmidt and Götz 1974, Hellinger 1977, Lohnes and Hopkins 1982, Rein 1983). What we typically find in contrastive publications of this time are isolated observations about, or juxtaposed descriptions of, two languages, without any major generalizations about similarities or contrasts being made.

A fresh breeze of air was brought into the discussion by John Hawkins' monograph *A Comparative Typology of English and German: Unifying the Contrasts* (Hawkins 1986) and some subsequent work based on or referring to this book (e.g. Rohdenburg 1990, Mair 1992, Mair and Markus 1992). Hawkins severs the link between contrastive analyses of two languages and the pedagogical goals initially associated with it and regards contrastive analysis as a limiting case of a specific type of comparative linguistics, i.e. language typology. In typology a broad range of unrelated languages is compared with the aim of identifying patterns and limits of cross-linguistic variation (cf. Comrie 1989, Croft 2003, Song 2010, Moravcsik 2013, Aikhenvald and Dixon 2017). Given the enormity of the task – typological studies are often based on samples of more than 200 languages – typological comparisons typically involve only a small fragment of language structure such as constituent order, gender, reflexivity, etc. (Dryer and Haspelmath 2013). One of the major results this research programme has come up with is the demonstration that languages do not differ from each other in random and unlimited ways, but exhibit clear patterns and limits of variation that can be captured in terms of correlations or implicational relations ('If a language has property A, it will also have property B'), and in terms of implicational hierarchies, which can be regarded as chains of such implications (see for instance Corbett 2010).

A contrastive analysis can be seen as the complement of a typological study (cf. also König 1990, 1996, 2012; see also van der Auwera 2012 on contrastive investigations as 'pilot studies' for linguistic typology). Instead of comparing a large number of languages with respect to a specific subsystem or a single variant property (constituent order, case marking, passive constructions, etc.), only two languages are compared with respect to a wide variety of properties. Such comparisons may be carried out for purely theoretical reasons, e.g. if one is interested in the specific ways in which grammatical subsystems interact, or in questions concerning the connections among various contrasts between two languages. For instance, a richer inflectional morphology has been claimed to come with greater freedom of constituent order.

By taking a typological approach we can also try to subsume various contrasts under higher-level generalizations and pursue the question of whether there is a certain unity among the contrasts describable in terms of a holistic typology or characterology for the relevant languages. In addition to Hawkins (1986), recent attempts to provide answers to this question can be found in Fischer (2013), Berg (2014) and Hawkins (2018).

The 'typological turn' reflected in Hawkins (1986) and follow-up work represents an important reorientation of contrastive linguistics after the 'contrastive hypotheses' outlined on page 1 had been abandoned, but it is not the only major development in the field. In the 1980s and 1990s the range of topics covered in contrastive studies was broadened, e.g. by including matters relating to discourse studies and rhetorics (Purves 1988, Connor 1996), (cross-cultural) pragmatics (Wierzbicka 1985, 1992, Oleksy 1989), intercultural communication (Scollon and Scollon 1995) and sociolinguistics (Hellinger and Ammon 1996).

In the 1990s contrastive linguistics moreover started to extend its empirical and methodological basis by using data from multilingual corpora (e.g. translation corpora, parallel corpora; see for instance Hartmann 1996, Sinclair et al. 1996, Johansson 1998, Krug 1998, Altenberg and Granger 2002, Aijmer and Altenberg 2013). 'Contrastive Interlanguage Analysis' relies on texts produced by second language learners for the identification of learning difficulties (Granger 1996, 2015). The use of multilingual corpora has also led to a cross-fertilization of contrastive linguistics and translation studies (cf. for instance Aston 1999, Granger et al. 2003, Xiao 2010, Gast 2015). Corpus-based contrastive studies are moreover increasingly making use of methods from computational linguistics and machine translation (cf. Steiner 2017 and other contributions to Czulo and Hansen-Schirra 2017), also bringing new research topics into the picture (e.g. Kunz 2010, 2015 on nominal coreference and cohesion and Neumann 2013 on contrastive register studies).

1.2 What our book is and what it is not

While the field of contrastive linguistics has taken several turns since its beginnings in the 1950s and is far from homogeneous, any contrastive study – theoretical or applied, qualitative or quantitative – needs to be based on solid descriptive foundations, i.e. a comparison of the languages under analysis in a broad range of linguistic domains. With the publication of the first edition of the present book in 2007, as well as the extensions added and revisions made in later editions, we intended to provide such a basis, as a frame of reference and a point of departure for more specific investigations.

Our book follows the spirit of Hawkins (1986) in its comprehensive character, the focus on the linguistic system (rather than language use) and its pursuit of generalizations (rather than individual observations about similarities or differences). It has a descriptive orientation and is intended to serve as input for practical applications as well. In spite of some overlap in content it differs significantly from Hawkins (1986) and the more recent monographs by Fischer (2013) and Beck and Gergel (2014). The major focus of Hawkins (1986) is on constituent order and reordering transformations as well as extraction phenomena within and across clauses. Such aspects will be dealt with in only three chapters of our book (Chapters 11–13). Our chapter on morphology (Chapter 4), which also has a counterpart in Hawkins (1986), is more detailed, and most chapters of our book have no counterpart in Hawkins (1986) at all. Another major difference between the two books is that the comparison in this book is more semantically based than the one in Hawkins (1986). Among the two more recent monographs mentioned above, Fischer (2013) relates directly to Hawkins (1986), addressing his theoretical claims concerning processing, efficiency and complexity, and accordingly focusing on argument structure and valency. Beck and Gergel (2014) provide analyses of matters concerning syntax and sentence semantics within the framework of Generative Grammar, using the English and German data primarily for illustrative purposes.

What our book aims at is providing a comprehensive description of the major contrasts in the grammar and lexicon of English and German based on relevant comparative and non-comparative work on the two languages, both traditional and recent. In addition to that, our contrastive study is based on a variety of insights and generalizations formulated within relevant typological work. Understanding the space of variation across languages in the domain of possessive constructions (König 2001) or reflexivity (König and Siemund 2000b), for example, is extremely helpful for the task of describing the position that English and German occupy within such typologies (cf. Chapters 8 and 10).

A further characterization of what the reader can reasonably expect from this book can be given in negative terms, i.e. by spelling out what the book does not contain:

• The book does not contain comprehensive descriptions of either English or German and therefore cannot be used as a reference grammar for either of these languages. There is a broad range of reference works for both languages which can be used for this purpose (e.g. Quirk *et al.* 1985, Huddleston and Pullum 2002, Biber *et al.* 1999 for English, and Engel 1988, Zifonun *et al.* 1997, Eisenberg 2006a,b, Schäfer 2016 for German, to name just a few of the major books; cf. also Lang and Zifonun 1996, Gunkel *et al.* 2017a,b for descriptions of German from a comparative point of view). What is presented in this book is a comprehensive description of general differences between the two languages.

- Major similarities between the two languages will be mentioned only in passing and will not be discussed in much detail. English and German are both members of the Western branch of the Germanic language family and thus closely related genealogically. It is therefore to be expected that there are still features manifesting this relatedness, even though English has considerably moved away from these common roots during the last 1,500 years. For example, both languages manifest the distinction between weak (regular) and strong (irregular) verbs (e.g. Engl. *wash, washed, washed* vs. *sing, sang, sung*), and both exhibit a gradual reduction of the latter group in favour of the former.

- The focus being on major contrasts between English and German, not much will be said about minor or isolated contrasts in this book. Of course, there are many differences of this kind: For instance, in contrast to its German counterpart *eigen* the Engl. adjective *own* can only occur in combination with a possessive determiner or a genitive phrase (*ein eigenes Auto* vs. *a car of your own*), the only exception being the combination *an own goal*. Many examples of this kind could be given and some of them will come up in our questions and exercises, but they do not constitute the primary matter of the book.

- A book such as this cannot cover the whole range of variation found within English or German, but has to focus on the standard varieties. Many statements about contrasts would look very different if the whole range of variation found in English were taken into consideration (cf. Kortmann *et al.* 2004; see Siemund 2013 for a typological perspective on varieties of English). But then, our whole enterprise would hardly have been possible if such a broad perspective had been taken. We therefore decided to mention regional or social variation in English or German only in those cases where it highlights or relativizes a particular contrast (see for instance the discussion of vowels in Scottish Standard English in Chapter 2).

- Given all the restrictions mentioned so far, there will be many aspects of English or German grammar about which our book has nothing to say. This also applies to subsystems where the contrasts are fairly obvious and well-known. There are also topics, however, which we intend to cover in future editions of this book. e.g. complex sentences (adverbial clauses and complement clauses) and contrasts in information structure (e.g. topicalization structures and cleft sentences; see for instance Gast 2010, Gast and Wiechmann 2012, Gast and Levshina 2013).

- The book concentrates on the linguistic systems of English and German, not the use of specific options in discourse. We will therefore not make any quantitative statements as can be found in corpus-based contrastive publications like those mentioned above. In cases where frequencies are relevant readers will be pointed to the relevant literature with a more specific focus.

1.3 Establishing comparability

The problem of establishing comparability and of finding a 'third of comparison' (*tertium comparationis*) is a major issue in any kind of comparative work (cf. Haspelmath 2010). Typically, both functional/semantic and form-related criteria are applied. For example, we use general semantic notions – 'comparative concepts' in terms of Haspelmath (2010) – such as 'temporal relations', 'inalienable possession', 'co-reference' and 'understood subjects' in our chapters on tense and aspect, on possessive constructions, on reflexivity and on non-finite subordination, respectively. A major challenge for this procedure of establishing comparability has recently come from what may be called advocates of 'neo-relativism', holding the view that linguistic systems are entirely self-contained. According to this line of reasoning, linguistic elements are only defined relative to the systems they form part of and are therefore incommensurable (cf. Haspelmath 2010 for discussion).

Given the close genealogical relationship of the two languages under comparison, we can use formal criteria of comparability in addition to functional ones, e.g. in the discussion of tense and aspect systems in Chapter 5. While differing in terms of their functions, the English *Present Perfect* and the German *Perfekt* exhibit a parallel formal make-up, consisting of a possessive verb (*have, haben/sein*) and a participial form, both of which derive from common (West Germanic) ancestor categories. For the same reason, we can compare formal elements and categories such as phonemes, gender, case etc. Even though the historical processes have led to mutual unintelligibility of English and German, there is a certain amount of shared distributional or functional ground providing the basis for comparison and the identification of differences.

In spite of the close genealogical relation between English and German, we obviously have to be careful to avoid overgeneralizations, as even in closely related languages structural similarities may be misleading. An interesting example is provided by the structures typically discussed under the label 'tough movement', exemplified in ⟨1⟩ (cf. Chapter 13):

⟨1⟩   a. John is hard to understand. ('tough movement')

        b. It is hard to understand John. (assumed underlying structure)

Such structures are often assumed to be derived by a process of promoting an underlying object (here, *John*) to subject function (cf. Section 13.2). In other words, ⟨1b⟩ is regarded as the more basic structure, and ⟨1a⟩ is taken to be derived from it. If we look at *prima facie* parallel German examples like ⟨2a⟩ and related structures as illustrated in ⟨2b⟩, the same analysis seems to be called for:

⟨2⟩   a. Hans ist schwer zu verstehen.

        b. Es ist schwer, Hans zu verstehen.

In contrast to English, however, there are modal uses of infinitives in German, expressing either possibility or necessity/obligation (cf. ⟨3⟩), and sentences of type ⟨2a⟩ could also be analyzed as expansions of such 'modal infinitives', as illustrated in ⟨4⟩ (cf. Brdar and Brdar 1992, Demske-Neumann 1994). Such an analysis would not be possible for English. In spite of the seemingly parallel structures, it is thus possible that (German) examples of the type of ⟨2a⟩ instantiate fundamentally different structures from (English) examples of type ⟨1a⟩.

⟨3⟩   a. Das ist zu schaffen. (possibility)

       b. Das ist zu erledigen. (necessity)

⟨4⟩   a. Das ist (leicht/mühelos/ohne Schwierigkeiten . . .) zu schaffen.

       b. Das ist (gut/schnell/sofort . . .) zu erledigen.

We will not pursue such problems of comparability any further at this point. As mentioned above, in many cases we can rely on direct historical links between English and German (a criterion which is not available in large-scale typological studies). Ultimately, our approach must be judged against the quality of our contrastive observations and generalizations.

As far as the theoretical framework used in our analysis is concerned, we will draw both on more traditional descriptive and functional views of grammatical organization and on insights gained within the framework of Generative Grammar. Our goal of presenting our findings in a way that is intelligible to a wide audience excludes, of course, any attempt to adopt the terminology of a specific theory of grammar. The book, which was primarily written as a textbook for BA or MA modules for programmes in English or German, should be intelligible to any student in the second or third semester.

1.4 The structure of the book

The topics selected for comparison in this book are grammatical domains which manifest a strikingly different organization in the two languages: phonology (Chapters 2 and 3), morphology (Chapter 4), tense and aspect (Chapter 5), modality (Chapter 6), grammatical relations (Chapter 7), (internal and external) possession (Chapter 8), diathesis (Chapter 9), reflexivity and intensification (Chapter 10), constituent order (Chapter 11), wh-movement and relativization (Chapter 12), and non-finite subordination (Chapter 13). Moreover, four chapters deal with contrasts in the lexicon, i.e. Chapter 14 on content words, Chapter 15 on compounding, Chapter 16 on derivation and Chapter 17 on function words. Chapter 18 contains some concluding remarks and addresses some of the more general questions raised above.

2 Phonology I: Phoneme inventories

In comparison to other languages of the world, English and German are both characterized by a relatively complex phonology. In particular, they have rich vowel inventories and permit considerably complex syllable structures. These attributes are characteristic of most Germanic languages, i.e. they are 'family traits'. The common Germanic origin of English and German is also reflected in a number of other phonological features. The consonant systems, for example, are structured by similar parameters of classification and overlap to a considerable extent, and phonotactic restrictions are largely parallel. However, there are striking differences as well. The vowel systems are structured in completely different ways, and a comparison of rules for stress placement reveals a number of significant contrasts, too. Since such differences are due to divergent diachronic developments, we will occasionally make reference to historical processes in our comparison, including the different situations of language contact.

We will start with a comparison of the consonant systems in Section 2.1. The vowel inventories will be compared in Section 2.2. Section 2.3 contains a short summary. Since most of what is said is a matter of general consensus, no specific references are provided in the text (but see the 'Further reading' section for relevant literature).

2.1 The consonants of English and German

2.1.1 Parameters of consonant classification

As is common practice in phonetics and phonology, consonants will be described in terms of three parameters: (i) the place of articulation, (ii) the manner of articulation, and (iii) the question of whether or not the vocal folds produce phonation during articulation ('voicing'). The **places of articulation** can be characterized with reference to the active and passive articulators involved. Table 2.1 surveys the places of articulation that are relevant to a description of English and German, as well as the technical terms used in this book. In those cases where the active articulator can be inferred from the passive one mentioning the former is redundant. For instance, instead of 'dorso-velar' we can simply say 'velar', since all velar consonants of English and German are dorsal. Such terms redundantly indicating the active articulator are put in parentheses in Table 2.1 and will generally be omitted. As will be seen, however, in some cases it is convenient or even necessary to consider the active articulators involved. For example, 'dorsal fricatives' – i.e. palatal, velar and

active articulator	passive articulator	TECHNICAL TERM	
lower and upper lips	–	BILABIAL	
lower lips	upper teeth	LABIO-	DENTAL
tip of the tongue (*apex*)	upper teeth	APICO-	DENTAL
	alveolar ridge	(APICO-)	ALVEOLAR
blade of the tongue (*lamina*)	alveolar ridge / hard palate	LAMINO-	POSTALVEOLAR
body of the tongue (*dorsum*)	hard palate	(DORSO-)	PALATAL
	soft palate (*velum*)	(DORSO-)	VELAR
	uvula	(DORSO-)	UVULAR
glottis	–	GLOTTAL	

Table 2.1 Technical terms used to refer to places of articulation

uvular fricatives – form a natural class in German insofar as they are phonetically similar and in complementary distribution, i.e. they are allophones. English does not have dorsal fricatives at all. When two sounds are produced at the same place of articulation, they are said to be 'homorganic'.

The second central parameter that we need in order to classify consonants is the **manner of articulation**. Consonants can be grouped into two major categories: OB-STRUENTS and SONORANTS (vowels are also sonorants, but they are not relevant at this point). There are three classes of obstruents: PLOSIVES, FRICATIVES and AFFRICATES. The status of affricates is disputed. For reasons to become apparent below they are included in the present discussion. The group of consonantal sonorants comprises the three major categories of NASALS, APPROXIMANTS and VIBRANTS. Approximants can be further be subdivided into LATERALS (or 'lateral approximants') and GLIDES (or 'semi-vowels'), and the class of vibrants comprises TRILLS and TAPS. Vibrants and laterals can be subsumed under the more general term 'liquids'. A classification of consonants based on the manner of articulation is provided in Table 2.2, with one example for each type of consonant in the last row.

CONSONANTS							
OBSTRUENTS			SONORANTS				
				APPROXIMANTS		VIBRANTS	
PLOS	FRICAT	AFFRIC	NASALS	GLIDES	LATERAL	TRILL	TAP
[p]	[f]	[tʃ]	[m]	[w]	[l]	[r]	[ɾ]

Table 2.2 Manners of articulation

The **transcriptions** provided in this section will manifest varying degrees of narrowness. We will generally focus on those aspects of articulation that are most central in the relevant context. Phonemes will be represented by typical phonetic realizations, written between slanting brackets (e.g. /ð/ for a voiced dental fricative), but the use of a phonetic symbol (here, ð) should not be taken to express that phonemes are phonetic entities.

2.1.2 The inventories of consonants

Nasals and plosives Both English and German have fully symmetric series of plosives, which can be characterized in terms of the places of articulation BILABIAL, ALVEOLAR and VELAR. Plosives are either voiced or voiceless. Nasals can be classified using the same places of articulation, but they are always voiced. The plosives and nasals of English and German are summarized in Table 2.3.

		BILABIAL	ALVEOLAR	VELAR
PLOSIVES	[– VOICED]	p	t	k
	[+ VOICED]	b	d	g
NASALS	[+ VOICED]	m	n	ŋ

Table 2.3 The plosives and nasals of English and German

Fricatives The fricative inventories of English and German are likewise relatively similar, but we will see that there are two important contrasts. English fricatives cover the whole range of places of articulation from labio-dental to apico-postalveolar in Table 2.1. In addition, there is a glottal fricative (/h/). With the exception of (voiceless) /h/, all fricatives of English are fully symmetric with regard to voicing, i.e. for each place of articulation there is both a voiced and a voiceless phoneme. The dental fricatives /θ/ and /ð/ are sometimes said to be in complementary distribution, but both sounds clearly have a phonemic status because there are contexts in which they make a difference in meaning. For example, the (voiceless) final [θ] in *teeth* ([ti:θ]) contrasts with the (voiced) [ð] in the verb *to teethe* ([ti:ð]). The same differentiation can be observed in the pairs *sheath/(un)sheathe, loath/loathe* and *wreath/wreathe*. Although the number of minimal pairs showing a phonemic contrast between [θ] and [ð] is small, and although phonemic contrasts can only be found in a final position, we consequently have to list both sounds in the phoneme inventory of English separately. The voicing opposition between the two dental fricatives carries very little functional load, though.

The **voiced postalveolar fricative** /ʒ/ is a relatively young phoneme with a severely restricted distribution. In general, it does not occur in word-initial or word-final position and is found only medially (e.g. *measure* → [mɛʒə], *usual* → [ju:ʒʊəl]). Even there, its distribution is restricted insofar as it occurs only in unstressed syllables and is in complementary distribution with the combination of /z/ and /j/ (which, in turn, occurs only in stressed syllables; e.g. *presume* → [prɪˈzjuːm], but not *[prɪˈʒuːm], in RP). It therefore seems reasonable to assume that the contrast between /zj/ and /ʒ/ is not distinctive. However, there are some more recent borrowings from French where we do find /ʒ/ in word-initial or word-final position, and where it is thus clearly phonemic, e.g. in *gigue* ([ʒiːg]) and *garage* (if it is pronounced [gəraːʒ]). We will consider such 'loan phonemes' to be part of the phoneme inventory of a language, but in lists and summaries they will be put in parentheses indicating their non-native status.

The standard varieties of English do not have **dorsal fricatives**, i.e. fricatives that are produced with the body of the tongue (e.g. [ç], [x]). These consonants were still part of the sound inventory of Middle English (they were allophones of /h/), but they later changed into other sounds or disappeared completely. The existence of those fricatives in Middle English is still reflected in the orthography of Modern English, where the sequence <gh> does not have a uniform phonological interpretation (cf. *laugh* → [lɑːf], *though* → [ðəʊ]). In Chaucer's works, <gh> stands for palatal and velar fricatives, very much like <ch> in Modern German. Accordingly, *right* was pronounced [rɪçt], which parallels the pronunciation of the German cognate *recht* ([rɛçt]). Likewise, the Modern English spelling of the verb *laugh* (cf. Germ. *lachen*) reflects the former presence of a velar fricative in that root (cf. *laugh* → [lauxx] in Middle English). While the standard varieties of English have completely lost palatal and velar fricatives, certain regional varieties have preserved at least some traces of these phones. The Scottish pronunciation of the famous 'Loch Ness' ([lɔx nɛs]) as opposed to its pronunciation in RP ([lɒk nɛs]) is a case in point.

German has all the fricatives of English except apico-dental /θ/ and /ð/. Moreover, it has preserved the **palatal** and **velar fricatives** mentioned above, which have been lost in English. These fricatives exist only in their voiceless variants and are in complementary distribution, i.e. they are allophones of a single phoneme. We will assume that this consonant phoneme has three allophones (note that there is considerable idiolectal variation in the distribution of these allophones): (i) after front vowels it is realized as [ç] (e.g. *Licht* → [lɪçt]), (ii) after back vowels it is realized as (velar) [x] (*suchen* → [zuːxən]), and (iii) after (central) /a/ it is realized as (uvular) [χ] (*Dach* → [daχ]). We can classify this phoneme according to the active articulator involved as a 'voiceless dorsal fricative'.

Like in English, the **voiced postalveolar fricative** /ʒ/ does not occur in the native German vocabulary and is found only in loan words (e.g. *Garage*, *Hommage*, *genant*). In initial and final positions, this phoneme is considerably more frequent in German than in English, where we regularly find the postalveolar affricate instead (e.g. *homage* → [hɒmɪdʒ] and *garage* if it is pronounced [gærɪdʒ]). The contrasts between English and German fricatives are summarized in Table 2.4. Each cell corresponds to one place of articulation and one manner of articulation. Within the cells, a distinction is made between the voiceless phonemes on the left hand side and the voiced ones on the right hand side. As can be seen from Table 2.4, the main differences can be summarized in two sentences: Only English has dental fricatives, and only German has dorsal fricatives.

	labio-dental		apico-dental		alveolar		post-alveolar		dorsal		glottal	
English	f	v	θ	ð	s	z	ʃ	(ʒ)	÷	÷	h	÷
German	f	v	÷	÷	s	z	ʃ	(ʒ)	ç x χ	÷	h	÷

Table 2.4 The fricatives of English and German

Affricates The phonological status of affricates has been a matter of debate for many years. Some phonologists assume that we can do without affricates as a category of their own, and that affricates should be regarded as combinations of a plosive and a fricative. However, the consideration of affricates may be illuminating from a historical point of view. There are a number of systematic correspondences in the vocabularies of English and German which can be explained on the basis of the 'Second' or '**High German Sound Shift**', which took place between the fifth and the eighth century AD and which affected southern varieties of German. In the course of the High German Sound Shift, the voiceless plosives /p/ and

	English	German
/p/ vs. /pf/	pan	Pfanne
	penny	Pfennig
	pipe	Pfeife
	post	Pfosten
	pool	Pfuhl
/t/ vs. /ts/	ten	zehn
	twig	Zweig
	tie	ziehen
	to	zu
	twitter	zwitschern

Table 2.5 Correspondences between plosives and affricates

/t/ changed into the relevant homorganic affricates /pf/ and /ts/ in a syllable-initial position, in gemination and after consonants, and into the corresponding fricatives /f/ and /s/ after vowels. The velar plosive /k/ was retained at the beginning of a syllable, but changed into /x/ between vowels (e.g. Old Saxon *makon* vs. Modern German *machen*). Since these changes have not occurred in English, they can help us to understand a number of lexical correspondences, some of which are listed in Table 2.5.

English only has the two **postalveolar affricates** /tʃ/ and /dʒ/. In words containing more than one morpheme, the sequence [ts] is also found (e.g. in plural forms such as *cats*), but since there is always a morpheme boundary between /t/ and /s/, these combinations should not be considered instances of a (phonological) affricate. The German affricates can be grouped into three major categories: first, there is the aforementioned class of affricates which was created during the High German

Sound Shift, viz. /pf/ and /ts/. Second, German has an affricate /tʃ/, which is basically restricted to a syllable-final position, but which sporadically occurs in the onset, too (e.g. *tschüss, tschechisch, Tscherkasse*). This affricate is often found in onomatopoetic words (*Quatsch, Matsch, flutsch*). It is ironic that German is sometimes said to have no postalveolar affricate, given that this very consonant forms part of the adjective *deutsch*. The third affricate of German is a loan phoneme (/dʒ/). It occurs in a number of borrowings, most of them from English (*Junkie, joggen*). The affricates of English and German are summarized in Table 2.6.

closure	labial	alveolar	alveolar
release	labio-dental	alveolar	postalveolar
Engl.	÷	÷	÷	÷	tʃ	dʒ
Germ.	pf	÷	ts	÷	tʃ	(dʒ)

Table 2.6 The affricates of English and German.

Laterals, glides and R-variants In addition to the major classes of consonants described above, there are three minor groups: laterals, glides and the different R-sounds. With regard to the former two classes, English and German show only few contrasts. Both languages have only one lateral, viz. /l/. As far as glides are concerned, the German inventory is a subset of the English one. Not counting /r/, English has two glides: bilabial /w/ (*word* → [wɜːd]) and palatal /j/ (*yes* → [jɛs]). German only has the palatal glide /j/ as in *ja*.

The various **R-allophones** of English and German encompass a broad class of sounds which differ in both manner and place of articulation. There are not only striking contrasts between the major standard varieties of English and German, there is also considerable language-internal (basically diatopic) variation in both languages. In RP, /r/ is best described as an apico-postalveolar approximant, represented phonetically as [ɹ]. For most American varieties it can be characterized as an apico-palatal (or 'retroflex') approximant ([ɻ]). However, there are further R-variants. In Scottish English, /r/ is often pronounced as an alveolar tap [ɾ], similar to the one of Spanish and Italian. The same pronunciation can be found in some African and Asian varieties of English. German /r/ is likewise subject to considerable diatopic variation. In Standard German, it is (ideally) a voiced uvular trill ([ʀ]), but in actual pronunciation it is often devoiced or pronounced as a fricative (e.g. *Regen* → [ʁeːgən] or [ʁeːgən]). Moreover, /r/ is vocalized in specific contexts, and is realized as a weak vowel similar to, but more open than, schwa ('open schwa'). This vowel is phonetically represented as [ɐ] (e.g. *hier* → [hiɐ]). In some southern varieties (e.g. Bavarian), /r/ is realized as an alveolar trill ([r]).

Summary The consonant inventories of English and German are summarized in Table 2.7. Only phonemes of the most important standard varieties are taken into account, i.e. Received Pronunciation (RP) and General American (GA) for English, and the standard pronunciation for German (so-called 'Modern High Standard German'). Allophonic variants are connected by hyphens (Engl. [ɹ]-[ɻ] and Germ. [x]-[ç]-[χ]). The contrasts between English and German are highlighted by shading the relevant cells.

	labial		apical				dorsal			
	bilabial	labio-dental	apico-dental	alveolar	post-alveolar	retroflex	palatal	velar	uvular	glottal
E										
PLOS	p b			t d				k g		
FRIC		f v	θ ð	s z	ʃ (ʒ)					h
AFFR					tʃ dʒ					
NAS	m			n				ŋ		
LAT				l						
GLIDE	w				ɹ - ɻ		j			
TRILL										
G										
PLOS	p b			t d				k g		
FRIC		f v		s z	ʃ (ʒ)		ç - x - χ			h
AFFR	pf			ts	tʃ (dʒ)					
NAS	m			n				ŋ		
LAT				l						
GLIDE							j			
TRILL									R	

Table 2.7 The consonants of English and German

2.1.3 Phonetic differences between phonologically corresponding consonants

English and German consonants do not only differ in their feature specifications, there are also considerable phonetic differences between certain consonants with identical features. The most striking non-phonemic contrasts can be found in the realization of the following types of consonants: (i) voiced obstruents are regularly devoiced in a syllable-final position in German but not in English ('Auslautverhärtung', i.e. 'final devoicing'); (ii) voiceless plosives have some allophonic variants in English that are absent from German (unreleased and glottalized plosives); (iii) the English lateral /l/ exhibits a kind of allophonic variation which German /l/ lacks (velarization); and (iv) the allophonic variants of the velar nasal /ŋ/ are distributed differently in English and German.

Voiced obstruents and final devoicing in German Final devoicing is a highly regular process in German that does not exist in English. As a phonetic rule, it can be described as follows: *Voiced obstruents are devoiced when occurring in syllable-final position.* As mentioned above, the class of obstruents comprises fricatives, plosives and affricates. For example, the final /d/ in *Rad* is devoiced ([ʀaːt]), so *Rad* cannot be distinguished from *Rat* in purely phonetic terms. The phonemic contrast between the /d/ of *Rad* and the /t/ of *Rat* becomes audible only if we consider other forms of those words in which the relevant plosives do not occupy a syllable-final position. For example, the /d/ of the plural form *Räder* is phonetically realized as [d]. Here, it does not form part of the first syllable, but occurs in the onset of the second one ([ʀɛː.dɐ]). By contrast, the [t] in *Räte* is voiceless, just like the one in *Rat*. Pairs like *Rad/Räder* can be established for all voiced obstruents (e.g. *Stab/Stäbe*, *Flug/Flüge*, *Los/Lose*, etc). Final devoicing must consequently be regarded as a phonetic process that is independent of any particular phoneme.

Voiceless plosives The phonetic realization of voiceless plosives may vary according to the following parameters: they may be (i) either aspirated or unaspirated, (ii) either released or unreleased, and (iii), when unreleased, they may be either glottalized or unglottalized. As far as **aspiration** is concerned, English and German behave similarly: syllable-initial voiceless plosives are generally aspirated (and aspiration is stronger in stressed syllables than in unstressed ones). Therefore, Engl. *pan* can be represented as [pʰæn], and Germ. *Panne* as [pʰanə], where aspiration is indicated by a superscript [ʰ]. The degree of aspiration cuts across English and German accents and is related to the geographical positions of the relevant varieties. As a general tendency, aspiration of initial voiceless plosives is stronger in British English than in Standard German, but it is stronger in Standard German than in American English. Within German varieties there is a north-south cline with regard to the degree of aspiration: initial voiceless plosives are more heavily aspirated in northern dialects of German, whereas some southern varieties (e.g. Austrian German) show a complete absence of aspiration.

In **non-initial positions** voiceless plosives are generally unaspirated in both English and German. For example, the [p] in *Spule* ([ʃpuːlə]) differs from that in *Pudel* ([pʰudəl]) in that it lacks aspiration. The same difference obtains between *pain* ([pʰeɪn]) and *Spain* ([speɪn]) in English. A contrast between English and German can be observed when voiceless plosives occur in a word-final position. Here, aspiration is generally stronger in German than in English. For example, the final [t] of *Hut* ([huːtʰ]) is usually aspirated, while the [t] in *hat* ([hæt]) is generally unaspirated. It should be noted, though, that aspiration of plosives in German is generally weaker in a word-final position than word-initially – for example, the [tʰ] in *Topf* is more strongly aspirated than the one in *Pott*.

If a plosive is followed by certain other consonants, it is often **not released** in either English or German. The absence of a release is phonetically represented by the diacritic [̚]. For example, *Zeltlager* can be transcribed as [tsɛlt̚laːgɐ], since the closure produced by the final [t] of *Zelt* is at the same time the starting point of the following [l]. Likewise, the English word *butler* will usually be pronounced [bʌt̚lə]. A difference between English and German can, again, be observed in a word-final position. While voiceless final plosives may be unreleased in English, this is not a common phenomenon in German. For example, [nʌt̚] is a possible pronunciation of the English word *nut*, but the German word *Hut* can, in isolation, not be pronounced [huːt̚]. Differences can also be observed in consonant clusters. In German, both /k/ and /t/ in *Akt* can be released, whereas this would be rather uncommon in the English word *act*.

If English final plosives are unreleased, they are often also **glottalized**. This means that, simultaneously with the closure produced in the oral cavity, the glottis is closed and thus obstructs the air stream. This additional closure can be represented by including a glottal stop in the relevant phonetic representation. For instance, the conjunction *but* can be represented as [bʌt̚] if the final [t] is not released, and as [bʌʔt̚] if it is additionally glottalized. Occasionally, the closure of the glottis may completely replace the alveolar closure, so *but* is often actually pronounced [bʌʔ] (e.g. in Cockney). This kind of phonetic substitution can also be found word-internally, for instance when *bottle* is pronounced [bɒʔl].

When considering allophony in the domain of plosives it should also be mentioned that General American differs from both RP and Standard German in the range of allophonic realizations of the **alveolar plosives** /t/ and /d/. They are often pronounced as taps in an intervocalic position or when following /r/ (e.g. in *eating* → [iːɾɪŋ], *party* → [pɑɾɾi]). The same phenomenon can be found in Western parts of England and in Australia. Some dialects of German show a similar kind of allophonic variation (e.g. the ones spoken in Hamburg and Hussia/Hessen).

Velarization of /l/ in English   The third major phonetic difference between English and German consonants concerns the realization of /l/. Most varieties of English display a systematic allophony which German lacks: /l/ is realized with varying degrees of 'velarization', which means that the *dorsum* is raised towards the *velum* during articulation. As a general rule, velarization is strongest in a syllable-final position, weakest at the beginning of a syllable, and intermediate between vowels.

For example, the [l] in *light* is generally not velarized, and consequently transcribed as a 'clear l' ([laɪt]). The final consonant of *tall*, by contrast, is represented as a 'dark /l/' ([tʰɔːɫ]). The central [l] in *silly* typically displays a degree of velarization which is weaker than that of the [ɫ] in *tall*, but stronger than that of the [l] in *light*.

Realizations of the velar nasal In both English and German, the velar nasal /ŋ/ only occurs after vowels. In English, its realization varies with the context according to the following rules: when occurring at the end of a morpheme, it is phonetically realized as [ŋ] (e.g. *sing*); morpheme-internally [g] is regularly inserted, so the resulting realization is [ŋg] (e.g. *finger* → [fɪŋgə]/*[fɪŋə]). In morphologically complex words like *sing-er* or *sing-ing* we find, again, the morpheme-final allophone ([sɪŋə], [sɪŋɪŋ]). However, there are exceptions to this rule: in comparative and superlative forms, /ŋ/ is realized as [ŋg], i.e. these words are (phonologically) treated as if they were mono-morphemic (e.g. *long-er* → [lɒŋgə]).

The distribution of /ŋ/-variants in German is different. The phonetic realization as [ŋ] is only found word-finally (e.g. *Gang*, *Dung*) and before schwa (i.e. [ə] or [ɐ]; e.g. *Zange* → [tsaŋə], *Finger* → [fɪŋɐ]). Before all other vowels, [g] is inserted (e.g. *Bingo* → [bɪŋgo]/*[bɪŋo], *Hangar* → [haŋgaʀ]/*[haŋaʀ], *Ungarn* → [ʊŋgaʀn]/*[ʊŋaʀn]). It is therefore reasonable to assume that [ŋ] and [ŋg] are also allophones in German. The relevant distributional rules obviously differ from those of English, especially insofar as the distribution of the /ŋ/-variants is not sensitive to the morphological status of the relevant syllables. For instance, the final consonant of *Strang* is realized as [ŋ] in the plural form *Sträng-e* (where it precedes schwa), whereas it is [ŋg] in *strang-ulier-en* (where it precedes a full vowel).

Summary The most important phonetic differences between English and German in the realization of phonologically similar (final) consonants are summarized in Table 2.8.

type of consonant	process	E	G
voiced obstruent	final devoicing	NO	YES
voiceless plosive	aspiration of word-final vcl. plosives	NO	YES
	lack of release of word-final vcl. plosives	OFTEN	NO
	glottalization of syllable-final vcl. plosives	OFTEN	NO
lateral	velarization of syllable-final /l/	YES	NO
velar nasal	[ŋg] within morphemes	YES	NO
	[ŋg] before vowels other than schwa	NO	YES

Table 2.8 Phonetic contrasts between English and German consonants

2.2 The vowels of English and German

2.2.1 Parameters of vowel classification

If we want to understand the systematicity underlying a vowel system, it is important to distinguish between two different methods of vowel classification: first, vowels can be classified according to phonetic parameters (**phonetic classification**); and second, they can be classified in terms of their distribution (**distributional classification**). As will be seen, the two classifications are closely interrelated, and we will make use of both kinds of criteria. It is nevertheless important to bear in mind that there is a fundamental difference between them. For a phonetic classification at least the following parameters are relevant:

⟨1⟩   a. the position of the tongue (height and advancement);
        b. lip rounding (rounded vs. unrounded);
        c. tension (tense vs. lax);
        d. length (long vs. short).

The first two parameters do not present any major difficulties. The **position of the tongue** can be described with reference to the (primary or secondary) vowel chart, which indicates, in an idealized way, the position of the highest point of the tongue during articulation. We will assume four degrees of height (close vowels, close-mid vowels, open-mid vowels, open vowels), and three degrees of tongue advancement (front vowels, central vowels, back vowels). The **rounding** parameter is binary, i.e. every vowel is either rounded (the lips are rounded during articulation) or unrounded (the lips are spread or relaxed). In the primary vowel chart, the front vowels and the lowest back vowel (ɑ) are unrounded, while the remaining vowels are rounded (ɔ, o and u). In the secondary vowel chart the rounding parameter is reversed, so the front vowels and the lowest back vowel are rounded, while the remaining back vowels are unrounded. The vowel charts with the primary and secondary cardinal vowels are displayed in Figure 2.1. The central/close vowels [ɨ] and [ʉ] are not taken into account, as they are not relevant to a description of English and German. Lip rounding is indicated by a circle enclosing the relevant vowels.

Two of the vowels in Figure 2.1 are marked with an asterisk. The reason is that there is a somewhat unfortunate **ambiguity** in the use of the relevant symbols. First, [a] is used to represent a cardinal vowel with the articulatory features unrounded, open and front. However, in phonetic transcriptions of German [a] often stands for a central vowel like the one in *Bann* ([ban]), especially in dictionaries. In order to avoid confusion, we will adopt this lexicographic convention commonly made in German linguistics, since it is probably familiar to most students. A front vowel like the one in English *hand* will be represented using the symbol [æ]. The second unfortunate mismatch between the cardinal vowel chart and diverging transcription techniques concerns the use of the vowel symbol [ʌ]. As a cardinal vowel, it is

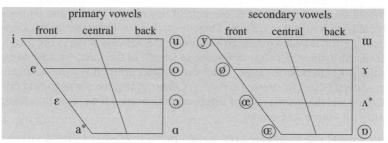

Figure 2.1 The primary and secondary cardinal vowel chart

the unrounded counterpart of the rounded open-mid back vowel [ɔ]. However, in phonetic descriptions of English it is generally used to represent the vowel in *but*, which is best described as a *central* open or open-mid vowel. This convention is so well established that it would make no sense to deviate from this practice here. The ambiguity of the two vowel symbols 'a' and 'ʌ' should thus be kept in mind.

The position of the tongue and the rounding parameter allow us to make categorical distinctions between certain pairs or groups of vowels. For example, the vowel in *Stiehle* is an unrounded close front vowel and contrasts with the *rounded* close front vowel in *Stühle*, and the *rounded* close *back* vowel in (*dem*) *Stuhle*. However, an additional distinction is needed in order to capture the difference between the vowels in *Stiehl* and *still*. They are both unrounded close front vowels, but they are clearly distinct phonologically, as they can make a difference in meaning.

Such contrasts are often described with reference to the physiological criterion of **tension**. Roughly speaking, the term 'tension' refers to the amount of muscular energy spent during articulation: The pronunciation of the vowel in *Stiehl* requires more effort than the production of the vowel in *still*. Tense and lax vowels also differ in quality: lax vowels are generally more central than tense vowels ('centralized'), which is related to the relative muscular relaxation associated with them: [ɪ] is 'more central' or closer to schwa than [iː]. Some phoneticians have explained the contrast between tense and lax vowels by saying that the former are produced with an 'advanced tongue root', since the root of the tongue (which is situated immediately over the larynx) is pushed forward during the articulation of such vowels.

In German, the contrast between tense and lax vowels can be established relatively straightforwardly, and each vowel can be assigned either a tense or a lax counterpart. The following minimal pairs illustrate this: *Stiehl* vs. *still*, *buhlen* vs. *Bullen*, *fühlen* vs. *füllen*. Moreover, muscular tension clearly correlates with another phonetic parameter of vowel phonology. As can be heard when we pronounce the aforementioned minimal pairs, there is always a difference in the **length** of the relevant vowels: tense vowels are generally longer than lax vowels. This rule, however, applies only to stressed syllables. For example, the first two vowels of *Schokolade* are tense, but nevertheless short.

It should be noted that there is one pair of vowels in German that do not differ noticeably with regard to tension: There is no obvious difference in the amount of muscular effort required for the articulation of the vowel in *Bahn* as opposed to that in *Bann*. Still, there is a clear difference in length. In this case, we have to assume that the vowel in *Bahn* is 'tense' in a more abstract sense: it is tense insofar as it is long when it occurs in stressed syllables. Consequently, the physiological criterion of tension and the acoustic one of length are both needed if we want to exhaustively classify the vowels of German.

While tension and length are very useful criteria to classify German vowels – for example, we can now categorically distinguish between the vowels in *Stiehl* and *still* by saying that the former is a *tense* unrounded close front vowel while the latter is a *lax* unrounded close front vowel – such a classification is more difficult to justify in English. The differences between the vowels in *feel* and *fill* and those in *fool* and *full* could reasonably be regarded as being instances of tension contrasts, but there are other vowels for which it is much more difficult to decide whether they are tense or lax. Is [æ] as in *bad* produced with as much muscular energy as the vowels in *feel* and *fool*, or does it pattern with the vowels in *fill* and *full*? And what about the vowel in *hawk*? Since there are no clear pairs of vowels that have the same specifications for height, advancement and rounding, and that differ only in their degree of tension or centralization, the distinction between tense and lax vowels seems to be more difficult to motivate. Length is not a very reliable criterion for a classification of English vowels either, since the length of those vowels varies with the context. In particular, all vowels are short when occurring before final voiceless obstruents. For example, the vowels in *feet* and *boot* are shorter than those in *feed* and *mood* and display a degree of length which is similar to that of the vowels in *fit* and *put*.

In view of such difficulties, most phonologists prefer to take **distributional criteria** into account in the classification of vowels. In both English and German, there is an important contrast between those vowels that can occur in word-final stressed open syllables and those vowels that can occur only before consonants. In German, the first, 'privileged' group of vowels comprises the following elements: /iː/ (*sie*), /yː/ (*früh*), /eː/ (*Reh*), /øː/ (*Bö[e]*), /ɛː/ (*zäh*), /aː/ (*ja*), /oː/ (*so*) and /uː/ (*Schuh*). In English (RP), there are only five monophthongs that can occur in final stressed open syllables: /iː/ (*fee*), /ɑː/ (*spa*), /ɔː/ (*law*), /uː/ (*shoe*) and /ɜː/ (*sir*).

Since the set of German vowels listed in the previous paragraph is identical to the class of vowels that we called 'tense' on the basis of phonetic criteria, we can assume that the feature of muscular tension and the ability to occur in final stressed open syllables go hand in hand. We can now simply define **tense vowels** as follows: *Tense vowels are those vowels that can occur in final stressed open syllables.* The advantage of this definition is that it can easily be applied to both English and German and thus provides a means of comparison. In phonemic representations, tense vowels will always be followed by the phonetic symbol indicating length, [ː].

This convention is justified by the fact that tense vowels are always long when they are stressed, as long as no phonological rule interferes (e.g. the shortening of tense vowels before voiceless obstruents in English). Consequently, the vowel in *feel* will phonologically be represented as /i:/, and the vowel in *fill* as /ɪ/.

While the consonant inventories of English and German are relatively similar, the vowel systems differ considerably. These differences go beyond the mere existence or non-existence of a given phoneme in one language or the other and concern the entire make-up of the systems. Since German is more conservative than English – the vowel system of Modern English has developed from a system that is similar to the German one – we will start with a consideration of the German vowels in Section 2.2.2 and turn to the English ones in Section 2.2.3.

2.2.2 The vowels of German

The vowels of German form a **concentric system** of tense and corresponding lax vowels. The tense/lax distinction is thus a central feature organizing German vowel phonology. Such a bipartition of vowels can be found in most Germanic languages. In addition to tension, lip rounding is distinctive, and German differentiates between rounded and unrounded front vowels. In order to describe all vowels of German, one needs only six tongue positions, the feature [± tense] and the rounding parameter [± rounded]. German has eight tense and seven lax monophthongs, i.e. there is almost a one-to-one correspondence between tense and lax vowels. There is only one neu-

position		RD	TN	V	ex.
front	close	−	+	/i:/	Stiehl
		−	−	/ɪ/	still
		+	+	/y:/	fühlen
		+	−	/ʏ/	füllen
	close-mid	−	+	/e:/	hehlen
		+	+	/ø:/	Höhlen
		+	−	/œ/	Höllen
	open-mid	−	+	/ɛ:/	Stähle
		−	−	/ɛ/	Ställe
central	open	−	+	/a:/	Bahnen
		−	−	/a/	bannen
back	close-mid/	+	+	/o:/	Wohle
	open-mid	+	−	/ɔ/	Wolle
	close	+	+	/u:/	buhlen
		+	−	/ʊ/	Bullen

Table 2.9 The monophthongs of German

tralization: the tense vowels /e:/ and /ɛ:/ both correspond to the lax vowel /ɛ/. Therefore, no difference can be heard between the second vowel in *Gefälle* and the first one in *Felle*, which are both pronounced [ɛ]. The **monophthongs of German** are summarized in Table 2.9 ('RD' stands for 'rounded' and 'TN' for 'tense'). Note that /o:/ and /ɔ/ differ in height (close-mid vs. open-mid), but this difference can be considered as following from the different specifications with regard to the tension parameter. In other words, both vowels can be viewed as corresponding to a single tongue position, which is between open-mid and close-mid. In addition to the 15 'pure vowels' listed in Table 2.9 there are only three **diphthongs** ('gliding vowels'): /aɪ/ as in *Hai*, /aʊ/ as in *Sau* and /ɔɪ/ as in *Heu*. All of these diphthongs are closing, i.e. the tongue moves upwards during articulation.

The symmetry of the German vowel system can be illustrated by considering the positions of the vowels in the **vowel chart**. This is done in Figure 2.2. Unlike in the cardinal vowel chart on p. 19, the oral space is divided by three horizontal lines in Figure 2.2, thus giving rise to four vertical partitions. This is done in order to emphasize the correspondence between the classification given in Table 2.9 on p. 21 and the positions of the relevant vowels in the cardinal vowel chart. For example, the top right field in the vowel chart corresponds to the class of close back vowels in Table 2.9, and the top left field to the category of close front vowels. Vowels from the secondary vowel chart (rounded front vowels) have been added to the primary vowels, separated from the latter by a slash (e.g. iː/yː). The left hand side of Figure 2.2 emphasizes the relationship between tense vowels and corresponding lax vowels. In the central diagram of Figure 2.2 it can be seen that alternatively, we can divide the oral space into an outer circle of tense vowels and an inner circle of lax vowels (although this is questionable in the case of /aː/ and /a/, which show little or no difference with regard to the position of the tongue). Given that the space is more reduced in the inner circle, it is unsurprising that we find less phonemes here. The articulation of the three German diphthongs is illustrated on the right hand side of Figure 2.2.

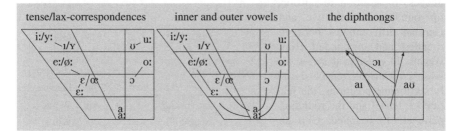

Figure 2.2 The vowels of German

2.2.3 The vowels of English: Received Pronunciation

It is much more difficult to systematically describe the vowels of English than those of German. There are two main reasons for that: first, varieties of English differ considerably in their vowel inventories. It is thus impossible to speak of *the* English vowel system. The second reason is that most of the individual vowel systems cannot easily be described in terms of a few phonological parameters like those used for

German, and that they have the appearance of an **unordered set** rather than a system. This is due to certain historical processes that occurred during the development from Middle English to Modern English. In particular, the system of tense vowels has changed considerably, while the lax vowels have remained relatively stable. As a consequence, the status of tension or length as a phonological feature has changed: rather than distinguishing one vowel from another (like in German /aː/ vs. /a/), the tension parameter is relevant only to a number of phonological rules relating to syllable structure and stress assignment. Although the tension specification of a vowel is thus important, it is not, in itself, distinctive.

The first problem mentioned above – the considerable degree of variation within Modern English – can be side-stepped by taking into account only a specific selection of **varieties**. We will focus on Received Pronunciation (RP) in our comparison with German, but the vowel systems of two further varieties (General American [GA] and Scottish Standard English [SSE]) will also briefly be considered in the subsequent sections. As for the second problem, it will be seen that the status of tension as a non-distinctive feature in English and the considerable asymmetry that characterizes English vowel phonology are themselves important aspects of a comparison of English and German.

RP has five tense and six lax **monophthongs**, which are summarized and classified according to position, tension and rounding in Table 2.10. There are only four front vowels (/iː/, /ɪ/, /ɛ/, /æ/). The open-mid front vowel /ɛ/ is often represented as (close-mid) /e/, since it is acoustically in between the two corresponding cardinal vowels. The two central vowels /ɜː/ and /ʌ/ are here classified as open-mid and open, respectively. /ʌ/ is relatively high for an open vowel, and in some classifications

position		RD	TN	V	ex.
front	close	–	+	/iː/	feel
		–	–	/ɪ/	fill
	open-mid	–	–	/ɛ/	bed
	open	–	–	/æ/	bad
central	open-mid	–	+	/ɜː/	sir
	open	–	–	/ʌ/	but
back	open	–	+	/ɑː/	spa
		+	–	/ɒ/	got
	open-mid	+	+	/ɔː/	law
	close	+	+	/uː/	shoe
		+	–	/ʊ/	full

Table 2.10 The monophthongs of RP

it is described as open-mid (in that case, /ɜː/ would be classified as either mid or close-mid in order to maintain a phonological distinction). The largest group of vowels in RP is made up of the five back vowels. Two of these back vowels are open (rounded /ɒ/ and unrounded /ɑː/), one is open-mid (rounded /ɔː/), and two are close (/uː/ and /ʊ/).

The set of **diphthongs** is considerably larger than the German one: there are eight diphthongs, which are all tense in the sense that they can occur in final stressed open syllables. These diphthongs can be grouped into two major categories: 'closing diphthongs' (the tongue moves upwards during articulation) and 'centring diphthongs', which end in schwa. Closing diphthongs can further be subdivided into the 'fronting diphthongs' /eɪ/ (*say*), /aɪ/ (*sigh*) and /ɔɪ/ (*boy*), and the 'backing diphthongs' /əʊ/ (*so*) and /aʊ/ (*now*). The class of centring diphthongs comprises /eə/ (*bare*), /ɪə/ (*beer*), and /ʊə/ (*sure*). Closing diphthongs can take an additional schwa and thus form triphthongs (e.g. /aɪə/ as in *fire*).

The positions of the vowels of RP on the vowel chart are indicated in Figure 2.3.

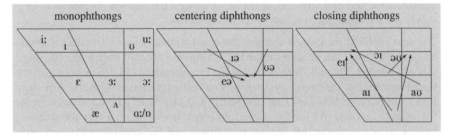

Figure 2.3 The vowels of Received Pronunciation

2.2.4 The vowel systems of English and German

If we compare the vowel inventories of RP and German, a number of striking differences can be observed. The first noticeable contrast is that the underlying 'organization' is completely different. German vowels can be characterized as a concentric system of tense and corresponding lax vowels. Such a neat bipartition cannot be established for RP. Tense and lax monophthongs are unevenly distributed over the vowel chart, and for most vowels it is impossible to assign either a tense or a lax counterpart to them. Neither do the lax vowels /ɛ/, /æ/, /ʌ/ and /ɒ/ have tense correlates, nor can the tense vowels /ɑː/, /ɔː/ and /ɜː/ clearly be assigned to any particular lax vowels. The only tense-lax correspondences that could reasonably be assumed in RP are those between /iː/ and /ɪ/ and between /uː/ and /ʊ/, but it would hardly be helpful to assume that length or tension is distinctive in RP, given that it applies only to four of eleven vowel phonemes. Remember that it is nevertheless necessary to classify all vowels as either tense or lax since this feature is relevant to a number of phonological rules.

The second important difference between RP and German concerns the **density of vowels**, i.e. the number of vowel phonemes relative to the different fields or areas in the vowel chart. In German, nine of fifteen monophthongs are front vowels, while in RP, the major group of vowels is that of back vowels (five back vowels vs. four front and two central vowels). We can say that German is 'front vowel biased' while English is 'back vowel biased'. This asymmetry also becomes visible when we consider the relevance of the rounding parameter in relation to vowel quality: in German, rounding oppositions can be found only among front vowels (e.g. /yː/ and

/ʏ/ as opposed to /iː/ and /ɪ/), while the only rounding opposition in RP distinguishes two back vowels from one another (open/unrounded /ɑː/ vs. open/rounded /ɒ/; note that these vowels also differ in tension). This contrast between RP and German is as expected: rounding oppositions are typically found in those areas where the 'density' of vowels is relatively high (conversely, we can of course say that the presence of rounding opposition results in a high density of vowels).

The third striking difference between the two vowel systems is that the **ratio of monophthongs to diphthongs** is quite different. German has five times more monophthongs than diphthongs (fifteen monophthongs as opposed to three diphthongs), while in RP the number of diphthongs is relatively high in comparison to the number of monophthongs (eleven monophthongs vs. eight diphthongs).

Having provided a bird's eye picture of the major contrasts between RP and German, we can now carry out a more fine-grained comparison. We will consider front vowels, central vowels and back vowels in turn.

Front vowels As pointed out above, one of the central contrasts between the front vowels of RP and those of German is that RP lacks rounded front vowels. This fact has been related to differences in vowel density: German has nine front vowels (five of them unrounded and four of them rounded), while RP has only four (all of them unrounded). In view of this disparity, one might be led to expect that the front vowels of RP are a subset of the German ones, but this expectation is not borne out. There are three front vowels that are common to both languages: /iː/ (*feel*/*Vieh*), /ɪ/ (*kin*/*Kinn*) and /ɛ/ (*bet*/*Bett*). However, even these vowels are not phonetically identical. The close vowels are higher in German than in English, and English /ɛ/ is slightly higher than German /ɛ/ (remember that this phonetic difference is reflected in the fact that the symbol [e] is often used to represent the English vowel in *bet*). In addition to these phonetically and distributionally similar vowels, German has two further unrounded front vowels which are both tense (/eː/ as in *Beeren* and /ɛː/ as in *Bären*), whereas RP has only the open lax vowel /æ/ (*bad*), which has no counterpart in German (note that some varieties of German neutralize the contrast between /eː/ and /ɛː/ so that *Bären* and *Beeren* are not differentiated). A contrastive overview of the front vowels of RP and German is given in Table 2.11.

	close				close-mid				open-mid		open	
	[−RD]		[+RD]		[−RD]		[+RD]		[−RD]		[−RD]	
	tns	lax	tns	lax	tns	lax	tns	lax	tns	lax	tns	lax
G	/iː/	/ɪ/	/yː/	/ʏ/	/eː/	/ɛ/	/øː/	/œ/	/ɛː/	(/ɛ/)	÷	÷
E	/iː/	/ɪ/	÷	÷	÷	/ɛ/	÷	÷	÷	÷	÷	/æ/

Table 2.11 The front vowels of RP and German

Central vowels RP and German have two central vowels each. While the German vowels /a/ (*Lamm*) and /aː/ (*lahm*) differ only in length, English /ʌ/ (*bud*) and /ɜː/ (*bird*) differ also in quality (height). German /a/ and English /ʌ/ have the same feature specifications in the classifications used here – they are lax, open, unrounded and central – but they differ phonetically insofar as Engl. /ʌ/ (*hut*) is higher than Germ. /a/ (*hat*). The RP central-mid vowel /ɜː/ is completely absent in German, and there is no comparable German vowel either.

Back vowels As mentioned above, back vowels are more numerous in RP than in German (five vs. four). The close vowels /uː/ and /ʊ/ exist in both languages. In addition to those, German has two more back vowels that RP lacks: /oː/ (*Ofen*) and /ɔ/ (*offen*). The absence of /oː/ from RP mirrors the lack of a tense close-mid front vowel, i.e. /eː/. Early Modern English still had these monophthongs, but they were later either raised (/eː/ → /iː/, e.g. *feed*; /oː/ → /uː/, e.g. *root*) or diphthongized (/eː/ → /eɪ/, e.g. *steak*; /oː/ → /oʊ/ → /əʊ/, e.g. *stone*). The second back vowel of German that RP lacks is the lax mid-open vowel /ɔ/ (*Bonn*). English only has a tense vowel with the features back, rounded and open-mid, viz. /ɔː/ as in *born*. This vowel, in turn, is absent from German. A certain similarity can be observed between English /ɔː/ and German /ɔ/ when the latter precedes /r/ (e.g. *Horn* → [hɔːn]), but the resulting sound should not be analyzed as a single phoneme. The other two back vowels of RP which German lacks are /ɑː/ (*part*) and /ɒ/ (*pot*). German does not have open back vowels at all. As will be seen, /ɒ/ does not exist in a number of other varieties of English either (e.g. GA and SSE). The contrasts between the back vowels of RP and German are summarized in Table 2.12. A comparative overview of all monophthongs of RP and German is provided in Table 2.13 on p. 27.

	close		close-mid		open-mid		open			
	rounded						unrounded		rounded	
	tense	lax	tense	lax	tense	lax	tense	lax	tense	lax
RP	/uː/	/ʊ/	÷	÷	/ɔː/	÷	/ɑː/	÷	÷	/ɒ/
German	/uː/	/ʊ/	/oː/	÷	÷	/ɔ/	÷	÷	÷	÷

Table 2.12 The back vowels of English and German

2.2.5 Other varieties of English: GA and SSE

The vowels of General American The vowel system of General American differs from that of RP in two important respects: first, GA has only ten monophthongs. The one vowel that is absent in GA is the rounded open back vowel /ɒ/. British words containing that vowel usually have /ɑː/ in GA. For instance, *god* is pronounced [gɑːd] and *stop* [stɑːp] or [stɑp].

		front		central		back	
		– RND	+ RND	– RND	+ RND	– RND	+ RND
Received Pronunciation							
close	tense	/iː/					/uː/
	lax	/ɪ/					/ʊ/
close-mid	tense						
	lax						
open-mid	tense			/ɜː/			/ɔː/
	lax	/ɛ/					
open	tense					/ɑː/	
	lax	/æ/		/ʌ/			/ɒ/
German							
close	tense	/iː/	/yː/				/uː/
	lax	/ɪ/	/ʏ/				/ʊ/
close-mid	tense	/eː/	/øː/				/oː/
	lax		/œ/				
open-mid	tense	/ɛː/					
	lax	/ɛ/					/ɔ/
open	tense			/aː/			
	lax			/a/			

Table 2.13 Contrasts between the vowels of RP and German

The second important difference between GA and RP concerns the number of **diphthongs**. Since GA is a rhotic accent, it does not have centring diphthongs. For instance, *pure* is pronounced [pjʊɹ], *beer* [bɪɹ] and *pair* [pɛɹ]. The remaining diphthongs are identical to those of RP, with the exception of /oʊ/, which corresponds to /əʊ/ in RP. Here, GA represents the more conservative state, since the former monophthong /oː/ first developed into /oʊ/ and later, in RP but not in GA, into /əʊ/. The rhoticity of GA is also responsible for another difference in the vowel inventories of GA and RP: the tense central vowel /ɜː/ as in *sir*, *fur* and *(in)fer* is absent in GA. What we find instead is a vocalized /r/. Since the resulting sound is pronounced in a central position (similar to schwa), it is generally transcribed as [ɚ] – a retroflex schwa, as it were. Phonologically, this vowel counts as a tense vowel, and is therefore here represented as /ɚː/. The vowels of GA are summarized in Table 2.14, and their positions on the vowel chart are indicated in Figure 2.4 on p. 28.

position		RD	TN	V	ex.
front	close	–	+	/iː/	feel
		–	–	/ɪ/	fill
	open-mid	–	–	/ɛ/	bed
	open	–	–	/æ/	bad
central	close-mid	–	+	/ɚː/	sir
	open	–	–	/ʌ/	but
back	open	–	+	/ɑː/	spa
	open-mid	+	+	/ɔː/	law
	close	+	+	/uː/	shoe
		+	–	/ʊ/	full

Table 2.14 The monophthongs of GA

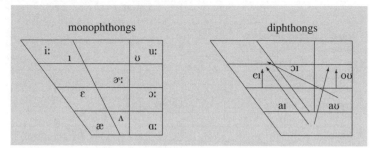

Figure 2.4 The vowels of General American

When we compare the vowels of GA to those of German, the basic observations are almost the same as those made in our comparison of German with RP. However, the inventory of back vowels in GA is more similar to the German one. As mentioned above, GA, like German, does not have a rounded open back vowel (/ɒ/). Consequently, there are as many back vowels in GA as there are in German (four), although two of the vowels are still different (GA /ɑː/ and /ɔː/ vs. German /oː/ and /ɔ/). Moreover, GA does not have centring diphthongs, so there are only five diphthongs altogether. This also makes GA a bit more similar to German than RP.

The vowels of Scottish English So-called 'Scottish Standard English' (SSE) shows even more striking deviations from RP than GA and is, in some respects, more similar to German than either of the major standard varieties. Some of the SSE-specific features are conservative, while others are innovative in comparison with RP and GA. The first important difference concerns the presence of close-mid monophthongs in SSE. While the Early Modern English monophthongs /eː/ and /oː/ have been raised or diphthongized in GA and RP, SSE has retained /oː/, and EModE /aɪ/ has been monophthongized to /eː/, thus re-establishing the symmetry in the system. For instance, *hello* is pronounced [heˈloː] in SSE, as opposed to [hɛˈləʊ] and [hɛˈloʊ] in RP and GA respectively. Likewise, the vowel in *rain* is a monophthong in SSE ([ɹeːn]). As a consequence, the system of tense vowels is more symmetric in SSE than it is in RP and GA.

The second important feature that distinguishes SSE from the two major standard varieties is that three pairs of vowels are **neutralized** in SSE: no phonological difference is made between /ɑː/ and /æ/, between /ɒ/ and /ɔː/, and between /uː/ and /ʊ/. Consequently, the following pairs of words are indistinguishable: *Sam* and *psalm* (both [saːm]), *fool* and *full* ([fuɫ]), and *caught* and *cot* ([kɔt]). As far as the neutralized vowel in *full* and *fool* is concerned, it is moreover important to note that it is often fronted and therefore pronounced [ʉ] or even [y]. Since this is an instance of free variation, however, we will assume that the relevant phoneme can be characterized as a rounded close back vowel.

Given that pairs of tense and lax vowels have merged in SSE, the question arises whether the resulting mergers count as tense or lax. Since all vowels resulting from the mentioned neutralizations can occur in final stressed open syllables, they are classified as tense and will be represented as such (i.e. /aː/, /ɔː/ and /uː/). In actual pronunciation, however, they are often short, in accordance with the **Scottish Vowel-Length Rule**: tense vowels are long before voiced fricatives, /r/ and word boundaries while they are short elsewhere. Some examples illustrating the 'Scottish Vowel-Length Rule' are given in Table 2.15.

vowel	example	long	short
/iː/	breathe	[bɹiːð]	
	keen		[kin]
/eː/	wave	[weːv]	
	waif		[wef]
/aː/	halve	[haːv]	
	half		[haf]
/uː/	smooth	[smuːð]	
	youth		[juθ]
/oː/	loathe	[loːð]	
	loath		[loθ]
/ɔː/	pause	[pɔːz]	
	bought		[bɔt]

Table 2.15 The 'Scottish Vowel Length Rule'

It is difficult to decide whether SSE has a **central vowel** phoneme like RP /ɜː/ and GA /ɚː/. In most varieties of Scottish English, a distinction between <er>, <ir> and <ur> is maintained, so *pert*, *bird* and *hurt* are pronounced [pɛɹt], [bɪɹd] and [hʌɹt], respectively. In other varieties (e.g. the 'Middle Class Accent' of Edinburgh), these vowels have merged into a vocalized /r/, sometimes represented as [ɝ].

The **diphthongs of SSE** differ considerably from those of RP, too. It has been assumed that SSE makes an additional distinction between two diphthongs, but this is questionable. In SSE, there is a clear phonetic difference between the diphthong in *side* ([sʌid]) and the (longer) one in *sigh-ed* ([saˑɪd]; [ˑ] indicates a half-length), and between the ones in *rice* ([ɹʌis]) and *-rize* ([raˑɪz]). However, it is

position		RN	TN	V	ex.
front	close	–	+	/iː/	beat
		–	–	/ɪ/	hit
	close-mid	–	+	/eː/	bait
	open-mid	–	–	/e/	bet
central	open	–	+	/aː/	bad
		–	–	/ʌ/	but
back	open-mid	+	+	/ɔː/	law
	close-mid	+	+	/oː/	boat
	close	+	+	/uː/	shoe

Table 2.16 The monophthongs of SSE

questionable whether we should really assume two different diphthongs here. As for the first pair, it is important to note that there is a morpheme boundary in *sigh-ed* but not in *side*. The second pair might be explained in terms of the Scottish Vowel-Length Rule. Still, the SSE diphthong in *side* is different from its counterpart in RP, and is usually represented as /ʌi/. The other closing diphthongs also differ qualitatively from their counterparts in RP: the vowel in *now* is usually represented as /ʌu/, and the diphthong in *boy* as /ɔe/. The vowels of SSE are listed in Table 2.16, and their positions on the vowel chart are indicated in Figure 2.5. Since SSE (like GA) is a rhotic accent, there are no centring diphthongs.

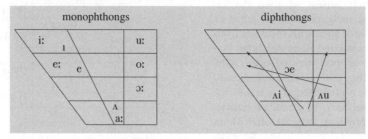

Figure 2.5 The vowels of SSE

When we compare the vowels of SSE to those of German, it becomes apparent that there are more parallels between those two systems than between German and either RP or GA. The SSE monophthongs /eː/ and /oː/ correspond closely to the relevant German vowels, both phonologically and phonetically, and the central vowel /aː/ is also similar in both languages. Furthermore, both SSE and German have three diphthongs that are similar, though not identical, in quality. Most of the parallels between SSE and German can be explained in terms of the relative conservativeness of both languages. The phonological innovations of SSE, however, have led to considerable differences as well. For example, the mentioned neutralizations of three vowels have severely reduced the Scottish vowel inventory, so the number of vowel phonemes is higher in German than it is in SSE (fifteen vs. nine).

2.3 Summary

As has been seen, the consonant inventories of English and German are structured very similarly and differ only with respect to the presence or absence of specific phonemes. In particular, German lacks dental fricatives and a bilabial glide, while English lacks dorsal fricatives and a series of affricates. The /r/-sounds of English and German differ phonetically, with both languages showing some diatopic variation, but they are more or less equivalent phonologically. More fundamental contrasts can be observed in the domain of vowel phonology. While (Standard) German exhibits a symmetrical system that is structured by specific (binary) features such as tension and rounding, the English vowels represent a rather unordered set of sounds and are difficult to learn for any foreign language learner. The lack of features structuring the English vowel system is probably also responsible for the relatively broad range of variation that can be found even among major varieties of English. It should be mentioned, however, that the vowel system of Standard German as described in this section differs considerably from the systems found in many dialects of German as well, where specific phonological oppositions are neutralized. For example, many (esp. southern) varieties do not distinguish between rounded and unrounded front vowels.

Revision, questions and exercises

1. Compile a list of English words representing different pronunciations of the letter sequence <gh>. How many different pronunciations are there? Are there any regularities with regard to the environments in which the relevant pronunciations can be found? Try to find a German cognate for each English word.

2. Try to find five pairs of English and German words (other than those given in Table 2.5 on page 12) that can be related to one another via the High German Sound Shift. Give examples involving both alveolar and bilabial plosives or affricates.

3. It has been mentioned that /θ/ and /ð/ are sometimes assumed to be in complementary distribution. For certain positions within the syllable or word this is actually true. Which are these positions? Can we make any generalizations concerning the environments where these two sounds contrast?

4. How do you pronounce the German words *Lügner* and *Stieglitz*? And how do you pronounce *Bagdad* and *Magdalena* in German? Consider whether the internal plosives are devoiced or not, and discuss whether your findings are expected against the background of the rule of final devoicing as described on p. 15.

5. What happens if Germans apply the rule of final devoicing in English? And what happens if native speakers of English fail to do final devoicing in German? Where could we have misunderstandings?

6. Speakers of northern varieties of German sometimes feel that Austrians fail to make a difference between voiced and voiceless plosives, e.g. they hear no or little difference between *Kern* and *gern*. Can you explain why?

7. Which vowels do German learners of English often substitute for /ɜː/ and /ɒ/? Think of the notorious *Happy Birthday*-song and the way Germans pronounce the word *pop music*.

8. Which sounds do native speakers of English often substitute for the tense close-mid monophthongs of German? Explain why it is precisely these sounds that are chosen as 'substitutes', and consider both phonetic and distributional aspects in your answer. (Consult Table 2.13 on p. 27.)

9. Explain: Why do Germans often have difficulties in differentiating between English /ɛ/ and /æ/, e.g. in *bed* vs. *bad*?

10. Which phonetic rule can you derive from the following minimal pairs: *rise* vs. *rice*, *raise* vs. *race*, *feed* vs. *feet*? Is there a corresponding rule in German?

Further reading

Surveys of English phonology can *inter alia* be found in Kreidler (1997, 2004), Roach (2010), Giegerich (1992), Cruttenden (2014), Carr (2015) and Davis (2015). The phonological systems of non-standard varieties of English are described in Kortmann *et al.* (2004). On the phonology of Scottish English see also Kamińska (1995). For descriptions of Standard German phonology see Wiese (1996), Hall (2000) and Schäfer (2016: Chs. 3+4). Early contrastive surveys of English and German phonology were provided by Moulton (1962), Kufner (1971), Burgschmidt and Götz (1974: Ch. 6) and Hellinger (1977: Ch. 4).

3 Phonology II: Phonotactics and stress

3.1 Syllable structure and phonotactic rules

3.1.1 The structure of the syllable

A syllable can be analyzed as a hierarchical structure which is made up of three parts: the **onset**, the **nucleus** and the **coda**. For reasons to become apparent below, the nucleus and the coda are regarded as forming a 'constituent' within the syllable which is referred to as **rhyme**. The syllable *pɪn* can thus be represented as shown in Figure 3.1 (the Greek letter σ stands for a syllable).

Every language has a set of rules concerning syntagmatic relations that tell us which combinations of phonemes are possible and which are impossible. Such restrictions on the placement of phonemes are called 'phonotactic rules', and the branch of phonology concerned with such rules 'phonotactics'. Given that a full treatment of phonotactic rules is beyond the scope of this book, we will restrict our attention to the placement of phonemes within a syllable, addressing questions like the following.

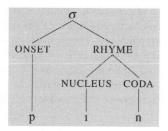

Figure 3.1 The syllable *pɪn*

1. Which phonemes can (co-)occur in which parts of the syllable?
2. Which types of phonemes are required by which syllable positions?

Although there are universal tendencies concerning possible and impossible syllable structures, **phonotactic rules** are basically language-specific. For example, Slavic languages permit types of syllables that are impossible in English or German, as in the Russian word *xleb* ('bread'). Likewise, the Classical Nahuatl verb *tlasoʔtla* ('love') would not be possible in English or in German, where syllables cannot begin with a consonant cluster of the form /tl/. It is crucial to see that words like *xleb* or *tlasoʔtla* are not simply non-existent in English and German; they are phonologically impossible because of phonotactic rules disallowing such syllable structures. It is consequently necessary to make a distinction between (a) actually existing syllables, (b) phonologically possible but non-existing syllables, and (c) phonologically impossible syllables.

Like most other rules of grammar, phonotactic rules are subject to **language-internal variation**, both diachronic and diatopic. Old English allowed some combinations of phonemes which are impossible in contemporary English. For example, the Old

English cognate of the mentioned Russian word *xleb* is *hlāf* (cf. Mod. Engl. *loaf*), which likewise exhibits a syllable structure that is disallowed in the standard varieties of Modern English, where /h/ cannot precede any other consonant. However, some varieties of English have preserved structures of the form /hw/ in the onset. For instance, in some conservative varieties from New England, but also in parts of Scotland and Ireland, a distinction is maintained between *witch* ([wɪtʃ]) and *which* ([hwɪtʃ]). In the following discussion we will be concerned only with the standard varieties of English and German.

Before considering the phonotactic rules of English and German, a remark should be made on the **relationship between phonology and morphology**. In some linguistic research traditions it is common practice to completely separate morphological from phonological rules and to regard them as pertaining to two different 'modules' of grammar. However, such a strict separation is not convenient for the present purposes. Many phonological rules of English and German are sensitive to morphological properties of a word. This concerns, in particular, rules of stress placement, but also issues of syllable structure: syllables in morphologically composite words may be more complex than syllables in morphologically simple words (or 'mono-morphemes'). For example, a structure like [tɛksts] is possible only through the addition of a plural /s/ to a simple morpheme, but no mono-morphemic English word could possibly end in a consonant cluster as complex as /ksts/. Since it would take us too far to describe the manifold interactions between phonology and morphology, we will consider only the structure of syllables in simple morphemes.

3.1.2 Distributional restrictions on phonemes

As a first step towards the description of syllable structure, we can try and see for each phoneme in which of the three positions of a syllable it can occur. The most relevant set of rules determining the distribution of phonemes relative to syllable positions concerns the **placement of consonants**. Vowels are not particularly interesting here because they are confined to occurring in the nucleus (there is a distributional restriction on vowels insofar as lax vowels cannot occur in final stressed open syllables; but this rule can better be accounted for in the context of [im]possible rhymes; cf. Section 3.2). What we have to do, thus, is determine for each consonant phoneme whether it can occur both in the coda and in the onset or only in one of the two positions.

Both English and German have a phoneme that can occur only after (lax) vowels (cf. Section 2.1.3): the **velar nasal** /ŋ/. A word such as *[ŋu:]* is therefore impossible in both languages. Another way of putting this generalization is to say that /ŋ/ can only occur in the coda. However, it should be pointed out that /ŋ/ does occur in the onset when it is, at the same time, part of the coda of a preceding syllable. This situation is called '**ambisyllabicity**' and is indicated by a dot on top of the relevant (ambisyllabic) consonant. For instance, the [ŋ] in *Menge* forms part of both the coda of the first syllable and the onset of the second, so the word is transcribed [mɛŋə]. Rather than saying that /ŋ/ cannot occur in the onset we should thus say that it must always occur in the coda of a syllable.

An apparently similar, but actually different type of distributional restriction applies to the **voiceless alveolar fricative** /s/ in German but not in English: it cannot occur in the onset of a stem-initial syllable if it is followed by a vowel. Therefore, a word like *[sɪŋən] is illicit in Standard German (in some southern varieties of German alveolar fricatives in the onset are always voiceless, so that [sɪŋən] is the only option there). However, unlike /ŋ/, /s/ is sensitive to its morphological environment, as it is barred only from stem-initial syllables. It may occur in syllable onsets when it is not stem-initial, e.g. in *Buße* ([buː.sə]). In this position voicing is distinctive, as is shown by the minimal pair *Muße* ([muː.sə]) vs. *Muse* ([muː.zə]).

A morpho-phonological rule quite parallel to the one described in the preceding paragraph restricts the distribution of the **dorsal fricative** of German, i.e. [ç]/[x]/[χ]. This sound does not regularly occur in stem-initial positions either, though relevant examples can be found among loan words (e.g. *Chirurg*, *Chiasmus*). Before consonants, back vowels and /a/, the grapheme <ch> is usually realized as [k] where the (typically Greek) source lexemes have [x] (*Charakter*, *Chrysantheme*). In examples like *Chirurg* and *Chiasmus*, the [ç]-allophone is often replaced with [ʃ] or [k] in some varieties of German, so that *Chemie* is pronounced [ʃemiː] or [kemiː]. The velar and uvular allophones do not occur at all in the onset. Note that – like /s/ – /x/ is only barred from stem-initial positions and is regularly found in the onset of non-stem-initial syllables, e.g. in *Buche* ([buː.xə]) or *Lache* ([laː.χə]).

Finally, there is one consonant which is confined to occurring at the beginning of a syllable in both English and German: the **glottal fricative** /h/. This consonant is also special in two other respects: it occurs only in stressed syllables, and it does not productively combine with other consonants to form clusters. We qualify this statement by including the adverb 'productively' because /h/ does occur before /j/ in certain English words, e.g. in *human*. However, the cluster /hj/ is possible only before close back vowels. In the sections dealing with consonant clusters (Sections 3.3–3.4), /h/ will therefore not be taken into account.

3.1.3 The Sonority Hierarchy

In the foregoing section we looked at some of the consonant phonemes described in Section 2.1, and we determined to what extent their distribution is restricted relative to the positions of a syllable. We can now, conversely, consider what types of phonemes are permitted or required by the positions of a syllable. This will also allow us to address the question of possible and impossible combinations or clusters of phonemes.

It has been mentioned that rules determining possible and impossible syllable structures are basically language-specific. This is not to say, however, that such rules may vary randomly from one language to another. Phonologists have observed that there is a strong correlation between the positions of a syllable, on the one hand, and the manner of articulation of the sounds forming part of a syllable, on the other. Classes of speech sounds can be ordered on a scale according to their degree of '**sonority**', and the degree of sonority of a given sound crucially determines its distribution. This scale is commonly referred to as the 'Sonority Hierarchy'. ⟨1⟩ offers a relatively simple version of the Sonority Hierarchy:

⟨1⟩   The Sonority Hierarchy:
plosives < fricatives < nasals < liquids < glides, close vowels < open vowels

The Sonority Hierarchy makes several predictions about the syllable structures allowed by a given language. For example, if a given speech sound can function as a syllable nucleus in a language, then all speech sounds which are higher on the scale of sonority can likewise occur in the nucleus (cf. Section 3.2). A second generalization that can be made using the Sonority Hierarchy concerns possible **consonant clusters** in the onset and in the coda: consonant clusters are generally structured in such a way that the more sonorous sounds are closer to the nucleus than the less sonorous ones. Therefore, clusters of the form ⌊plosive + lateral⌋ (e.g. /pl/) are allowed in the onset but not in the coda, while the mirror image ⌊lateral + plosive⌋ (e.g. /lp/) can be found only in the coda (we will use the symbols '⌊' and '⌋' to enclose constituents of syllables). As we will see, the Sonority Hierarchy can only make approximate predictions about syllable structures, but is nevertheless very useful as a frame of reference and classification. We will now consider the various constituents of the syllable in turn.

3.2   The syllable nucleus

In stressed syllables, the nucleus always requires a vowel, but in unstressed syllables /m/, /n/ and /l/ are also possible syllable nuclei if there is a homorganic consonant in the onset. This is in accordance with the generalization derived from the Sonority Hierarchy which says that the types of speech sounds permitted in the nucleus form an uninterrupted sequence on that hierarchy which starts from the rightmost elements.[1] To illustrate the phenomenon of **consonantal nuclei** with some examples, Germ. *Anden* is usually pronounced [an.dn̩] in connected speech, so the second syllable is made up of the onset /d/ and the nucleus /n/ (the diacritic [̩] underneath the [n] indicates its status as a syllable nucleus). Similarly, the second syllables of *Stumpen* ([ʃtʊm.pm̩]) and *Hantel* ([han.tl̩]) contain the 'syllabic consonants' /m/ and

---

[1]   Note that the various /r/-sounds can also occupy a position in the nucleus, but in this case they are usually vocalized; cf. Section 2.1.

/l/ respectively (if no schwa is inserted). Instances of such consonantal nuclei in English can be found in *handle* ([hæn.dl̩]), *piston* ([pɪs.tn̩]) and *wampum* ([wɒm.pm̩]). As far as the nucleus is concerned, we do consequently not find any noticeable contrasts between English and German.

3.3 The onset

3.3.1 An 'exceptional' segment: The prependix

Before considering the structural properties of English and German onsets we first need to slightly revise the syllable structure introduced in Figure 3.1 at the beginning of this chapter. English and German syllables may not begin with more than three consonants. In such maximal (triple) consonant clusters the type of consonant permitted in the first position is restricted so severely that it is usually assigned a special or even exceptional status. In English, the first element of such clusters is always /s/ (e.g. *string*). In German, it is always /ʃ/ in a stem-initial position (e.g. *Strang*), except before /k/, where German

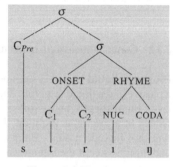

Figure 3.2 The prependix

behaves like English insofar as it allows only /s/ (*Skrupel*). Word-medially, German also has /s/ (e.g. *abstrakt*). Initial segments such as /s/ in *string* and /ʃ/ in *Strang* are called '**prependices**' (singular 'prependix', cf. Ewen and van der Hulst 2001). They can be regarded as combining with a syllable to form another syllable. This is illustrated in Figure 3.2, which provides a structural description of the syllable *string*, the prependix being represented as 'C_{Pre}'. Note that alternatively, the prependix can be assumed to be part of the onset. Since it is an open question which of these analyses is most adequate from a theoretical point of view, we will here adopt the analysis which seems more convenient to us from a didactic point of view, i.e. the one represented in Figure 3.2.

The representation given in Figure 3.2 will help us to describe the syllable structures of English and German in a highly systematic way. In particular, the onset of a syllable – i.e. the constituent made up of C_1 and C_2 in Figure 3.2 – is formed according to a rule relating to the Sonority Hierarchy (the '**Principle of Sonority**'): C_1 in the onset is always less sonorous than C_2 (cf. also Section 3.3.2). Note that prependices are not only found before clusters of consonants but also before single consonants. For instance, the initial segments of clusters like /sp/ (Engl. *spoon*) or /ʃt/ (Germ. *Steuer*) are also regarded as prependices, since such combinations of consonants would not conform to the Principle of Sonority.

The near complementarity of /s/ and /ʃ/ in prependices of English and German words (only /s/ in English, only /ʃ/ in German, except before /k/) is the result of a process of historical change which can neatly be related to the Sonority Hierarchy. Proto-Germanic had only /s/ before consonants in the onset, and the introduction of /ʃ/ in that position is an innovation of (High) German. This innovation started in the context of liquids (/sl/ became /ʃl/), then affected /s/ followed by a nasal, and finally carried over to onsets containing /s/ plus /t/ or /p/. This last change has not taken place in some northern varieties of German, where <sp> and <st> are still pronounced [sp] and [st] respectively. The whole process of change has been 'incomplete' in Standard German insofar as it has not taken place before /k/.

We will now consider the most important combinations of consonants in the onset.

3.3.2 Consonant clusters in the onset

Plosive + liquid A rather frequent type of consonant cluster in the onset comprises a plosive and a liquid (e.g. /pl/, /br/, /tr/, /kl/, etc.). This combination is very common cross-linguistically and is often referred to as *muta cum liquida*, a term adopted from Latin grammar tradition (but unlike in that tradition, our class of 'liquids' does not include nasals). English and German allow all combinations of plosives and liquids except the homorganic formations */tl/ and */dl/.

Plosive + nasal A categorical contrast between English and German can be observed when we consider combinations of a plosive and a nasal: such combinations are impossible in English, while German allows the combination of a plosive with /n/ and has /kn/ (*Knecht, knarren, Knie*), /gn/ (*Gnom*) and in loan words also /pn/ (*Pneumonie*). That such clusters are really phonologically impossible rather than accidentally non-existent in English can be seen from the fact that the relevant words have undergone a systematic phonological change, either in the course of their historical development or in the process of borrowing: the plosive has simply been dropped. Therefore, *pneumonia* is pronounced [njuːməʊnjə], *knight* [naɪt] and *gnome* [nəʊm].

Plosive + fricative A similar restriction can be observed in combinations of plosives and fricatives. While German allows /ps/ (*Psychologie* → [psyçologiː]) and /kv/ (*Quelle* → [kvɛlə]), in addition to the affricates /pf/ and /ts/, English does not have any combination of (non-homorganic) plosives and fricatives whatsoever. Again, loan words with such structures in the onset are altered phonologically in such a way that the plosive is dropped (e.g. *psychology* → [saɪkɒlədʒɪ], *pseudo* → [sjuːdəʊ]). A recent tendency to pronounce such clusters in accordance with their orthography can probably be attributed to hyper-correction, or at least a strong influence of reading and writing habits on the spoken language.

Fricative + liquid or nasal In clusters made up of a fricative and a liquid the fricatives involved are always apical or bilabial and usually voiceless, so formations like /vr/ are rare (e.g. Germ. *wringen*). As far as contrasts between English and German are concerned, there is a **partial complementarity** between /s/ and /ʃ/: English has /sl/ (*slide*), while /ʃl/ occurs only in loan words (*shlep*). German has /ʃl/ (*Schlange*), while /sl/ is basically restricted to proper names and loan words (*Slowakei, Slang*). When there is /r/ in the second position of such clusters, English and German behave in a parallel fashion: they both have /ʃr/ (Engl. *shrine*, Germ. *Schrein*) but not /sr/. In combinations of fricatives and nasals, English and German are, again, complementary: English allows only ⌊/s/ + nasal⌋ (e.g. *snow, smear*) while German has only /ʃ/ before nasals (*Schnee, schmieren*).

Glides in the second position There is an apparently striking contrast when we consider onsets whose second positions are occupied by a glide. Such structures are possible in English (e.g. *twin* → [twɪn], *pure* → [pjʊə]), but impossible in German. However, this contrast is not as important as it may appear to be. German does not have a bilabial glide /w/ anyway, so the only glide that is relevant to a phonotactic comparison of English and German is /j/. And this glide has a rather restricted distribution in English too: it occurs only before close back vowels. The contrast concerning glides in the second position thus boils down to the fact that English has syllables beginning with ⌊consonant + /juː/⌋ (*new*) or ⌊consonant + /jʊ/⌋ (*pure*) while such syllables are impossible in German.

Summary Possible combinations of consonants in the onset are summarized in Table 3.1.

		glide	liquid	nasal
plos.	E	all except */bw/, */pw/	all except */dl/, */tl/	–
	G	–	all except */dl/, */tl/	/gn/, /kn/, /pn/
fric.	E	/fj/, /vj/, /θw/, /sj/, /sw/, /zj/	/fl/, /fr/, /sl/, /ʃr/, /θr/	/sm/, /sn/
	G	–	/fl/, /fr/, (/sl/), /ʃl/, /ʃr/	/ʃm/, /ʃn/
nas.	E	/mj/, /nj/	–	–
	G	–	–	–
liq.	E	/lj/	–	–
	G	–	–	–

Table 3.1 Consonant clusters in the onset

3.4 The rhyme and the coda

To a certain extent, the structure of the coda mirrors that of the onset: while in the on-set less sonorous segments precede more sonorous ones, the mirror-inverted order is found in the coda. For example, /pl/, /kl/ and /tr/ are good onsets but impossible codas, while /lp/, /lk/ and /rt/ are good codas but impossible onsets (in English and German). However, the coda cannot simply be described as the mirror image of the onset. For example, /nd/ is allowed in the coda but */dn/ is not allowed in the onset. Moreover, there are 'additional' segments at the right margin of the word which are similar to the prependix, but which differ from the latter in terms of the type and number of consonants allowed. A further difference concerns the relationship between the coda and the nucleus, which is much tighter than the one between the onset and the nucleus. Before considering possible and impossible consonant clusters in the coda in Section 3.4.3, we will briefly address these two aspects of phonotactic analysis in Sections 3.4.1 and 3.4.2.

3.4.1 The right margin of the syllable

As has been pointed out, the coda, like the onset, can systematically be related to the Sonority Hierarchy, but it cannot simply be described as the mirror image of the onset. A similar situation obtains when we consider the right margin of the syllable more generally. Just as there is an 'additional' segment of the syllable be-fore the onset (the prependix), there is a slot for additional phonological material behind the coda. Such 'additional' seg-ments on the right margin of the syllable are called '**appendices**'. As has been men-tioned, there is an important difference between the prependix and the appendix:

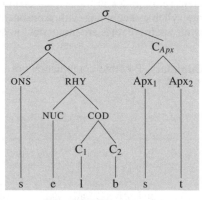

Figure 3.3 The appendix

while there can only be one consonant in the prependix, the appendix comprises two consonant positions. For instance, in the German word *selbst*, the coda is made up of two consonants (/lb/), and the appendix contains another two consonants, i.e. /s/ and /t/. The two positions of the appendix are labeled 'Apx$_1$' and 'Apx$_2$' in Figure 3.3, where the entire structure of the syllable *selbst* is illustrated. The appendix is represented as C$_{Apx}$. In English, both of the two positions in C$_{Apx}$ can be taken by only one consonant, namely /s/ (Apx$_1$) and /t/ (Apx$_2$). In German, Apx$_1$ is usually taken by /s/, but in some cases to be detailed below we also find /ʃ/. C$_4$ is always taken by /t/, just as in English.

3.4.2 The rhyme

One respect in which the coda is more restricted than the onset is that the question of which consonants and consonant combinations are allowed in the coda depends on the nature of the vowel in the nucleus. As has been pointed out, the existence of rules relating to the structure of both the nucleus and the coda has led phonologists to assume that the nucleus and the coda form a constituent within the syllable, which we call 'rhyme'. If there is a tense vowel in the nucleus, consonant clusters in the coda are possible only under very specific circumstances, for example when both of the consonants are alveolar. Therefore, Germ. *Mond* (/moːnd/) and *Freund* (/frɔɪnd/) as well as Engl. *fiend* (/fiːnd/), *old* (/əʊld/) and *aunt* (/ɑːnt/) are possible while syllables like */iːŋk/ and */uːlp/ are illicit. Such rules can be regarded as restrictions on the formation of rhymes. Another rule of this type concerns the velar nasal /ŋ/: it can occur only after short vowels. Therefore, [θɪŋ] is a good English word while *[θiːŋ] is phonologically impossible. Otherwise, codas with a single consonant are generally allowed (with the mentioned exception that /h/ cannot occur in the coda at all). When there are two consonants in the coda, a number of restrictions similar to those determining the structure of the onset apply. These restrictions will be described in Section 3.4.3.

3.4.3 Consonant clusters in the coda

Liquid + obstruent The combination ⌊liquid + plosive⌋ is unrestricted in both languages under comparison, i.e. /l/ and, in German as well as in rhotic accents of English, /r/ may co-occur with all plosives (/lp/, /lg/, /rt/, …). ⌊Liquid + fricative⌋ is more restricted: while it is generally possible with voiceless fricatives (/ls/, /rf/, etc.), only specific voiced fricatives may combine with liquids. Interestingly, the combinations allowed in English and German are complementary: while English has /lv/ (*valve*) and (in rhotic accents) /rv/ (*starve*), Standard German does not permit these clusters but has /lz/ and /rz/ instead – which, in turn, are not allowed in English. It should be noted that in German the presence of the phoneme /z/ in such clusters is not immediately obvious, since in mono-morphemes it is always (phonetically) devoiced, as a result of final devoicing. For example, one may think that the final consonant in *Hals* ([hals]) and *Vers* ([fɛrs]) is /s/. However, the plural forms *Hälse* ([hɛlzə]) and *Verse* ([fɛrzə]) reveal that the correct phonological representations of these words are /halz/ and /fɛrz/ respectively.

A phonetic, though not necessarily phonological, contrast between English and German can be observed when we consider combinations of a liquid and a postalveolar fricative. In English such formations are phonetically non-existent, but it is not quite clear whether they are also phonologically impossible. The clusters [lʒ] and [rʒ] are not attested, but combinations with the corresponding affricates in the second position are relatively frequent ([ldʒ] as in *bulge* and [rdʒ] as in *large*). It is difficult to decide whether these words incorporate phoneme clusters of the form /lʒ/ and /rʒ/, which are realized phonetically as [ldʒ] and [rdʒ] respectively (as a result of **epenthesis**), or whether /d/ forms part of the phonological representations too. Under the assumption that it is generally desirable to assume as little phonological material as possible, the first hypothesis is certainly preferable, but a definitive solution to this problem needs to be based on much more thorough considerations.

Liquid + nasal or liquid Liquids may occur in the coda together with nasals, but such combinations are possible only with /m/ (e.g. Engl. *helm* and Germ. *Film*) or /n/ (e.g. Engl. *barn* or Germ. *Harn*), while */lŋ/ and */rŋ/ are illicit. The combination /ln/ is very rare in both languages. It can be found in English *kiln*, and in German place names or proper names like *Köln* and *Hochfelln*. Two liquids may also be combined, with /r/ preceding /l/, for example in Germ. *Kerl* and Engl. *curl*.

Nasal + obstruent If the first consonant of a cluster in the coda is a nasal, the following one is either a plosive or a fricative. English allows such sequences only if the nasal and the plosive are **homorganic** (/mp/ as in *hemp*, /nt/ as in *hunt*, /nd/ as in *hand*, /ŋk/ as in *sink*). There is one homorganic formation that is disallowed, namely /mb/ (cf. *limb* → [lɪm]). German allows ⌊/m/ + alveolar plosive⌋ in addition to the mentioned homorganic clusters, for example /mt/ as in *Zimt* and /md/ as in *Hemd*. In codas of the form ⌊nasal + fricative⌋ German also permits more of the logically possible combinations than English. English has only the homorganic formations /nz/ as in *bronze* and /ns/ as in *dance*, as well as ⌊/n/ + postalveolar fricative/affricate⌋ in *punch* and *fringe*. Non-homorganic clusters can be found only exceptionally (e.g. /mz/ in *Thames* → [tɛmz]). German generally allows /m/ or /n/ to combine with labial and apical voiceless fricatives (e.g. /ms/ as in *Sims*, /nf/ as in *Hanf*, /nʃ/ as in *Mensch*, etc.). In homorganic formations, a plosive is sometimes (phonetically) inserted (e.g. [ntʃ] as in *Mensch*; cf. the discussion of Engl. *bulge* and *large* above).

Fricative + plosive In English, ⌊fricative + plosive⌋ is generally allowed if the fricative is /s/ and the plosive is voiceless (e.g. /st/ as in *fast*, /sp/ as in *wasp*, /sk/ as in *flask*). In addition to these combinations there is also /ft/ (as in *loft*). German permits such clusters only if the second consonant is /t/, which may co-occur with /s/ (*Mast*, *Hast*), /f/ (*Haft*, *Kraft*) and /x/ or /ç/ (*Macht*, *Pflicht*). The sequence /ʃt/ is possible but rare (e.g. *Gischt*).

Summary Possible combinations of consonants in the coda are summarized in Table 3.2.

		plosive	fricative	nasal	liquid
liquid	E	all combinations	all except */lð/, */lz/, */rð/, */rz/	liquid + /m/ or /n/	/rl/
	G	all combinations	all except */lv/, */lʒ/, */rʒ/, */rv/	liquid + /m/ or /n/	/rl/
nasal	E	/mp/, /nd/, /nt/, /ŋk/	/ns/, /nz/, /n(t)ʃ/, /n(d)ʒ/	–	–
	G	/mp/, /mt/, /nd/, /nt/, /ŋk/	/m/ or /n/ + vcl. fricative	–	–
fricative	E	/ft/, /sk/, /sp/, /st/	–	–	–
	G	/ft/, /st/, /ʃt/, /xt/	–	–	–

Table 3.2 Consonant clusters in the coda

3.4.4 The appendix

Although we have assumed that the structure of the appendix is basically identical in English and German, there is a crucial difference between the two languages: English permits maximally three consonants at the end of a syllable, while in German there are up to four consonants in this part of the syllable. Relevant examples from German are *Herbst* and *selbst*. We might thus consider assuming different syllable structures for English and German. However, this would be misleading. English and German syllables have identical structures insofar as there are two consonant positions in the coda (abiding by the Principle of Sonority) plus an appendix consisting of /s/ and /t/ (CC-st). The fact that English allows maximally three consonants at the end of the syllable is an independent rule. In other words, English has the same type and number of consonant positions as German but it does not allow speakers to 'exhaust' the structural slots available. This means that, in syllables with three consonants, there are maximally two consonants in the coda and one in the appendix, or one consonant in the coda and two in the appendix. English *corpse* (in rhotic accents) provides an examples of the former structure (-⌊rp⌋-⌊s⌋), while *text* is an instance of the latter type (-⌊k⌋-⌊st⌋).

In German, /s/ (in Apx$_1$) may be added to all voiceless plosives. We find /ps/ as in *Schnaps* and /ks/ as in *Box*. The homorganic cluster /ts/ is also possible, but it should be regarded as an affricate. After /p/, /ʃ/ is allowed in Apx$_1$ too (*hübsch* → [hypʃ]). This type of alternation between /s/ and /ʃ/ in the appendix is reminiscent of the situation found in the prependix (*springen* vs. *Skrupel*). English allows a more restricted range of consonant clusters of the form ⌊plosive + fricative⌋ in the coda.

The only fricative allowed in Apx$_1$ is /s/. Given that English has no affricate /ts/, there are only two types of clusters: /ks/ as in *fix* and /ps/ as in *corpse* or *mumps* (note that [tʃ] and [dʒ] are regarded as affricates, and hence as single consonants).

A final /t/ (in Apx$_2$) may be added either to a single plosive in the coda (e.g. /pt/ as in Engl. *apt* or Germ. *Abt*, /kt/ as in Engl. *act* or Germ. *nackt*), or to specific clusters that emerge from the addition of /s/ in Apx$_1$ to a plosive in C$_2$ of the coda: German has /pst/ (*Herbst* → /hɛrpst/), /kst/ (*Text* → /tɛkst/, *Axt* → /akst/) and /tst/ (*Arzt* → /artst/, with an affricate). English permits only /kst/ (*text*, *next*). Note that /dst/ is attested in *amidst*, but it is questionable whether this word is mono-morphemic since *amidst* can be related to *amid*, analogously to *among/among-st*, so we could assume a morpheme boundary here (*amid-st*).

Summary A summary of English-German contrasts in the appendix is provided in Table 3.3. Affricates and codas containing an affricate are put in parentheses because they could be considered as different types of consonant clusters, since affricates are usually regarded as single consonants.

C$_1$	C$_2$	Apx$_1$	Apx$_2$	English	German
	plosive	s/ʃ		/ps/, /ks/	/ps/, /pʃ/, /ks/
	plosive		t	/pt/, /kt/	/pt/, /kt/
	plosive	s	t	/kst/	/pst/, /kst/
liquid	plosive	s	t	–	/lpst/, /rpst/

Table 3.3 Codas and appendices in English and German

3.5 Stress assignment

3.5.1 External language history and stress

Providing a comparative survey of stress placement in English and German is a rather difficult undertaking. The rules determining where the main stress of a word falls are complex in both languages, and even in their most sophisticated form they generally allow for exceptions. The complexity of the two rule systems has historical reasons: on the one hand, English and German have Germanic roots, and hence obey Germanic rules of stress assignment. One of the most important rules is the following:

⟨2⟩ Germanic stress rule:
Words are stressed on the first syllable of the root.

On the other hand, both languages have **borrowed** a great many words from other (non-Germanic) languages, and thereby have 'imported' new rules and idiosyncratic patterns into their lexicons and sound systems. In German, new lexical items have often preserved the stress pattern of the source language. *Oktober* (< Lat. *október*), *Arena* (< Lat. *aréna*) and *Museum* (< Lat. *mūséum*), for example, have simply inherited their stress patterns from their Latin precursors and do therefore not abide by the Germanic rule as stated in ⟨2⟩. If we wanted to explain why such words are stressed the way they are, we would consequently have to consider the exact phonological make-up of the relevant Latin source lexemes. We would have to take into account whether the nucleus of the penultimate syllable (i.e. the second syllable from the end) is long or short, since short vowels may be unaccented in this position in Latin while long vowels invariably attract stress. Therefore, [e] in Lat. *línea* ('line', cf. Germ. *Linie*) and [ɪ] in *praemium* ('booty, price', cf. Germ. *Prämie*) are unaccented while the long [ō] in *octóber* bears stress.

New types of stress pattern may arise when the lexico-phonological material of a loan word is (basically) preserved, but the word is altered morphologically. For example, in the German nouns *Person* (< Lat. *persóna*), *Figur* (< Lat. *figúra*), and *Advent* (< Lat. *advéntum*) the main stress falls on the same syllable as in the source lexemes, but the Latin endings have been dropped. This leads to final stress, which is (originally) alien to both Germanic and Latin phonology. The emergence of such new stress patterns has been sporadic in German, and has led to a relatively high number of lexical items with **unpredictable stress**, but not to new stress rules. English, by contrast, has not only imported new stress patterns along with borrowed vocabulary, but has also undergone more systematic rearrangements in its phonotactic rules. In particular, English has developed regular final stress in verbs, as a result of language contact with (Norman) French. As far as nouns are concerned, new vocabulary has generally been adapted to the English rules. Quite a number of English and German loan words that are of identical origin therefore have different stress patterns: Germ. *Restaurant* is stressed on the last syllable, imitating the French pronunciation, whereas Engl. *restaurant* is stressed on the first syllable, in accordance with the English rules (cf. Section 3.6.2). The same divergence can be observed in the following pairs of words: Engl. *student* vs. Germ. *Student* (< Lat. *studens*, pl. *studéntes*), Engl. *patent* vs. Germ. *Patent* (< Lat. *patens*, pl. *paténtes*), Engl. *abstract* vs. Germ. *abstrakt* (< Lat. *abstráctum*), and more common words like Engl. *person* vs. Germ. *Person* and Engl. *figure* vs. Germ. *Figur*.

Although many stress patterns could best be explained with reference to historical changes, a number of synchronic rules, with varying degrees of reliability, can also be established. In order to describe these rules, we need a certain repertoire of technical terms that allow us to refer to specific types of syllables in terms of their structural characteristics, as well as to their position within a word. These terms will briefly be introduced in the next section. Moreover, some additional remarks concerning the relationship between morphology and phonology will be made which are necessary for an understanding of the rules described below.

3.5.2 Words, syllables and affixes

The position of a syllable in a word Every word is made up of at least one syllable. If a word contains two syllables, it is 'disyllabic', if it contains three syllables,
we say that it is 'trisyllabic' – and so on for 'tetrasyllabic' words (four syllables),
'pentasyllabic' words (five syllables), etc. Since mono-morphemic words do generally not have more than three syllables, the last two of these terms are not relevant
in the present context.

In most Indo-European languages, rules of stress assignment relate to the number
and order of syllables. Some languages have rules in which syllables are 'counted'
from left to right (e.g. the Germanic rule 'stress the first syllable of the root', cf.
⟨2⟩), while other languages determine the stress patterns of their words from right
to left (e.g. 'stress the second syllable from the end'). In order to describe rules
of the latter form, a terminology has established itself that allows us to refer to
syllables in terms of their 'distance' from the right margin of a word. The last
syllable is commonly referred to as the 'final' or **ultimate syllable**'; the next syllable
to the left is the 'penultimate syllable' or, for short, the **penult**'; and the third one
is the 'antepenultimate syllable' or **antepenult**'. For the next syllable preceding
the antepenult we can simply add another prefix 'pre-' in order to avoid recursion
of *ante-* (the 'pre-antepenult' rather than the 'ante-antepenult'). The use of this
terminology can be illustrated using the word *propensity*:

⟨3⟩ prə   pɛn   sɪ   ti
     pre-antepenult antepenult penult ultimate syllable

Heavy syllables, light syllables and hybrid syllables In order to describe rules
of stress placement, it is useful to distinguish three types of syllables: (a) 'heavy
syllables', (b) 'light syllables' and (c) 'hybrid syllables'. Heavy syllables have a
tense vowel in the nucleus and/or at least two consonants in the coda. For example,
the syllables /iːz/, /ɪnt/ and /mɛlt/ are heavy. Light syllables have a lax vowel or
a syllabic consonant in the nucleus and are open, i.e. they have an empty coda –
syllables like /pæ/, /mʊ/ and /bɪ/ belong in this group. Finally, the term 'hybrid
syllable' subsumes a class of syllables that share properties with both heavy and
light syllables. It refers to syllables with a lax vowel in the nucleus and exactly one
consonant in the coda (e.g. /pɪt/, /mɛn/, etc.).

Remarks on the phonological status of affixes In the context of phonotactics
it was mentioned that phonological rules are not completely independent of morphological properties of the relevant words. An additional aspect of the relationship between these two levels of linguistic analysis becomes relevant when we
consider rules of stress placement: Phonological rules often apply in such a way
that **morpheme boundaries** are assumed where in a strictly morphological analysis

we would not find any. This means that some words are treated as being morphologically complex even though they cannot be so analyzed from a semantic point of view. Let us consider an example: the verb *beget* is, morphologically, mono-morphemic. If we assume a morpheme boundary between the two syllables *be* and *get*, this gives us a prefix with an inchoative/causative function (cf. *be-friend*, *be-witch*) and a verbal base with the meanings 'receive', 'obtain', etc. But we cannot possibly derive the meaning of *beget* ('give existence to [a child]' or 'bring about') from these components. Yet, the word clearly *looks as if it were morphologically complex* and is also treated as such by the phonological component of grammar – otherwise it would be pronounced ['bɛgət]. It is therefore necessary to make the following assumption:

⟨4⟩ Rules of stress placement apply on the basis of morphological structures that are not necessarily semantically transparent.

The reasons for the principle stated in ⟨4⟩ are manifold. In part, they certainly have to do with diachronic developments (e.g. some verbs were formerly poly-morphemic but have become morphologically unanalyzable as the result of semantic change), but the synchronic principle of analogy certainly also plays a role (e.g. *be-get* is treated on a par with *be-friend* because the phonological structures of the two words are largely parallel).

3.6 Stress rules for mono-morphemic words

3.6.1 Disyllabic words

As has been pointed out, both English and German are characterized by a **'blend' of stress rules** from Germanic and Romance. In English, the strongest Romance influence came from (Norman) French, while in German most of the relevant loan words are from Latin. These historical facts are reflected in rules of stress assignment.

Stress in disyllabic words can be assigned quite straightforwardly in German. Since in Latin it is always the penult or the antepenult that is stressed, and since the penult is also the first syllable in disyllabic words, Germanic and Latin rules of stress assignment happen to coincide here. Therefore, the following rule provides a reasonable approximation to rules of stress placement in German:

⟨5⟩ In German, disyllabic words are stressed on the first/penultimate syllable.

The rule given in ⟨5⟩ is not sensitive to the lexical class of a word: *Arbeit*, *schlafen*, *aber*, *neben* and *gerne* are all stressed on the first or penultimate syllable. However, there are also disyllabic words that do not conform to the rule stated in ⟨5⟩. As has been mentioned, some words that have been **borrowed** from Latin have preserved their stress patterns while the original suffixes have been dropped. Therefore, *Person*, *Advent* and *Pedal* are stressed on the ultimate syllable. As a result, stress placement cannot be predicted on the basis of purely synchronic information but always depends on the historical source of the relevant items.

The English stress rules accounting for disyllabic words are more complicated, but, on the whole, more systematic. First, a distinction is made between rules for verbs, on the one hand, and rules for nouns, on the other. (We will see that adjectives manifest an intermediate behaviour, as far as stress placement is concerned.) And secondly, stress placement in verbs is sensitive to the structure of the syllables involved. The basic stress rule for English **nouns** is identical to the one established for German disyllabic words in ⟨5⟩. It is given in ⟨6⟩ (note that here we write 'penult' rather than 'first' because all English stress rules can better be described as right-to-left). Like in German, there are some exceptions to this rule in English too, *hotel* and *police* probably being the most frequent ones. Some examples of nouns that abide by the rule given in ⟨6⟩ are provided in ⟨7⟩:

⟨6⟩   In English, disyllabic nouns are stressed on the penult.

⟨7⟩   *accent, bacon, chimney, doctrine, envy, facet, gargoyle, harvest, luggage, minute, nipple*

The rules of stress placement for **verbs** are more complex than those for nouns. In general, the stress pattern of a verb depends on the structure of the ultimate syllable: if it is heavy, stress will usually be final; otherwise – i.e. if the ultimate syllable is either light or hybrid – it will be stressed on the penult, irrespective of its make-up. This is summarized in ⟨8⟩. Some examples illustrating ⟨8a⟩ are given in ⟨9⟩.

⟨8⟩   English disyllabic verbs are stressed:
   a. on the ultimate syllable if it is heavy;
   b. on the penult if the ultimate syllable is not heavy (i.e. light or hybrid).

⟨9⟩   *carouse, esteem, fatigue, foment, lament, maintain*

We can now look at verbs whose ultimate syllable is not heavy. Some relevant examples are given in ⟨10a⟩ and ⟨10b⟩ for hybrid and light final syllables respectively. (In rhotic accents, the examples in ⟨10a⟩ belong to the same category as those in ⟨10b⟩.)

⟨10⟩   verbs with a hybrid or light ultimate syllable
   a. *ambush, banish, brevet, cancel, cosset, covet, debit, drivel, finish, happen, menace, notice, posit*
   b. *alter, answer, cover, foster*

The rules given in ⟨8⟩ do not apply to verbs like *beget* or *upset* because these are regarded as morphologically complex (cf. Section 3.5.2). Still, there are some

exceptions to ⟨8⟩. First, verbs ending in *-ow* (*bellow, borrow, follow, swallow*) 'should' be stressed on the final syllable in accordance with ⟨8a⟩, since diphthongs are categorized as tense vowels and the relevant syllables are therefore heavy. But they are actually stressed on the penult. There are two ways of explaining these exceptions. On the one hand, we could argue that there is a suffix *-ow* (/əʊ/) which is never stressed. This (morphological) explanation would be analogous to the one given for the apparently exceptional stress pattern of *beget*. On the other hand, we could argue (phonologically) that syllables ending in /əʊ/ could be classified as hybrid if we regard the final segment of those syllables as a glide. But such explanations hardly have any theoretical value. It therefore seems reasonable to simply assume an additional rule which stipulates that (specific) 'disyllabic verbs ending in /əʊ/ are stressed on the penult'.

While the explanations given for the stress pattern of verbs like *borrow* may not be particularly striking, there is a second set of apparent exceptions that can clearly be explained on the basis of morphological considerations. The verbs *balance, harvest, license* and *warrant* should be stressed on the ultimate syllable, in accordance with their phonological make-up. However, these verbs are stressed on the penult. The reason is that they are clearly derived from nouns and can be used in a verbal function only as the result of **conversion** (i.e. derivation without any morphological indicator).

Cases of conversion like those discussed in the previous paragraph must be distinguished from pairs of words that have identical segments but differ in their stress patterns. Often, the lexical class of such words can be determined on the basis of stress: when used as nouns, the main stress falls on the first or penultimate syllable, and when used as verbs, they have final stress. The words in ⟨11⟩ represent only a selection of such items whose lexical class varies systematically with stress positions:

⟨11⟩   *contrast, extract, import, record, subject, progress, project*

Let us now consider **adjectives**. The stress rules for (disyllabic) adjectives are particularly difficult to describe because there is a chimera haunting the phonological literature which says that adjectives generally behave like verbs. This generalization is based on adjectives like the ones in ⟨12⟩: they have a heavy ultimate syllable, and they are stressed on that syllable. This, apparently, parallels the behaviour of verbs.

⟨12⟩   *alert, alive, correct, divine, immune, obscene, serene*

However, there are two problems with this generalization: first, some of the examples in ⟨12⟩ are not very well chosen: *alert* and *alive* belong to a well-defined series of adjectives beginning with *a-*, one of whose most salient characteristics is that most of them cannot occur in an attributive function (cf. *a-wake, a-top, a-kin*, etc.). These words are clearly morphologically complex. And second, there are also numerous disyllabic adjectives with a heavy ultimate syllable that are stressed on the penult. A selection of such alleged 'exceptions' is provided in ⟨13⟩.

⟨13⟩   *ancient, fragile, hollow, narrow, perfect, pleasant*

The trouble is that there are hardly any disyllabic adjectives which are clearly mono-morphemic from a phonological point of view, i.e. disyllabic adjectives that do not incorporate any segments that could be analyzed as derivational affixes. Therefore, stress assignment is generally a function of the relevant **affixes**. For example, disyllabic adjectives ending in *-ant*, *-ient* and *-ow* are generally stressed on the penult, while endings like *-eme* and *-ene* attract stress. Some of the endings that are usually associated with specific stress patterns are listed in ⟨14⟩.

⟨14⟩   a.   stress on the penult:
            -ant: *flagrant, pleasant, pregnant, regnant, stagnant, vacant*
            -ow: *callow, hollow, mellow, narrow, shallow, yellow*
            -ient: *ancient, patient, sentient*
            -ous: *anxious, famous*
       b.   stress on the ultimate syllable:
            -eme: *extreme, supreme*
            -ene: *obscene, serene*

The very few 'atomic' disyllabic adjectives that we can identify in the lexicon of English seem to pattern with nouns (e.g. *stubborn*). Moreover, there is an additional indication that in some sense, adjectives are more akin to nouns than to verbs: in ⟨11⟩, we saw that certain lexical items can function as both nouns and verbs, depending on the stress pattern. If nouns or verbs can also be used as adjectives, they usually exhibit the stress pattern of a noun in their adjectival uses, not that of a verb. Some relevant examples are given in ⟨15⟩.

⟨15⟩   *concrete, desert, present, subject, suspect*

3.6.2 Trisyllabic words

In German, it is virtually impossible to describe the stress patterns of trisyllabic words in purely synchronic terms. Such rules could be provided only with reference to the historical origins of the relevant words. As pointed out above (cf. ⟨2⟩), words of Germanic origin tend to be stressed on the first syllable, which is a relatively widespread pattern among trisyllabic words as well (e.g. *Ameise, Herberge, Bräutigam*). Also, it has been mentioned that words of non-Germanic origin have often preserved the stress pattern of the relevant source lexeme (e.g. *Oktober, Museum*), and that in many cases final stress has resulted from the loss of some ending (e.g. *Appetit, Apparat*). If we wanted to find general rules of stress placement for these words, we would have to classify each of them according to its **historical origin**. There are three major classes: (i) words of Germanic origin, (ii) words of Latin origin that have basically remained unchanged, and (iii) words of Latin origin whose endings have been dropped. However, this would be a mere lexicographic exercise which would certainly not be helpful for learners of German. We will therefore assume that stress in trisyllabic words is lexical and has to be learnt with each word separately. It is probably just a small comfort that the problem of trisyllabic words is basically restricted to nouns: there seem to be no trisyllabic basic German verbs or adjectives.

Turning to English, the situation is different. Rules of stress assignment for trisyllabic words are relatively straightforward; only they are just as complex as those for disyllabic words. Again, we have to consider two factors if we want to determine where the main stress falls: (i) the lexical class of the relevant item, and (ii) the types of syllable involved. Let us begin with **nouns**: if the penult of a noun is heavy or hybrid, then it is stressed (e.g. *advántage*); if the penult is light, the main stress falls on the antepenult (e.g. *cítizen*). This rule is summarized in ⟨16⟩:

⟨16⟩   English trisyllabic nouns are stressed:
   a.   on the penult if it is not light (i.e. heavy or hybrid);
   b.   on the antepenult if the penult is light.

Let us consider some examples. ⟨17a⟩ gives a list of trisyllabic nouns with stress on the penult (the penult is heavy or hybrid), and ⟨17b⟩ provides a list of nouns with light penults:

⟨17⟩   a.   stress on penult: *appendix, banana, intestine, mosquito, synopsis, tomato, veranda, utensil*
   b.   stress on antepenult: *asterisk, citizen, cinema, hospital, institute, paragraph, parliament, restaurant, telescope*

The rules for trisyllabic **verbs** likewise stand in a close relationship to those for disyllabic verbs: the 'critical' syllable is also the last one here. If it is heavy, the main stress falls on the antepenult; if the ultimate syllable is not heavy (i.e. light or hybrid), it is the penult that is stressed. These rules are summarized in ⟨18⟩, and some examples are given in ⟨19⟩.

⟨18⟩   In English, trisyllabic verbs are stressed:
   a.   on the penult if the ultimate syllable is not heavy;
   b.   on the antepenult if the ultimate syllable is heavy.
⟨19⟩   a.   ultimate syllable is not heavy (stress on penult):
        abandon, accomplish, elicit, establish, imagine
   b.   ultimate syllable is heavy (stress on antepenult):
        analyze, celebrate, culminate, dominate, emphasize

In comparison to disyllabic verbs, trisyllabic ones show a relatively regular behaviour with regard to their stress patterns. Still, there are some cases that require at least some further considerations and might be regarded as exceptions. For example, *benefit* has a hybrid ultimate syllable and should thus be stressed on the penult (cf. *elicit*), but is actually stressed on the antepenult. Conversely, *contribute* should be stressed on the antepenult, in accordance with ⟨19b⟩, but is usually stressed on the penult. As far as *benefit* is concerned, we could argue that it is basically a noun and becomes a verb only via conversion. The stress pattern of *contribute* (with stress on the penult) can be explained if we assume that it is poly-morphemic (cf. *at-tribute*). Note that this explanation presupposes that the verbal base is derived from the noun *tribute*, since a verb *tribute* would have to be stressed on the final syllable. Those speakers who stress *contribute* on the first syllable seem to treat that word as a basic lexical item (so ⟨18b⟩ applies).

The last lexical class to be considered in this section is, again, that of **adjectives**. As we saw above, disyllabic adjectives show stress patterns that locate them somewhere in between nouns and verbs, although they are more akin to the former. For trisyllabic adjectives, general rules of stress assignment are even more difficult to determine. In many cases, the actually existing patterns can be explained on the basis of rules for either verbs or nouns. For example, *difficult* would have to be stressed on the antepenult according to both of the relevant rules, and the same applies to *arrogant* and *elegant*. As we have seen, it moreover makes sense to assume that many adjectives are morphologically complex (or at least behave as if they were complex). For example, *important* can be related to the verb *import*, and *abundant* to *abound*. In view of the low number of trisyllabic adjectives that are clearly mono-morphemic we will not make any further generalizations concerning their stress patterns.

Summary The rules for stress assignment in mono-morphemic English and German nouns and verbs can be summarized as shown in Table 3.4.

POS	*n*-syllabic	English	German
N	disyllabic	penult	penult (ultimate)
	trisyllabic	(a) penult if penult is not light (b) antepenult if penult is light	idiosyncratic
V	disyllabic	(a) ultimate syllable if it is heavy (b) penult if ultimate syllable is not heavy	penult
	trisyllabic	(a) penult if ultimate syllable is not heavy (b) antepenult if ultimate syllable is heavy	–

Table 3.4 Stress rules in mono-morphemes

3.7 Stress in morphologically complex words

Morphologically complex words behave similarly in English and German. There are three classes of derivational affixes: (i) those that change the stress pattern of a word, (ii) those that leave the original stress pattern intact and are themselves unstressed, and (iii) those that do not affect the stress pattern of the base and bear an additional (primary or secondary) accent. The first type of morpheme is called 'stress-shifting' and the second 'stress-neutral'. For the third type of affix we will use the label 'stressed' affixes. While English and German show few contrasts in the domain of stress-shifting and stress-neutral affixes, an important difference will be pointed out concerning the phonological behaviour of stressed affixes.

3.7.1 Stress-neutral and stress-shifting suffixes

As a general rule, most suffixes of **Germanic** origin are **stress-neutral**. For example, the English suffixes *-ship* (*partnership*) and *-hood* (*likelihood*) never change the stress pattern of their bases. In some cases, the addition of such stress-neutral suffixes to a verbal, adjectival or nominal base gives rise to stress patterns that would be impossible in mono-morphemes: when a stress-neutral suffix is added to a trisyllabic word with main stress on the antepenult, the resulting word is stressed on the pre-antepenult (e.g. *cómpromis-ing, cháncellor-hood*). Parallel examples can be found in German (e.g. *Kléinbürger-tum, Ánalphabeten-tum*). **Stress-shifting** affixes are typically of **Romance** origin. We can distinguish two types: (i) affixes that attract stress (e.g. the English suffix *-ation* as in *declar-átion* and Germ. *-ant* as in *Liefer-ánt*), and (ii) affixes that are associated with fixed stress positions but that are not themselves stressed (e.g. the English suffixes *´-ify* and *´-ity* as in *solídify* or *solídity*; they always derive words with stress on the antepenult). This class of stress-shifting affixes is sometimes also called 'stress-changing'. Some examples of stress-neutral and stress-shifting suffixes are listed in Table 3.5.

English	German
stress-neutral	
apprais(e)-*al*	Lobpreis-*ung*
announc(e)-*er*	Faulenz-*er*
cheap-*en*	Ungereimt-*heit*
resent-*ful*	freud-*voll*
likeli-*hood*	Wahrscheinlich-*keit*
compromis(e)-*ing*	Abschwäch-*ung*
fever-*ish*	fieber-*haft*
humour-*less*	humor-*los*
coward-*ly*	überschwäng-*lich*
question-*able*	verwert-*bar*
partner-*ship*	Partner-*schaft*
stress shifting	
triangu-*lar*	defizit-*är*
solid-*ify*	Liefer-*ant*
declar-*ation*	Stabili-*tät*
question(n)-*aire*	form-*ell*
employ-*ee*	form-*al*
honor-*ific*	praktik-*abel*
economi-*cs*	Idiot-*ie*

Table 3.5 Stress-neutral and -shifting affixes in English and German

3.7.2 Stress-neutral and stressed prefixes

While the derivational suffixes of both English and German are either stress-shifting or stress-neutral, prefixes are either stress-neutral or stressed. The class of **stress-neutral prefixes** includes affixes such as *de-* in Engl. *de-fer* and *ver-* as in Germ. *ver-laufen*. Stressed affixes introduce an additional stress position into the word. Since one of the resulting accents is stronger than the other, a distinction is made between '**primary**' and '**secondary stress**'.

The German negative prefix *un-* forms part of the class of **stressed affixes**. When it is prefixed to the adjective *glücklich*, the resulting pronunciation is [ˈʊnˌɡlʏklɪç], i.e. the prefix attracts primary stress, but the stress position of the (adjectival) base is not deaccented completely and retains a secondary stress. Such instances of 'double stress' are commonly known from compounds like *Hausmeister* ([ˈhaʊsˌmaɪstɐ]). Therefore, some phonologists assume that stressed affixes exhibit the phonological behaviour of free morphemes. Other relevant examples of such affixes are *sub-* as in *súb-òptimal* and *in-* as in *ín-akzeptàbel*.

Like German, English has some stressed affixes too – for example, the prefix *un-* as in *un-happy*. However, there is a crucial difference between English and German as far as the distribution of primary and secondary stress within the derivate is concerned: in English, the main stress remains on the root, and the affix only bears secondary stress. Therefore, *unhappy* is pronounced [ˌʌnˈhæpi]. Secondary stress on derivational prefixes can also be observed in *ìn-advértently*, *sùb-cónsciously* and *ùnder-cóver*.

Stressed prefixes are much more numerous in German than in English. In particular, there is an extensive class of verbal stressed prefixes (or 'verbal particles') that do not have correlates in English, for example *an-* in *an-fahren*, *ab-* in *ab-fahren* and *aus-* in *aus-laufen*. The closest English near-equivalents of those elements are verbal particles like *out* in *go out* (cf. Germ. *aus-gehen*).

German prefixes like *ab-* and *an-* are also called '**separable**' because they are separated from the verbal root in main clauses when the main verb is finite (*Ich gehe jetzt aus*). Separable affixes contrast with 'non-separable' ones, which are always contained in the verb (e.g. *ver-laufen*, *ent-laufen*), and which are generally stress-neutral. Some German affixes have both a 'separable' and a 'non-separable' use, and their meaning varies accordingly. For instance, the prefix *um-* means *around* when used as a non-separable prefix while it means *over* as in *knock over* when it is separable. The following sentence (which is standardly quoted in that context) has therefore two different meanings, depending on whether *um-* is stressed or not: *Bitte den Verkehrspolizisten von hinten umfahren!*

3.8 Summary

In this chapter we have considered some fine-grained differences between English and German in the domain of 'syntagmatic' phonology (phonotactics) and stress. While the syllable structures of English and German are relatively similar, considerable differences have been found in rules of stress assignment. These contrasts can be clearly related to differences in 'external' language history, as the more flexible or innovative rules of English are certainly not unrelated to the considerable amount of language contact that this language has been exposed to.

Revision, questions and exercises

1. Many phonotactic restrictions of English and German can be explained in terms of general principles. Consider the following rules: (a) /tl/ and /dl/ are the only combinations of a plosive and a liquid that are disallowed in the onset; and (b) /pw/ and /bw/ are the only combinations of a plosive plus /w/ that are illicit in the English onset. Can you generalize over these facts?
2. All combinations of nasals and plosives in the English coda are homorganic. To what extent is this expected, against the background of question 1.?
3. Onset clusters involving a prependix are categorically disallowed in some Romance languages like Spanish. What do speakers of those languages do when they pronounce words like *spain* or *strong*?
4. Given that so-called 'separable' prefixes in German may be detached from the verb, the question arises whether we should call these elements 'affixes' at all. Discuss some pros and cons of this assumption, considering both phonological and morphological/syntactic facts.

Further reading

There is a large body of literature on phonotactics and stress, most of which is theoretically oriented rather than descriptive, however. Overviews of English syllable structure can be found in Giegerich (1992: Ch. 6) and Carr (2015: Ch. 7). For stress placement in English see Giegerich (1992: Ch. 7) and Carr (2015: Ch. 8) (cf. also Kreidler 1997 and, for a radically different view of stress theory, Burzio 1994). The syllable structure of German is described in Wiese (1996: Ch. 3), Hall (2000: Ch. 8) (see also Hall 1992) and Schäfer (2016: Ch. 4). For stress placement in German see Wiese (1996: Ch. 8), Hall (2000: Ch. 9) and Schäfer (2016: Ch. 4). Berg (1997) is a contrastive study with a focus on proper names, Domahs *et al.* (2014) is a (theoretical) comparative study of English, German and Dutch, where additional pertinent references can be found.

4 Inflectional morphology

> "I heard a Californian student in Heidelberg say, in one of his calmest moods, that he would rather decline two drinks than one German adjective."
>
> (M. Twain, *The Awful German Language*)

There are two major systems of expressive devices distinguishable in every language: (a) the **lexicon**, i.e. the inventory of basic units of meaning, and (b) the **grammatical system** of a language. Communication without grammar, or with very little grammar, is possible and can be found in early stages of (first and second) language acquisition, in pidgins and the language use of migrant workers. The full command of a language also requires mastery of the grammatical system and its three subsystems intonation, constituent order and morphology. It is the last of these subsystems and its structure in English and in German that will be discussed in this chapter.

In contrast to other domains of grammatical structure, there are no difficulties in **establishing comparability** in this domain. By and large, the inflectional categories typically distinguished in grammars of German can also be distinguished in English and vice versa, and the major contrasts between the two languages concern the realization of these categories and perhaps also the extent to which these categories still play a role in the synchrony of both languages. The focus of our analysis will be on inflectional morphology. As far as the organization of the chapter is concerned, we can make a first division between the three major lexical categories that inflect both in English and in German: (i) nouns and pronouns (as well as articles), (ii) adjectives and (iii) verbs. All other word classes (adverbs, prepositions, conjunctions, etc.) do not inflect in German or in English.

4.1 Nouns and pronouns

4.1.1 The inflection of nouns and articles in German

The inflection of nouns is traditionally discussed in combination with the inflectional behaviour of pronouns and that of articles. Pronouns such as *er*, *sie*, *es*, etc. can roughly be defined as expressions that are substituted for noun phrases under specific grammatical or contextual conditions and depend on those noun phrases for their interpretation. The **subclasses of pronouns** usually distinguished in grammars include the following: (i) personal pronouns, (ii) possessive pronouns, (iii) reflexive pronouns, (iv) relative pronouns, (v) interrogative pronouns, (vi) demonstrative pronouns, (vii) indefinite pronouns and (viii) impersonal pronouns. Articles (e.g. *der*, *die*, *das*) typically derive from demonstrative pronouns and combine with nouns to form a noun phrase (NP) or, according to more recent views, a determiner phrase (DP).

In German, **nouns** inflect for case and number. Articles moreover exhibit gender inflection. This is illustrated by the paradigms in Table 4.1 (strong inflection). As can be seen from this table, there are four cases (nominative, accusative, dative and genitive) and two number categories (singular and plural). Three (grammatical) gender categories are distinguished in the singular (masculine, feminine, neuter), but there are no gender distinctions in the plural. Feminine nouns do not inflect for case, and case distinctions are indicated only by the article here. In the strong inflection, there is no morphological distinction between nouns in the nominative and nouns in the accusative in any of the gender categories. In the weak inflection (*der Junge*, *den Junge-n*, *dem Junge-n*, etc.), a distinction is made between the nominative singular form, on the one hand, and all other forms, on the other.

Table 4.1 also illustrates that in the nominal paradigm there is massive '**syncretism**', i.e. formal identity of different categories, and that most of the categorical distinctions are made by articles, or by the combination of a specific article with a given nominal form. In the strong inflection, there are only two different suffixes attaching to nouns in the singular (*-es, -e*), and only one of them is commonly used in contemporary German (genitive *-es*). In the weak inflection, there is only one suffix (*-n*). In either case, there are six different forms of the definite article for the twelve cells in the table. A specific form – for instance, the article *die* – may have a variety of inflectional features: feminine, singular, nominative and feminine, singular, accusative as well as plural for all genders. However, when we consider specific combinations of an article and a noun, most of the ambiguities vanish. In other words, inflection is 'distributed' over the determiner and the noun, so that it

NUM	CASE	MASC		FEM		NEUT	
SG	Nom	der	Mann	die	Puppe	das	Haus
	Acc	den	Mann	die	Puppe	das	Haus
	Dat	dem	Mann-(e)	der	Puppe	dem	Haus-(e)
	Gen	des	Mann-es	der	Puppe	des	Haus-es
PL	Nom	die	Männ-er	die	Puppe-n	die	Häus-er
	Acc	die	Männ-er	die	Puppe-n	die	Häus-er
	Dat	den	Männ-er-n	den	Puppe-n	den	Häus-er-n
	Gen	der	Männ-er	der	Puppe-n	der	Häus-er

Table 4.1 Inflection of German articles and nouns

is NPs (rather than articles or nouns) that are morphologically specified for gender, number and case. In Table 4.1, only three singular NPs are ambiguous: *die Puppe* (nominative and accusative singular), *der Puppe* (genitive and dative singular), and *das Haus* (nominative and accusative singular). Thus, there are nine different NPs for the twelve cells in the upper half of the paradigm.

4.1.2 Plural formation in German

The precise form of inflectional markers (of case and number) may vary (*die Männ-er, die Bräuch-e, die Oma-s,* etc.). This fact is captured by distinguishing several noun classes. We will not go into this problem in great detail, and we will restrict ourselves to some remarks concerning the formal expression of plurality in German. On the face of it, there seem to be very many patterns of plural formation in German; but if one takes some phonological information into account, the

plural marker		SG	PL	
I	-(e)n	die Zeit	die Zeit	-[ən]
		die Ampel	die Ampel	-[n]
II	(-e)	der Hund	die Hund	-[ə]
		das Pendel	die Pendel	-∅
III	¨(-e)	der Kran	die Krän	-[ə]
		der Apfel	die Äpfel	-∅
IV	(¨)-er	das Haus	die Häus	-[ɐ]
		das Kind	die Kind	-[ɐ]
V	-s	das Auto	die Auto	-[s]

Table 4.2 German plural formation

enormous variation in plural formation can be reduced to five basic types (cf. Wegener 1999). There is a regular correspondence between specific suffixes (allomorphs) which is sensitive to the phonological make-up of the stem: if the last syllable of a word contains schwa (e.g. *die Ampel*), there is never an additional schwa in the ending (*die Am*[pəln] rather than *die Amp[ələn]). This process is called '**schwa-deletion**'. Taking this rule into account we can distinguish only five strategies of plural formation (cf. Table 4.2):

(i)   the plural in -[(ə)n] (*die Zeit → die Zeiten*); schwa-deletion applies regularly, e.g. in *Ampel → Ampel-n*;

(ii) the plural in [ə] (*Hund → Hunde*); if the final syllable of the word contains schwa, the suffix is phonologically empty (schwa-deletion), e.g. *Pendel → Pendel*;

(iii) plural formation of type (ii) plus *umlaut* (*Floh → Flöhe*); schwa-deletion applies (*Vogel → Vögel*);

(iv) *umlaut* + [ɐ] (*Wald → Wälder*); *umlaut* applies only to /a/, /o/ and /u/ (*Kind → Kind-er*);

(v)   -s (*Auto → Auto-s*).

While in many cases it simply has to be learnt what kind of plural formation applies to a given word, there are some regularities as well. For instance, feminine nouns ending in schwa always form their plural by adding [n] (*Pause-n*, *Birne-n*, etc.).

As mentioned above, there is a certain 'division of labour' between articles and nouns in the marking of case, gender and number in NPs. This division of labour can be regarded as an **economy principle** which says that grammatical categories need not be marked redundantly within an NP. As will be seen below, such a principle can also be observed in the case marking of adjectives. That it is also relevant to number marking can be seen from the following observation (cf. Wegener 1995: 23): nouns with a zero-marked plural always have either masculine or neuter, but never feminine gender. This fact can be regarded as being related to a more general economy principle because masculine and neuter nouns mark the plural in the article (*der/das* vs. *die*) whereas the feminine article is ambiguous between singular and plural. Consider the following masculine (cf. ⟨1⟩) and neuter (cf. ⟨2⟩) nouns which do not show any indication of plural marking on the noun (i.e. they are of type II in Table 4.2):

⟨1⟩ a. *der Löffel* – *die Löffel*
     b. *der Zettel* – *die Zettel*
     c. *der Schlüssel* – *die Schlüssel*
     d. *der Erker* – *die Erker*
     e. *der Füller* – *die Füller*
     f. *der Kiefer* – *die Kiefer*
⟨2⟩ a. *das Pendel* – *die Pendel*
     b. *das Mündel* – *die Mündel*
     c. *das Banner* – *die Banner*

The feminine nouns in ⟨3⟩, by contrast, do exhibit a morphological indicator of plurality (*-n*); they are of type I:

⟨3⟩ a. *die Schüssel* – *die Schüssel-n*
     b. *die Nadel* – *die Nadel-n*
     c. *die Gabel* – *die Gabel-n*
     d. *die Feder* – *die Feder-n*
     e. *die Ader* – *die Ader-n*
     f. *die Mauer* – *die Mauer-n*
     g. *die Kiefer* – *die Kiefer-n*

Inherent vs. non-inherent features There is a further point illustrated by Figure 4.1 above that is worth mentioning: the values for case and number assigned to the different cells are a property of the relevant word-form, whereas gender is a property of the whole paradigm (or lexeme). For instance, the lexeme HUND has the gender 'masculine' in all its possible forms. This difference in the status of the categories 'case' and 'number', on the one hand, and 'gender', on the other, is often captured in grammars by classifying the former as 'non-inherent' features (*Einheitenkategorien*) and the latter as 'inherent' features (*Wortkategorien*; cf. Eisenberg 2006a).

Gender assignment in German Gender has a semantic basis in German, but it is not fully predictable: nouns denoting male humans are generally masculine, and nouns denoting female humans are usually feminine, but there are some exceptions (e.g. *das Weib*). One of the most difficult tasks for any (first or second language) learner of German is to learn what gender classes the other nouns belong to. Though it is often said that gender assignment in German is completely arbitrary, a series of studies (e.g. Köpcke 1982, Zubin and Köpcke 1989) have shown that a number of generalizations are in fact possible. Apart from the typical associations between **derivational affixes** and gender (*-heit, -keit, -ung, -schaft* → feminine; *-ling, -er* → masculine, *-chen* → neuter) there are lexical subsystems in German which oppose masculine and feminine subordinate terms to a neuter superordinate term (*der Apfel, die Birne* vs. *das Obst*). Moreover, there are expressions with derivational suffixes like *-mut* or *-nis*, which may have one of two genders (*der Wagemut, der Übermut* vs. *die Anmut, die Wehmut*) and whose assignment seems to correlate with the parameter '**extroversion**' vs. '**introversion**' (Zubin and Köpcke 1989), which has been related to stereotypically male and stereotypically female properties:

⟨4⟩ 'introverted'
    a. die Anmut 'gracefulness'
    b. die Zagemut (obsolete) 'timidity'
    c. die Wehmut 'melancholy'

⟨5⟩ 'extroverted'
    a. der Hochmut 'arrogance'
    b. der Übermut 'foolhardiness'
    c. der Wagemut 'bravado'

In German, gender distinctions show up in agreement between nouns, articles and adjectives and in the selection of pronouns. In the latter case, there is one more interesting example illustrating the semantic motivation of formal categories: the stressed, **deictic** use of personal pronouns is completely determined by semantic principles. *Er* and *sie* can only refer to male or female humans or higher animals:

⟨6⟩   a. Mir gefällt dieser Tisch. Ich nehme ihn.
        b. Welchen Tisch nehmen sie jetzt?
            – *Ich nehme IHN (pointing gesture).
            – Ich nehme DIESEN DA.

A similar phenomenon is illustrated by ⟨7⟩. Only an anaphoric pronoun that refers to a human being or animal can follow a preposition. An anaphor relating to a noun phrase with an inanimate referent can be spelled out as *da*-PREP (e.g. *da-mit, da-von*, etc.).

⟨7⟩ Karl hat einen Ball/Hund bekommen und hat den ganzen Tag damit/mit ihm gespielt.

In a major grammar of German (Eisenberg 2006a), the term 'Wortkategorie' is also used for some other properties of nouns that have repercussions on their inflectional behaviour: the distinction between proper names and common nouns, and the distinction between count nouns and mass nouns among the latter. In addition to gender, a second inherent category ('Wortkategorie') is therefore assigned to nouns, namely that of '**individuation**', which can assume one of three values: 'proper name' (e.g. *Paul, Maria*), 'count' (*Berg, Hund*), or 'mass' (*Wasser, Zeit*). These distinctions play a role in the rules for the genitive and the plural (e.g. *des Hund-es* vs. *Paul-s*), in the use of articles or quantifiers (*zwei Berge* vs. **zwei Wasser*) as well as in the semantic interpretation of the relevant expressions.

4.1.3 The inflection of pronouns in German

The different subclasses of pronouns do not manifest a uniform inflectional behaviour, and most of the forms are suppletive (and therefore not segmentable). As far as the personal pronouns (summarized in Table 4.3) are concerned, a number of facts are

CASE	1	2	3		
NOM	ich	du	er	sie	es
ACC	mich	dich	ihn	sie	es
DAT	mir	dir	ihm	ihr	ihm
GEN	meiner	deiner	seiner	ihrer	seiner

Table 4.3 Personal pronouns of German

noteworthy: while the nominative forms seem to be completely idiosyncratic (*ich, du, er, sie, es*, etc.), the other case forms seem to exhibit specific morphological characteristics, at least in the first and second persons. The relevant accusative forms are associated with a stem *-ich* as in *m-ich* and *d-ich*. Interestingly, it is the reflexive pronoun *sich* that patterns with these forms morphologically in the third person, while the anaphoric third person pronouns *ihn, sie, es* are, again, idiosyncratic (cf. Gast and Hole 2003). The situation is slightly different in the dative, where the feminine form in the third person *ihr* is similar to the first and second person forms, whereas the masculine and neuter form *ihm* is clearly different (*mir, dir, ihr* vs. *ihm*). The reflexive pronoun *sich* is also used in the dative.

The genitive forms are based on the possessive pronouns *mein, dein*, etc. plus a suffix *-er*. Note that it is important to make a distinction between **genitive pronouns** and **possessive pronouns**: While the former are of category NP and consequently have the relevant distribution (cf. ⟨8⟩), possessive pronouns are nominal modifiers and have more or less the distribution of a determiner (cf. ⟨9⟩).

⟨8⟩   a. Ich erinnere mich deiner/seiner/ihrer, etc.

       b. Er gedenkt meiner/deiner/seiner/ihrer, etc.

⟨9⟩   Dies ist mein Auto.

A fact that is remarkable from the perspective of English is that there are two types of **possessive pronouns** or 'determiners' in German: (i) *sein/ihr*, and a form corresponding to the genitive of the demonstrative pronouns (*dessen/deren*). There is a semantic contrast between these two forms which may be exploited for purposes of **reference tracking**: the demonstrative forms are used whenever the possessor in question is not topical or expected, e.g. if it is not the subject of the same clause:

⟨10⟩   a. Plötzlich sah Otto ...

          ... seinen Freund mit seiner Frau.

          ... seinen Freund mit dessen Frau.

       b. Maria liebt ...

          ... ihre Nichte und ihre Freunde.

          ... ihre Nichte und deren Freunde.

In ⟨10a⟩ *seine Frau* could be the wife of *Otto*, whereas *dessen Frau* can only refer to the wife of his friend, and a parallel contrast can be observed in ⟨10b⟩. In English, a distinction as illustrated in ⟨10⟩ cannot easily be made. This is related to the fact that English does not have mono-morphemic demonstrative pronouns for

	MASC	FEM	NEUT	PL
NOM	dies-er	-e	-es	-e
ACC	dies-en	-e	-es	-e
DAT	dies-em	-er	-em	-en
GEN	dies-es	-er	-es	-er

Table 4.4 German demonstrative pronouns

animate reference and uses the demonstrative determiners *this* or *that*, sometimes combined with the pronoun *one* (*this one*, *that one*, etc.). The inflectional paradigm of German demonstrative pronouns is given in Table 4.4.

The only genuine reflexive pronoun of German (*sich*) is used for the third person. It does not inflect for gender, number or case. A more comprehensive discussion of reflexive marking in German and English is provided in Chapter 10. Indefinite and generic pronouns will be dealt with in Chapter 17.

4.1.4 The inflection of pronouns and nouns in English

Given the **poverty of nominal inflection** in English, this section is considerably shorter than the previous one. Within the noun phrase only nouns and pronouns (and, to a very limited degree, adjectives) inflect, while articles are invariant. But even (pro)nominal inflection is severely reduced, in comparison to German and Old English. As in German, nouns inflect for number (singular vs. plural, where only the plural is marked overtly), but plural inflection is much more uniform in English. The vast majority of nouns takes the suffix *-s*, which may take three different forms, depending on the final sound of the noun ([s], [z] or [ɪz]). The other plural markers (in particular, *-ren/child-ren*, *-en/ox-en*, 'vowel gradation'/*ablaut* as in *foot/feet*, *mouse/mice*, and 'zero marking'/*fish*) only show up with a small number of nouns and can be regarded as genuine irregularities, whereas the different ways of plural formation distinguished for German in Section 4.1.1 can be considered as regular.

Gender is only relevant for the choice of pronouns in English (in other words, English has a pronominal gender system). If we neglect minor details, we can simply say that the choice of a pronoun for a noun phrase in Standard English is determined by natural sex distinctions and metaphorical extensions thereof (*ships, countries*, etc.). These semantic rules may, however, be overridden by emotive and affective factors and in some dialects of English (for instance, in Somerset, Newfoundland, Tasmania) the count vs. mass distinction (degree of **individuation**) plays a role (cf. Wagner 2003, 2004, Siemund 2008). In Somerset dialects, for instance, non-human count nouns are replaced by masculine pronouns, whereas mass nouns are invariably neuter, cf. the often quoted example in ⟨11⟩:

⟨11⟩   a.   Pass the bread – it's over there.

      b.   Pass the loaf – he's over there.

Analogously to the gender system of Old English, the case system has also been subjected to loss and attrition so that it is even controversial whether one can still speak of 'case' distinctions in English. As far as noun phrases are concerned it is the suffix *-s* (the **Saxon genitive**) that may still be regarded as a case suffix and would then be part of a two-term system of case (genitive vs. common case):

⟨12⟩   a.   John's car is brand new.

      b.   I never read yesterday's paper.

The problem with this analysis is that the *s*-suffix can also combine with phrases, in contrast to normal case markers (cf. ⟨13⟩). In recent descriptions *-s* is therefore often analyzed as a **phrasal clitic** or postposition, i.e. as an adposition that can be attached to a noun phrase.

⟨13⟩   a.   [NP The girl who lives next door]'s dog bit me.

      b.   He had taken [NP somebody else]'s car.

The formal distinctions found for **personal pronouns** in English seem to show the vestiges of a former three-term system comprising the genitive (*his, her, my*) in addition to a subjective (*he, she, I*) and an objective case (*him, her, me*). As is well-known, the dative and the accusative collapsed in Middle English, a development which resulted in a three-term system, with different neutralizations in the various person-gender combinations (cf. Table 4.5). However, even here it is highly problematic to regard the relevant distinctions as elements of a case paradigm, since the choice between these different forms of a pronoun is determined by prosodic and syntactic considerations, which do not normally play a role for the differentiation between different cases (cf. Hudson 1995). The data that are problematic for the view that English still has a morphological case system include the following:

⟨14⟩   a.   Who is it? – It is me.
       b.   George is taller than me / I am.
       c.   Me betray my best friend? – Never!
       d.   Yeah but me and Catherine don't talk about it you know. [BNC]

The last example seems to represent the only possible pattern for most young people in Britain and in the U.S. In contrast to many other languages the alleged subjective form *I* can only be used in English if it is the subject of a tensed verb. But even in such contexts *I, he, she*, etc. are excluded if they occur in coordinations. The conclusion to be drawn from these observations could simply be that

	SUBJ	OBJ	POSS
1		I	me	my
2		you		your
3MASC	he	him	his
3FEM	she	her	
3NEUT		it		its

Table 4.5 English pronouns

I and *me* are forms of a personal pronoun which are selected by a lexical rule that is "sensitive to the word's function and also to coordination" (Hudson 1995: 390). According to this view, it is highly doubtful whether the distribution of different pronominal forms should still be described in terms of a case system.

The contrasts discussed so far can be summarized as in Table 4.6. 'Yes' in the cells pronouns/case and pronouns/gender for English is put in parentheses because, as has been shown, the choice of a given 'case' form is only partly determined by the grammatical relation of the relevant element, and because the gender system of English is semantically motivated and moreover restricted to pronouns.

		NUMBER	CASE	GENDER	INDIV
English	pronouns	yes	(yes)	(yes)	no
	nouns	yes	no	no	yes
	articles	no	no	no	no
German	pronouns	yes	yes	yes	no
	nouns	yes	yes	yes	yes
	articles	yes	yes	yes	no

Table 4.6 Inflectional categories in English and German

So far nothing has been said about contrasts involving the word category 'individuation'. Unlike in English, proper names can be combined with the definite article in German, even if some speakers are aware of a certain southern flavour in this usage. This suggestion of clear identifiability generally associated with the definite article is particularly exploited in utterances addressed to children:

⟨15⟩   a. Ich bin der Peter.

       b. Der Karl würde so etwas nicht tun.

The constraints on using the plural or quantifiers in combination with **mass nouns** are identical in English and in German and so are the semantic effects of overriding these constraints: the resultant noun phrase is interpreted as referring either to a specific quantity or to a type (e.g. *two chocolates*). In German the relevant constraints on the use of quantifiers typically relate to the choice between singular and plural. English often uses different lexical expressions for count and mass nouns:

⟨16⟩   a. wenig/er Geld – little/less money

       b. wenige/r Scheine – few/er notes

⟨17⟩   a. viel/mehr Brot – much/more bread

       b. viele/mehr Brötchen – many/more rolls

4.2 Adjectives

4.2.1 The inflection of adjectives in German

In contrast to other Germanic languages like Norwegian or Swedish, adjectives do not inflect in predicative position in German. In attributive position they inflect for case, number and gender. The precise form of their inflectional behaviour is determined by syntactic factors. Traditionally a distinction is made between two basic paradigms of inflection, 'strong inflection' and 'weak inflection', and a third, mixed type. The **strong inflection** is found whenever there is no determiner preceding the adjective. Here the inflection corresponds more or less to the 'pronominal inflection' illustrated in Figure 4.4 above. The only difference can be found in the genitive singular masculine and neuter (*Der Geruch heißen Kaffees*; cf. Table 4.7).

NOM	heiß-er Kaffee	weiß-e Sahne	kalt-es Bier
ACC	heiß-en Kaffee	weiß-e Sahne	kalt-es Bier
DAT	heiß-em Kaffee	weiß-er Sahne	kalt-em Bier
GEN	heiß-en Kaffee-s	weiß-er Sahne	kalt-en Bier-es

Table 4.7 Strong adjectival inflection in German

The **weak inflection** is manifested by attributive adjectives when they follow a definite determiner. Here we only have the choice between schwa and [(ə)n]. The affix is schwa for all nominative singular forms and for the accusative form in the feminine and neuter gender. In all other cases we find [(ə)n]:

⟨18⟩   a.   MASCULINE
           der heiße Tee, des heißen Tees, dem heißen Tee, den heißen Tee
       b.   FEMININE
           die große Tat, die große Tat, der großen Tat, der großen Tat
       c.   NEUTER
           das weite Tal, das weite Tal, dem weiten Tal, des weiten Tales

After **indefinite determiners** or possessive pronouns such as *ein, kein, mein*, etc. we find the strong inflection in the nominative singular and in the accusative singular neuter ([*ein*] *großes Glück*). The weak inflection is used for all other cases. When indefinite or possessive pronouns combine with an adjective in the weak inflection, gender is marked only once in the NP. For instance, the adjectives in *einer großen Frau* und *einem großen Mann* are identical. The differences between the three paradigms can thus be explained in terms of an **economy principle** (cf. the remarks made in the context of number marking above): gender is generally marked either on the determiner or on the adjective. In the third (mixed) type of paradigm the determiners have no suffix in the nominative (*kein-Ø* vs. *dies-er*). Consequently, the gender marker appears on the following adjective (*ein klein-er Mann*).

The inflectional distinctions used in German to mark the **comparative** and the **superlative** forms are highly regular, apart from a few suppletive forms (e.g. *gut/besser*): *-er* is the suffix marking the comparative and *-est* is used for the superlative.

⟨19⟩   intelligent – intelligent-er – am intelligent-est-en

4.2.2   The inflection of adjectives in English

In English, adjectives inflect neither in predicative nor in attributive position. They do, however, attach the marker *-ly* when they are in construction with a verb (adverbs of manner, cf. ⟨20a⟩), with another adjective (adverbs of degree, cf. ⟨20b⟩) or with the whole sentence ('disjuncts', 'sentence adverbials', cf. ⟨20c⟩):

⟨20⟩   a.   John drives very carefully.
       b.   That solution is highly problematic.
       c.   Obviously, he was not well informed.

In colloquial **American English** the suffix *-ly* is absent in many cases where it would appear in standard British English (cf. Tagliamonte and Ito 2002):

⟨21⟩   a.   It tastes real good.

       b.   It tastes really good.

⟨22⟩   a.   She drank it down quick.

       b.   She drank it down quickly. (cf. Tagliamonte and Ito 2002: 249)

As Tagliamonte and Ito (2002) have shown, there is a sharp decline in the use of zero forms (i.e. adverbs without -*ly*) even in American English. Moreover, bare adverbs are preferred by older speakers. In some cases, a functional differentiation between zero forms and *ly*-forms has established itself. For instance, the adverbs *sure* (typically American) and *surely* (typically British) also differ in terms of their syntactic and semantic properties. *Surely* often conveys uncertainty (e.g. in questions) whereas *sure* usually conveys certainty (and often occurs in exclamations):

⟨23⟩   a.   You surely went along to talk to him?

       b.   He sure (?surely) is an idiot!

Genuine dialect differences can be observed in the use of *really* and in some instances of adverbs which could also be analyzed as predicative adverbs, e.g. *to play aggressive(ly)* or *to look at s.o. strange(ly)* (cf. Rohdenburg and Schlüter 2009).

Whether -*ly* is a derivational or an inflectional suffix is a matter of some debate (cf. Quirk *et al.* 1985). The fact that this suffix changes the word class of the stem to which it is added is an argument for the former view, but given that -*ly* can be very generally added to an adjective in a grammatical environment requiring an adverb, it can be regarded as inflectional, especially since it can be added to nearly every adjective and is completely regular in the contribution that it makes to the meaning of the resultant form.

The only other inflectional forms we find for adjectives are the comparative and superlative forms, which are quite similar to those found in German:

⟨24⟩   a.   big – bigger – biggest

       b.   happy – happier – happiest

In contrast to German, however, there are two strategies for deriving comparative and superlative forms, viz. the inflectional ('**synthetic**') one just mentioned and the '**periphrastic**' or '**analytic**' one. In the latter case the comparative or superlative form of the adverb *much* is placed before the relevant adjective:

⟨25⟩   a.   beautiful – more beautiful – most beautiful

       b.   difficult – more difficult – most difficult

The analytic strategy is the younger one of the two and another manifestation of the tendency, visible throughout the history of English, to lose inflectional contrasts and to replace them by periphrastic constructions and thus move in the direction of an 'isolating' (or 'analytic') language (cf. Siemund 2004). The two strategies of comparative formation are often described as being in complementary distribution, but in reality they overlap in many contexts. The factors determining the choice between them are often seen in phonological (including prosodic) properties of the relevant adjectives, in particular the number of syllables, the location of stress and the structure of the syllables involved:

⟨26⟩   a. monosyllabic adjectives
            → synthetic strategy (plus a few cases of suppletion);
        b. adjectives with three or more syllables
            → analytic strategy (except for adjectives with prefixed *un-*);
        c. disyllabic adjectives
            → both strategies are admissible depending on syllable structure, on stress and some other factors.

Quite obviously, it is with **disyllabic adjectives** that most difficulties may arise, though monosyllabic ones also pose some problems (cf. below). Disyllabic adjectives with penultimate stress usually take the synthetic strategy when the last syllable is open or contains a syllabic consonant (e.g. /l/, /n/; cf. ⟨27a⟩), but the analytic strategy is often also available. Disyllabic adjectives with closed final syllables often require the analytic strategy (cf. ⟨27b⟩). Disyllabic adjectives with final stress usually form an analytic comparative, but synthetic forms are, again, also often available (cf. ⟨28⟩):

⟨27⟩   a. funnier, narrower, feebler, prettier, simpler
        b. more famous, more pleasant

⟨28⟩   more polite (politer), more obscure (??obscurer)

There seems to be an overall tendency for the analytic forms with *more* and *most* to expand their range of contexts. A detailed analysis of current usage has shown that apart from the generalization stated in ⟨26b⟩ there is a wide variety of factors that determines the choice between the two strategies of comparative formation in addition to the phonological factors mentioned above: the syntactic position, the syntactic complexity, the frequency, meaning, etc. of an adjective (cf. Mondorf 2009). For instance, adjectives that are rarely used in the comparative typically occur in the analytic strategy and so do adjectives with complements:

⟨29⟩   a. It might be more true to say that there is a constant quantity of reporters.
        b. He was prouder. / He was more proud of her.

Depending on their meanings, even monosyllabic adjectives alternate between the synthetic and the analytic strategy. Mondorf (2007) has shown that the adjectives *blunt*, *clear*, *cold*, *dark*, *fresh*, *light* and *round* may occur with either strategy of comparative formation, and that most of the analytic cases are adjectives with an abstract meaning:

⟨30⟩ a more fresh taste, a more blunt approach, a more clear thought, a more cold look, a more dark character, etc.

Finally, there is one further factor, clearly illustrated by ⟨29a⟩, namely the distinction between propositional and **meta-linguistic** uses of adjectives, and it is this factor which also provides a bridge to the situation in German and to a plausible historical origin of the analytic strategy. In German, analytic comparative forms with *mehr* and *eher* are perfect and in fact the only option if the adjective is used in a meta-linguistic sense:

⟨31⟩ a. Heute war ich eher gelangweilt.

b. Karl ist mehr zögerlich als abwartend.

4.3 Verbs

4.3.1 The inflection of verbs in German

The general picture presented above with respect to the inflectional categories of nouns and noun phrases also holds true for verbs. As a result of **morphological attrition** most of the categories found in earlier stages of English have been lost, whereas German has preserved most of the inflectional contrasts found in earlier stages of its history, even if the precise phonological form has changed. In German, verbs inflect for person, number, tense and mood. Table 4.8 provides a succinct survey of the possible forms.

finite verbs									
imperative	non-imperative								
	person			number		tense		mood	
SG	PL	1	2	3	SG	PL	PRES	PAST	IND	CONJ

Table 4.8 Inflectional categories of the German verb

The distinction between weak and strong verbs is part of the genetic heritage of English and German and is still relevant in both languages. **Strong verbs** are found in the domain of the most elementary and most frequent vocabulary, and the number of (basic) strong verbs is very limited and is furthermore slowly decreasing. The figures given in grammars for the number of strong verbs in both English and German vary between 160 and 180, and in both languages there are about 30 verbs that oscillate between a strong and a weak (regular) use. Well-known examples of German verbs changing over into the class of weak verbs are *backen*, *bewegen*, *gären*, *schallen*, *saugen*, *klimmen*, etc. In English, regularization can be observed in connection with *abide*, *bust*, *chide*, *cleave*, *creep*, *dive*, *gild*, *grind*, *hoist*, *shear*, *shine*, *slay*, *strive*, to mention just a few (see also Krug 1998).

Weak verbs, by contrast, form an open subclass of verbs in both English and German. They are not only much more numerous than strong verbs, but also provide the template for all additions to the lexicon. Table 4.9 provides the inflectional paradigm for weak verbs in German. As can be seen from this table, suffixal markers can be isolated for temporal and modal information: the suffix *-t* indicates past tense and the suffix *-e* (actually, -[ə]) indicates *Konjunktiv* mood. There are two sets of person markers: *-e*, *-st*, *-t* for present indicative and *-(e)*, *-(e)st*, *-(e)* for all other singular forms. In the plural, there is only one paradigm of person markers, namely *-(e)n*, *-(e)t*, *-(e)*. The phonological parsimony in this system is striking: only the coronals /n/, /t/ and /s/ as well as schwa are used to convey modal and temporal information.

	present tense			past tense		
		SG	PL		SG	PL
INDIKATIV						
1.		-e	-en		-e	-en
2.	leg	-st	-t	leg-t	-est	-et
3.		-t	-en		-e	-en
KONJUNKTIV						
1.		-Ø	-n		-Ø	-n
2.	leg-e	-st	-t	leg-t-e	-st	-t
3.		-Ø	-n		-Ø	-n

Table 4.9 Weak verbal endings in German

In contrast to the regularities found in Romance languages, the use of the *Konjunktiv* is not obligatory in specific contexts, but can be chosen relatively freely, and the choice between *Indikativ* and *Konjunktiv* is usually meaningful. The *Konjunktiv I* is typically used to express wishes and, in indirect speech, to avoid any commitment to the content of a particular statement. A sentence like ⟨32a⟩ conveys the view of the quoted speaker:

⟨32⟩   a.   Der Kanzler behauptet, die Reformen seien ein voller Erfolg.

       b.   Wenn ich Geld hätte, würde ich mir ein Auto kaufen.

The *Konjunktiv II* is typically used for counterfactual statements (as in ⟨32b⟩ above). In indirect speech, it can be used to distance oneself from the content of a sentence, and expresses even more distance than the *Konjunktiv I*. For instance, ⟨33⟩ indicates that the speaker disagrees with what is said in the quotation, while ⟨32a⟩ merely avoids any commitment to the truth of the embedded sentence:

⟨33⟩   Der Kanzler behauptet, die Reformen wären ein voller Erfolg.

As in all Germanic languages only the distinction between the present (non-past) and the past tense is marked by inflectional forms. The implications of this fact for the analysis of the tense systems in the two languages will be discussed in a separate chapter (Chapter 5).

4.3.2 The inflection of verbs in English

In English, verbs inflect for tense and marginally also for person and number (3rd person singular present -s). Each verb has maximally four (weak verbs) or five (strong verbs) inflectional forms, if the non-finite forms are included. The only exception is the copula *be*, which manifests a full paradigm of different forms. There is thus no point in representing verbal paradigms in the usual fashion. The inventory of forms can be represented as in Table 4.10 (cf. Huddleston 1984: 125).

	tensed			non-tensed		
	present		past	base form	*ing*-form	past
	3rd prs.	other				participle
weak verbs	*walks*	*walk*	*walked*	*walk*	*walking*	*walked*
strong verbs	*steals*	*steal*	*stole*	*steal*	*stealing*	*stolen*

Table 4.10 Inflectional categories of the English verb

The **past tense** morpheme has three allomorphs -t, -d and -ed, quite analogously to the plural marker. There is one genuine **subjunctive** form left in English, viz. *were* in combination with first person subjects:

⟨34⟩   If I were you I would not do it.

In all other cases non-indicative verbs are either simple base forms (cf. ⟨35a⟩ and ⟨35b⟩), past tense forms (cf. ⟨35c⟩) or combinations of verbs with modal verbs (cf. ⟨35d⟩ and ⟨35e⟩):

⟨35⟩   a. I insist that he go immediately.
   b. God save the queen.
   c. If you had been more careful you would not be in such trouble right now.
   d. May all your dreams come true.
   e. It is only natural that he should despise his followers.

The use of '**quasi-subjunctive**' base forms as in ⟨35a⟩, which was long considered a feature of American English ('colonial lag') and of formal language, is presently gaining ground in British varieties of English as well. Four contexts can be distinguished where such 'quasi-subjunctive' base forms are regularly found:

⟨36⟩ a. Active/present
          I demand that he go there.
      b. Active/past
          I demanded that they go there.
      c. Passive
          I demand that I/he/they be supported.
      d. Negation
          I demand that they not go there.

On the basis of these four contexts, the differences between British and American English can be described in more precise terms (cf. Schlüter 2009): while in American English 'quasi-subjunctive' uses of base forms do not show an affinity to any particular syntactic or semantic context, they are most widely used with the copula or passive auxiliary *be* in British English. Quasi-subjunctive base forms in the context of a negator as in ⟨36d⟩ are relatively rare in both major varieties.

It is an interesting question to what extent English can be said to have a grammatical category of 'subjunctive mood'. The fact that there still is one genuine subjunctive form (*were*) might suffice for justifying the assumption of that category for English. Moreover, the use of base forms with a subjunctive implication could be regarded as being indicative of the subjunctive being a grammatical category in its own right, since infinitive base forms can be distinguished from subjunctive base forms on distributional grounds. But then, the very fact that no morphological distinction is made between infinitives and (alleged) subjunctives can be interpreted as being another instance of the tendency for English to abandon the morphological marking of grammatical categories, and to develop into an isolating language. Viewed from this perspective, mood distinctions are on the verge of disappearing in English, since only subjunctive *were* could be regarded as a modal form in its own right.

4.4   Economy of form: The English suffix *-ing*

The inventory of phonemes used in inflectional affixes of German is very limited, the only vowel being schwa and the consonantal inventory comprising only the coronals mentioned above as well as /m/ and /r/ (e.g. dative/masculine *-m* in strong adjectival inflection and comparative *-er*). The inventory of possible forms is also quite limited, but not nearly as much as it is in English, where we find only six inflectional suffixes: *-er* (comparative), *-est* (superlative), *-s* (3rd person non-plural), *-ed* (past tense/participle), *-th* (ordinal numbers) and *-ing* (Progressive aspect, gerunds, etc.). The last of these suffixes is used in a variety of functions, which is not surprising, given the low number of inflectional devices available. Consider the examples in ⟨37⟩.

⟨37⟩ a. Deverbal adjective
This is very interesting.
b. Progressive aspect
I am not talking to you.
c. Adverbial participle
Walking along the river, I suddenly saw a crane.
d. Gerund(ive nominal)
Not reading poetry impoverishes your life.
e. Non-finite relative clause
The guy talking to George is my boss.
f. Action nominalization
No reading of poetry is good enough for Mary.
g. Deverbal preposition
Concerning your recent proposal, I think ...

The verbal *ing*-form in the examples given above is used differently in each case and thus provides a superb example of the **parsimony** in the formal inventory of English morphology, on the one hand, and the vast potential of using these forms, on the other.

The first point to be illustrated in the following is that the uses exemplified above do in fact differ from each other semantically and/or syntactically, even though they are morphologically indistinguishable. This will be established on the basis of some tests which reveal the essential properties of the different uses of the *ing*-suffix.

4.4.1 Deverbal adjectives

Our first example is a clear case of word formation. The verbs combining with the suffix *-ing* are transitive verbs with human objects and are often called '**psych-verbs**'. The resultant forms combine with degree adverbs, comparative markers, occur in both attributive and predicative position and are thus clear cases of (derived) adjectives. More examples are given in ⟨38⟩:

⟨38⟩ a. This is very amusing / exciting / depressing / annoying / terrifying / boring / reassuring. (predicative)
b. A barking dog is a nuisance. (attributive)

The productivity of the derivational process is clearly limited. Apart from the aforementioned selectional property concerning the object (cf. the term 'psych-verbs') there is also a restriction which excludes phrasal verbs with the required subcategorization and selectional features (*This turns me on, He let me down* but **This is on-turning, *He is down-letting*, etc.). The contribution made to the meaning of the resultant adjective by the suffix seems to be quite regular. The derived adjectives allow the suppression of the Experiencer argument and thus the implication that the referent of the subject has the property of provoking the reaction expressed by the verb in human beings generally:

⟨39⟩   a. This worries me.

         b. This is worrying.

Note furthermore that the derived adjectives often permit the choice between two different prepositional phrases and thus allow for the possibility to make a distinction between a more objective (*for*) and a more subjective (*to*) construal:

⟨40⟩   a. That was very interesting for me.

         b. That was very interesting to me.

4.4.2 The Progressive aspect

The second example of the list in ⟨37⟩ is an instance of the aspectual category called 'Progressive'. The relevant forms are in paradigmatic opposition to the morphologically unmarked simple forms. Verbal *ing*-forms are always preceded by a form of the copula *be*. The following examples are further instances of this use of *-ing*:

⟨41⟩   a. I was just sitting down for dinner when the telephone rang.

         b. If you fail to plan you are planning to fail.

What we find here is clearly a matter of inflectional morphology and syntax. The resultant form is verbal just like the basis. Apart from a few stative verbs (e.g. *contain, consist of, belong, own*), there are hardly any verbs that do not combine with the Progressive and the contribution made by the discontinuous aspectual markers *be + -ing* seems to be quite regular, even if it may manifest a certain degree of polysemy. The function of the Progressive aspect is described in Chapter 5.

4.4.3 Adverbial participles

The third type of example listed in ⟨37⟩ is traditionally called a 'participial' construction, but terms like 'adverbial participle', 'free adjunct' or 'converb construction' differentiate these examples more clearly from the rest. Unfortunately, terminology differs widely in different traditions of grammar writing. Latin grammar uses the term 'participium conjunctum', in French the term *gérondif* and in Italian the label *gerundio* are used for analogous structures. Note that the phrase introduced by the *ing*-form may contain objects, adverbs and the negator *not*. Moreover, the non-finite form of the verb may have its own subject (cf. ⟨42c⟩). Otherwise the subject of the main clause is the understood subject of the participle:

⟨42⟩ a. Using a sharp axe, he fought his way into the building.
b. Not seeing anybody, he went back into the building.
c. The Dean turned and went out, his gown billowing darkly behind him. (absolute construction/Lat. *ablativus absolutus*)

The term '**free adjunct**' captures the fact that these participles do not occupy argument (valency) positions in the main clause, but have an adverbial function and are thus freely omissible. Note also that adverbial participles are unspecific and vague in the contribution they make to the meaning of a sentence. In German, participial constructions are hardly used unless they are not more complex than a simple verbal form (*Hans kam fröhlich singend ins Zimmer*). A translation of such participles from English into German typically requires spelling out the relationship implicitly signalled by the participle in terms of a conjunction:

⟨43⟩ a. Not knowing the artist, he bought the picture.
b. Da / obwohl er den Künstler nicht kannte, kaufte er das Bild.

4.4.4 Gerunds

Gerunds have exactly the same internal structure as adverbial participles: the phrase that they introduce is a verb phrase, they may contain objects, the negation particle *not*, adverbs, etc. Like participles, gerunds may have their own subjects, which are either realized as possessive phrases (cf. ⟨44a⟩) or in the objective case (cf. ⟨44b⟩):

⟨44⟩ a. Their reluctantly signing the treaty took us by surprise.
b. I remember him rebuilding the barn.

Gerunds differ from adverbial participles in their distribution: they are governed by specific verbs or prepositions and only occur in **argument positions**. Thus, they cannot be omitted without making the sentence ungrammatical:

⟨45⟩ a. Reading poetry is fun. (*_____ is fun.)
b. I enjoy reading poetry. (*I enjoy _____.)
c. I look forward to reading your poetry. (*I look forward to _____.)

Note furthermore that gerunds are **hybrid** constructions: while their external syntax is that of an NP, they manifest the internal properties of a VP. Because of this hybrid character they are often regarded as separate parts of speech in traditional grammar ('verbal nouns'). Whereas gerunds can occur quite freely in subject position and as prepositional complements, they only co-occur with certain verbs in object position, where they are in contrast with infinitives (e.g. *regret*, *remember*, *try*, *love* and *enjoy* allow both infinitives and gerunds; *risk* and *avoid* only allow gerunds). Even though there seems to be a certain tie-up between the use of a gerund and a factual situation, the correlation is by no means perfect (cf. Chapter 13).

There are no gerunds in German. English gerunds in subject or in object positions typically correspond to infinitives in German:

⟨46⟩ a. Poesie zu lesen macht Spaß.

b. Ich freue mich (darauf), Ihre Gedichte zu lesen.

In prepositional phrases the valency position is usually saturated by a proform spelled out as *da-* (+ PREP), often followed by an infinitive or finite clause:

⟨47⟩ a. I insist on your taking that medication.

b. Ich bestehe darauf, dass du dieses Medikament nimmst.

4.4.5 Non-finite relative clause

The participial construction exemplified by ⟨37e⟩ is totally parallel in its formal make-up to adverbial participles and even to gerunds except for the fact that they do not have their own subjects, the understood subject being the head of the noun phrase they form part of. The difference between these uses of *ing*-forms is again purely a matter of distribution. Non-finite relative clauses are a constituent of a noun phrase. They can therefore only be moved together with their head noun, in contrast to adverbial participles, which can either occur at the beginning or the end of the clause. Like adverbial participles these phrases are used as adjuncts.

⟨48⟩ a. I will ask the woman (living across the street).

b. Annie is now dating the man (owning a Bugatti).

c. Anyone (owning a bike) is welcome to our club.

4.4.6 Action nominalizations

The derived nominals exemplified by ⟨37f⟩ are like gerunds in their distribution, i.e. they occur in argument positions, but they exhibit all the characteristics of nominal constructions (they may combine with adjectives, they take objects introduced by *of*, they combine with the negator *no*, they allow the use of articles) instead of verbal constructions (adverbs with *-ly*, direct objects, negation with *not*, no articles). Both their external syntax and their internal syntax is that of a noun phrase:

⟨49⟩   a.   No reading of literature is good enough for me.

            b.   I enjoy a thorough reading of poetry. (action nominalization)

In a gerundive construction corresponding to ⟨49b⟩ an adverb has to be used instead of the adjective, which is an indication of the more verb-like characteristics of gerunds in comparison to action nominalizations:

⟨50⟩   I enjoy reading poetry thoroughly. (gerund)

4.4.7 Deverbal prepositions

Examples such as ⟨37g⟩ are a special case of adverbial participles acquiring the status of prepositions. This development can be observed in so-called '**absolute constructions**', i.e. in participial constructions with their own subjects. A change in the sequential order of participle and subject indicates a reanalysis of the participle as preposition. In free adjuncts such as ⟨37g⟩ it is not the subject of the main clause, but an unspecified generic subject or the whole main clause itself that is the understood subject of the participle, which is another clear indication of a development from deverbal participle to preposition. The list of deverbal prepositions developing or having developed into prepositions includes the following expressions: *barring, concerning, following, owing to, regarding, saving, considering, including, notwithstanding, facing, past*, etc. (cf. Kortmann and König 1992). These developments are clear cases of grammaticalization.

⟨51⟩   a.   They sold the company, notwithstanding my objections.

            b.   Considering her age, she has published a lot.

Many of the prepositions derived from adverbial participles are also used as postpositions, i.e. they follow their nominal complements:

⟨52⟩   They sold the company, my objections notwithstanding.

The difference between prepositional and postpositional uses of elements such as *notwithstanding* is at least partly one of dialect: American English prefers postpositional *notwithstanding*, whereas British English prefers the prepositional variant (cf. Berlage 2009).

4.5 Summary

We will conclude this chapter with some more general points concerning the contrasts described above:

(a) In the course of its historical development English has lost most of its inflectional categories. Whether this **morphological attrition** was due to intensive contact with Celtic and Scandinavian languages, to a reduction of unstressed syllables or to a combination of several causes is not perfectly clear. What is clear, however, is that this drift towards the invariable word led to a massive reduction of morphological paradigms and ultimately to a loss of many categories. Many of those categories are now expressed by separate verbs (modals) or adverbs (*more*, *most*) preceding the former stems of the relevant suffixes. As a result English is developing, or has already developed, into an isolating (analytic) language. Modern German, by contrast, has preserved most of its categorical distinctions despite some drastic simplifications within the inflectional paradigms.

(b) Inflectional distinctions in English are typically **binary** and **privative oppositions**, i.e. contrasts between two forms, only one of which has a morphological representation, the other one being zero:

⟨53⟩   a. person → 3rd person.SG.present (*-s*) vs. others (∅)

        b. number → plural (*-s/-en*) vs. SG (∅)

        c. aspect → Progressive (*be* + *-ing*) vs. non-progressive (∅)

        d. tense → past (*-ed*) vs. present (∅)

There are more distinctions in each paradigm in German, even though German has also collapsed some of its categories. It is a characteristic feature of English that multiple use is made of six different suffixes.

(c) As pointed out in several reviews of John Hawkins' book, the view expressed in Hawkins (1986: 11ff.) that the morphological distinctions drawn in English are a **subset** of those found in German is generally correct. However, the Progressive form, the adverbial marker *-ly* and the person, number and gender distinction manifested by reflexive pronouns in English have no counterpart in German.

Revision, questions and exercises

1. Give a general characterization of inflectional morphology in English. Which inflectional categories have disappeared in the historical development of English?
2. Why is it problematic to assume that the so-called (Saxon) genitive *-s* is a case marker in English?
3. Are the morpho-syntactic (inflectional) categories of English really a subset of those found in German? Give reasons for your answer!
4. Under what conditions does an adjective combine with the suffix *-ly*? Is this an inflectional or a derivational affix?

5. Describe the conditions for the use of different comparative markers in English.

6. In English, non-finite verbal forms with -*ing* can be used as reduced relative clauses. How do such reduced relatives like ⟨54a⟩ differ from participial constructions as in ⟨54b⟩ or ⟨54c⟩? Why would it be wrong to say that these *ing*-forms are reduced Progressive forms?

   ⟨54⟩   a. I would like to meet the man owning that dog.

            b. She sat down, saying nothing.

            c. Living in Canada, John goes skiing every week.

7. What grammatical (and also semantic) factor determines the choice between the members of pairs like the following: *much – many, little/less – few/fewer*, etc.?

Further reading

Overviews of inflectional morphology in English can be found in major reference grammars such as Quirk *et al.* (1985) and Huddleston and Pullum (2002), as well as in handbooks such as Bauer *et al.* (2013) (see also Carstairs-McCarthy 2009, Schmid 2011, Blevins 2006, Don 2014). Pronominal gender in English has been described by Siemund (2008). Mondorf (2009) investigates the formation of adjective comparison in English against the background of theories of processing. The several types of *ing*-forms have been described by Blevins (1994, 2005). Kortmann and König (1992) deal with the reanalysis or grammaticalization of *ing* forms as (deverbal) prepositions. For German see the grammars by Zifonun *et al.* (1997), Eisenberg (2006a) and Schäfer (2016), and the morphological surveys by Hentschel and Vogel (2009), and Elsen (2011). A comprehensive overview of nominal inflection in the context of a comparison with other European languages can be found in Gunkel *et al.* (2017b). Hawkins (1986) contains a survey of English-German contrasts.

5 Tense and aspect

A woman accompanied her husband to the doctor's office. After his check-up the doctor called the wife into his office alone. He said: "Your husband is suffering from a very severe disease, combined with horrible stress. If you don't do the following, your husband will surely die: Each morning fix him a healthy breakfast. Be pleasant and make sure he is in a good mood. For lunch make him a nutritious meal he can take to work. For dinner prepare an especially nice meal for him. Don't burden him with chores, as he probably had a hard day. Don't discuss your problems with him, it will only make his stress worse. Try to relax your husband in the evening by wearing lingerie and giving him plenty of back rubs. Encourage him to watch some type of team sporting event on TV. And most importantly, make love with your husband several times a week and satisfy his every whim. If you can do this for the next ten months to a year, I think your husband will regain his strength completely."

On the way home, the husband asked his wife: "Oh, by the way, what did the doctor say?" – "You are going to die," she replied.

5.1 Introduction

In order to describe the location of something or to identify an object or event in space and time, we need points of reference (orientation). The location can then be described in relation to that point (*five miles to the north of Cambridge, at the beginning of 2003, a year ago today*, etc.). As far as orientation in space is concerned, many points of reference, man-made and natural ones, are available: lakes, mountains, trees, towns, buildings, streets, etc. For orientation in time we use salient events as such reference points. Calendar time is established on the basis of some major event in a particular culture, the birth of Jesus Christ for Christians ('200 BC', '2005 AD', etc.), the flight of Mohammed from Mekka to Medina for Muslims and the beginning of a dynasty of emperors in Japan. There is, however, another salient point of orientation that plays a crucial role for such notions as 'past', 'current/present' and 'future' as well as for tense distinctions in languages, viz. the **moment of utterance**, which simply divides time into two spheres: everything before it (the past) and the time following it (the future). This point of orientation is invoked by every act of utterance and the rough divisions it provides play the most fundamental role for temporal orientation in natural languages.

The meaning of **tense** is both relational and deictic. It can be characterized as locating a situation (or 'event', 'eventuality') in time relative to (before, around, after) the moment of utterance. A first rough differentiation of tense systems is therefore often made in terms of a three-term distinction between 'past tense', 'present tense' and 'future tense', depending on whether a situation is located before, around or after the moment of speech. This, however, is only a first rough systematization, which does not do justice to the complexity of most systems found in languages and is based on notional rather than formal criteria. The formal theories proposed for German, on the one hand, and English, on the other, are more complex than that and require more basic ingredients than simply a moment of speech, specific points or intervals[1] at which certain situations or events happen and sequential relation such as 'before', 'after' and 'included in'. All of these basic terms are needed, but in addition at least one more basic point (or interval) is required, viz. a point of reference, a point from which a situation is viewed, or alternatively, a point about which a claim is made or about which a question is raised. The terms 'point of reference' (Reichenbach 1947) or 'topic time' (Klein 1994: 3–9) are frequently used as labels for this third basic argument of temporal relations.

Aspect, by contrast, is not a deictic category and has nothing to do with location in time. According to widely accepted traditional definitions, aspect concerns the different perspectives a speaker can take and express with regard to a situation (eventuality), or "different ways of viewing the internal temporal constituency of a situation" (Comrie 1976: 3). The situation can be seen as completed from a point of view posterior to, i.e. outside of, the situation or it can be seen from inside as ongoing. These definitions are intuitively appealing, but they are also entirely metaphorical in nature (cf. Klein 1994: 27ff.). Whether and how it is possible to make these vague definitions more precise will be discussed later. For the time being these vague characterizations must suffice.

In addition to these two basic terms (tense, aspect) there is a third one that is needed as a basis for a comparative analysis of tense-aspect systems and of any discussion of tense and aspect in general, namely the term *aktionsart* (or 'actionality'), which is often subsumed under the term 'aspect'. It will be shown below that the overall contribution of a tense or an aspect to the meaning of a sentence may vary with the meaning of the predicate and that there are restrictions on the use of specific formal categories (such as the Progressive aspect) depending on the type of predicate. What is relevant here is not the meaning of individual predicates, but general aspects of the meaning of four, five, six or more general classes of predicates; it is not the meaning of verbs, but the meaning of larger constituents that also include the objects and maybe also subjects. The four types of *aktionsarten*

---

[1] A point-in-time can be regarded as a special case of an interval, which is thus the more basic notion.

typically distinguished are the following: (i) **states**, (ii) **activities** (or 'processes'), (iii) **instantaneous events** (or 'achievements') and (iv) **protracted events** (or 'accomplishments'; cf. Vendler 1967, Klein 1994: 30–35). States are non-dynamic situations, and they are 'homogeneous' insofar as every part of a state is also a state (e.g. *live, own a bike*). Activities (processes) share with states the property of being homogeneous (*march, work, eat apples*), but they are dynamic and involve volitional agents. Events, by contrast, involve a change of state, which can be either instantaneous (achievements, e.g. *lose some money, win a match*) or gradual (accomplishments, e.g. *write an essay, eat an apple*, etc.). Events are not homogeneous. A part of writing an essay is not writing an essay. *John wrote an essay* can only be said when the essay has come into existence as a result of John's writing. In describing certain regularities in the use of tense and aspect forms as well as in the contrasts between the two languages, we will need to use these distinctions.

5.2 Establishing comparability

Traditions of grammar writing differ from language to language and often also between different 'schools' (or 'theories') of grammar. If we take the inventory and the system of tense-aspect distinctions found in major grammar handbooks of English (Quirk *et al.* 1985: 176, Huddleston and Pullum 2002) and those found in handbooks of German grammar (e.g. Schäfer 2016) as a starting point, there is hardly any basis for carrying out a comparison: on the basis of purely morphological distinctions only two tenses are typically distinguished for English, namely (i) a **'Past tense'** and (ii) a **'Non-Past'** (**Note:** When referring to (formal) tense categories of specific languages, these categories will be capitalized: 'Past [tense]', 'Present [tense]', 'Progressive [aspect]', etc.):

⟨1⟩ a. John repair-s cars. (Non-Past)
b. John repair-ed cars. (Past)

There is, on this analysis, no Future tense in English, the alleged 'future forms' simply being combinations of auxiliary verbs in the Present (Non-Past) tense with main verbs. Sentences like the following are analyzed as sentences in the Present tense with future reference.

⟨2⟩ a. He will$_{\text{PRESENT}}$ write an essay.
b. He is$_{\text{PRESENT}}$ going to write an essay.

Nor are there complex past tenses, the relevant forms being combinations of the Perfect marker *have* + *-en*, *-ed*, etc. (past participle) and one of the two tenses or the auxiliaries mentioned before. The **compositional** nature of these forms is clearly reflected by the terminology (Present + Perfect):

⟨3⟩   a. John has written an essay. (Present Perfect)
      b. John had written an essay. (Past Perfect)
      c. John will have written an essay. (Future Perfect)

The picture found in grammars of German is very different. **Six tenses** are usually distinguished (*Präsens, Präteritum, Futur I, Perfekt, Plusquamperfekt, Futur II*; see e.g. Eisenberg 2006a: 196), even if we find an analysis here and there that departs from that traditional picture (e.g. Thieroff 1992).

Note, however, that the usual analyses given for the system in English specify (at least) six different forms, even though they do this in a combinatorial fashion, viz. the two forms given in ⟨1⟩ (Present and Past tense), the one (or two) illustrated by ⟨2⟩ (Future tense) and the three given in ⟨3⟩ (Present Perfect, Past Perfect, Future Perfect). This inventory of possible formal distinctions thus seems to be quite parallel in the two languages and it is exactly this inventory that we will take as a basis of comparison. Note, furthermore, that there is an older tradition of grammar writing, based on the model of Latin grammar and also frequently used for didactic purposes, that distinguishes exactly six tenses also for English.

As a first step in our contrastive analysis we can therefore say that we find an inventory of almost **parallel formal distinctions** in the two languages, whose individual items may require different (combinatorial or holistic) analyses and may also have a very different meaning and use. Table 5.1 illustrates the relevant formal inventories of tense distinctions in English and German (note that the traditional terminology used for German [*Plusquamperfekt, Futur II*] does not suggest that the complex forms are the result of combining categories in any way).

German		English	
Präsens	*Ich schlafe.*	*I sleep.*	Present
Präteritum	*Ich schlief.*	*I slept.*	Past
Futur I	*Ich werde schlafen.*	*I will sleep.*	Future
Perfekt	*Ich habe geschlafen.*	*I have slept.*	Present Perfect
Plusquampf.	*Ich hatte geschlafen.*	*I had slept.*	Past Perfect
Futur II	*Ich werde geschlafen haben.*	*I will have slept.*	Future Perfect

Table 5.1 Six tenses in English and German

Within Table 5.1 two points require a detailed comparison and discussion: (i) the Present Perfect and the *Perfekt*, which are parallel in form but differ dramatically in their meaning and use, and (ii) the 'future' tenses. In the latter case the question has to be discussed whether there is a Future tense in English at all and which of all expressions with future time reference can be considered as such. The question of differences in the meaning and use of these forms is also a major problem.

As far as aspect is concerned, a fully grammaticalized aspectual opposition (Progressive vs. Non-Progressive) in English corresponds to the modest beginnings of a developing aspectual system in German. The Progressive in English may combine with all the 'tenses' listed in Table 5.1 and therefore does not constitute a tense category, as the label 'continuous tenses' misleadingly suggests. Moreover, the choice between the Progressive aspect and the formally unmarked Non-Progressive has to be made for every sentence. In German, there are expressive devices that may express a similar meaning as the Progressive form in English. But these devices are more lexical than grammatical, there are several such devices and they are not obligatory in the relevant contexts (cf. also Section 5.5):

⟨4⟩   I was driving home when the accident happened.

    a.   Ich fuhr (gerade) nach Hause, als der Unfall passierte.

    b.   Ich war auf dem Heimweg, als der Unfall passierte.

5.3   Future time reference

The (epistemic) status of the future is very different from that of the present or the past. The future is essentially open. Our statements about the future are a matter of probability rather than certainty. We nevertheless talk about the future, reflecting on our intentions as well as making predictions concerning courses of events outside our control. Typically there is a modal element involved. Future tenses usually contribute more than pure future time reference.

5.3.1   Future time reference in German

In German, the Present tense (*Präsens*) can be used for future reference in most contexts and according to frequency counts it is the device most frequently used for that purpose. Alternatively, the auxiliary verb *werden*, originally a copulative verb expressing a change of state, can be used and is traditionally regarded as the marker of Future tense. The contrast between the use of the *Präsens* and the use of *werden* is subtle and relates *inter alia* to the degree of certainty with which a statement is made: the *Präsens* sometimes seems to convey more certainty than the *Futur I*:

⟨5⟩   *Präsens*

    a.   Morgen beginnen die Vorlesungen.

    b.   Im nächsten Jahr schließe ich mein Studium ab.

    c.   Wenn wir uns nicht beeilen, kommen wir zu spät.

⟨6⟩   *Futur I*

    a.   Durch den Streik werden morgen viele Menschen zu spät zur Arbeit kommen.

    b. Im nächsten Jahr werde ich mein Studium abschließen.

    c. Eines Tages wirst du noch den Kopf verlieren.

Such a use of the *Präsens* for future time reference is restricted to 'scheduled events' in English, i.e. to predictions made on the basis of timetables and schedules (*The first train to Berlin leaves at 6.30 a.m.*, cf. Section 5.3.2).

5.3.2 Future time reference in English

There are more strategies for referring to future events in English than there are in German:

***will/shall* + infinitive** The modal verb *will* has almost completely lost its basic volitional meaning ('want', 'be willing') and is thus "the nearest approximation to a 'neutral' or 'colourless' future" in English (Quirk *et al.* 1985: 213). The volitional component, however, is still present in certain 1st person contexts. It is also in those contexts that *shall* comes close to expressing mere prediction, at least in British English:

⟨7⟩   a. Will you let me know in time?

       b. Tomorrow's weather will be cold and cloudy.

       c. We will know by tomorrow.

       d. I shall look into this myself.

***be going to* + infinitive** Originally the Progressive form of a verb of motion, *be going to* has lost all implications of motion and is the next most important means of referring to future time in English after *will*. Together with *will* this expression is often analyzed as a genuine future marker. Its meaning is often described as indicating 'future fulfillment of present intention' or of 'present cause', rather than pure prediction:

⟨8⟩   a. It is going to rain. (Look at the clouds!)

       b. Are you going to play tennis today? (Is that your intention?)

Simple Present As already mentioned, this strategy is used in English only for situations determined by schedules, regularities, habits, etc., and the Simple Present cannot normally be used with future time reference. Two examples are given in ⟨9⟩.

⟨9⟩   a. Mary starts her new job on Tuesday.

       b. When does the train leave?

Present Progressive Like the Simple Present, the Present Progressive can also be used for future reference. In contrast to the other expressive devices discussed before, sentences like the following imply that arrangements, plans or programmes have been made at the moment of speaking. In other words, the relevant situation is already under way:

⟨10⟩   a. Are you playing tennis tomorrow?
　　　 b. I am taking Mary to the theatre tonight.

In contrast to ⟨8b⟩, ⟨10a⟩ amounts to asking whether the addressee has booked for a court and ⟨10b⟩ suggests that Mary has been invited out, which would not be implied by a pure intentional statement with *going to*.

will/shall **+ Progressive** The rarest form of all is a combination of two devices already discussed. If we are dealing with a straightforward combination of the Progressive and *will* (or *shall*, which is basically restricted to first person subjects and British varieties of English), the meaning of the complex expression can be derived from the meaning of the two parts:

⟨11⟩   We will soon be landing in Paris.

There are, however, also clear cases where the overall meaning is not compositional and is often described as 'future as a matter of course', i.e. the situation is not specifically intended or planned but the consequence of some other action. In certain contexts such sentences can therefore be more cautious than a sentence without the Progressive:

⟨12⟩   a. You can come with me. I'll be driving through Windermere anyway.
　　　 b. When will you be paying back the money?

Summary As is shown by the preceding observations, the discussion about a 'Future tense' in English is not only complicated by the fact that the alleged future markers are separate auxiliary verbs and have preserved some of their older meanings in certain contexts, but also by the existence of several candidates for the status of a Future tense marker, which also differ in meaning and nearly always have semantic implications over and above mere prediction. Even if one discards the view that only inflectional affixes can be regarded as tense markers, there is still the problem of whether *will* or *be going to* or both should be regarded as markers of Future tense. Instead of pursuing this issue further at this point we will briefly summarize the main semantic features differentiating the different strategies of referring to the future in English:

- *Will* typically expresses a **contingent future**, a prediction with a hidden conditional (*We'll miss the train* [*if we don't hurry up*].). This ties up nicely with the observation that *going to* is rarely used in the main clause of a conditional. *Going to*, by contrast, expresses an **absolute prediction**, based as it is on present intentions or present causes. A further consequence of these implications is that *going to* tends to refer to the near future, while the distant future tends to be expressed by *will* (*When will they ever learn?*).

- The futurate use of the Present Progressive typically signals that the relevant situation already holds at the moment of speech, since the relevant **arrangement** has already been made.
- In contrast to German, the Simple Present can only be used for future time reference in English if the situation in the future is determined by general rules or **schedules**.

5.4 The German *Perfekt* and the English Present Perfect

In spite of a largely parallel formal make-up, the use of the German *Perfekt* and the use of the Present Perfect in English are very different. The major contrast between the two languages is due to the fact that the German *Perfekt* has developed, or is developing, into a **narrative tense** and thus can also co-occur with adverbials denoting definite moments in the past. This development is more pronounced in the spoken language than in the written one, more in the south than in the north and more in sentences with main verbs than in finite sentences with auxiliary verbs. To describe the relevant contrast by saying that the *Perfekt* and the *Präteritum* are interchangeable in German, whereas their counterparts in English are not, would be an inadmissible simplification, however.

5.4.1 The German *Perfekt*

Two major uses can be distinguished for the German *Perfekt*: (i) a **resultative** use with respect to the moment of utterance (cf. ⟨13⟩), and (ii) a **narrative** use (cf. ⟨14⟩):

⟨13⟩ a. Schau mal, es hat geschneit.

b. Die Maschine aus Paris ist gelandet.

⟨14⟩ Gestern sind wir ins Kino gegangen. Wir haben uns den neuesten Film von Wim Wenders angesehen. Anschließend haben wir bei einem Italiener gegessen.

Given that the *Präsens* may be used with future time reference as well, the *Perfekt* may also have a resultative meaning with respect to some event in the future and in this case has a function similar to that of the *Futur II*, which suggests less certainty than the simple *Perfekt*:

⟨15⟩ a. Wenn du das nächste Mal kommst, sind wir schon umgezogen (werden wir schon umgezogen sein).

  b. Morgen Abend habe ich dieses Kapitel abgeschlossen.

The resultative use of the German *Perfekt* has a clear parallel in English. It is therefore not surprising that the same term is used in descriptions of English. It is the narrative use that makes the German *Perfekt* very different from the Present Perfect in English. In examples like ⟨14⟩ we find reference to **definite moments in the past** which are separated from the moment of utterance, i.e. a typically narrative use. In such contexts only the Past tense is admissible in English. Note, however, that many speakers of Standard German still hesitate to use auxiliary verbs (*sein, haben, müssen, können*, etc.) and some main verbs (*heißen*) in the *Perfekt*. The following sentences are regarded as regionally and stylistically marked by many speakers of Standard German:

⟨16⟩ a. Wie hat er doch gleich geheißen.

  b. Er hat nicht kommen gekonnt.

The absence of *Perfekt*-forms in cases such as ⟨16b⟩ can also be regarded as being due to the fact that most modal verbs do not have a participial form. The formation of a *Perfekt*-form is possible with infinitives:

⟨17⟩ Er hat nicht kommen können.

The narrative use of the German *Perfekt* is the result of a change still in progress today. As a result of this change the *Präteritum* and the *Perfekt* are interchangeable in those contexts where the Past tense is used exclusively in English. The difference between pairs like the following is only a stylistic one:

⟨18⟩ a. Karl arbeitete gestern den ganzen Tag.

  b. Karl hat gestern den ganzen Tag gearbeitet.

⟨19⟩ a. Im letzten Jahr besuchte ich China.

  b. Im letzten Jahre habe ich China besucht.

⟨20⟩ a. Plötzlich ging das Licht aus und es wurde stockdunkel.

  b. Plötzlich ist das Licht ausgegangen und es ist stockdunkel geworden.

As is normally the case with older forms, the use of the *Präteritum* is more formal and more frequent in the written language whenever there is a choice between the two tenses (i.e. basically in the narrative uses). Contrasts arise, however, when the *Perfekt* is used with a resultative meaning, in which case the *Präteritum* is inadmissible:

⟨21⟩ a. Unser Hund ist weggelaufen. Wir müssen schnell etwas tun. (?Unser Hund lief weg.)

  b. Warte, bis ich das Geschirr gewaschen habe.
    (?? ... bis ich das Geschirr wusch.)

There is one more recent development in German that deserves special mention, even though it has no counterpart in English. In southern dialects (specifically, in Bavarian) the *Präteritum* has completely disappeared even in those contexts where it is still used in informal speech in the north (auxiliary verbs). As a result of this, the *Plusquamperfekt* has also disappeared and has been replaced by a **'double'** *Perfekt*, as the following example shows:

⟨22⟩   a. I hob des scho g'lesen g'hobt.
    b. Ich hab' das schon gelesen gehabt.

A related, though distinct, phenomenon is observable in northern dialects: a kind of *plusqueparfait surcomposé* also found in colloquial French:

⟨23⟩   Ich hatte das Buch schon gelesen gehabt, als ich es geschenkt bekam.

The preceding examples are instances of non-standard speech. What is remarkable, however, is that this double *Plusquamperfekt* or *plusqueparfait surcomposé* is perfectly acceptable in the *Subjunktiv* and even contrasts in meaning with the normal *Subjunktiv*, as shown by the following minimal pair (O. Leirbukt, p.c.):

⟨24⟩   a. Meine Mannschaft hätte einen Punkt verdient.
    b. Meine Mannschaft hätte einen Punkt verdient gehabt.

The first sentence would be said during a match by a coach whose team is losing, whereas the second sentence could be said by the same coach after his team lost the match.

5.4.2 The English Present Perfect

Whenever the Present Perfect is used in English a time interval is under consideration that goes up to and includes the moment of utterance. The situation described is not seen as cut off from the moment of speech and therefore only such **adverbials of time** can be combined with that tense form whose reference can include the moment of utterance (*so far, until now, as yet, to this day, this morning, this year,* etc.). Adverbs which locate a situation at a definite point before the moment of utterance, by contrast, cannot combine with the Present Perfect.

⟨25⟩   a. Until now we have been able to cope.
    b. I have not had breakfast today / this morning / *at eight
       (said before noon).

In making a claim with a sentence in that tense form one is also saying something about the moment of speech, e.g. that some state continues to be the case, that there is a result or an experience of the subject referent at that point, etc. Such an experience or result is only possible of course if the referent of the subject still exists at the time of speaking. An **existential presupposition** of this type is particularly obvious in examples like the following (cf. McCawley 1971).

⟨26⟩ a. Oxford has been visited by Einstein.

b. ?Einstein has visited Oxford.

⟨27⟩ a. Britain has had many able rulers.

b. ?Assyria has had many able rulers.

Depending on the exact nature of the implications expressed relative to the moment of utterance and depending on the distance between the situation and the moment of speech, several **uses of the Present Perfect** are usually distinguished. The number of uses and the terminology may differ from author to author (cf. Leech 1971: 30–50, Comrie 1976: 56ff., Quirk *et al.* 1985: 192). The following notions are commonly found: 'universal use', 'existential use', 'resultative use' and 'hot-news perfect'. The different use types of the Present Perfect are tied to specific properties of verbs or verb phrases, in particular their *aktionsart*/actionality.

The universal use The so-called 'universal' (or 'continuative', 'continuous') use of the Present Perfect (state/habits-up-to-the-present) is mainly used with state verbs and activity verbs.

⟨28⟩ a. Bill has been ill for more than two years now.

b. John has worked for that company all his life.

Sentences like those in ⟨28⟩ assert the continuation of a state, a habit or an activity up to the moment of speech. In German, both the *Präsens* and the *Perfekt* can be used in such contexts, but only the *Perfekt* implies that the situation does not extend beyond the moment of speech.

⟨29⟩ a. Ich habe seit zehn Jahren nicht mehr getanzt. Bitte entschuldigen Sie, wenn ich Ihnen auf die Füße trete.

b. Ich tanze seit zehn Jahren nicht mehr.

With state verbs, universal instances of the Present Perfect in English are usually translated by the *Präsens* in German:

⟨30⟩ a. I have lived here for many years.

b. Ich lebe hier seit vielen Jahren.

Existential use The existential use of the Present Perfect (or 'perfect of experience') is used with bounded events in the past that are not located in time ('indefinite past'):

⟨31⟩ a. I have played tennis, but not very often.

b. Have you ever been to America?

In these contexts the *Perfekt* is also possible in German (cf. ⟨32⟩). In some cases a tense difference in English is expressed by using lexical means in German. The existential presupposition expressed by the first sentence in ⟨33⟩ ('Gerhard Schröder lives') is signalled by the contrast between *schon* and *erst* in German (cf. ⟨34⟩):

⟨32⟩ Ich habe auch schon mal Tennis gespielt.

⟨33⟩ a. I have met Gerhard Schröder only once.

b. I met Willy Brandt only once.

⟨34⟩ a. Ich bin Gerhard Schröder erst einmal begegnet.

b. Ich bin Willy Brandt nur einmal begegnet.

Resultative perfect This use of the Present Perfect mainly occurs with change-of-state verbs (i.e. achievements and accomplishments): In such contexts the *Perfekt* is the only option in German (cf. ⟨36⟩).

⟨35⟩ a. Someone has taken my car.

b. John has lost his keys.

⟨36⟩ a. ??Jemand stahl mein Auto.

b. ??Johann verlor seinen Schlüssel.

Hot-news perfect Sometimes the Present Perfect is used for an event in the very recent past that is unknown to the hearer:

⟨37⟩ Chancellor Schröder has resigned after all (12 October 2005).

5.4.3 Summary

As the preceding discussion has shown, shared features and contrasts between the system of tense distinctions in German and that of English are better represented by Table 5.2 than by Table 5.1 above. For each of the formally corresponding tenses (*Präsens*/Present tense, *Präteritum*/Simple Past, etc.) a specific number of uses is distinguished, and the table shows which of these uses are available in English and which are in German. It also shows which tense is used in case the relevant use is not available in one of the languages.

As can be seen from Table 5.2, there are four major contrasts: (i) German has a futurate use of the *Präsens* which English lacks, (ii) there are two future tenses in English corresponding to the German *Futur*, (iii) occurrences of the universal use of the Present Perfect with stative verbs are usually translated by the *Präsens* in German, and (iv) the German *Perfekt* has a narrative use which the English Present Perfect lacks.

USE	GERMAN	ENGLISH
PRÄSENS/PRESENT TENSE		
non-past	*Ich schlafe von 12 bis 7.*	*I sleep from midnight to seven.*
futurate	*Morgen weiß ich das.*	→ future tense
PRÄTERITUM/SIMPLE PAST		
past time	*Ich schlief den ganzen Tag.*	*I slept the whole day.*
FUTUR I/FUTURE TENSE		
future time	*Ich werde schlafen.*	*I will sleep.*
		I am going to sleep.
PERFEKT/PRESENT PERFECT		
resultative	*Jemand hat mein Auto gestohlen.*	*Someone has stolen my car.*
existential	*Ich habe (schon mal) Tennis gespielt.*	*I have played tennis.*
hot news	*Kanzler Schröder ist zurückgetreten.*	*Chancellor Schröder has resigned.*
universal	→ Präsens	*I have lived here for two years.*
narrative	*Ich bin gestern im Theater gewesen.*	→ Past tense
FUTUR II/FUTURE PERFECT		
future result	*Ich werde das bis morgen erledigt haben.*	*I will have done this by tomorrow.*
PLUSQUAMPERFEKT/PAST PERFECT		
pre-past	*Ich hatte geschlafen.*	*I had slept.*

Table 5.2 Use of tenses in English and German

5.5 Some remarks on aspect

However interesting the question of assigning the perfect forms to the tense system or the aspectual system might be from a theoretical perspective, it is of limited relevance for our contrastive analysis. We have therefore treated the Present Perfect, the Past Perfect and the Future Perfect as relative tenses and opposed them to formally similar forms in German. We thus take the more traditional view that there is only one system of aspectual contrasts in English, which comprises the Progressive and the Non-Progressive.

Since this system is not part of the system of tense distinctions, it may combine with all the tenses discussed above. In English this system has been **fully grammaticalized**, so that for each sentence a choice has to be made between these two forms, a choice that has clear consequences for the resultant interpretation. In German there are lexical expressions that may be used for the Progressive in English, but their use is optional and the distinction made in English can simply be neutralized in German. The options available in German for expressing overtly what is encoded by the Progressive in English can be illustrated by the following English examples and their translations into German (cf. Krause 2002: 22ff.):

⟨38⟩ Charles is working.
   a. Karl arbeitet gerade.
   b. Karl ist am Arbeiten.
   c. Karl ist beim Arbeiten.
   d. Karl ist arbeiten.

⟨39⟩ I was just taking a walk when the bomb exploded.
   a. Ich ging gerade spazieren, als die Bombe explodierte.
   b. Ich war (gerade) beim Spazierengehen, als die Bombe explodierte.
   c. Ich war gerade am Spazierengehen, als die Bombe explodierte.
   d. Ich war gerade dabei, spazieren zu gehen, als die Bombe explodierte.

There are several interesting points to be made about these expressive devices. Formally, we find an adverb (*gerade*), prepositions (*am*, *bei*) with combinations of a fused definite article and a nominalization of the relevant verb,[2] an infinitive construction with a proform (spelled out as *da*) saturating the valency position of the preposition *bei* and the combination of a copula and a verb. A second interesting point is that these different expressions are not equally permissible in all grammatical and lexical contexts. The use of the adverb *gerade* is generally possible and often accompanies the use of the other expressions. The prepositions seem best with intransitive verbs, and a complex predicate consisting of a verb and an incorporated object is often used to create such an intransitive predicate (*Er war beim/am Äpfelpflücken*). The infinitive with *zu* seems best with transitive verbs and verbs denoting events (changes), as the following contrast shows:

⟨40⟩ a. Ich war dabei, meinen Aufsatz abzuschließen, als du kamst.
   b. ?Ich war dabei, zu schlafen/zu arbeiten/Äpfel zu essen, als du kamst.

Thirdly, these different expressive devices are not completely equivalent in the contribution they make to the meaning of a sentence. Forms with the copula and

---

2   Another preposition that is sometimes found is *in/im* (*Diese Dinge sind im Kommen / Anmarsch / Verschwinden.*). This construction is very rare, however, and mainly occurs with verbs of motion (cf. Krause 2002: 239ff.).

the plain verb imply that a person has gone somewhere and is doing something at the appropriate place, an implication also frequently suggested by the preposition *bei*, though not by *am* (cf. ⟨41⟩). Because of this property de Groot (2000) coined the term '**absentive**' for such constructions.

⟨41⟩ Karl ist einkaufen/schwimmen.

Another differential feature concerns the choice of subjects: The construction with *beim* + nominalization tends to license only agentive subjects.

⟨42⟩ a. Ich bin am/*beim Verhungern.

b. Die waren da noch beim Aufbauen. (Krause 2002: 146)

As far as the frequency of these 'emergent progressives' in German is concerned, the following scale can be set up on the basis of the figures given in the literature:

⟨43⟩ $am + V_{nom} > dabei + \text{inf.} > beim + V_{nom} > im + V_{nom}$

Note, furthermore, that at least one of the German counterparts of the English Progressive has a regional and non-standard flavour. The expression with *am*, in particular, is typically found in parts of Germany adjacent to the Netherlands and may well be the result of contact between Dutch and German (cf. *Hij is aan het tuinieren* 'He is gardening'), though parallel constructions are commonly used in southern varieties of German as well. The infinitive construction after *dabei* tends to denote the beginning of an event (*Ich bin dabei, das Essen zuzubereiten.*).

Of course, none of the expressions listed above is obligatory and the plain verb can be used in all cases. So what we find in German is modest beginnings of grammaticalization of an aspectual opposition with several competitors for the status of Progressive aspect, which manifest clear contextual restrictions. Moreover, it is only in the core contexts of the Progressive that the relevant German expressions can be used: (i) in contexts where **current happenings** are described (cf. ⟨44⟩) and (ii) in Jespersen's well-known context of **temporal frames** (cf. ⟨45⟩).

⟨44⟩ a. John is washing his car.

b. Who's calling?

⟨45⟩ a. He was sipping a beer when the call came through.

b. The owner of the restaurant was cleaning the yard when the bomb exploded.

These two cases are really instances of the same use type, which constitutes the core area of the different uses found for progressive forms across languages (cf. Bybee and Dahl 1989): a more or less punctual event (a telephone call, an explosion, the speech event, etc.) is surrounded by a more extended situation, whose temporal bounds are not specified. In addition to these core contexts the English Progressive is found in a wide variety of further contexts that do not require or even permit one of the German forms discussed above. The following examples are instances of different use types frequently distinguished in the literature (cf. Leech 1971, Scheffer 1975, Schopf 1974, König 1980):

⟨46⟩ Backgrounding
Marian listened distractedly to Effingham. They were standing at the window of the drawing room.

⟨47⟩ Possible incompleteness
The latest report on cancer has shown that more people are dying of cancer this year than in previous years.

⟨48⟩ Interpretative use
If you fail to plan you are planning to fail.

⟨49⟩ Emotive use
He is always doing stupid dance moves that have no rhythm.

⟨50⟩ Futurate use
I am going out tonight.

⟨51⟩ Restricted habit
John has a new girlfriend. Guess who is buying his clothes now?

At first sight these examples may appear to instantiate different uses, but on closer examination at least some of them are just special instances of the use type discussed above. A more extended situation surrounding a less extended one may be seen as a kind of background (cf. ⟨46⟩) and examples like ⟨47⟩ are just special instances of an extended situation framing the speech event in which the event in question is associated with a change of state. Since a sentence with the Progressive only looks at a part of a larger whole, the final outcome is not described in the relevant sentence. Sentence ⟨47⟩ could thus be used by a statistician in November describing the death toll due to cancer in the relevant year, noting that the figure reached is higher than the one in previous years. The remaining four uses seem to be genuine extensions of the core uses.

Finally we may note that the Progressive in English does not only combine with verbs but also with **adjectival** and **nominal predicates**. Such structures are not only absent from German, they are also extremely rare in other languages of the world (cf. König 1995, Ljung 1980):

⟨52⟩ a. I am not simply being perverse when I say that the best also comes from John Jackson.

b. You are being rude/trite/polite/brave/obnoxious.

c. Johnny is being a policeman.

Sentences with nominal predications as in ⟨52c⟩ imply play-acting, while the adjectival cases describe temporary wilful behaviour. The adjectival structures in ⟨52a⟩ and ⟨52b⟩ could also be subsumed under the interpretative use of the Progressive aspect, however. What is expressed by such examples is typically another, more far-reaching interpretation over and above the interpretation that is obvious. Example ⟨48⟩ is a clear case of such an interpretative use with a verbal predication. The sentence says that not planning amounts to planning one's failure. 'Failing to plan' is the basic interpretation, which receives a further interpretation 'planning to fail'.

5.6 Summary

Starting from the observation that the tense systems of English and German are formally parallel, but partly different in their meanings and uses, we have identified four major contrasts in the domain of tense (cf. Table 5.2 on p. 92). The situation is different in the area of aspect, since here the two languages display different formal inventories for encoding the relevant meanings. While English has one (fully grammaticalized) formal category for the expression of the Progressive aspect (copula plus -ing), German uses different, partially lexical, devices to express those meanings, which are moreover optional (e.g. *gerade*) and associated with specific regional varieties (e.g. *Ich bin am Arbeiten*).

Revision, questions and exercises

1. The tense systems of English and of German look strikingly similar in their formal inventories. What are the main differences?
2. How can future time reference be expressed in English and German? Give an overview and provide examples for illustration!
3. Describe the different expressive devices for referring to future time in English. Are there any differences in their meaning and use? Give examples!
4. What is wrong with the following sentences and why are they typical mistakes made by German learners?

    ⟨53⟩ a. *If you do this you get into trouble.

          b. *We have to hurry up. Otherwise, we are running out of time.

5. Among the different uses of the Present Perfect in English there is one use (illustrated by the examples in ⟨54⟩) that has to be translated using the Present tense (*Präsens*) in German. How can we distinguish this use from the others?

    ⟨54⟩ a. I have known the Smiths for many years.

          b. I have lived in this house for more years than I care to remember.

     c. John has been married since 1984.

     d. Mary has owned this car for two years now.

6. What are the main differences between the German *Perfekt* and the *Präteritum*?

7. What are the main differences between the Present Perfect and the Simple Present in English?

8. Try to summarize the main differences between the German *Perfekt* and the English Present Perfect in three or four sentences.

9. The meaning of the Present Perfect in English is partly determined by the *aktionsart* of the verb. Identify some correlations between specific *aktionsarten* and readings of the Present Perfect and provide examples for illustration!

10. Describe four major use types of the Progressive aspect in English and give three examples for each use type.

11. Is there anything in German corresponding to the opposition between the Progressive and the Non-Progressive aspect in English?

12. Discuss: Is there an 'absentive' in English?

13. To what extent are constructions like the following allowed in your dialect?

    ⟨55⟩   a. Ich bin gerade am Biertrinken.

          b. Ich bin gerade beim Abwaschen.

          c. Ich bin gerade dabei, abzuwaschen.

14. Try to find the English translations of the German time adverbial *mit der Zeit* in sentences like the following:
(i) Mit der Zeit wird Karl ein wertvoller Mitarbeiter werden.
(ii) Mit der Zeit erhärtete sich der Verdacht.
Can we use the same translation in both cases? Which contextual feature is relevant for the selection of a correct translation?

15. Which use/s of the Progressive is/are exemplified by the following dialogue taken from Coetzee, *Disgrace*, p. 58:
– "You're confusing issues, David. You are not being instructed to repent ... You are being asked to issue a statement."
– "I am being asked to issue an apology about which I may not be sincere."
– "The criterion is not whether you are sincere ... "
– "Now we are really splitting hairs ... "

16. Is it possible to use the Progressive in imperatives?

Further reading

Analyses of the English tense system can be found in Leech (1971), Comrie (1985), Declerck (1991, 2006) and Klein (1994). The German system is described in the major reference grammars by Eisenberg (2006a), Zifonun *et al.* (1997) and Schäfer

(2016) as well as more specific monographs such as Thieroff (1992), Welke (2005) and Heinold (2015). Aspect in general is the topic of a monograph by Bernard Comrie (Comrie 1976). Aspect systems have also been analyzed by Hatav (1993). Schopf (1974) deals with aspect in English more generally, and Scheffer (1975), König (1980, 1995) and Ljung (1980) deal with uses and meanings of the Progressive aspect more specifically. German structures corresponding to the English Progressive aspect are discussed by Krause (2002). A formal comparison of tense and aspect in English and German is provided by Beck and Gergel (2014: Ch. II-7).

6 Modality and modal verbs

> Wer es mag, der mag's wohl mögen.
> 'Those who like this kind of thing will
> find this the kind of thing they like'

6.1 Introduction

To define the semantic concept of modality in terms of more elementary notions is not an easy matter. For the purpose of this chapter it will suffice to say that modal expressions change the meaning of a sentence from a basic descriptive statement (*John walks his dog every day*) into a statement about necessities, possibilities, obligations, abilities, etc. (*John must walk his dog every day*), or into a statement expressing a conclusion or inference (*John must be walking his dog at the moment*). Note that in the latter case the speaker does not have enough knowledge to make a simple non-modal statement (*John is walking his dog at the moment*).

Modality can be expressed by a wide variety of expressive devices: by derivational affixes (Engl. *-able*, Germ. *-bar*), by verbal participles (Engl. *be obliged to, be supposed to*, Germ. *verpflichtet sein*), by adjectives (Engl. *necessary, possible, likely*, Germ. *unumgänglich, notwendig, wahrscheinlich*), by infinitive constructions (Engl. *This is to be done immediately*; Germ. *Das ist sofort zu erledigen*), and by (specific classes of) verbs (Engl. *must, have to*; Germ. *müssen*).

The expressions to be discussed and compared in this chapter, i.e. **modal verbs**, fall squarely into this semantic domain of modality. Unlike some of the other expressions, they can be defined on the basis of clear formal criteria. This subclass of modal verbs comprises the following expressions in English and in German:

1. modal (auxiliary) verbs$_E$ = {*can, may, will, shall, must (need, dare, ought)*}

2. modal verbs$_G$ = {*können, müssen, dürfen, sollen, wollen, mögen, (brauchen)*}

Among the modals of English, a differentiation is often made between the 'central' members of that class and the 'marginal' ones, i.e. *need* and *dare*, which are here put in parentheses. The latter class is also often taken to include *ought* (*to*) and *used* (*to*).

Historically, most of these verbs derive from the so-called '**preterite-presents**' of Proto-Germanic, i.e. verbs with past tense forms and a present-tense meaning, and this shared history is still visible in similarities of form and of meaning. Starting out from this identical origin, the modal verbs of English and German have moved apart considerably in the course of their historical development, with respect to both formal and semantic criteria. What they still share, however, is the fact that they form a special subclass of verbs in the two languages under comparison, and that they can be defined in terms of formal and semantic properties.

Following this brief introduction we will turn to a comparison of the syntactic and morphological properties of modal verbs in Section 6.2. In Section 6.3, the major dimensions of meaning in the domain of modality are introduced. Section 6.4 deals with combinations of modals and their interaction with negation. In Section 6.5, the interactions between form and function in the domain of modality are discussed, with particular reference to the types of readings available for each modal and their interaction with negation (internal vs. external). In Section 6.6, devices for the encoding of modality other than modal verbs or auxiliaries are discussed, and an additional dimension of interpretation – the centre of orientation or *origo* in the sense of Bühler (1934) – is introduced. Section 6.7 summarizes the major English-German contrasts discussed in this chapter.

6.2 Formal properties of modal verbs

6.2.1 Auxiliary verbs in English

The most striking grammatical property of modal verbs in English is the restriction that they cannot be used as the sole predicate of a sentence. Together with a small set of other verbs (the 'primary auxiliaries' *be*, *have*, *do*), they form the class of '**auxiliary verbs**' and manifest specific properties in connection with the placement of negation, their position relative to the subject, in elliptical constructions and in connection with the emphatic assertion of a sentence as opposed to its negation (*verum focus*, cf. also Section 17.3). The collective term for these four properties, used in many grammars of English, is the acronym **NICE** (Negation, Inversion, Code, Emphasis; cf. Huddleston and Pullum 2002: 92):

(I)   **N**: Placement of *not* (negation)

In contrast to German *nicht*, the negator *not* is restricted in its syntactic position and is usually placed after the first auxiliary verb in a sentence.

⟨1⟩   John may not have been interrogated.

(II)   **I**: Inversion of verb and subject

In declarative sentences subjects normally precede the finite verb. The only verbs that can precede a subject under certain conditions (in interrogative sentences, in conditionals and in the scope of initial negative adverbs) are auxiliary verbs.

⟨2⟩   a.   Can you hear me?

      b.   Had I known this, I would have left immediately.

(III)   **C**: Post-verbal ellipsis (code)

Identical parts of complex sentences may be reduced in their verbal constituents. What is eliminated in those cases are the objects and the main verb; the auxiliary verbs are kept, or even inserted in the case of *do*-support. Such post-verbal ellipsis is also found in question tags.[1]

⟨3⟩   a.   I am not sure that he stole the money, but he may have (stolen it).

      b.   I enjoyed the play very much and Ed did (enjoy it), too.

      c.   Anne will stay and so will Barbara.

      d.   You will help him, won't you?

(IV)   **E**: Emphasis (*verum focus*)

If the truth of a statement is emphatically asserted (focused) in contrast to its negation, the stress invariably falls on an auxiliary verb.

⟨4⟩   a.   I doubt that Bill stole the money

      b.   Well, he DID steal it.

⟨5⟩   a.   You don't really speak Mandarin, do you?

      b.   I DO speak Mandarin.

There are two other properties of auxiliary verbs, which will only be mentioned in passing: Specific adverbs (*often*, *certainly*, *twice*, etc.) tend to precede lexical verbs, but to follow auxiliaries, and quantificational expressions ('floating quantifiers') like *both*, *all*, *each*, etc. exhibit the same ordering properties:

⟨6⟩   a.   He has often complained about his situation.

      b.   He often complains about the situation.

⟨7⟩   a.   They can all/both do what they want.

      b.   The players all took a card.

---

[1]   See Huddleston and Pullum (2002: 93) for an explanation of the somewhat opaque term 'code' for this type of ellipsis.

6.2.2 Modal auxiliaries in English

The four properties subsumed under the acronym NICE are properties exhibited by all auxiliary verbs, i.e. both by the modal auxiliaries and the other three auxiliary verbs (*have*, *be*, *do*), which, however, can also be used as main verbs:

⟨8⟩   a.   How do you do?
             b.   Don't be so mean!
             c.   I am having a bath.

Have and *be* are especially used in different temporal (perfect) and aspectual (progressive) forms of main verbs, and the meaningless auxiliary verb *do* is introduced into a basic structure whenever an auxiliary verb is needed for the placement of negation, for inversion, for post-verbal ellipsis or for the emphatic assertion of truth (*verum focus*). On the basis of the NICE-properties, *need* and *dare* can also be considered as auxiliary verbs (though peripheral ones). In addition to the four NICE-properties modal auxiliaries exhibit some additional properties which distinguish them from main verbs and other auxiliaries:

(V)   Modal auxiliaries are always **tensed**

There are neither infinitive forms nor participles (present or past). This implies, of course, that they cannot be combined anymore, as was still possible in earlier stages of English and is still found in some dialects (e.g. Southern American English, Scottish). Thus an English expression like *must* corresponds to inflected forms in German like (*ich*) *muss*, (*du*) *musst*, (*ihr*) *müsst*, etc., rather than the infinitive *müssen*. Complex tenses (Present Perfect, Past Perfect) cannot be formed with modal verbs, either, since there is no past participle. Moreover, if a modal auxiliary occurs in a sentence in combination with other auxiliary verbs, it must always be the first one, since it has to carry tense inflection:

⟨9⟩   He may have been being interrogated by the police for many hours.

As is shown by the example in ⟨9⟩, the following order of auxiliaries is found in a sentence of English if several auxiliaries are combined. Each auxiliary verb determines the form of the auxiliary following:

⟨10⟩   modal *may* → infinitive
                      ↓
         perfect *have* → past participle
                          ↓
             progressive *been* → -*ing*
                              ↓
                 passive *being* → past participle
                                  ↓
                     main verb *interrogated*

This syntactic constraint has led to a few constructions where the modal verb occurs first, even though it is really in the scope of (i.e. modified semantically by) a later verb:

⟨11⟩   a.   I can't seem to stand on my own two feet.
          ~ 'I seem to be unable to stand on my own two feet.'
       b.   John could have written to her.
          ~ 'John had the possibility to write to her, but he did not'.
          or 'John probably wrote to her.'

(VI)   Modal auxiliaries show **no agreement** (*-s*) with a third person singular subject. In other words, there is no person-number contrast for these verbs.

⟨12⟩   a.   John can swim very fast. – They can swim very fast.
       b.   John swims very fast. – They swim very fast

(VII) Modal auxiliaries are followed by the **bare infinitive** without *to*. *Ought* is an exception to this generalization.

⟨13⟩   a.   You must go now.
       b.   You ought to go now.

(VIII) There is **no clear present-past opposition** for many of these verbs.

There is no past tense form for *must, might* is not a past tense form of *may* in all of its uses, nor is *should* a past tense of *shall* in all of its uses, etc. It is a consequence of this unsystematic relationship between such pairs as *may* and *might* that these expressions are discussed as separate entries in dictionaries. In order to express past time reference in combination with modality, a **semi-auxiliary** such as *have to* or some lexical expression (e.g. *be bound/allowed to*) can be used.

⟨14⟩   a.   This must be the mailman.
       b.   This had/was bound to be the mailman.
⟨15⟩   a.   May I come in?
       b.   John asked me whether he was allowed to come in.

(IX)   Some modal auxiliaries can express a remote (unreal) **conditional** or an **unreal past tense** (esp. *would, should* [Br.]).

These uses often correspond to the *Konjunktiv II* in German or the subjunctive mood in Romance languages.

⟨16⟩ a. I would have come back if I'd been given the choice.
(cf. Germ. ... *wäre*$_{\text{KONJ. II}}$ *zurückgekommen* ...)
b. I regret that he should do such a thing.
(*should* after verbs of emotion, cf. Fr. *Je regrette qu'il soit*$_{\text{SUBJ}}$ *parti.*)

All of these properties characterize the inflectional paradigm of modal verbs in English as defective. Some of the constraints mentioned above do not hold in Early Modern English or in some English dialects, as the following examples from Shakespeare's plays (⟨17a⟩ and ⟨17b⟩) and Scottish English (⟨18⟩) show:

⟨17⟩ a. I must away to-day, before night come.
(*must* as a main verb, from *The Taming of the Shrew*)
b. I know thee not, old man. (negation without auxiliary, from *Henry IV*)

⟨18⟩ You have to can drive to get that job. (*can* as main verb; cf. Miller 2004)

6.2.3 Modal verbs in German

In German the modal verbs listed above have not developed into auxiliaries, but they do have specific inflectional and syntactic properties, so that they, too, can be analyzed as forming a special subclass of verbs. With their counterparts in English they share the property of having no distinctive inflectional form for the first and third person singular in the present tense. The simple stem form is used instead. The example below illustrates the difference between modal verbs and other verbs in connection with the minimal pair *sollen* ('shall') – *rollen* ('roll'):

⟨19⟩	a. ich soll	ich roll-e
	b. du soll-st	du roll-st
	c. er soll	er roll-t

Also like their English counterparts, German modals combine with the **plain infinitive** rather than using the infinitive marker *zu*.

⟨20⟩ a. Karl will Brot kaufen.
b. Karl beabsichtigt, Brot zu kaufen.

This exhausts the parallels, however. The modal verbs of German neither share the general properties of auxiliary verbs in English, nor do they share the other specific characteristics of a defective paradigm. They have infinitive and participial forms and can therefore be combined (cf. ⟨21⟩), they show a clear number contrast in their inflection, as well as clear present-past tense opposition. As far as the 'participial' forms are concerned, two peculiarities are found in Standard German, however (regional varieties may differ from Standard German though). Whenever the modals combine with verbs, the infinitive takes the place of the past participle in the complex tenses *Perfekt* and *Plusquamperfekt* ('perfect infinitive', *Ersatzinfinitiv*; cf. ⟨22⟩). The usual past participles are found whenever a modal verb combines with a nominal complement, as in ⟨23⟩.

⟨21⟩   a.   Karl muss arbeiten können.
             'Karl must be able to work.'

       b.   Ich weiß, dass er arbeiten können muss.
             'I know that he must be able to work.'

⟨22⟩   Karl hat arbeiten müssen/wollen/dürfen.
       'Karl had/wanted/was allowed to work.'

⟨23⟩   Karl hat das gekonnt/gemocht/gewollt/gedurft.
       'Karl was capable of doing that.'

Moreover, present participles with modal verbs are very rare in German. They are occasionally found in fiction or in journalese and have a formal and archaic flavour:

⟨24⟩   a.   Was aber bringt die Jugend dazu, diesen grausamer nicht sein können-
             den Bilanzen in so großer Zahl zu lauschen? (*Die Zeit*, 29.10.1999)
             'But what makes young people listen in large numbers to these balance
             sheets (end results) which couldn't possibly be worse?'

       b.   Irritierend blieb allenfalls die nicht schwinden wollende Erinnerung an
             jenen ... Jungen ... (Günter Grass, *Beim Häuten der Zwiebel*, p.7)
             'What remained irritating was the memory of this young man which did
             not (want to) fade away.'

What also makes modal verbs differ from other verbs in German are the restrictions in their combinatorial potential as far as non-verbal complements are concerned. All German modal verbs combine with pronominal objects relating to a preceding verbal complement or VP:

⟨25⟩   a.   Karl soll wieder arbeiten, aber er darf/kann (es/das) nicht.

       b.   Karl is required to return to work, but he cannot/is not allowed to.

As far as non-verbal complements are concerned, three subgroups can be distinguished: *Wollen* and *mögen* may combine with concrete referents (objects) as in ⟨26a⟩ and with directional complements as in ⟨26b⟩. *Können* combines with directional complements (cf. ⟨26b⟩) as well as specific skills, in particular languages (cf. ⟨26c⟩). *Müssen, dürfen* and *sollen* are most restricted insofar as they can only be combined with directional complements. Note that all three semantic types of directional complements are admissible for the modals *müssen, dürfen, sollen*, i.e. complements referring to a Source, to the Path and those referring to a Goal. This is illustrated by ⟨26d⟩. The combinability of modal verbs with non-verbal complements can thus be summarized as shown in ⟨27⟩:

⟨26⟩   a. Karl will/mag ein Eis. 'Karl wants an ice cream.'

       b. Karl will/mag/kann/darf/soll jetzt nach Hause.
          'Karl wants to/can/may/is expected to go home now.'

       c. Karl kann Russisch. 'Karl speaks Russian.'

       d. Ich muss hier weg/durch einen dunklen Wald/nach Hause.
          'I have to get away from here/to go through a dark forest/to go home.'

⟨27⟩   *mögen, wollen* >   *können*   > *müssen, dürfen, sollen*
      ——————————— directional complements ———————————
      —— skills (esp. languages) ——
      — objects —

All the properties described above show that modal verbs constitute a special and distinct subclass among German verbs, but are still much more similar to the other verbs than their counterparts in English. Translations of sentences with modal verbs from German into English therefore pose many problems for the learner, and sometimes different (e.g. adjectival) expressions of modality have to be used. We will return to these problems in Section 6.6.

6.3 Dimensions of meaning and use

6.3.1 Circumstantial and epistemic uses of modal expressions

However different the meanings and uses of individual modal verbs in English and in German may be, there is one general property that the members of the relevant classes in the two languages share: Each member of the two classes has at least two different meanings or uses. In describing this polyfunctionality as 'different meanings or uses' we want to indicate that it is a matter of some controversy whether this should be regarded as a question of polysemy (multiple meanings) or of vagueness, i.e. as a manifestation of a univocal meaning that results in different interpretations depending on the context.

Two major use types can be distinguished for both possibility modals (*can, may*) and necessity modals (*must, have to*). We will call these uses '**circumstantial**' and '**epistemic**'. Circumstantial modals, alternatively called 'situational' or 'root' uses, indicate possibility or necessity following from some fact, state of affairs, event, etc. conditioning some other fact, state of affairs, or event. Relevant examples are given in ⟨28⟩ for circumstantial possibility and in ⟨29⟩ for circumstantial necessity.

⟨28⟩ **Circumstantial possibility**
   a. With this new swimming pool I can swim all day.
   b. Seit Karl in Paris wohnt, kann er auch am Sonntag im Büro arbeiten.

⟨29⟩ **Circumstantial necessity**
   a. To survive in the desert, organisms must learn how to reduce heat.
   b. Karl muss im Büro arbeiten, denn zu Hause ist es zu laut.

While the 'circumstances' in ⟨28⟩ and ⟨29⟩ refer to 'physical' conditions such as the presence of a swimming pool or proximity to one's place of work, in ⟨30⟩ below the modals express that the future actions of the subject depend in some way on background assumptions about duties, obligations, principles of conduct, permission, etc. The action expressed in the sentence (without a modal verb) follows in some sense from these background assumptions. Such uses will be called **deontic**, and they will be regarded as special cases of circumstantial modals.

⟨30⟩ **Deontic possibility**
   a. May I come in?
   b. Auf der Terasse kannst du rauchen.

⟨31⟩ **Deontic necessity**
   a. You must be more careful in the future.
   b. Du solltest jetzt nach Hause gehen.

Another special case of circumstantial modality is provided by uses of modals where some possibility or necessity follows from the abilities or, more generally speaking, the 'disposition' of a referent. Such uses are associated with specialized modals in many languages, e.g. *savoir* in French (*Il sait nager* 'He can swim').

⟨32⟩ **Dispositional possibility**
   a. Little Johnny can already swim.
   b. Hans kann sich schon alleine anziehen.

⟨33⟩ **Dispositional necessity**
   a. If you MUST smoke, at least you could use an ashtray.
   b. Karl musste plötzlich auf die Toilette gehen.

A dimension of meaning and use that differs strikingly from the examples given in ⟨28⟩–⟨33⟩ above shows up in examples like ⟨34⟩ and ⟨35⟩ below. In these examples the modal verbs indicate that the speaker does not have adequate knowledge to make a statement without modal qualification. Such statements are based on conclusions and inferences rather than first-hand evidence and established knowledge. Based on the Greek word for 'knowledge' (*epistēmē*), this use is called the '**epistemic**'. The examples given in ⟨34⟩ show that this use can be found with several, if not all, modal verbs in English. For all examples of this type paraphrases like (*it is*) *possibly true, probably true, likely, necessarily true*, etc. are found in dictionaries and grammatical descriptions.

⟨34⟩ **Epistemic possibility**
    a. You might be right.
    b. John may have already left.
    c. He cannot be more than fifty years old.

⟨35⟩ **Epistemic necessity**
    a. John must be at least eighty.
    b. The house ought to be here somewhere.
    c. My students should have no problem with this test.

The fact that modal verbs in English and in German have a double (circumstantial and epistemic) meaning and use, thus relating to different background assumptions or discourse contexts, does not mean that concrete utterances are always ambiguous. Even though two interpretations are possible for some sentences if we disregard the situational context, it is the grammatical context which more often than not determines or at least favours one of the interpretations available. For example, a circumstantial interpretation is unlikely if the predicate of the sentence denotes a state of affairs in which some human referent participates without having control over it (cf. ⟨36⟩), whereas it is preferred in the case of an action predicate (cf. ⟨37⟩):

⟨36⟩ Epistemic interpretation preferred
    a. You may be wrong. (nominal predication)
    b. You must be kidding. (progressive aspect)
    c. You must have worked very hard yesterday. (perfect)

⟨37⟩ Circumstantial (deontic) interpretation preferred
    a. You may take as many as you like.
    b. You must/should/ought to work a little harder.
    c. You should leave her alone.

The preceding examples show that tense and aspect also play a role in disambiguation. The progressive aspect and the perfect, both of which are associated with 'stativity', result in a preference for an epistemic interpretation, as in ⟨36b⟩ and ⟨36c⟩. However, a circumstantial/deontic interpretation is not entirely ruled out in combination with stative predications, as is illustrated in ⟨38⟩.

⟨38⟩   a.   Don't forget: You must be working when the boss comes in.
       b.   You must have finished all the work by the time the day is over.

Still, the aspectual properties of a predication in the scope of a modal operator play
an important role, as do other tense and mood specifications (cf. Section 6.5).

6.3.2 Other uses of modals

In both English and German, modals are also used in contexts where they do not
primarily express possibility or necessity. For example, English *can* sometimes
expresses existential quantification as in ⟨39⟩, and it is used in combination with
predicates of 'inert perception' (Leech 1971) to express the actual instantiation of
a stative event, as opposed to its mere possibility (cf. ⟨40⟩).

⟨39⟩   Welshmen can be tall.
       ∼ 'Some Welshmen are tall'

⟨40⟩   I can see the moon.
       ∼ 'I see the moon', stative reading of *see*

While existential and stative uses of possibility modals as in ⟨39⟩ and ⟨40⟩ are
found in both languages under comparison, there are at least two uses that show up
in only one of the languages. Both of these uses represent extensions of modals that
originally expressed volition (the so-called 'bouletic' modals *will* and *wollen*), or
deontic necessity (*shall*/*sollen*). Note that the members of each pair are semantically
related. Germ. *sollen* can often be paraphrased in terms of *wollen*:

⟨41⟩   Du sollst dafür bezahlen.
       ∼ 'I want you to pay for this.'

German *sollen* and *wollen* have developed a '**quotational**' use, in which they are
used to describe a claim made by the subject of the sentence in the case of *wollen*,
or by some third party in the case of *sollen*:

⟨42⟩   a.   Karl will Michael Jackson gekannt haben.
            'Karl claims to have known Michael Jackson.'
       b.   Karl soll Michael Jackson gekannt haben.
            'Karl is said to have known Michael Jackson.'

This use can certainly be regarded as a specific sub-case of the epistemic use, since
it indicates that the available knowledge is not sufficient for the speaker to make a
simple claim. However, these modal verbs do not express likelihood or probability

but indicate the source of information. Note that this use is even found in combination with complex tenses like the *Perfekt* (*Karl hat krank sein sollen* 'Karl was said to be ill').

The English counterparts (*will* and *shall*) of the two German modal verbs just discussed have taken a different development. They have been grammaticalized to markers of future time reference (cf. ⟨43a⟩/⟨43b⟩). The slightly archaic flavour of the example with *shall* in ⟨43b⟩ shows that this use is marginal at best in American English and even in British English the futurate use of *shall* is only found in connection with first person subjects (cf. ⟨43c⟩).

⟨43⟩ a. When will you ever learn?
       b. We shall overcome one day.
       c. I/*he shall know more about this by tomorrow.

How *will* and *shall* (in their futurate uses) differ from other markers of future time such as *going to/gonna* is discussed in the chapter on tense and aspect (Chapter 5).

6.4 Combinations of modal verbs and interaction with negation

As already mentioned, the combination of two modals is excluded in (Standard) English, since there are no non-finite forms. In German, by contrast, such combinations are possible and so the question of possible interactions between different types of modals can be raised. If we look at the possible interpretations of sentences like those in ⟨44⟩, we note that the combination of two circumstantial interpretations (a disposition as a necessary condition in ⟨44a⟩) is possible, as is the combination of an epistemic with a circumstantial interpretation (cf. ⟨44b⟩):

⟨44⟩ a. Karin muss Gitarre spielen können (um diese Rolle zu bekommen).
           'Karin must be able to play the guitar (in order to get that role).'
       b. Karin muss Gitarre spielen können (sonst hätte sie sich kein neues Instrument gekauft).
           'Karin must (be able to) play the guitar (otherwise she would not have bought herself a new instrument).'

In the latter case, i.e. in combinations of epistemic and circumstantial interpretations, it is almost always the epistemic one that is expressed by the first and higher modal, whereas the circumstantial modal occurs in the non-finite form. If the relevant sentences occur as subordinate clauses the order is reversed, but it is still the epistemic modal that occurs in a finite form:

⟨45⟩ Ich meine, dass Karin [[[Gitarre spielen] können$_{DISP}$] muss$_{EPIST}$].

Semantically speaking, we can say that epistemic modals 'take scope over' circumstantial ones. This is also true of English sentences where a modal auxiliary cooccurs with a non-finite form of a semi-modal, as in ⟨46⟩.

⟨46⟩ I may have to work this weekend.

The question of '**scope**' is also relevant if we consider the interpretation of negation in combination with modals. Note first that in infinitival complementation, a negative marker such as Engl. *not* or Germ. *nicht* may relate either to the finite (superordinate) predicate or to the non-finite (embedded) one. The two possibilities are not easily distinguished in spoken German, where intonational means (such as a pause or some specific intonation contour) may be used for disambiguation. In the written language, the placement of a comma clearly indicates the scope relationships:

⟨47⟩ a. Karl beabsichtigt, nicht zu kommen.
          intention > NOT > come
       b. Karl beabsichtigt nicht, zu kommen.
          NOT > intention > come

In English the insertion or omission of the auxiliary *do* in the counterparts of ⟨47a⟩ and ⟨47b⟩ differentiates between such cases:

⟨48⟩ a. John intends not to come.
       b. John does not intend to come.

In sentences with modal auxiliaries, however, the auxiliary *do* is never inserted, since these verbs are themselves auxiliaries. As a result, the same ambiguities concerning the relationship of the negator *not* to the rest of the sentence as illustrated in ⟨47⟩ for German may also arise: *Not* can relate either to the modal ('**external negation**'), or to the second verb ('**internal negation**'). The following examples illustrate these two possibilities for the epistemic use of *can* and *may* in ⟨49a⟩ and ⟨49b⟩. ⟨49c⟩ is an example with two negations:

⟨49⟩ a. It can't have been Tom.
          external: NOT > POSS > it was Tom
       b. It may not have been Tom.
          internal: POSS > NOT > it was Tom
       c. I can't NOT go.
          external and internal: NOT > POSS > NOT > I go
          'I kann (doch) nicht einfach NICHT hingehen.'

Both English and German exhibit a more or less systematic relationship between the reading of a modal (circumstantial vs. epistemic) and the interpretation of negation in the case of possibility modals: While circumstantial possibility modals are normally interpreted in the scope of negation, epistemic ones may take scope over negation. German often uses a **Konjunktiv II** form of the modal in order to indicate that an epistemic reading is intended (cf. also Section 6.5):

⟨50⟩ Epistemic, POSS > NOT

    a. He may not be home yet.

    b. Er könnte noch nicht zu Hause sein.

⟨51⟩ Deontic, NOT > POSS

    a. You may not go home yet.

    b. Du darfst noch nicht nach Hause gehen.

This is different with the necessity modal *must*, however. While English *must* invariably takes scope over negation, Germ. *müssen* is interpreted in the **scope of negation**. Identical looking sentences like those in ⟨52⟩ therefore differ systematically in their interpretation:

⟨52⟩   a. You must not run away/use the elevator. (NEC > NOT)

    b. Du musst nicht weglaufen/den Aufzug benutzen. (NOT > NEC)

These two sentences contain lexical elements which have an exact counterpart in the other language, arranged in the same linear order, and still they are not translational equivalents. The English sentence translates as ⟨53a⟩ and the German sentence has ⟨53b⟩ as its translational equivalent:

⟨53⟩   a. Du darfst nicht weglaufen/den Aufzug benutzen.

    b. You need not run away/use the elevator.

Both *need* and *brauchen* are specialized to '**non-affirmative**' contexts as in ⟨53⟩, i.e. they are 'negative polarity items'. Note that there is an important difference between the distribution of the two verbs. Both *need* and *brauchen* are used with and without an infinitival particle. While the difference in German is one of register – *zu* is required by prescriptive grammarians but often omitted in casual speech (cf. ⟨54⟩) – in English the particle *to* differentiates between a (positive polarity) main verb use of *need* and a (negative polarity) auxiliary use of that verb (cf. ⟨55⟩).

⟨54⟩ Du brauchst nicht so früh (zu) kommen.

⟨55⟩   a. You need not come so early.

    b. You need to come early (if you don't want to stand in line for an hour).

Note that the distributional behaviour of *need* is paralleled by that of another, more marginal member of the class of English modals, i.e. *dare*. While *dare* does not express possibility or necessity, it behaves distributionally like a modal auxiliary with a restriction to negative polarity contexts, very much like *need* (note that positive polarity uses of *dare* have been preserved in the archaic expression *I dare say*).

⟨56⟩   a. I dare not even think of this.

b. I dare to claim that the sole value of philosophy of science is its entertaining ability. (attributed to the philosopher Michael Ruse)

The interactions between polarity and the distribution or interpretation of a modal are put into a larger context in the next section, where a more detailed comparison of the various forms of English and German modals as well as their possible readings in specific contexts is provided.

6.5   Tense, mood and the interpretation of modals

6.5.1   Inventories of forms

In German, modal verbs occur in all the tense and mood forms available, and their interpretation varies more or less systematically with these categories. For each modal verb we find present and past tense forms and also a systematic distinction between indicative forms and *Konjunktiv II* forms. In Table 6.1 the four possible forms are illustrated with the modal verbs *können* and *müssen*.

Indikativ Präsens	Indikativ Präteritum	Konjunktiv I	Konjunktiv II
Er kann kochen.	Er konnte kochen.	Er könne kochen.	Er könnte kochen.
Er muss arbeiten.	Er musste arbeiten.	Er müsse arbeiten.	Er müsste arbeiten.

Table 6.1 Interaction with tense and mood: German

As will be seen below, the various forms of German differ in the types of modality that they can express. The tense and mood specifications are interpreted relatively straightforwardly in many cases, however. There is a clear past-vs.-non-past opposition (cf. ⟨57a⟩ vs. ⟨57b⟩). The *Konjunktiv II* forms express greater tentativeness and less certainty than the present indicative ones (cf. ⟨58⟩). In questions and requests, they are often used for the expression of consideration, politeness, tentativeness, etc. (cf. ⟨59⟩). The *Konjunktiv I* forms can only be used in indirect speech (cf. ⟨60⟩) and are very rare in the spoken language.

⟨57⟩   a. Das muss der Briefträger sein.
             'This must be the mailman.'
         b. Das musste der Briefträger sein.
             'This had to be the mailman.'

⟨58⟩   a. Das müsste der Briefträger sein.
             'This ought to be be the mailman.'
         b. Das dürfte der Briefträger sein.
             'This is bound to be the mailman.'

⟨59⟩   Dürfte ich nach Hause gehen?
         'May I go home?'

⟨60⟩   Karl meint, das müsse der Briefträger sein.
         'Karl thinks that this must be the mailman.'

The system of English modals seems at first sight to be also morphologically regular and transparent, more or less like the system of German. However, this regularity is only apparent, insofar as it concerns only the forms, but not their functions. The English modals are summarized in Table 6.2.

| present | can | may | will | shall | must | dare | need | – |
| past/remote | could | might | would | should | – | dared | – | ought |

Table 6.2 Inflectional forms of English modals

As Table 6.2 shows, some modal verbs (*must, ought, need*) do not distinguish past from present tense forms. *Ought* is originally a past tense form of *owe* and is therefore listed with the past tense forms, but it is only used with present time reference. Like *must*, it is only admissible in past contexts when occurring in indirect speech, as in ⟨61⟩.

⟨61⟩   John said the children must/ought to leave the building immediately.

In those cases where English makes a formal distinction between present tense forms and past tense forms, the latter are also used in 'remote' conditionals and in modally remote preterite forms, i.e. in contexts roughly corresponding to the *Konjunktiv II* in German:

⟨62⟩   a. If he came in time we could go out for dinner. (Germ. *käme*)
         b. Could you lift this suitcase? (Germ. *könntest*)

In what follows, we will focus on the most 'central' members of the class of modals in English and German. We will start with possibility modals in Section 6.5.2 and turn to necessity modals in Section 6.5.3.

6.5.2 Possibility modals: Forms and readings

In this section, we will consider what types of readings are available for what types of modals. We will focus on modals with a present time interpretation and disregard cases like *could* when it functions as an indicative past tense form of *can* (e.g. *He could play the piano*). What we are primarily interested in are the differences between modals like *could* (or *könnte*) and their 'basic' counterparts (*can/können* etc.) with respect to parameters such as circumstantial vs. epistemic readings, 'tentativeness' vs. 'assertiveness' and the interaction with negation (internal vs. external). We will start with the German modals, as they display a somewhat more systematic behaviour than their English counterparts.

The possibility modal *können* allows both epistemic and circumstantial interpretations for both mood categories (*Indikativ* and *Konjunktiv II*). The *Konjunktiv II* form suggests more tentativeness in each case:

⟨63⟩ a. Er kann/könnte schon zu Hause sein. (epistemic)

  b. Kann/könnte ich nun nach Hause gehen? (deontic)

However, the different mood forms of *können* behave differently with respect to the interaction with negation in their epistemic uses. While the *Indikativ* forms of *können* are normally interpreted with external negation (cf. ⟨64a⟩), negation in combination with *Konjunktiv II* forms is often internal in declarative sentences (cf. ⟨64b⟩), but external in questions like ⟨64c⟩.

⟨64⟩ a. Er kann jetzt noch nicht zu Hause sein. (NOT > POSS)

  b. Er könnte jetzt noch nicht zu Hause sein. (POSS > NOT)

  c. Könnte er das nicht vergessen haben? (NOT > POSS)

A more categorial difference can be observed between the mood forms of *dürfen*. The *Indikativ* form is invariably deontic, i.e. it always expresses permission. This reading is also available for the *Konjunktiv II* form, which is, again, more tentative and more polite (cf. ⟨65a⟩). However, *dürfte* also has epistemic uses which *dürfen* lacks (cf. ⟨65b⟩). Interestingly, *dürfte* expresses more certainty than *könnte* and is more or less equivalent to *müsste* (cf. ⟨65c⟩).

⟨65⟩ a. Darf ich jetzt nach Hause gehen? (deontic)

  b. Das *darf/dürfte jetzt der letzte gewesen sein. (epistemic)

  c. Das dürfte/müsste deine Mutter sein. (epistemic)

As was seen above, the *Indikativ* and the *Konjunktiv II* forms of *können* differ with respect to the scope of negation. A similar difference can be observed between the mood forms of *dürfen*. Negation in combination with (deontic) *dürfen* is always external (cf. ⟨66a⟩), while it is typically internal in combination with epistemic *dürfte* (cf. ⟨66b⟩).

⟨66⟩   a. Du darfst noch nicht nach Hause gehen. (NOT > POSS)
        b. Der dürfte jetzt noch nicht zu Hause sein. (POSS > NOT)

Among the English possibility modals, *can* is the most generic one, i.e. it has the broadest range of uses. It is regularly used in dispositional as well as deontic contexts (cf. ⟨67a⟩ and ⟨67b⟩, respectively).

⟨67⟩   a. Little Johnny can already swim. (dispositional)
        b. Can I go now? (deontic)

An idiosyncrasy can be observed in epistemic uses of *can*. Such uses are restricted to '**non-affirmative**' contexts, mostly negative ones:

⟨68⟩   a. He can't be home yet. (epistemic)
        b. *He can be (at) home by now.
            (no epistemic *can* in non-negative/declarative clauses)

Negation is always external in the case of epistemic *can*, so ⟨68a⟩ is interpreted as shown in ⟨69⟩:

⟨69⟩   It is NOT [POSSIBLE [that he is at home already]].

The 'remote' form of *can*, i.e. *could*, regularly allows epistemic uses in both positive and negative contexts, thus differing from the 'basic' form *can*:

⟨70⟩   He could be home by now. (epistemic *could*)

Negation in combination with epistemic *could* is typically external:

⟨71⟩   That couldn't be your parents at the door. (NOT > POSS)

Like *can*, *could* also has deontic uses (cf. ⟨72⟩); and just like German *könnte*, it expresses more tentativeness than the 'basic' form (remember that we disregard modals with past time reference):

⟨72⟩   Could I go now?

The second 'major' possibility modal of English, *may*, does not have dispositional uses and is mostly used in the deontic and epistemic domain (cf. ⟨73⟩). Deontic uses of *may* as in ⟨73a⟩ are basically restricted to questions, and even in this type of context they sound formal:

⟨73⟩   a. May I go now? (deontic)
        b. He may know this already. (epistemic)

The scope of negation varies systematically with the type of modality expressed by *may*. Deontic *may* combines with external negation (cf. ⟨74a⟩), epistemic *may* with internal negation (cf. ⟨74b⟩).

⟨74⟩   a. You may not go yet. (deontic, NOT > POSS)
        b. He may not know this yet. (epistemic, POSS > NOT)

The absence of a dispositional reading for *may*, as well as its tendency to express epistemic (rather than deontic) readings, is one of the main aspects of meaning distinguishing *may* from *can*. This distinction is a classical problem for German learners of English, as *can* and *may* often seem to correspond to the German verb *können*. The following minimal pair illustrates the difference between the two modals (cf. Leech 1971):

⟨75⟩   a. This road can be blocked. (dispositional)
        b. This road may be blocked. (epistemic)

Even though this generalization is a guideline rather than a strict rule, *can* in ⟨75a⟩ is typically interpreted as a dispositional modal, and *may* in ⟨75b⟩ as an epistemic modal. ⟨75a⟩ states that it is a property of the street in question that it can be blocked – the street is 'blockable', as it were. ⟨75b⟩ says more than that – it suggests that there is evidence to the effect that the street is in fact blocked. This difference can at least approximately be expressed with the use of different mood categories in German. The *Indikativ* suggests a dispositional reading while the *Konjunktiv II* suggests an epistemic reading:

⟨76⟩   a. Diese Straße kann man blockieren. (dispositional)
        b. Diese Straße könnte blockiert sein. (epistemic)

Unlike its basic counterpart *may*, *might* is very rarely used in a deontic function in contemporary English. It is basically an epistemic modal. As in the case of *may*, negation is internal here:

⟨77⟩   a. He might know this already. (epistemic)
        b. He might not know this yet. (POSS > NOT)

For a summary of the contrasts pointed out in this section it will be useful to distinguish a more generic and a more specific possibility modal for each language. The modals *can* and *können* are not only genetically related but also cover a similar range of functions, as they can be used in dispositional, deontic as well as epistemic contexts. The modals *may* and *dürfen* are more specialized and are primarily associated with the expression of permission (note, however, that the German cognate of *may* is of course *mögen*). In our summary we will thus compare *can* to *können* and *may* to *dürfen*. On this basis, three major contrasts between English and German possibility modals can be identified:

- German *können* has epistemic uses in all contexts, whereas English *can* is only used epistemically under negation and in other types of 'non-assertive' contexts (e.g. questions).

- English *may* has epistemic uses while German *dürfen* does not have such uses.

- Epistemic *dürfte* behaves more like a necessity modal and is basically equivalent to *müsste*, while English *might* is even more tentative than epistemic *could*.

6.5.3 Necessity modals: Forms and readings

The German forms *muss* and *müsste* behave similarly in many respects. They have dispositional as well as deontic uses. *Müsste* is more tentative or polite than *muss*:

⟨78⟩   a. Ich muss/müsste mal auf die Toilette gehen. (dispositional)
         b. Ich muss/müsste jetzt nach Hause. (deontic)

The mood distinction is associated with a distributional difference in the case of epistemic readings, however. Note first that *muss* is more 'definite' than *müsste*, which expresses a weaker epistemic commitment:

⟨79⟩   Der Unfallfahrer muss/?müsste betrunken gewesen sein.
⟨80⟩   a. Das muss so stimmen. (strong commitment)
         b. Das müsste so stimmen. (weak commitment)

A second difference concerns the cooccurrence of the modals with negation. Negation with *muss* is external (cf. ⟨81a⟩). *Müsste* does not normally combine with negation (cf. ⟨81b⟩), and a form of *können* is mostly used instead (cf. ⟨82⟩; note again the difference in the scope of negation).

⟨81⟩   a. Es kann, muss aber nicht so sein. (NOT > NEC)
         b. *Es müsste so nicht stimmen.
⟨82⟩   a. Es kann so nicht stimmen. (NOT > POSS)
         b. Es könnte so nicht stimmen. (POSS > NOT)

As mentioned above, the English counterpart to Germ. *müssen, must,* only has a present tense form. *Must* is a rather generic modal and has dispositional, deontic and epistemic uses. As has been seen, it always takes scope over negation in deontic cases (cf. ⟨83a⟩). This applies to epistemic uses of *must* as well (cf. ⟨83b⟩).

⟨83⟩   a.   You must not do that. (deontic, NEC > NOT)

        b.   He must not have read the safety instructions. (epistemic, NEC > NOT)

There are thus two main differences between Germ. *müssen* and Engl. *must*:

- Germ. *müssen* has a non-indicative form, while no such form is available for Engl. *must*.

- In its deontic readings, Germ. *müssen* is contained in the scope of negation (negation is external), whereas Engl. *must* invariably takes scope over negation (negation is internal).

6.5.4 Summary

As has been seen, the system of German modals is more 'transparent' than that of English, especially in terms of the interpretation of tense and mood categories. Even though there are also some (apparently idiosyncratic) asymmetries in the German system, the degree of lexical specialization exhibited by the English modals is higher. We can interpret this type of 'lexical specialization' as a tendency for the different forms of modals to develop into separate lexical entries. As has been mentioned repeatedly, this tendency is reflected in dictionaries of English, where each modal often has an entry of its own. By contrast, dictionaries of German rarely, if ever, provide different entries for *Indikativ* and *Konjunktiv* forms of modals.

6.6   Other means of modal marking and the *origo* of modality

6.6.1   Ways of expressing modality

As pointed out above, modal notions can be expressed by a variety of lexical elements other than (auxiliary) verbs, i.e. by adjectives (*able, capable, bound, likely, possible, probable, willing*), by past participles (*obliged to, forced to, allowed to*), by nouns (*need, permission*), by adverbs (*maybe, perhaps*) and, of course, by 'semi-auxiliaries' as well as main verbs (*have* [*got*] *to, manage,* etc.). As also pointed out above, these expressions do not share the polyfunctionality or polysemy with modal auxiliaries in English, but have one meaning or use only, either a circumstantial one (e.g. *capable, be permitted, be obliged*), or an epistemic one (e.g. *bound, likely, probable*). The double use as both circumstantial and epistemic expressions is evidently a specific property of modal verbs in Germanic languages.

The reason for extending our discussion of modality in English beyond the modal auxiliaries at that point is that the other expressive devices play a specific role in a contrastive study of modality in English and in German. Due to the defective paradigm of modal auxiliaries in English (no infinitive, no past participle, no combinations of modals), there are many contexts in which the German counterparts of the modal auxiliaries in English require a different translation. Such problems of equivalence in translation arise especially for the circumstantial use. Except for a few rare cases the epistemic use of modal verbs in German is only found in present and past time contexts. Here it is the past time contexts that require a translation into English without a modal auxiliary:

⟨84⟩   a. Das musste der Briefträger gewesen sein.
          'This was bound/had to be the mailman.'

        b. Das konnte der Briefträger sein.
          'This was possibly the mailman.'

The circumstantial use, by contrast, is semantically compatible with all tenses in German and since the paradigms for modal verbs are not defective, such meanings can be expressed by the specific modal verbs discussed in this chapter. In English, the relevant German sentences, which require a non-finite form of a modal verb, can only be translated with the help of some (non-auxiliary) **substitution form** like those listed in the preceding paragraph and in ⟨85⟩ below, where alternative expressions for the circumstantial uses of *must*, of *can* and of *may* can be found:

⟨85⟩   a. must: have (got) to, be obliged to, be forced to, etc.;

        b. can: be able, capable, prepared to; manage, have the possibility to, etc.;

        c. may: be allowed to, be permitted to, have permission to, etc.

The use of these forms for modal verbs in the past, in complex tenses or in combinations of modal verbs is illustrated by the following examples:

⟨86⟩   a. Wir mussten ihn bestrafen.
          'We had to punish him.'

        b. Wir werden ihn bestrafen müssen.
          'We will have to punish him.'

        c. Ich durfte die Geschenke noch nicht sehen.
          'I was not allowed to see the presents yet.'

        d. Ich hätte den ganzen Tag schwimmen können.
          'I would have been able to swim all day.'

  e. Ich hatte das schon immer tun wollen.
     'I had always wanted to do that.'

  f. Ein Schauspieler muss Klavier spielen können.
     'An actor must be able to play the piano.'

  g. Ich hätte das gerne tun mögen.
     'I would have liked to do that.'

The fact that these non-auxiliary expressions fill gaps in the defective paradigms of modal auxiliaries in English gives rise to the question of whether there is complete equivalence between these substitution forms and the modal auxiliaries they sometimes replace. Looking at the answers to these questions in detail reveals another interesting dimension in the meaning of modal auxiliaries and of modal expressions in general.

6.6.2 Specifying the *origo* of modality

Recall that the distinctions between the different uses of modal verbs were drawn in terms of obligation, volition, conclusion, supposition, inference, etc. What we have not considered at all so far is the question of where the obligation or the volition comes from, whose volition is expressed, or who it is that draws a conclusion. This question opens up an additional dimension in the semantic analysis of modal verbs. Modal verbs turn out to be 'indexical' expressions in many cases, i.e. they relate the content of a verb to a centre of orientation, an *origo* in the sense of Bühler (1934). The 'modal source' – for instance, the source of an obligation or the source of information – can often be due to the speaker or it can be attributed to somebody else. In epistemic uses of modal verbs we typically find conclusions or inferences drawn by the speaker, and in deontic uses obligation, permission and volition can also typically be ascribed to the speaker. But this is not necessarily the case.

Let us turn to some examples. According to major reference grammars of English (e.g. Quirk *et al.* 1985: 225), *must* and *have to* are not equivalent in those (present tense) contexts where they are interchangeable. The modal verb *must* often indicates that the obligation is imposed by the speaker, whereas the authority comes from somebody else or from the circumstances in the case of *have to* (cf. ⟨87⟩; see Depraetere 2008 for a critical assessment of this generalization). German does not seem to make that distinction and uses *müssen* in both cases.

⟨87⟩ a. I must have a hair-cut.

      b. I have to have a hair-cut.

⟨88⟩ Ich muss mir die Haare schneiden lassen.

Another well-known example is provided by orders, pieces of advice and similar directive speech acts. The modal *shall* is used in Shakespeare's plays in this function, contemporary English often uses *should* or *ought to*, especially in combination with 2nd person subjects:

⟨89⟩ ... you shall put this night's business into my dispatch ... (Macbeth I.5.65)

⟨90⟩   a. You should never give up.

      b. You ought to stay home.

This type of speech act can also be expressed by using *am/is/are to*. This '**modal idiom**' resembles the modal auxiliaries not only in its meaning, but also insofar as it does not have non-finite forms. None of the following forms is admissible in English: *to be to, *being to, *been to. If this expression is used, however, the directive speech act does not come from the speaker, but from some other source, such as a member of the family perhaps in examples like ⟨91a⟩. German typically uses *sollen* in such cases, which can also be used when the speaker is the *origo* of the modal predication, however:

⟨91⟩   a. You are to come home immediately. (3rd person *origo*)

      b. Du sollst sofort nach Hause kommen! (1st or 3rd person *origo*)

Table 6.3 summarizes some of the interesting contrasts that we find in English itself as well as some of the contrasts between English and German. It contains the modal verbs discussed in this chapter as well as some substitution forms (in parentheses). In the horizontal dimension we find the basic semantic content of a modal verb, the attitude or speech act expressed and in the vertical one a specification of the relevant *origo* or point of orientation. Note that Table 6.3 is not exhaustive, i.e. there are many combinations of *origo* and source of modality that are not mentioned in it.

	Source of ...				
	I	II	III	IV	V
↓ Origo	obligation	permission	volition	concession	claim
speaker	*must, should*	*you may*	–	*he may*	–
	muss(t), soll(st)	*du darfst*	–	*er mag*	–
subject	–	–	(*he wants to*)	–	(*he claims to*)
	–	–	*er möchte, will*	–	*er will*
neither	(*have to, are to*)	*you can*	(*you are to*)	–	(*he is said to*)
	muss(t), soll(st)	*du kannst*	*du möchtest*	–	*er soll*

Table 6.3 Modal expressions and their relation to an *origo*

Table 6.3 requires some further exemplification. In the deontic use of *may* the situation is analogous to that found for *must* and *shall* (cf. column II). The use of *may* in a permissive sense means that the speaker is the center of orientation, while *can* typically points to some third party (cf. ⟨92⟩). Similarly, in German *dürfen* is often used if the speaker is the *origo*, while *können* is more neutral in this respect (cf. ⟨93⟩).

⟨92⟩   a.   You may go now, James.
       b.   The boss doesn't need you anymore. You can go.

⟨93⟩   a.   Sie dürfen gehen, James.
       b.   Sie können nach Hause gehen. Sie werden nicht mehr gebraucht.

Möchten in German has two interesting uses, which seem to be totally unrelated, but turn out to be differentiated only in terms of the point of orientation. In both cases, a wish is expressed, but the wish may come either from the referent of the subject (cf. ⟨94⟩) or from a source that is different from both the speaker and the subject referent (cf. ⟨95⟩ and column III in Table 6.3):

⟨94⟩   a.   Ich möchte jetzt nach Hause gehen.
          'I would like to go home now.'
       b.   Sie möchten sicher nach Hause gehen?
          'You probably want to go home now.'

⟨95⟩   Du möchtest sofort zum Chef kommen!
       'You are to see the boss immediately!'

The 3rd person present indicative form of *mögen* may express a concession – quite similarly to English *may* – but the concession always comes from the speaker (cf. column IV):

⟨96⟩   a.   He may be a famous politician, but he is still an idiot.
       b.   Er mag ja ein bekannter Politiker sein, aber er ist ein Idiot.

⟨97⟩   ??Du sagst, er mag ein bekannter Politiker sein, aber ...

Finally, quotational *wollen* and *sollen* differ only insofar as the claim mentioned in the sentence comes from the subject in the former case and from somebody other than speaker and subject referent in the latter case (cf. column V and Section 6.3.2):

⟨98⟩   a.   Er soll ein guter Schachspieler gewesen sein, als er jung war.
          'He is said to have been a good chess player when he was young.'
       b.   Er will ein guter Schachspieler gewesen sein, als er jung war.
          'He claims to have been a good chess player when he was young.'

6.7 Summary

We are now in a position to summarize the major contrasts between English and German in the domain under investigation (cf. Table 6.4). In both languages the modal verbs form a specific subset of verbs with a similar historical development, with very similar meanings and with specific morphological and syntactic properties. In English these verbs have developed into auxiliary verbs and form highly defective inflectional paradigms. In German there are also some special properties, but the modal verbs are still considered as main verbs. In German only the 3rd person singular of modal verbs has a specific inflectional form and there is no past participle.

The dimensions of meaning relevant for the semantic analysis of modal verbs are basically the same in the two languages, even if we have one use in each language that has no counterpart in the other (quotational/German, futurate/English). In German, modal verbs interact in a more regular fashion with tense and mood than in English, and what used to be different forms of one modal in the latter language (e.g. *may/might*) is developing, or perhaps has developed, into different modals. Some differences in the interaction with negation and the range of interpretations associated with each modal verb have been noticed (*must not* vs. *muss nicht*, epistemic readings of *can/können* and *may/dürfen*). Finally, some more subtle contrasts have been shown to be related to the *origo*, i.e. the source of modality, in specific cases.

property of modal verbs	English	German
paradigm structure	no inflection	no 3Sg suffix (present)
	no non-finite forms	no participial forms
		($\rightarrow$ perfect infinitive)
combinations of modals	no	yes
main predicate of sentence	no	restricted possibilities
interaction with tense and mood	irregular	regular
quotational use	no	yes (*soll*)
futurate use	yes (*will*)	no

Table 6.4 Summary: Modal verbs in English and German

Revision, questions and exercises

1. How would you analyze the uses of the verbs *need* and *dare* in sentences like the following (auxiliary verb or main verb)?

    ⟨99⟩   a.   We need to get some more beer.
           b.   You need not go to that meeting if you don't want to.
           c.   Need this be true?
           d.   I don't need any of this.
           e.   I did not dare to do this.

2. In colloquial English both of the following interactions of *used to* with negation can be observed. How can we analyse these two cases?

    ⟨100⟩   a.   John didn't use to do this.
            b.   John used not to go there.

3. What kind of modality do we find in the following sentences without modal verbs?

    ⟨101⟩   a.   This fruit is not edible. This meal is very eatable.
            b.   This bed does not fold up.
            c.   It is necessary that we do this immediately.

4. How would you analyze the use of *will* in sentences like the following?

    ⟨102⟩   a.   You willed this to happen, didn't you?
            b.   He will leave his things lying all over the place and it makes me mad.

5. Why is it that the following German sentences sound odd? In what kind of context would they be acceptable?

    ⟨103⟩   a.   ?Ich will mit dem Papst gesprochen haben.
            b.   ?Ich mag ja recht haben, aber zugeben werden sie es sicher nicht.

6. What kind of negation (external or internal) do you find in the following sentences?

    ⟨104⟩   a.   You may not smoke in here.
            b.   It need not have been Tom.
            c.   It can't have been Tom.
            d.   He ought not to go there.
            e.   I will not hear this again.
            f.   You mustn't be telling lies.

7. Which interpretation of the modal (deontic, epistemic) is more plausible in cases like the following? Give reasons for your answers!

⟨105⟩ a. You must be kidding.
   b. You must be a very busy man.
   c. This should not be too difficult.
   d. What shall I do?
   e. Must you always be so noisy?
   f. Fred can be very charming.

8. The tags of tag questions typically repeat the modal verb of the preceding sentence or insert the auxiliary *do*, as in ⟨106⟩. How can we explain the form of the tag in examples like ⟨107⟩?

   ⟨106⟩ a. You can hear me, can't you?
      b. You know me, don't you?

   ⟨107⟩ a. Let's go to see a movie, shall we?
      b. Stay on the pavement, will you?
      c. You are coming with us, won't you?

9. On the basis of which criteria do English grammars draw a distinction between auxiliary verbs and main verbs? Why is such a distinction not normally drawn for German?

10. In both English and German we find conditional clauses introduced by verbs. In English this possibility is very restricted and only possible for a few verbs. Which are the verbs that allow this construction?

Further reading

The major reference grammars of English (Quirk *et al.* 1985, Biber *et al.* 1999, Huddleston and Pullum 2002) contain comprehensive information on modals. Leech (1971) provides a basic introduction. Palmer (1990, 2001) deals with modals and modality specifically. For German, reference grammars such as Eisenberg (2006b) and Schäfer (2016) can be consulted. In addition there is comprehensive literature on modals and modality in German, e.g. Öhlschläger (1989), Diewald (1999), Abraham and Leiss (2013) and Maché (forthcoming), to name just four major monographs. For comparative work on modals (in Germanic languages), see Abraham and Janssen (1989) and Abraham (1991, 2002), among others.

7 Grammatical relations

Der Werwolf, sprach der gute Mann,
Des Weswolfs, Genitiv so dann
Dem Wemwolf, Dativ wie man's nennt
Den Wenwolf, damit hat's ein End.

(from "Der Werwolf", by Ch. Morgenstern)

7.1 Identifying grammatical relations in English and German

'Grammatical relation' or 'syntactic function' is the general cover term for such notions as 'subject', 'object', 'predicate', 'adverbial' or 'attribute'. This chapter is concerned with the encoding of the major grammatical relations **'subject'** and **'object'** in English and in German. The question of whether the terms 'subject' and 'object' can be used in descriptions of all languages, and whether these relations belong to the formal universals of language is usually answered affirmatively, even though it has not been established beyond any doubt. What has been clearly established, however, is that these grammatical notions play an important role in grammatical descriptions of English and of German, even if the criteria for identifying subjects and objects in English and German are not identical. Among the criteria that can be used for the identification of subjects in both languages we find the following:

(i)   Subjects can be omitted and are typically omitted in **imperatives**:

⟨1⟩   a.   Take out the dog for a walk!

      b.   Geh und hol Bier für mich!

(ii) Identical subjects can be omitted in **coordinations**:

⟨2⟩   a.   John opened the door and Ø switched on the light.

      b.   Karl öffnete die Tür und Ø schaltete das Licht an.

(iii) If verbs take several arguments (have several valency positions), it is normally
      the **Agent** that is encoded as subject, provided there is one. The encoding
      of a different semantic role (Recipient, Theme, Patient) as subject typically
      requires some operation on the argument structure of a verb or a different
      verb altogether:

⟨3⟩ a. Charles wrote Mary a letter.

b. Mary received a letter from Charles.

c. A letter was written to Mary (by Charles).

⟨4⟩ a. Karl schickte Maria einen Brief.

b. Maria bekam einen Brief von Karl.

c. Ein Brief wurde (von Karl) an Maria geschickt.

(iv) **Subjects** can be left **unspecified** in embedded (subordinate) clauses if the understood subject of the embedded verb is given in the main clause:

⟨5⟩ a. John has promised me ＿＿ never to let me down again.

b. John asked me ＿＿ to help him.

⟨6⟩ a. Wir beabsichtigen, ＿＿ nach Kuba zu fliegen.

b. Der Chef hat mich beauftragt, ＿＿ die Rechnung zu prüfen.

(v) Verbs show **agreement** with their subjects in person and number. In English, this is visible only in the 3rd person singular. In German, by contrast, verbs inflect systematically for person and number in agreement with their subjects, although not all positions in the paradigm are clearly distinguished formally:

⟨7⟩ a. Joan takes dancing lessons.

b. The girls take physics as a major subject.

⟨8⟩ a. Er/ihr kauft Bücher.

b. Wir/sie kaufen Bücher.

In addition to these criteria, which can be applied to both languages under consideration, there are also criteria that are applicable to only one of the languages. Obviously, case marking is the most relevant factor in German. For example, the subject of the German sentence *Mich interessiert diese Sache* is not the initial constituent, which exhibits accusative case marking and is thus identified as a direct object (*mich*). The **nominative case** clearly identifies *die Sache* as the subject. There are, however, also a few criteria for identifying subjects in English which have no parallel in German (e.g. inversion, question tags), and these criteria can be used to identify subjects in some non-trivial cases such as sentences with **existential *there***. The verb after existential *there* normally agrees with the following noun phrase, which can therefore be considered as the subject of such sentences:

⟨9⟩ There are two students waiting outside.

On the basis of other (English-specific) criteria, however, it is *there* that is identified as subject. In polar (yes-no) interrogatives subjects change their position with the auxiliary verb ('subject-auxiliary inversion', cf. Chapter 11) and this criterion points in another direction:

⟨10⟩ a. Are the students working on their exams?

b. Are there two students waiting outside?

Further criteria that identify the existential marker *there* as subject are constituent order (subjects precede finite verbs) and the form of **question tags**. In these tags an interrogative sentence is reduced to its subject and its auxiliary verb. On the analogy of sentences like ⟨11a⟩, *there* can be analyzed as a subject:

⟨11⟩ a. The students are working on their exams, aren't they?

b. There are two students waiting outside, aren't there?

On the basis of considerations like these, we could assume that *there* is really the subject in existential sentences, and that it licenses both singular and plural agreement on the verb, depending on the semantics of the relevant noun phrase. Sentences with existential *there* are also discussed in the context of constituent order (cf. Section 11.1).

Objects or complements can be identified negatively with respect to the properties pointed out above: In English, objects follow the verb and in German they are marked by the accusative, the dative or the genitive case. As is well-known, a sentence may also include **adverbials** (adjuncts) in addition to a subject and to objects. The problem of drawing a clear distinction between complements and adjuncts (*Ergänzungen* vs. *freie Angaben*) is usually considered as one of the key issues of valency grammar and the argument structure of predicates. The most basic criteria relate to the omissibility of these constituents as well as to the question of whether their formal properties are in some way determined by a predicate: complements are typically required (non-omissible) and governed by a predicate, adjuncts are not:

⟨12⟩ a. (Luckily) John found his wallet (immediately).

b. Luckily John found *(his wallet) immediately.

Unfortunately, the criterion of omissibility is not fully reliable, since complements may be omitted when they are contextually given in order to create specific semantic effects:

⟨13⟩ a. Fred contributed generously (to the collection).

b. Fred writes (books).

c. This will help (you).

In research on valency, additional criteria have therefore been established to distinguish between complements and adjuncts. One of the most reliable tests is that adjuncts can usually be expressed in a clause of their own, for instance with the predicate *happen* or *geschehen* (the '*happen*-test' or '*geschehen*-Test'), while this is not possible in the case of complements:

⟨14⟩   a. Hans saß im Sessel.

       b. ??Hans saß, und dies geschah im Sessel.

⟨15⟩   a. Hans schlief im Sessel ein.

       b. Hans schlief ein, und dies geschah im Sessel.

These problems are well-known (see e.g. Storrer 2003, Hole 2015) and will not be considered in detail.

7.2   Encoding grammatical relations

7.2.1   Case marking and constituent order

There are several ways of encoding grammatical relations, two of which are exemplified by the languages under comparison. German uses **case marking** for that purpose. The nominative case identifies the subject, while objects are commonly encoded in the accusative (direct object) or the dative (indirect object; cf. ⟨16⟩). Some verbs require objects in the genitive case, but genitive case marking of objects is becoming rarer and is gradually being replaced by the dative or by prepositions in Present-Day German (cf. ⟨17⟩).

⟨16⟩   a. Mich interessiert diese Sache.

       b. Ich kenne den Lehrer.

       c. Ich gebe dem Lehrer einige Ratschläge.

⟨17⟩   a. Ich erinnere mich seiner. Ich erinnere mich an ihn.

       b. Ich schäme mich seiner. Ich schäme mich für ihn.

In English, by contrast, grammatical relations are identified by **linear order**. The subject is that constituent which precedes the finite verb, whereas objects follow the main verb (cf. ⟨18⟩). Deviations from this order are called '**inversion**' (cf. ⟨19⟩ and Ch. 11).

⟨18⟩   a. The monkey took the banana.

       b. Heathrow sees a plane take off or land every two minutes.

       c. This suit fits me beautifully.

⟨19⟩   Have you ever been there?

The availability of a four-term case system in German and the loss of case distinctions in English is clearly one of the major differences between the two languages, since several rules of German can be formulated in terms of case marking (e.g. constituent order).

Given that English lost its case system as early as the Middle English period, other grammatical means are used to encode grammatical relations. Constituent order is obviously the most important factor, but there is also a system of 'alternations' that determines the mapping from semantic roles to syntactic functions, especially in predications with more than two arguments.

7.2.2 Grammatical relations in ditransitive predications

As long as there is only one object in a predication, no further formal distinctions need to be drawn, even though there may also be differences between different types of single objects with regard to passivization and other syntactic changes (specific types of objects cannot be passivized, for instance). If there are two objects, the differentiation is, again, based on constituent order in English: The indirect object (IO) precedes the direct one (DO) in so-called '**double object constructions**':

⟨20⟩ Fred sent [Mary]$_{IO}$ [a letter]$_{DO}$.

As shown by the examples in ⟨16⟩ above, objects can be differentiated by case marking in German and are thus differentiated both paradigmatically, if there is only one object (cf. ⟨21⟩), and syntagmatically (in terms of constituent order), if there is more than one object (cf. ⟨22⟩):

⟨21⟩   a. Karl hat mich unterstützt.

       b. Karl hat mir geholfen.

       c. Karl hat sich meiner angenommen.

⟨22⟩   a. Karl gab seinem Professor die Seminararbeit.

       b. Der Arzt überwies den Patienten an einen Spezialisten.

Note that in German two objects normally differ in their case marking in addition to differing in their typical linear order (cf. Ch. 11). There are only very few verbs like *lehren, kosten, fragen* or *abfragen* ('**double accusative**' verbs) which assign the same case to two objects (e.g. *Karl lehrte mich das Skifahren, Das kostet mich nur ein Lächeln.*). But even in those cases the two objects sometimes behave differently. When such sentences are transformed into the passive voice, one of the two accusative objects often behaves like an indirect object (cf. Plank 1987). For instance, only one of the two objects taken by the verb *lehren* can be promoted to subject in a *werden*-passive, whereas the other object requires the *bekommen*-passive:

⟨23⟩   a. Lehrer Lampe lehrte mich das Fürchten.

       b. Damals wurde noch die Kunst des Singens gelehrt.

       c. ?Damals wurde ich das Fürchten gelehrt.

       d. Damals bekam man noch das Fürchten gelehrt.

Moreover, examples like those in ⟨24a⟩ show that one object can be more easily omitted than the other, just as is normally the case with indirect (often omissible) and direct objects (typically non-omissible).

⟨24⟩   a. Professor Lampe lehrte Latein an der Harvard Universität.

       b. ??Professor Lampe lehrte mich an der Harvard Universität.

On the basis of distributional considerations we can therefore say that the first (typically animate) object of 'double accusative verbs' (*mich* in ⟨23a⟩) behaves more like an indirect object even though there is no distinctive case marking.

7.2.3 Source and Recipient in predicates of transfer of possession

There is a minor but clear difference between English and German concerning the semantic role of the first object in a double object construction. In English this role must always be that of a Recipient or Beneficiary:

⟨25⟩   a. She wrote me a letter.

       b. Mary bought her husband a book.

       c. They gave me a generous sum of money.

In German, this role is also the typical one of indirect objects, as is shown by the following examples:

⟨26⟩   a. Die Frau gab dem Jungen etwas zu essen.

       b. Ich habe dir einen Brief geschrieben.

       c. Karl wollte sich ein Buch ausleihen.

In sentences describing a **transfer of possession** the dative may, however, also encode the Source (owner) of a transfer, rather than the Recipient (cf. ⟨27⟩). In English, prepositional objects have to be used in such cases. Example ⟨28a⟩ can only mean that the speaker will buy a bike *for* Carl, but not *from* him. In the latter case a sentence like ⟨28b⟩ would be appropriate:

⟨27⟩   a. Der angebliche Freund hatte ihm viel Geld gestohlen / entwendet / ge-
            raubt.

       b. Der Lehrer nahm dem Schüler das Handy weg/ab.

       c. Ich werde (dem) Karl das Fahrrad abkaufen.

⟨28⟩   a. I will buy Carl a bike.

       b. I will buy a bike from Carl.

7.2.4 Prepositional and non-prepositional objects: Alternations, case and derivation

The encoding of the third argument in ditransitive predications as a prepositional phrase is found in both languages, but it is more common in English than in German. Moreover, English is more 'liberal' in many cases insofar as it allows more alternative constructions. For instance, the verb *serve* licenses the double object construction as well as two options for encoding the Patient and the animate argument (Recipient or Beneficiary). Relevant examples are given in ⟨29⟩, ⟨31⟩ and ⟨33⟩. The sentences ⟨30⟩, ⟨32⟩ and ⟨34⟩ provide parallel examples with other verbs.

(a) Double object constructions: 'serve somebody something'

⟨29⟩ I served her a glass of wine and dropped to my knees

⟨30⟩ a. Uncle Jim gave Mary a present.

b. Uncle Jim bought Mary a drink.

c. Can you lend me some money?

(b) Inanimate/Patient objects: 'serve something to somebody'

⟨31⟩ Stavrakis served a glass of wine to Gleason not long before his heart attack.

⟨32⟩ a. Uncle Jim bought a drink for Mary.

b. Uncle Jim gave a present to Mary.

c. I owe this to a friend of mine.

(c) Animate objects: 'serve somebody with something'

⟨33⟩ The investigating team had this morning served her with a third notice asking her to be present at her residence for questioning.

⟨34⟩ a. He envied Mary for her success.

b. Mary blamed John for the broken picture.

c. Mary introduced John to linguistics.

In German these three options can be found, too, but there is no verb that displays the full range of possibilities. In many cases, corresponding verbs take different **derivational prefixes,** and sometimes specific prepositions are required (e.g. *jmdm. etw. überweisen* vs. *jmdn. an jmdn. verweisen* cf. ⟨35⟩).

⟨35⟩ a. Karl überwies mir einen größeren Betrag.

b. Karl überwies den Betrag an mich.

c. Karl verwies den Kunden an seinen Chef.

Even though there are thus no major and general qualitative contrasts in the syntax of trivalent verbs in English and German, there is a clear quantitative difference insofar as alternations of the type illustrated in ⟨29⟩–⟨33⟩ are more common and more frequent in English.

Another instance where derivation is required in German but not in English is provided by **alternations** in the argument structure of verbs involving locative or directional complements (Levin 1993, Laffut 2006):

⟨36⟩ a. Fred spread peanut butter on the sandwich.

b. Fred spread the sandwich with peanut butter.

⟨37⟩ a. She inscribed their names on the ring.

b. She inscribed the ring with their names.

⟨38⟩ a. Fritz strich Erdnussbutter auf das Brot.

b. Fritz bestrich das Brot mit Erdnussbutter.

In English we simply find an alternation in the mapping of thematic roles (Location and Locatum) onto grammatical functions. The participant role of Locatum is encoded as direct object in ⟨36a⟩, and the Location is encoded as a prepositional phrase. In ⟨36b⟩ it is the Location that is encoded as direct object and the Locatum is expressed by a prepositional phrase.

In German we find the **applicative prefix** *be-* in such cases, a marker which indicates that it is not the Theme but the Location that is encoded as direct object. *Beschreiben, beladen, bespritzen, bemalen, bekleben, befallen, betasten, belegen, bespielen, besprühen*, etc. are further examples of such applicative verbs. The applicative prefix *be-* may change the basic argument structure of a verb in one of two different ways (cf. Wegener 1985: 171; note that these observations are not restricted to verbs with a locative or directional complement):

(a) Three place predicates licensing dative and accusative objects alternate with three place predicates licensing accusative and prepositional complements:

⟨39⟩ a. jemandem etwas liefern – jemanden mit etwas beliefern

b. jemandem etwas neiden – jemanden um etwas beneiden

(b) A three place predicate is changed into a two place one by incorporating the basic accusative object:

⟨40⟩ a. jemandem Gnade gewähren – jemanden begnadigen

b. jemandem Waffen geben – jemanden bewaffnen

Moreover, a variety of non-separable and separable prefixes (e.g. *ent-, heran-, er-, ver-, über-*, etc.) have the effect of changing the case-marking associated with some verbs in German:

⟨41⟩ a. Karl winkte mir zu.

b. Karl winkte mich heran.

⟨42⟩ a. Karl bot mir viel Geld.

b. Karl überbot mich.

7.3 Case and semantic distinctions: Location vs. direction

The fact that German, in contrast to English, has preserved its system of case distinctions also has consequences for other aspects of grammatical organization in the two languages. This is not the place to enter into complex discussions as to whether case in German is largely structural or inherent; we will simply consider a few obvious cases of semantic distinctions carried by case marking in German and their translations into English.

One of the best-known phenomena is, of course, the distinction between '**location**' and '**direction**' expressed by the dative and the accusative in German:

⟨43⟩   a. Karl rannte in dem/im Park.
            'Charles was running in the park.'

        b. Karl rannte in den Park.
            'Charles ran into the park.'

Sentence pairs such as these differ in the case assigned by the preposition *in*, but this difference is a consequence of the grammatical function displayed by the prepositional phrases. In ⟨43a⟩ we find a **locative adverbial**, which like all adverbials is omissible without making the sentence incomplete, whereas we find a **directional complement** in ⟨43b⟩, which fills an argument position of the verb *rennen*. That these prepositional phrases are instances of an adjunct and a prepositional complement, respectively, can be shown using the *happen*-test:

⟨44⟩   a. Karl rannte, und das geschah im Park.

        b. ??Karl rannte, und das geschah in den Park.

A standard way of analyzing the difference in the **case assignment** to the object in examples ⟨43a⟩ vs. ⟨43b⟩ is to say that the dative is assigned by the preposition (*an, in, auf, vor, neben, unter, über, hinter, bei*, etc.), whereas the accusative case is assigned by the directional phrase that verbs of motion are subcategorized for. Such directional phrases are possible with any of the prepositions listed above (except *bei*), but also with purely dynamic prepositions like *durch*.

The case distinction in German examples like ⟨43a⟩–⟨43b⟩ may correspond to the choice between two different prepositions in English: *in* vs. *into*, *on* vs. *onto*.

⟨45⟩   a. Johnny is jumping on the table.

        b. Johnny is jumping onto the table.

At first glance prepositional oppositions between *in* and *into* or *on* and *onto* could be seen as making up for the loss of case distinctions in English, specifically for the loss of the dative–accusative distinction that was still used in Old English to differentiate between location and direction. Note, however, that the addition of the directional marker to a basic preposition is only possible for the two cases mentioned (*in*, *on*) and not for *near, under, over, across, behind, in front of*, etc. More often than not the distinction between location and direction is not overtly expressed in English, even in those cases where it could be made. The additional specification of a basically vague meaning comes from inherent semantic properties of the verb (stative or dynamic, cf. ⟨46⟩ and ⟨47⟩), but may also be indicated by other elements in the context, as for instance by the aspectual forms of the verb (cf. ⟨48⟩):

⟨46⟩   a.   The dog is under the table.
           'Der Hund ist unter dem Tisch.'
       b.   The dog ran under the table.
           'Der Hund rannte unter den Tisch.'
       c.   John put the car in(to) the garage.

⟨47⟩   a.   Where is John?
       b.   Where did he go (to)? (?Whither did he go?)

⟨48⟩   a.   John is sitting on the sofa.
           'John sitzt auf dem Sofa.'
       b.   John sat on the sofa.
           'John setzte sich auf das Sofa.'

The tendency of Modern English to neutralize the distinction between location and direction is most obvious in connection with **adverbs**, as the following examples illustrate (cf. Rohdenburg 1990):

⟨49⟩   a.   John is there, upstairs, outside, next door, everywhere.
       b.   John went there, upstairs, outside, next door, everywhere.

⟨50⟩   a.   Johann ist dort, oben, draußen, nebenan, überall.
       b.   John ging dorthin, nach oben / draußen / nebenan, überall hin.

These examples show that all of the following formal means can be used in German to express direction vs. location: (i) accusative vs. dative case (cf. ⟨51⟩), (ii) postpositions/particles (*hin* vs. Ø; cf. ⟨52⟩), and (iii) prepositional phrases (*nach* vs. Ø). Just as in English, the addition of a prepositional phrase may often contribute a motion component which is not contained in the predicate itself, especially with reflexive-causative constructions (cf. ⟨53⟩):

⟨51⟩   a.   Er raste in der Fabrikhalle (umher).
       b.   Er raste in die Fabrikhalle.

⟨52⟩   a.   Wärest du so freundlich, hier zu schwimmen?
       b.   Wärest du so freundlich, hierher zu schwimmen?

⟨53⟩   a.   Max Schmeling boxte in Amerika.
       b.   Max Schmeling boxte sich in die Herzen der Amerikaner.

7.4 The semantic versatility of grammatical relations

Examples like the following and their preferred translations into German illustrate another general contrast between English and German in the domain under discussion (cf. Rohdenburg 1974, 1990, Hawkins 1986: 53ff.):

⟨54⟩ a. This advert will sell us a lot of dog food.

b. Money can't buy everything.

c. This statement overlooks the fact that the situation has changed completely.

d. Tomorrow will be cloudy in most places.

e. Burke had been sandwiched with them and Philips, who was streaming blood, into a narrow foyer.

f. This hotel forbids dogs.

g. This loses us our best midfield player.

⟨55⟩ a. Mit dieser Werbung werden wir viel Hundefutter verkaufen.

b. Mit Geld kann man nicht alles kaufen.

c. Mit dieser Aussage übersieht der Autor, dass ...

d. Morgen wird es in den meisten Teilen stark bewölkt sein.

e. ... Philips, an dem Blut herunter strömte, ...

f. In diesem Hotel sind Hunde nicht zugelassen.

g. Damit verlieren wir unseren besten Mittelfeldspieler.

A first contrastive characterization of such sentences could simply point out that they manifest a peculiar selection of subjects. Rohdenburg (1974) speaks of 'secondary subjects', both in a historical and a systematic sense. More specifically, the remarkable nature of the subjects in ⟨54⟩ relates to the mapping of participant (thematic) roles (syntagmatic semantic relations) onto grammatical functions. Participant roles are determined by a construction and are labels for ways of participating in the process. In ⟨54a⟩–⟨54c⟩ and perhaps also in ⟨54g⟩ it is an Instrument that is selected as subject. In ⟨54d⟩ it is a temporal phrase and in ⟨54c⟩ and ⟨54f⟩ it is a Location.

In German such subjects are rare, even though they are slowly creeping into journalese as a result of sloppy translations from English and of the influence English exerts on all languages. In other words, more literal translations into German are possible in these and analogous cases, but the results have a clearly non-idiomatic flavour. A detailed comparison between these English examples and their optimal translations into German reveals that they share one important aspect of information structure: The **topic**, i.e. the entity or referent the rest of the sentence is about, is the same in both cases. What differs is the encoding of this entity as subject in the case of English and as adverbial in German. What these examples show is that English manifests a greater freedom in mapping various participant roles onto grammatical relations. German, on the other hand, exhibits a strong preference for encoding an Agent as subject, but has the option of promoting any participant role to the topic position, i.e. to the position immediately preceding the finite verb.

In the descriptive study by Rohdenburg (1974), a detailed and comprehensive survey of this general contrast in the semantic diversity of grammatical relations in English and German is presented in terms of groups of predicates established on the basis of **lexical fields** (meteorological predicates, predicates of smelling, of motion, of financial transactions, of injuring, etc.). The following examples are a small selection from these lists. In each case the German translation is meant to illustrate the general contrast pointed out above:

⟨56⟩   a. Scarborough's sunny and a bit quiet because the season hasn't properly begun.

       b. In Scarborough wird es sonnig und ziemlich ruhig sein ...

⟨57⟩   a. The remainder of the Continent should be fair to cloudy.

       b. Im übrigen Teil des europäischen Festlandes dürfte das Wetter heiter bis wolkig sein. (Der andere Teil dürfte sonniges und heiteres Wetter haben.)

⟨58⟩   a. The roof of the tunnel was seeping water.

       b. Wasser tropfte von dem Dach des Tunnels.

⟨59⟩   a. The Langdon (river) could and frequently did drown people.

       b. Im Langdon konnte man ertrinken, was übrigens häufig genug vorkam.

⟨60⟩   a. This paid the taxes and satisfied the owner.

       b. Damit wurden die Steuern bezahlt und der Eigentümer zufrieden gestellt.

⟨61⟩   a. The latest edition of the book has added a chapter.

       b. Zur letzten Ausgabe des Buches wurde ein Kapitel angefügt. (Die letzte Ausgabe des Buches enthält ein weiteres Kapitel.)

⟨62⟩   a. This lake prohibits motor boats.

       b. Auf diesem See sind Motorboote nicht zugelassen.

⟨63⟩   a. My guitar broke a string mid-song.

       b. An meiner Gitarre riss mitten im Lied eine Saite.

7.5 Summary

The following contrasts can be regarded as the most striking ones in the encoding of grammatical relations in English and German:

- Grammatical relations are encoded by case marking in German and by linear order in English.
- Objects are differentiated paradigmatically and syntagmatically in German, but only syntagmatically in English.
- In German, alternation patterns in the argument structure of three-term (trivalent) predicates are typically associated with prefixation.
- The first object in a double object construction cannot encode the Source in a transfer of possession in English, in contrast to German.
- The semantic contrast between location and direction is expressed by case marking (dative vs. accusative), by prepositions and postpositions in German, but not overtly marked in English in most cases.
- Grammatical relations (subject, object) are more diverse in their semantic interpretation in English than in German.

Revision, questions and exercises

1. Give definitions for the following grammatical relations in English and German: (i) subject, (ii) direct object and (iii) indirect object. Which criteria can be used in both languages and which ones are relevant to only one of the two languages?

2. What is the subject in the following German sentences?

    ⟨64⟩   a. Es tanzt der König mit der Magd.

           b. Es wird getanzt.

           c. Es gibt viele Fahrräder in Peking.

    Compare these sentences to their English counterparts. Which expressive devices correspond to German *es* in English?

3. What is the subject in the following sentences?

    ⟨65⟩   a. Mich friert.

           b. Mir ist langweilig.

           c. Mir wird ganz schwindclig.

    Use common tests and diagnostics for identifying subjects in your answer.

4. To what extent does the following parallelism contribute an argument to the analysis of *there* as a subject in sentences like ⟨66a⟩?

    ⟨66⟩   a. I expect there to be no major problems.

           b. I expect George to find a solution.

           c. I expect that there won't be any problems.

           d. I expect that George will find a solution.

5. Find five examples of double object constructions in a corpus of German (or in a newspaper) in which transfer of possession is expressed, and in which

the indirect object is the Source (e.g. *Ich stahl ihm ein Buch*). Translate these examples into English. What kind of structures do you use in English?

6. The following sentences are ambiguous:

⟨67⟩ a. The cat jumped on the table.
b. The boy crept under the bed.
c. Jack dived under the kayaks.

Explain the ambiguity. Does the same ambiguity arise in German? And is there a way of making the sentences unambigous in English?

7. Translate the following sentences into English:

⟨68⟩ a. An Freds Auto ging ein Kolben kaputt.
('Kolben': *piston*)
b. Plötzlich brannte in der Maschine eine Sicherung durch.
c. In der dritten Kurve platzte am Auto ein Reifen.

What general contrast between English and German do these examples illustrate?

Further reading

A comprehensive discussion of how to define subjects can be found in Keenan (1976) (cf. also Comrie 1989: Ch. 5 and Uhrig 2018). For the distinction between arguments (subjects, objects) and adjuncts and other parameters of valency, see for instance Storrer (2003), Herbst and Schüller (2008) and Hole (2015). For information on the use of German cases see the major reference grammars (Zifonun *et al.* 1997, Eisenberg 2006a, Schäfer 2016). The meaning and use of the dative has been described in much detail by Wegener (1985) and Hole (2014). Verb alternations in English are systematically discussed in Levin (1993). The relationship between semantic roles and syntactic functions (in particular subjects) has been studied in work done by Günter Rohdenburg (e.g. Rohdenburg 1974, 1990). Fischer (2013) contains a comprehensive contrastive treatment of valency structures in English and German.

8　Internal and external possessors

> A man passing by a house heard a woman's voice through an open window: "James, take off my coat. James, take off my shoes. James, take off my dress. James, take off my tights ... And don't let me catch you wearing them again!"

8.1　Introduction

Consider the German examples in ⟨1⟩ and their English translations in ⟨2⟩:

⟨1⟩　a.　Mir zittern die Knie.
　　　b.　Ich habe mir die Füße gewaschen.
　　　c.　Maria wäscht sich die Haare.
　　　d.　Du gehst mir auf die Nerven.
　　　e.　Sie gießt ihm Wasser auf den Hut.

⟨2⟩　a.　My knees are shaking.
　　　b.　I have washed my feet.
　　　c.　Mary is washing her hair.
　　　d.　You are getting on my nerves.
　　　e.　She is pouring water onto his hat.

There is a systematic contrast visible in each pair of sentences. The German examples all have one argument more than their English counterparts, and this additional argument is a dative NP. A second difference concerns the expressions denoting a body part or garment. In German, we find the definite article and in English the possessive determiner (pronoun). All sentences express situations that involve body parts or, more generally, objects possessed by a human being. If we neglect examples like ⟨1e⟩ and ⟨2e⟩ for the time being, we could also speak of '**inalienable possession**', i.e. of entities that are an integral part of the body.

Possession involves both an owner, which we will call the '**possessor**', and something owned, the '**possessum**'. On the basis of this terminological distinction we are now in a position to characterize the contrast exemplified by ⟨1⟩ and ⟨2⟩ more precisely. In the German examples in ⟨1⟩ the possessor and the possessum are not expressed by the same phrase but by two different arguments, a subject and a dative NP in ⟨1a⟩, a dative NP and an accusative NP in ⟨1b⟩ and ⟨1c⟩ and by a dative NP and a prepositional phrase in the two remaining sentences. In English, by contrast, possessor and possessum are expressed by one phrase, the possessor by the possessive determiner and the possessum by the noun. In keeping with fairly wide-spread terminological conventions, we will speak of '**external possessors**' in German examples like ⟨1⟩ and of '**internal possessors**' in cases like ⟨2⟩.

Given the valency (argument structure) of the verbs involved, the English constructions correspond more to what we expect. The verbs *wash* and *waschen* are transitive verbs, which usually combine with a subject and an object in both languages:

⟨3⟩   a.   John washed the dishes.

       b.   Karl wusch das Geschirr (ab).

What we find in German but not in English is thus a change in the argument structures of the verbs, i.e. an **increase in valency**. Examples like the following show that this operation is only possible if the possessor is human or a higher animal:

⟨4⟩   a.   Karin kämmte ihrem Kind die Haare.

       b.   Karl verband dem Hund die Pfote.

       c.   ?Karin wusch der Pflanze die Blätter ab.

       d.   ?Hans wusch dem Auto das Dach.

The terms used in the title of the chapter can now be defined as follows:

> **External possessor constructions** are constructions in which a semantic possessor-possessum relation is expressed (i) by coding the possessor as a core grammatical relation of the verb, and (ii) in a constituent separate from that which contains the possessum; (iii) despite being coded as a core argument, the possessor phrase is not licensed by the argument frame of the verb root itself. Internal possessor constructions express the possessor (pronoun) and the possessum (noun) in one noun phrase.

In the following sections the contrasts between English and German relating to inalienable possession will be discussed in more detail.

8.2   Constraints on external possessors

8.2.1 Syntactic constraints

As already mentioned, an external possessor is generally encoded by a dative object in German. The traditional term employed in grammars of German for this use of the dative is 'Pertinenzdativ' or '**dative of possession**'. Table 8.1 shows that the possessum may be expressed by any other argument depending on the verb.

			PSOR		PSUM	
(i)	Subj	V	Dat		Acc	*Er wusch ihm die Füße.*
(ii)	Subj	V	Dat		PP	*Karl trat ihm gegen das Schienbein.*
(iii)			Dat	V	Subj	*Mir schmerzen die Knie.*

Table 8.1 Syntactic function of the possessor in external possession

If our examples in ⟨2⟩ gave the impression that there are no external possessor constructions in English, we have to correct this impression here. Such constructions are marginally possible, but only if the possessum (typically a body part) is expressed by a prepositional phrase. The examples in ⟨5⟩ thus correspond to type (ii) in German (Table 8.1). Note, however, that all examples in ⟨5⟩ are possible without the prepositional phrases, which makes them very different from the German constructions of type (ii) in Table 8.1. For instance, *Ben punched Jim* and *She grabbed him* are good English sentences as well, whereas **Karl trat ihm* is incomplete.

⟨5⟩ a. Ben punched Jim on the nose.

　　 b. She grabbed him by the arm.

　　 c. He kissed her on the cheek.

　　 d. They dragged in the haggis by the tail.

The constraints relevant for German in addition to the syntactic regularities described in Table 8.1 can be stated in general semantic and/or cognitive terms and concern the following questions: (a) What are possible possessors? (b) What is a possible possessum? (c) What are possible verbs in these constructions? These questions will now be addressed one by one.

8.2.2 Constraints concerning the possessor

As briefly indicated above, possessors in the constructions under analysis must be **animate**. Higher animals are usually grouped together with humans. External possessor constructions with artefacts or plants are not ungrammatical, but attribute human-like qualities to these entities. For inanimate human bodies these constructions would only be used on the threshold between life and death:

⟨6⟩ a. Wir drückten dem Verstorbenen die Augen zu.

　　 b. Ich bin dem armen Hund auf die Pfote getreten.

　　 c. ?Ich berührte der Pflanze die Blüte.

　　 d. ?Ich trat dem Auto gegen den Kotflügel.

The constraint illustrated by the examples above is yet another manifestation of the well-known **Animacy Hierarchy**, which provides a suitable generalization for many constraints found across languages:

⟨7⟩ The Animacy Hierarchy
$1^{st}/2^{nd}$ pers. pron. > 3rd pers. pron. > proper name > other animate nouns > inanimate nouns

Many constructions are only possible with animate arguments and may even be restricted to human arguments. Moreover, the roles of speaker and hearer expressed by first and second person pronouns, respectively, are the most obvious manifestations of human existence and certain constructions like the 'ethical dative' in German (*Fass mir ja nicht den Hund an!*) are restricted to arguments in these highest positions. Applied to external possessors the hierarchy says that if a language allows such constructions for a possessor at any point in the hierarchy, it will also allow them for all possessors further to the left. The Animacy Hierarchy is one of the clearest manifestations of the anthropocentric nature of language.

8.2.3 Constraints concerning the possessum

We have already seen that the possessum in external possessor constructions must be inalienably possessed, i.e. it is typically a body part. In German all extensions of the body, e.g. clothes, covers, houses and even marginally land can also be found as possessum in these constructions. As we go down the following list of examples, the possessum becomes more and more remote from the human body. '**Personal sphere**' would be a general cover term for all these cases:

⟨8⟩ a. Ich habe mir die Haare verbrannt.

b. Karl hat mir die Brille zerbrochen.

c. Er ist mir auf den Mantel getreten.

d. Es regnete mir ins Zelt.

e. Sie haben mir das Haus über dem Kopf angezündet.

f. Der Feind war ihm ins Land eingefallen.

Of course, the English counterparts of all of these examples would have internal possessors. Note that in sentences with two different human referents and two different possessa we have multiple ambiguities in German:

⟨9⟩ a. Der Polizist steckte dem Verbrecher die Hände in die Manteltaschen.

b. The policeman put his hands into the coat-pockets of the criminal.

⟨10⟩ Maria legte Karl die Hände auf die Schultern.

In ⟨10⟩, possessors and possessa can be related in more than one way: either Maria lays Karl's hands on Karl's shoulders, or she lays her own hands on his shoulders. This ambiguity can be resolved by adding an internal possessor to the external one (cf. ⟨11⟩). In English such ambiguities do not arise because possessors are encoded internally anyway (cf. ⟨12⟩).

⟨11⟩   a.   Maria legte Karl ihre Hände auf die Schultern.

        b.   Maria legte Karl seine Hände auf die Schultern.

⟨12⟩   a.   Mary laid her hands on Carl's shoulders.

        b.   Mary laid Carl's hands on his shoulders.

8.2.4   Constraints on predicates

Examples like the following suggest that not all predicates lead to acceptable results in external possessor constructions. Verbs of perception and stative verbs seem to be deviant in this construction:

⟨13⟩   a.   *Ich betrachtete ihr das Gesicht. – Ich betrachtete ihr Gesicht.

        b.   *Ich hörte ihr die Stimme. – Ich hörte ihre Stimme.

⟨14⟩   a.   Ihm fiel ein Apfel auf den Kopf.

        b.   ?Ihm lag ein Apfel auf dem Kopf.

Verbs expressing a change of state or an action leading to some effect are best with external possessor constructions. What seems to be more important, however, is the requirement that the human possessor be **affected** (positively or negatively) in some way.

⟨15⟩   a.   Ein kalter Wind wehte mir ins Gesicht.

        b.   Ein wunderbarer Duft umwehte mir die Nase.

        c.   Zweige schlugen ihm ins Gesicht.

⟨16⟩   a.   Dir klebt Honig im Bart.

        b.   Warum starrst du mir andauernd auf die Beine?
            (?... die Handschuhe?)

The situation described in ⟨16b⟩ is much more likely to be construed as sexual harassment if the legs rather than the gloves are the target of the staring. The intuition already stated in Havers (1911) that external possessor constructions describe a situation which affects the human possessor wholly and completely seems to be highly relevant.

8.3   Meaningful choices in German: External versus internal possessors

Even though such sentences are relatively rare, internal possessor constructions are not excluded for contexts of inalienable possession and the personal sphere in German. What is more, in the semantic domain under discussion German allows a choice between these two constructions which is associated with a clear difference of meaning. Consider the counterparts of the examples in ⟨17c⟩–⟨17e⟩ with internal possessors:

⟨17⟩   a.   Ich habe meine Haare verbrannt. (cf. ⟨8a⟩)

b.   Er hat meine Brille zerbrochen. (cf. ⟨8b⟩)

c.   Er ist auf meinen Mantel getreten. (cf. ⟨8c⟩)

d.   Es regnete in mein Zelt. (cf. ⟨8d⟩)

e.   Sie haben mein Haus angezündet. (cf. ⟨8e⟩)

There is a subtle, but clear difference of meaning between minimal pairs of this type. While sentences like ⟨8b⟩ and ⟨8c⟩ above suggest that the items were worn at the time of the 'accident', ⟨17b⟩ and ⟨17c⟩ do not have such an implication. A sentence like ⟨17a⟩ gives us the impression that the hair in question was cut off or was part of a wig, whereas it is an integral part of the speaker in ⟨8a⟩. Finally, ⟨8d⟩ and ⟨8e⟩ suggest or imply that the speaker was inside the location given, whereas ⟨17d⟩ and ⟨17e⟩ do not. The difference in question is not easily captured in terms of truth conditions, but more plausibly in a preference for construing a situation in a certain way. With external possessors, i.e. with constructions in which the possessor is encoded as a separate argument, the situation is construed as **totally affecting** the person in question. This implication is lacking in the construction with internal possessors, where body parts and extensions of the body are treated as separate parts which do not concern the possessor. A further manifestation of this difference is that internal possessor constructions sound more aseptic and free of sexual connotations or personal involvement, and this is exactly what is exploited in many contexts:

⟨18⟩   a.   Der Arzt massierte den Rücken der Patientin.

b.   Der Arzt massierte der Patientin den Rücken.

⟨19⟩   a.   Der Augenarzt schaute in meine Augen.

b.   Karin blickte ihm liebevoll in die Augen.

The difference between internal possessor constructions and external possessor constructions is most striking when we turn to non-compositional (**idiomatic**) meanings. Such interpretations are invariably associated with external possessors in German, as the following examples show:

⟨20⟩ a. Ich habe ihm die Hammelbeine lang gezogen.
'I put him on the carpet.'

b. ?Ich habe seine Hammelbeine lang gezogen.

⟨21⟩ a. Diese Frau hat mir völlig den Kopf verdreht.
'This woman completely turned my head.'

b. ?Diese Frau hat völlig meinen Kopf verdreht.

⟨22⟩ a. Der Kerl hat sich meine Bücher unter den Nagel gerissen.
'He pinched my books.'

b. *Der Kerl hat meine Bücher unter seinen Nagel gerissen.

⟨23⟩ a. Mir kommt eine Idee. 'I have an idea.'

b. ?Meine Idee kommt.

⟨24⟩ a. Das liegt mir im Magen. 'This is something that worries me.'

b. ?Das liegt in meinem Magen.

⟨25⟩ a. Du musst ihm mehr auf die Finger schauen.
'You have to keep an eye on this guy.'

b. Du musst auf die Finger des Zauberers schauen.
'You have to watch the fingers of the magician.'

Not all b-examples are really ill-formed, but none of them has the idiomatic interpretations of their counterparts in a. The only interpretation they have is a literal one and that is pretty absurd in most cases.

The possibility of differentiating between literal and idiomatic interpretations in this way does not exist in English. The following examples with internal possessors can have both a literal and an idiomatic interpretation and thus provide the basis for puns:

⟨26⟩ a. They were only pulling your leg.

b. She has broken my heart.

c. She put the words right into my mouth.

d. This woman really turned my head.

e. You are getting on my nerves.

⟨27⟩ a. I was only pulling your leg, metaphorically speaking.

b. I scratch your back, you scratch mine.

Note, furthermore, that the joke at the beginning of this chapter is based on an ambiguity of internal possessor constructions in English which is lost in the (disambiguating) German translation.

8.4 Implicit possessors

The following cases could also be subsumed under the term 'external possessor construction', but the possessor is expressed by the subject, rather than by a dative object. We will therefore follow the relevant literature in using the term 'implicit possessor constructions' for such sentences in German. Note that English again uses possessive determiners where German uses a plain definite article:

⟨28⟩   a. Die Kinder hoben die Hand. – The children raised their hands.

       b. Der Minister senkte den Kopf. – The minister lowered his head.

       c. Ich kann mit den Ohren wackeln. – I can wiggle my ears.

       d. Ich öffnete die Augen. – I opened my eyes.

External possessors in the dative are excluded in those cases. Where they are possible, as in ⟨29⟩, the situation described is very unusual and clearly different from the spontaneous action described by ⟨28d⟩. A sentence like ⟨29⟩ could be used to describe a non-standard method of opening one's eyes (with one's hands, for example) after excessive consumption of alcohol.

⟨29⟩   Ich öffnete mir die Augen.

English uses internal possessor constructions for these situations, too:

⟨30⟩   a. She lowered her eyes.

       b. He gnashed his teeth.

       c. He shook his head.

       d. I ground my teeth.

       e. He licked his lips.

The examples given so far illustrate a few other subtle differences between the two languages. An instrumental phrase in German often corresponds to a direct object in English:

⟨31⟩   a. Er schnalzte mit der Zunge.

       b. He clicked his tongue.

Note furthermore that in contrast to English the subject and the (possessor of the) object do not have to exhibit number agreement in German (i.e. there is no '**dependent plural**' in the latter language):

⟨32⟩   a. The children craned their necks.

       b. Die Kinder streckten die Zunge heraus.

⟨33⟩   a. The two blondes were still swaying their hips. [PN]

       b. Die zwei Blondinen wackelten immer noch mit der Hüfte.

8.5 Summary and historical remarks

Constructions with external possessors encoded in the dative are a characteristic phenomenon of European languages, both Indo-European and non-Indo-European (for instance, they are found in Basque, Hungarian and Maltese as well). However, such constructions are not found in Indo-European languages at the periphery of Europe (English, Celtic), nor are they commonly found in Indo-European languages outside of Europe (e.g. Indic languages). Such constructions also existed in Old English, but disappeared with the loss of case inflections. Similar developments are observable in Scandinavian and in Dutch. Dutch lost its external possessors in general, but still has traces of such constructions in idiomatic expressions.

The contrasts discussed in this chapter are yet another manifestation that after similar beginnings English and German moved into different directions. With the loss of case marking, English also lost the possibility of encoding inalienable possession through external possessors, thereby losing the formal means of distinguishing two meanings still kept apart in German.

The major differences discussed above can be summarized as shown in Table 8.2:

External and internal possessors	German	English
External possessors	yes	no (except with adjunct PPs)
Internal possessors	yes	yes
Implicit possessors	yes	no

Table 8.2 External possession in English and German

Revision, questions and exercises

1. Which general difference between English and German is illustrated by the following examples:

    ⟨34⟩   a. Mir tut der Kopf weh.

            b. My head is aching.

    ⟨35⟩   a. Er schnitt sich die Fingernägel.

            b. He cut his nails.

    Why are sentences like ⟨34a⟩ and ⟨35a⟩ remarkable from a syntactic point of view? (How many arguments/objects does *schneiden* normally take?)

2. Under which conditions is it possible to have external possessors in English? Give examples!

3. Which difference, if any, would you see in the following minimal pairs in German:

⟨36⟩   a.   Er schaut mir direkt ins Zimmer.

         b.   Er schaut direkt in mein Zimmer.

⟨37⟩   a.   Wir müssen dem Pianisten auf die Finger schauen.

         b.   Wir müssen auf die Finger des Pianisten schauen.

Is there a way of making a parallel distinction in English?

4.   Whenever sentences like ⟨38a⟩ have a non-literal (idiomatic) meaning, only the external possessor seems to be possible in German:

⟨38⟩   a.   Die Polizei sitzt mir im Nacken.

         b.   *Die Polizei sitzt in meinem Nacken.

Try to find five other examples which confirm or disconfirm this hypothesis.

5.   Describe the German-English contrast illustrated by the following examples:

⟨39⟩   a.   Karl kann mit den Ohren wackeln.

         b.   Charles can wiggle his ears.

⟨40⟩   a.   Er knirschte mit den Zähnen.

         b.   He gnashed his teeth.

⟨41⟩   a.   Er schnalzte mit der Zunge.

         b.   He clicked his tongue.

Further reading

General overviews of the encoding of external and implicit possession can be found in the volume edited by Payne and Barshi (1999). A typological survey is provided by König (2001). König and Haspelmath (1997) and Haspelmath (1999) focus on the distribution of external possessor constructions in Europe. External possession in German is dealt with by Krohn (1980), Wegener (1985) and Hole (2014). A contrastive analysis of the use of articles is contained in Ebert (1982).

9   Voice: Active and passive

There is in Melbourne a man who probably knows more about poisonous snakes
than anyone else on earth. His name is Dr.
Struan Sutherland, and he has devoted his
entire life to a study of venom. "And I'm
bored with it," he said when we went along
to see him the next morning. "Can't stand
all these poisonous creatures, all these
snakes and insects and fish and things. Stupid things biting everybody. And THEN
people expecting me to tell them what
to do about it. I'll tell them what to do.
DON'T GET BITTEN IN THE FIRST PLACE.
That's the answer."

(Douglas Adams, *Here be chickens*, Ch. 2)

9.1   Basic concepts

In its widest possible use, the term **'voice'** (or **'diathesis'**) relates to the argument
structure of predicates, i.e. the relationship between thematic roles like Agent, Patient, Instrument and grammatical functions like subject and object, as well as to
the alternations found between different argument structures. One of the relevant
structures is generally taken as basic. In this sense not only alternations like the ones
in ⟨1⟩ but also those in ⟨2⟩, ⟨3⟩ and ⟨4⟩ could be subsumed under this grammatical
category:

⟨1⟩   a. John washed his shirt. (active)
       b. The shirt was washed by John. (passive)
       c. This shirt washes well. (middle voice, mediopassive)

⟨2⟩   a. John spread peanut butter on the sandwich.
       b. John spread the sandwich with peanut butter.

⟨3⟩   a. John sent a letter to Maria.
       b. John sent Maria a letter.

⟨4⟩   a. Fido bit me.
       b. Fido bites.

In the more narrow sense of the term only the first three structures are subsumed under the term voice and traditional descriptions of English and of German often distinguish between the active and passive voice. We will use the more restricted concept of voice and only discuss the active voice, the passive voice and the middle voice, especially since the major contrasts between English and German are found in this more restricted domain.

There is general agreement on the fact that the **active voice** is the basic voice in English and German. It is more frequent and uses less morphological material than the passive voice, which is expressed by an auxiliary verb (*be* or *get* in English, *werden* or *bekommen* in German) and a participial form of the verb. The argument of less morphological complexity cannot be used for the active relative to the middle voice, but it is obvious that at least the majority of verbs that may occur in structures like ⟨1c⟩ are basically transitive and thus derived from an active construction like ⟨1a⟩ (argument omission).

The active voice and the passive voice are easily identifiable in both English and German and there is thus no problem of establishing comparability in this domain. In going from an active to a passive structure three changes have to be made, as is shown by ⟨1a⟩ and ⟨1b⟩ above:

(i)   The **subject** of the active structure is **demoted** to the status of an adjunct (or oblique argument) that is introduced by *von* in German and with *by* in English. Like all adjuncts these prepositional phrases are omissible and it is precisely this omissibility of the Agent that is a desirable stylistic option in many communicative contexts (cf. ⟨5⟩).

(ii)   An **object** and sometimes also an adverbial noun phrase is **promoted** to subject status. The combined effect of (a) and (b) is thus a **valency reduction** by one argument: monotransitive verbs (*wash*) are changed into intransitive ones (*be washed*), and ditransitive ones (*give s.o. sth.*) into monotransitive ones (*be given sth.*). In German, intransitive predications may also be passivized, thus becoming subjectless (cf. below).

(iii)   An **auxiliary** verb is introduced (*be* or *get* in English; *werden* or *bekommen* in German, depending on the case of the object promoted).

⟨5⟩   a. It has been shown in this essay that ...

          b. Mention must also be made of the fact that ...

          c. John was born in York and buried in Paris.

          d. John was said/reputed to be a good teacher.

The omission of the Agent is relevant as a stylistic norm *inter alia* in scholarly texts (cf. ⟨5a⟩–⟨5b⟩), but is also frequently found in cases where the identity of the Agent is of no interest whatsoever (e.g. the undertaker in a burial, cf. ⟨5c⟩), or is not easily specifiable, as in ⟨5d⟩. Active and passive sentences differ also in their *topic*, i.e. in terms of what the sentence is about, and are thus not substitutable for each other in texts despite their basic semantic equivalence.

9.2 Passivization in English

9.2.1 Monotransitive verbs

Which active sentences have a passive counterpart in English? Which structural properties must an active sentence have in English in order to be transformable into a passive one? Note, first of all, that only sentences with two arguments, typically sentences with transitive verbs, have a passive counterpart in English:

⟨6⟩ a. Sir Norman Forster built this library.

b. This library was built by Sir Norman Forster.

Given that passivization reduces the valency of the basic verb, it follows that passives of underlying intransitive verbs are inadmissible in English, quite in contrast to German (e.g. *Hier lebt es sich gut. Heute wird gefeiert.*; cf. below). This restriction is linked to the fact that English – unlike German – does not allow subjectless sentences (*Mich friert. Mir wird übel.*). The vast majority of passive sentences in English are based on verbs taking only one (non-prepositional) complement:

⟨7⟩ a. A famous architect built this house.

b. This house was built by a famous architect.

⟨8⟩ a. John regards Bill as a friend.

b. Bill is regarded as a friend by John.

⟨9⟩ a. John painted the wall white.

b. The wall was painted white by John.

⟨10⟩ a. This spray drives away insects.

b. All insects have been driven away.

Since English does not differentiate the objects of transitive verbs, a passive construction is in principle possible for all transitive verbs, including of course the relevant phrasal verbs. There is, however, a **semantic restriction**. Passive constructions require a 'true Patient', i.e. the subjects of these constructions must have been affected (or even created) by the relevant event in some way. It is for this reason that active sentences like the following have no counterpart in the passive voice:

⟨11⟩ a. John has three sons.

b. The package contained a present. (* ... is contained by the package.)

    c. The bottle holds ten quarts.

    d. My sister lacks money.

    e. The dress becomes her.

    f. The French word *maison* means 'house'.

In some cases a passive construction is possible for only one of two uses of a verb:

⟨12⟩   a. A stranger approached me. – I was approached by a stranger.

      b. A train approached me. – *I was approached by a train.

As illustrated by all the examples discussed so far, the auxiliary verb used normally and most frequently in English is the **copula verb** *be*. In combination with other auxiliary verbs the passive auxiliary occupies the position closest to the verb:

⟨13⟩   The prisoner may have be-en be-ing interrogated all night long.
                         Perf Prog Pass

In addition to this auxiliary another one has been developing as an alternative with a subtle but clear difference in meaning, the **verb** *get*:

⟨14⟩   a. I was stung by a bee.

      b. I got stung by a bee.

⟨15⟩   a. I was arrested.

      b. I got arrested.

⟨16⟩   a. He was run over by a bus.

      b. He got run over by a bus.

Apart from a difference in register ('stylistic value') there is a clear semantic difference between such pairs: The passive with *get* implies a partial responsibility of the Patient for the action in question. This responsibility can be underlined, as in the following cases and is most obvious in passive imperatives, which are only possible with the auxiliary *get* (*Get lost!*, *Don't get bitten in the first place!*):

⟨17⟩   a. He got himself arrested.

      b. Don't get arrested.

      c. I'll try and get arrested.

      d. The students got (themselves) arrested to prove their point.

      e. He went and got himself arrested.

      f. The student got arrested to prove his point.

In addition to this difference there is also one of attitude. The *get*-passive may express a certain **emotional involvement** of the speaker or an unfavourable attitude towards the relevant action. This is quite obvious in pairs like the following where the passive with *be* expresses a neutral question about the manner of an action, whereas the *get*-passive expresses a critical comment:

⟨18⟩ a. How did that window get opened?
       (... It should have been left shut.)
    b. How was that window opened?
       (... Which tools did they use?)

Finally, *get*-passives are marginal at best with ditransitive verbs, where the *be*-passive is usually the only option:

⟨19⟩ a. John was given a book by his sister.
    b. *John got given a book by his sister.
⟨20⟩ a. Power was given him to rule the country.
    b. *Power got given him to rule the country.

9.2.2 Ditransitive verbs

As pointed out in Section 7.2.2, ditransitive verbs, i.e. verbs with three argument positions may occur in three different constructions in English, not all of which are, however, possible for each verb:

(i) a **double object construction,** where both the Recipient or Beneficiary of an action and the Patient (typically an object transferred by the action) are encoded as objects: *to serve somebody something*;

(ii) a construction where the Patient is encoded as direct object and the Recipient as prepositional phrase: *to serve something to somebody* (**prepositional object construction**);

(iii) a construction like (ii) but with a different order of arguments: The Recipient or Beneficiary is expressed as direct object and the Patient as PP: *to serve somebody with something* (**prepositional alternation**).

As a consequence of these alternations, sentences with ditransitive verbs also allow several passive constructions. In these passive sentences it is usually the object immediately following the verb in the active sentence that is promoted to the status of subject:

⟨21⟩ a. Bill offered John a cigar.
    b. John was offered a cigar (by Bill).
    c. Bill offered a cigar to John.
    d. A cigar was offered to John (by Bill).

⟨22⟩   a. John blamed Bill for the accident.

       b. Bill was blamed for the accident (by John).

       c. John blamed the accident on Bill.

       d. The accident was blamed on Bill (by John).

For sentences instantiating the double object construction as in ⟨21a⟩ there is also the possibility of promoting the direct object to subject status and leave the indirect object unaltered. This construction is felt to be somewhat dated, however, and occurs rarely in the spoken language:

⟨23⟩   And power was given him over every tribe and people and tongue and nation. [Apocalypse 13]

9.2.3 Passivization of prepositional verbs

Given that all (structural types of) transitive verbs permit passive constructions, it is totally unremarkable that we should also find passive constructions with **phrasal verbs** like *make up, carry out, take away, push around*, etc. Such verbs are just one special type of transitive verb whose two components may be separated in certain constructions, but which exhibit otherwise all the properties typical of transitive verbs:

⟨24⟩   a. We immediately carried out our plan.

       b. Our plan was immediately carried out. (...wurde ...ausgeführt.)

⟨25⟩   I don't like to be pushed around. (...herumgeschubst zu werden.)

What is remarkable from the perspective of German, however, is the possibility of passive counterparts for verbs with **prepositional objects** like *refer to, rely on, lie to, laugh at*, etc.:

⟨26⟩   a. This book has been referred to many times.

       b. I have been lied to many times.

       c. Our house was broken into.

       d. Hard drinks are best abstained from.

In general, such passive constructions are only admissible with primary, i.e. simple prepositions, but deverbal prepositions and even complex ones can also be found in such sentences:

⟨27⟩   I don't like to be sat in front of at the movies.

Like for all passive constructions in English the subject must be a real Patient in such passives, i.e. the referent of the subject must be clearly affected by the action in question.

9.2.4 Directional complements and locative adjuncts

In contrast to German and many other languages, passive constructions in English can also be derived from active sentences with directional complements and locative adjuncts such as ⟨28⟩. Note that in cases like ⟨29⟩ the prepositions have their normal locative sense and that the prepositional phrases in the corresponding active sentences are not objects or complements of the relevant verbs.

⟨28⟩ a. Many people have gone across this lake.
    b. This lake has been gone across many times in winter.
      (It is perfectly safe.)

⟨29⟩ a. This bed has been slept in.
    b. Somebody has slept in this bed.

⟨30⟩ a. This cup has been drunk out of.
    b. Somebody has drunk out of this cup.

The semantic condition mentioned above is also relevant here. The referent of a passive subject must somehow be **affected** in some significant way by the action. The bed is not properly made up in ⟨29a⟩ and the cup is dirty in a situation described by ⟨30a⟩.

The passive constructions described above show that in English passive formation is not restricted to predicates with direct objects. Prepositional objects and even the noun phrases of locative complements and adjuncts can be promoted to subjects in passive constructions as long as the semantic condition on the meaning of the resultant constructions is met. Another striking contrast to German that follows from the first one is the fact that prepositions are separated from the NPs they occur with in the relevant active sentences, i.e. they are stranded behind the verb. **'Preposition stranding'** has established itself as a term for this phenomenon which is wide-spread in English (cf. also Section 12.2.1), but only marginally possible in German:

⟨31⟩ a. I have been lied to many times.
    b. All tastes will be catered for.
    c. I was laughed at in public.
    d. This chair must not be sat on.

9.2.5 Multi-word predicates

Preposition stranding can also be observed in passive constructions derived from the following active sentences, which are furthermore special insofar as they allow two passive forms:

⟨32⟩   a. Somebody took advantage of Bill.

      b. Advantage was taken of Bill.

      c. Bill was taken advantage of.

These options, which are also (by and large) available in connection with verbal expressions like *to keep track of, to lose sight of, to make a fool of, to take care of, to take stock of, to make fun of,* etc., are obviously a consequence of the fact that either the light verbs *take, make, keep,* etc. can be analyzed as the main predicates or a whole sequence such as *take advantage of.* In the first case, passives as in ⟨32b⟩ are formed. In the second case, the relevant verbs together with the following noun (which is never preceded by an article) can be analyzed as complex predicates selecting a prepositional object, so that passive constructions analogous to ⟨26⟩ are possible (cf. ⟨32c⟩). These two different analyses can be described as shown in ⟨33a⟩ and ⟨33b⟩.

⟨33⟩   a. [$_{NP}$ They] [$_{VP}$[$_V$ made] [$_{NP}$ fun] [$_{PP}$ of Bill]]

      b. [$_{NP}$ They] [$_{VP}$[$_V$ made fun] [$_{PP}$ of Bill]]

Finally, mention should be made of the fact that passive constructions may also be based on complex active sentences with clausal objects and structures with '**exceptional case marking**' (S-O raising; cf. Ch. 13). The passive constructions based on raising structures are not found in German because exceptional case marking is marginal in that language (cf. ⟨34e⟩–⟨34h⟩):

⟨34⟩   a. The authorities believe that the IRA planted the bomb.

      b. The authorities believe that the bomb was planted by the IRA.
         (passive in object clause)

      c. That the IRA planted the bomb was believed by the authorities.
         (passive in main clause)

      d. It was believed by the authorities that the IRA planted the bomb.
         (extraposition)

      e. The authorities believed the IRA to have planted the bomb.
         (S-O raising)

      f. The IRA was believed (by the authorities) to have planted the bomb.
         (S-S raising)

      g. The authorities believed the bomb to have been planted by the IRA.
         (passive and S-O raising)

      h. The bomb was believed (by the authorities) to have been planted by the IRA. (passive and S-S raising)

9.3 Passivization in German

9.3.1 Accusative objects and dative objects

Passive formation in German is case-dependent: only sentences with accusative objects have a regular **passive with *werden*** and a subject that corresponds to the direct object in the corresponding active sentence:

⟨35⟩   a. Die Abwehr erkannte den Agenten.
      b. Der Agent wurde erkannt.

⟨36⟩   a. Viele Dichter haben ihre Schönheit beschrieben.
      b. Ihre Schonheit ist von vielen Dichtern beschrieben worden.

The restriction mentioned above with regard to the transitivity of the verb and the affectedness of the Patient in English also applies to German. Verbs like *kennen, wissen, besitzen, haben* are hardly ever found in the passive voice. The verbs that do not occur in the passive voice are often assigned to certain semantic subgroups (cf. Eisenberg 2006b: 127): (i) verbs of possession (e.g. *haben, bekommen*), (ii) verbs of measurement (e.g. *wiegen, kosten*) and (iii) verbs of emotion (e.g. *erstaunen, verwundern*).

Passives with a subject corresponding to a dative object in the active voice may form passives with the **auxiliary *bekommen/kriegen*** (cf. ⟨37⟩; see Leirbukt 1997). These constructions belong more to informal, spoken German than to the written language, especially with *kriegen* as auxiliary. In the English counterparts of such sentences the auxiliary *have* is sometimes used (cf. ⟨38a⟩ and ⟨38b⟩).

⟨37⟩   a. Maria hat alle diese Bücher geschenkt bekommen/gekriegt.
         'Mary was given all those books.'
      b. Dann bekam ich neue Aufgaben zugewiesen.
         'Then I got some new assignments.'

⟨38⟩   a. Karl bekam gestern die Haare geschnitten.
         'Karl had his hair cut yesterday.'
      b. Dann bekam er die Pistole weggenommen.
         'Then he had his pistol taken away from him.'

As is shown by the preceding examples, the resultant passives are fine with verbs governing both an accusative and a dative object, with the dative in the role of Recipient or Beneficiary. The *bekommen*-Passiv is only marginally possible with some verbs governing only a dative object, and in some cases it is ungrammatical:

⟨39⟩   a. (*)Er bekam geholfen. (acceptable in some dialects)
      b. *Er bekam gefolgt.

In contrast to English, passives do not occur in the imperative mood in German, even though *werden* does combine with the imperative in adjectival predications (cf. ⟨40b⟩):

⟨40⟩ a. *Werde nicht überfahren! → Lass dich nicht überfahren.
'Don't get run over by a car!'

b. Werde ja nicht krank!
'Don't get ill!'

In addition to the passive auxiliaries pointed out so far (*werden* and *bekommen/kriegen*), there are at least three further elements that may be used to form passives, each of them with specific distributional restrictions and semantic properties. First, combinations of the **copula** *sein* with past participles are often regarded as instances of a passive which is used to describe states rather than processes (*Zustandspassiv* vs. *Vorgangspassiv*). This distinction is not made in English, and both types of passive predication are translated using the *be*-passive:

⟨41⟩ a. Das Fenster sollte geschlossen sein.
'The window should be closed.'

b. Das Fenster sollte geschlossen werden.
'The window should be closed'.

There is a special case of the *Zustandspassiv* which indicates the continuation of a state. It is often used when a change of state is expected or in some way under discussion. This passive is named after the auxiliary used and is therefore called '*bleiben*-Passiv':

⟨42⟩ a. Das Fenster blieb geschlossen. 'The window remained closed.'

b. Der Brief blieb ungeschrieben. 'The letter remained unwritten.'

Finally, the verb *gehören* may also function as a passive auxiliary in German. This use, which originated in legal language, is primarily found in prohibitive modal statements (*Modalpassiv*).

⟨43⟩ a. Das gehört verboten.
'This ought to be forbidden.'

b. Der Kerl gehört eingesperrt.
'This guy ought to be put into jail.'

9.3.2 Passivization of intransitive verbs

In contrast to English, intransitive verbs may also be passivized in German. These sentences lack subjects.

⟨44⟩   a. Heute wird gefeiert und getanzt.
          'There will be celebrating and dancing today.'
       b. Jetzt muss gehandelt werden.
          'What is needed now is action.'
       c. Hier wird nicht geraucht.
          'Smoking is not allowed here.'

Demoted Agent phrases with *von* are extremely rare in such '**impersonal passives**', in which the dummy pronoun *es* has to fill the Forefield position if no other constituent does. The prototypical cases of such passives contain verbs with Agent subjects and *haben* as perfect auxiliary. A special subgroup among those verbs is the group of inherently (obligatorily) reflexive verbs:

⟨45⟩   a. Jetzt wird sich wieder vertragen. 'It is now time to make up.'
       b. Hier wird sich nicht beklagt.
          'Nobody is going to complain at this place.'

So-called '**unaccusative verbs**' like *sterben, einschlafen, verschwinden, ankommen*, etc., which typically select Patient subjects and form their *Perfekt* with *sein*, are not as easily compatible with the passive voice, but by no means totally excluded:

⟨46⟩   a. In den großen Städten des Irak wird auch weiterhin gestorben.
          'People are still dying in the major cities of Iraq.'
       b. Hier wird nicht eingeschlafen. 'Don't you fall sleep here.'

Finally, **modal infinitives** can also be counted among the passive constructions in German. Depending on the adjective, this construction may either express deontic necessity, possibility or both. The English translations are regular passives:

⟨47⟩   a. Diese Aufgabe ist bis morgen zu erledigen.
          'This task is to be completed by tomorrow.'
       b. Das ist durchaus zu schaffen.
          'This can certainly be done.'

9.4 The middle voice

9.4.1 Basic properties of the middle voice

The term 'middle voice' has a clear definition in languages like Classical Greek or Sanskrit, but is difficult to characterize precisely when it is used as a general category for all languages or for languages like English and German. Most attempts at defining this term in a general fashion are based either on semantic or on syntactic criteria. Kemmer (1993: 763) defines the middle voice as a grammatical means for the expression of situation types which are neither clearly two-participant events nor one-participant events, and other attempts speak of 'actions carried out by Agents for their own benefit'. A cross-linguistic definition based on syntactic criteria uses the term 'middle voice' for those cases (not subsumed under the term 'passive') where a basically transitive predicate is used intransitively. In what follows we will use this formal definition, in the more restricted sense in which it is typically applied to English and partly also to German, namely for constructions also called 'modal passives' or 'facilitatives' in the literature and exemplified by ⟨48⟩:

⟨48⟩   a. This shirt washes well.

       b. Dieses Hemd wäscht sich gut.

⟨49⟩   a. This bread doesn't cut.

       b. Dieses Brot lässt sich nicht schneiden.

In addition to these 'modal passives', the following constructions are often also subsumed under the term 'middle voice', whose common denominator with the examples in ⟨48⟩ and ⟨49⟩ is that a basically transitive verb is used intransitively (→ **'derived intransitivity'**), and that they employ the reflexive pronoun in German but not in English:

⟨50⟩   a. Karl streckte sich. (non-translational motion)

       b. Charles stretched.

⟨51⟩   a. Karl setzte sich hin. (change of body posture)

       b. Charles sat down.

⟨52⟩   a. Die Türe öffnete sich. (anti-causatives)

       b. The door opened.

Having made this comparative statement, we can now entirely concentrate on **'modal passives'** as the only instances of derived intransitivity to be discussed here.

The basic properties of middles are non-controversial and easy to describe, but such a characterization does not tell us anything about the complexity of these constructions, their constraints and overall meaning. For the time being we will also disregard the numerous and subtle contrasts between English and German. The following properties are central:

(i)   Verbs in the middle voice take **Patients as subjects**; subjects correspond to the objects of their transitive counterparts (*John wanted to translate Shakespeare, but Shakespeare does not translate.*)

(ii)   There is an **implied generic Agent** which cannot be expressed overtly. German middles with *lassen* are an exception to this generalization (*Das Gerät lässt sich auch von Kindern gut bedienen.*)

(iii) Middle verbs involve a **modal meaning**, roughly describable in terms of 'letting' and 'hindering'; they express 'doability' or, more precisely, 'conduciveness'. Middles express the speaker's judgement that the subject referent does or does not block the type of event denoted by the predicate. The implication that the entities denoted by their subjects have specific properties which make them accessible to specific interactions with human Agents makes these constructions particularly suitable for advertising.

(iv) The tense of these constructions is typically the **simple present**. (*Referees bribe easily.*)

(v) Middle verbs often require the presence of an adverbial, a negation, an emphatic *do*, etc. (*But much of it would not translate, not the puns.*)

The following comparative analysis of middle constructions is organized around two questions:

(i) What are the constraints on the predicates found in middle constructions in the two languages?

(ii) What are the differences between the two middle constructions (the 'plain middle' and the *lassen*-middle) in German and how do they relate to their English counterparts?

9.4.2 Constraints on verbs

The constraints frequently formulated in the literature (e.g. transitivity, objects must be affected [but not effected], only with verbs denoting activities and accomplishments, only verb meanings implying inherent properties which create a primary responsibility for the activity in question) certainly provide a reasonable characterization of the core cases. All the verbs in the following examples are basically transitive, none of the relevant objects are effected objects, i.e. they do not denote things that are created by the activity in question. Furthermore, none of the verbs are stative and all of the sentences can be read as implying certain properties of the subject referents which are responsible for or facilitate the situation under discussion. These observations apply more or less to both English and German. The following examples also show, however, that the English middles have two different counterparts in German (plain *sich*, *lassen* + *sich*):

⟨53⟩ a. This book sells extremely well.
   b. Dieses Buch verkauft sich sehr gut.

⟨54⟩ a. This car drives easily.
   b. Dieses Auto fährt sich sehr gut.

⟨55⟩ a. You've got the same shoes I have. They wear like iron, don't they?
   b. Du hast dieselben Schuhe wie ich. Die tragen sich wie Eisen, nicht wahr?

⟨56⟩   a. The bed folded up against the wall.

        b. Das Bett ließ sich gegen die Wand klappen.

As is shown, however, in some studies of the middle voice in English (e.g. Heyvaert 2003: Ch. 6, Davidse and Heyvaert 2007, Hundt 2007), there are **exceptions** to all of these generalizations about constraints on predicates. Intransitive verbs are possible in middle constructions, and what is promoted to subject function in such cases is some adjunct, mostly a locative one (cf. the sporting verbs in ⟨57⟩); the subject referent is not necessarily affected by the activity (cf. ⟨58⟩); not all activity or accomplishment verbs are possible (cf. ⟨59⟩); and there are many examples which cannot possibly attribute a certain responsibility to the subject referent:

⟨57⟩   a. [...] the routes are designed to bycicle in a few hours.

        b. The new tartan track runs much faster.

        c. This artificial snow does not ski badly.

        d. The course is riding well.

        (Hundt 2007: 17)

⟨58⟩   a. She photographs extremely well.

        b. Much of it wouldn't translate, not the puns.

⟨59⟩   *That terrain explores easily. (Dixon 1991: 332)

What clearly emerges from these discussions is that no clear constraint on admissible verbs can be formulated for English, since the complete predication including adverbs, negation and other specifications also contribute to the grammaticality of an example.

What can we say about the relevant constraints in German? The most clearly visible contrast certainly is that the two German middle constructions, the **plain middle** and the *lassen*-**middle**, correspond to one middle construction in English. The *lassen*-middle is clearly less constrained than the plain middle in German and can replace the latter in most cases. The precise relationship between these two constructions will be discussed in the next section. Another contrast relates to intransitive verbs. In contrast to English, all intransitive verbs with agentive subjects and several others forming their perfect with *haben* are admissible with both types of middles. Also in contrast to English, the relevant constructions are impersonal and select the dummy subject *es*:

⟨60⟩   a. Hier lebt/wohnt/tanzt/träumt es sich sehr gut.

        b. Mit Worten lässt (es) sich trefflich streiten.

What we find here once again is a valency reduction of basic intransitive verbs, just as in impersonal passives. Since subjectless sentences are generally excluded in English, impersonal middles are not admissible either.

9.4.3 The distribution of middle constructions in German

As already mentioned, the *lassen*-middle is by far the less constrained, more productive and more frequent of the two middle constructions in German. Of the types often distinguished in the literature for English only the facility-oriented middle corresponds to the plain middle in German. In other words, plain middles in German require an adverbial specification, as is illustrated by ⟨48⟩, ⟨53⟩–⟨55⟩ and ⟨60a⟩. Whenever an evaluative adverb is missing, the *lassen*-middle is the only option:

⟨61⟩ a. The laces of this shoe won't tie.

b. Die Schnürsenkel von diesen Schuhen lassen sich nicht zubinden.

⟨62⟩ a. This paint applies evenly.

b. Diese Farbe lässt sich gleichmäßig auftragen.

⟨63⟩ a. [about a shoe chest] Stows on floor or shelf.

b. Lässt sich auf dem Boden oder im Regal abstellen.

⟨64⟩ a. This material won't wash.

b. Dieses Material lässt sich nicht waschen.

Other factors that seem to exclude the use of simple middles are the complexity of the predicate (*analysieren* vs. *lernen*) and the possibility of an active interpretation:

⟨65⟩ a. Diese Vokabeln lernen (*analysieren) sich leicht.

b. Diese Sätze lassen sich leicht analysieren.

⟨66⟩ a. Bureaucrats bribe easily.

b. Beamte lassen sich leicht bestechen. (* ... bestechen sich leicht.)

As far as their formal properties are concerned, *lassen*-middles also differ from plain middles in allowing Agent-phrases introduced by *von*, just like passives, and in allowing the omission of the expletive *es* in the Middle Field (cf. ⟨60b⟩).

9.5 Summary

English and German differ in the auxiliaries that they use for passivization, and in the type of grammatical marking that passivization (as a diathetic operation) interacts with. This contrast is obviously related to more general differences in the ways grammatical relations are encoded in English and German (cf. Chapter 7). English allows the passivization of indirect objects with the same auxiliary that is also used for direct objects (*be*), while German uses different auxiliaries for the passivization of direct and indirect objects (*werden* vs. *bekommen*; note that the *bekommen* passive is diatopically restricted). Moreover, English and German show considerable differences in the types of diathetic marking that we have subsumed under the term 'middle (voice)'. The major contrasts pointed out in this section are summarized in Table 9.1.

	English	German
PASSIVIZATION		
auxiliaries	*be, get*	*werden, bekommen*
tie up	with linear order	with case marking
subjects corresponding to ...		
direct objects	yes	yes
indirect objects	yes (only *be*)	yes (only *bekommen*)
prepositional objects	yes	no
adjuncts	yes	no
formed from intransitive verbs	no	yes
imperative	yes (with *get*)	no
MIDDLE VOICE		
Number of constructions	one	two (plain, *lassen*)
Formal marking	argument omission	*sich/sich lassen*
Dummy subjects	no	yes

Table 9.1 Major contrasts in diathesis: Passivization and the middle voice

Revision, questions and exercises

1. Which types of promoting non-subjects to subject status are there in German and English? Which of the operations are possible only in one of the two languages?
2. Try to give a concise definition of the grammatical category 'voice'/'diathesis'!
3. What are the most important differences between the *be*-passive and the *get*-passive?
4. What are the most important differences between the *werden*-passive and the *bekommen*-passive in German? What can you say about the *gehören*-passive?
5. Would you expect the following sentence to be possible? Give reasons for your answer!

   ⟨67⟩ This house has been looked at by the Duke of Edinburgh.

6. Which restrictions in German exclude passive structures like the following in English:

   ⟨68⟩ a. Last night the Kremlin was broken into.
   b. This table has been sat at by Prince Charles.

7. How can we explain the possibility of having two passive counterparts for the following active sentence in English?

⟨69⟩ a. They made a fool of me.
       b. A fool was made of me.
       c. You have been made a fool of.

8. How would you translate the following sentences into German?

⟨70⟩ a. I don't like to be sat in front of at the movies.
       b. This chair has been sat on by Prince Charles.

9. Characterize the meaning of sentences with passives derived from intransitive predicates in German. Give some examples.

10. Summarize the most important characteristics of the middle voice ('modal passives') in English and German.

11. How can certain contrasts in word formation (*employer – employee, trainer – trainee, examiner – examinee*) and contrast expressed by prepositions (*in, on* vs. *under: in control – under control, under attack / pressure / occupation / construction*) be discussed in terms of voice?

Further reading

A general treatment of the category 'voice' can be found in Fox and Hopper (1994). For voice in English see the major reference grammars (Quirk *et al.* 1985, Biber *et al.* 1999, Huddleston and Pullum 2002) and Svartvik (1966), Herbst and Schüller (2008). Cross-linguistic studies of the passive can be found in Siewierska (1984), Shibatani (1985) and Abraham and Leisiö (2006). More specific investigations of the English passive include the following: Bolinger (1977) and Couper-Kuhlen (1979) (prepositional passive), Davison (1980) (on 'peculiar passives') and Hundt (2001) (on the *get*-passive). Preposition stranding is discussed in great detail in Takami (1992). The German passive is described in the major reference grammars (e.g. Zifonun *et al.* 1997, Eisenberg 2006b, Schäfer 2016). For a more detailed treatment of the *bekommen*-passive see Leirbukt (1997). A comprehensive analysis of the middle voice from a cross-linguistic perspective can be found in Kemmer (1993). The middle voice in English is dealt with in Fellbaum (1989), Dixon (1991), Fagan (1992), Davidse and Heyvaert (2007) and Hundt (2007). For the middle voice in German see Kunze (1996), Steinbach (2002) and Kaufmann (2004). Fischer (2013) contains a comprehensive contrastive treatment of valency structures in English and German (cf. also Fischer 1997, 1999).

10   Reflexivity and intensification

> Je m'aime beaucoup et réciproquement.
> (P. Geluck, *Le Chat*)

10.1   Introduction

The term 'reflexive' can be applied to structures or constructions ('reflexive constructions'), to verbs ('reflexive verbs') or to pronouns ('reflexive pronouns'). If we want to establish comparability in the domain of reflexivity, we cannot simply take reflexive pronouns as defined in major handbooks of English grammar as our starting point and basis of comparison. More often than not the term 'reflexive pronoun' is simply applied to all uses of **self-forms** in English (*myself, yourself, himself,* etc.), regardless of whether or not they meet criteria relevant to a cross-linguistic definition of reflexivity. As will be shown below, there are at least two different uses of *self*-forms in English, which need to be distinguished by categorical labels and which have no parallel in German. Nor can we take the German reflexive pronoun *sich* and its different uses as the sole starting point, because again, we will find differentiations in the use of this expression that have no parallel in English. What we need to take as a basis are formal and semantic criteria applicable to both languages that will at least identify a **prototype of reflexivity** or reflexive markers. Let us take the following two sentences, which are clear cases of reflexive structures, as a starting point:

⟨1⟩   a.   John is looking at himself in the mirror.
       b.   Johann betrachtet sich im Spiegel.

Generalizing from these examples, we can say first of all that reflexivity is typically found in connection with verbs taking two or more arguments (monotransitive or ditransitive verbs). A predicate will be called 'reflexive' whenever two of its arguments ('co-arguments') refer to the same person (i.e. when there is **'co-reference'**). The expressions indicating this co-reference are traditionally called 'reflexive pronouns'. In ⟨2b⟩ the insertion of a *self*-form into the position of the direct object results in such a reflexive structure.

⟨2⟩   a.   The royal scandal has distracted media attention from the economic crisis. [PONS, s.v. *distract*]
       b.   He was distracting *himself* with his job, distracting himself from having to talk to her. [WSM 433]

Reflexive pronouns (or 'reflexive markers', 'anaphors')[1] can thus roughly be defined for English and German as follows:

D1 Reflexive pronouns are expressions indicating that an argument of a predicate is co-referent with another argument of the same predicate (a co-argument), typically with the subject. This co-argument is called the '**antecedent**' of the reflexive pronoun.

The structure of this chapter is as follows: It will first be shown that there are two uses of *self*-forms in English, only one of which can be subsumed under the label 'reflexive pronoun' (Section 10.2). The other use – that of 'intensifiers' – will be discussed in Section 10.3. In Section 10.4 an analogous distinction will be drawn for German, whose reflexive marker *sich* also has two uses, that of a reflexive pronoun and that of a middle marker. Our comparison in Section 10.5 will only be concerned with those contexts and uses where Engl. *self*-forms and Germ. *sich* overlap in their distribution and meaning. Section 10.6 contains some remarks on the historical development of reflexive markers in English, and Section 10.7 summarizes the results.

10.2 The use of *self*-forms in English

Armed with criterion D1 we should now be in a position to distinguish the reflexive use of *self*-forms in English from other uses and to establish a clear basis for comparing reflexives in English and in German. Unfortunately, such a procedure is not in line with the traditions of grammar writing in the two languages. Even in relatively recent reference grammars of English (Quirk *et al.* 1985: 355–61, Biber *et al.* 1999: 342, Huddleston and Pullum 2002: 1483ff.) reflexive pronouns are simply characterized in terms of their morphological make-up: "reflexive pronouns are inflectional forms of the personal pronouns, formed morphologically by the compounding of *self* with another form" (Huddleston and Pullum 2002: 1483). In Standard English there are two series of such *self*-forms: (a) one based on the object (originally the dative) forms of the personal pronouns (*himself, herself, itself, themselves*) and (b) one based on the possessive (genitive) forms (*myself, yourself, ourselves, yourselves*). Furthermore, there is the plain, generic form *oneself* and a hybrid form *themself* used in potentially sexist contexts. According to this definition all of the following examples would contain reflexive pronouns:

⟨3⟩ a. John was clearly protecting himself.

b. She poured herself another cup of tea.

---

[1] The term 'anaphor' is used in generative studies of reflexivity with a more or less precise definition, but we will continue to use the traditional term 'reflexive pronoun'.

⟨4⟩ a. It was the work of the rabbi's wardens, not of the rabbi himself.
   b. "All things must change," he said. "Sin itself must change."
   c. Miss Marple herself had wanted the case.

Even though the *self*-forms in the two sets of examples are completely parallel in their form – they inflect for number, person and in the third person also for gender in agreement with some other noun phrase in the sentence – a closer look at their distribution and meaning shows that there are some fundamental differences between the forms in ⟨3⟩ and those in the set of examples under ⟨4⟩:

(i)   The *self*-forms in ⟨3⟩ occur in **argument positions** (as objects) of transitive verbs, whereas those in ⟨4⟩ are adjuncts to some noun phrase. It follows from these distributional facts that the *self*-forms in ⟨4⟩ can be omitted without making the sentences ungrammatical, whereas those in ⟨3⟩ cannot be left out, since they fill a valency (argument) position.[2]

(ii) There is also a clear difference in meaning: The *self*-forms in ⟨3⟩ indicate that two participants in the relevant situations (Agent and Patient in ⟨3a⟩ and Agent and Recipient in ⟨3b⟩) have the same referent, i.e. they denote the same person. Such **co-reference** of *self*-forms with an antecedent, typically the subject of the same clause, is usually represented by assigning the same referential index to antecedent and reflexive (*Fred_i fancies himself_i*). The *self*-forms in ⟨4⟩, by contrast, do not express such co-reference.

(iii) In contrast to their counterparts in ⟨3⟩, the *self*-forms in ⟨4⟩ are always phonologically prominent, i.e. they are focused and therefore **stressed**. The semantic effect of such focusing is invariably the evoking of alternatives. In other words, what the *self*-forms in examples such as ⟨4⟩ do is bring alternatives to the value denoted by the preceding noun phrase into the discussion. In the examples given, these alternatives are in fact mentioned in the context, e.g. *the rabbi's wardens* as opposed to *the rabbi* in ⟨4a⟩.

(iv) Finally, we should note that the *self*-forms in ⟨3⟩ and those in ⟨4⟩ have different **translations** in German and in many other European languages: *sich* vs. *selbst* in German, *si/sé* vs. *stesso* in Italian, *sebja* vs. *sam* in Russian, to mention just a few examples.

The grammar handbooks mentioned above as well as numerous studies on reflexivity in English are of course aware of such differences and therefore distinguish a 'basic' use of reflexive pronouns from an 'emphatic' use ('emphatic reflexives'). The statement that reflexive pronouns may have a 'non-reflexive' or 'emphatic' use

---

[2] Note that this difference is completely parallel to the one found between two uses of *ing*-forms, as illustrated by the following two examples: (i) *I enjoyed reading your book*, and (ii) *Reading your book, I noticed that I had made a mistake*. The *ing*-form in (i) is not omissible, filling as it does a valency position, whereas the omission of the *ing*-form in (ii) does not render the sentence ill-formed. It is therefore only natural that two different terms (gerund vs. free adjuncts/adverbial participle) should be used for the relevant constructions (cf. Chapters 4 and 13).

seems to us an extremely unfortunate choice of terminology, especially since the basic reflexives of type ⟨3⟩ can also be focused and thus be used emphatically:

⟨5⟩   Instead of denouncing his opponents, he has clearly denounced HIMSELF.

We will therefore use the term INTENSIFIER for the *self*-forms in ⟨4⟩, keeping the term REFLEXIVE PRONOUN for the relevant forms in ⟨3⟩ (cf. Table 10.1). As a first result of our comparison we can therefore note that in English reflexive pronouns are identical in their form, though not in their distribution, to intensifiers. There is no such formal identity in German where intensifiers (*selbst*, *selber*) are invariant particles.

	REFLEXIVE PRONOUN	INTENSIFIER
English	*John hates himself.*	*I talked to the boss himself.*
German	*Johan hasst sich.*	*Ich sprach mit dem Chef selbst.*

Table 10.1 Reflexive pronouns vs. intensifiers

At this point it should also be mentioned that in describing the semantic effect of reflexive pronouns as expressing co-reference we are simplifying a much more complicated story. Such a description might be roughly adequate for examples like ⟨3a⟩ above, but it clearly is not for sentences like the following:

⟨6⟩   a.   Every professor admires himself.
      b.   Who wants to introduce himself?

These sentences are clearly different in meaning from the following ones:

⟨7⟩   a.   Every professor admires every professor.
      b.   Who wants to introduce who?

As is well known from elementary predicate logic, ⟨6a⟩ can roughly be analyzed as follows:

⟨8⟩   for all x, if x is a professor, then x admires x

In other words, the reflexive in ⟨6a⟩ stands for a variable that occurs twice in a sentence and is bound by an operator preceding it. If we want to test the truth of a sentence like ⟨6a⟩ or a proposition like ⟨8⟩, we have to substitute the same value for each occurrence of the variable x.

A general analysis of reflexivity must therefore be based on such complicated cases like ⟨6⟩, which are also applicable to simple structures like ⟨3a⟩. Having pointed this out we will continue to use the term 'co-reference' for easier comprehension.

10.3 The use and meaning of intensifiers

10.3.1 The adnominal use of intensifiers

Having thus narrowed down the subclass of reflexive pronouns among the more comprehensive class of *self*-forms, we are now in a position to take a closer look at the subclass of *self*-forms excluded above from the class of reflexive pronouns by various tests and criteria. The following examples provide additional exemplification of the use of *self*-forms as intensifiers:

⟨9⟩ a. Writers themselves, rather than their works, should be vetted for their sense of social responsibility.

b. Since cleansing river breezes never found their way through the walls, a patina of stone dust covered everything. Even the artist himself wore fine grey powder like a second skin. [WSM 9]

c. The paperwork, phone calls and political manoeuvring could take as much time as the investigation itself. [PFA 68]

d. You are kindness itself.

Exactly like the examples given in ⟨3⟩ and ⟨4⟩, the sentences in ⟨9⟩ show that there is no formal difference whatsoever between reflexive pronouns and intensifiers in English. Members of the two categories have the same formal make-up and both agree with a noun phrase in the same clause. It is this formal identity which has led many grammarians to assigning them to the same category, viz. that of reflexive pronouns, which are then analyzed as having two different uses, a basic reflexive use and an emphatic use. Where reflexive pronouns and intensifiers differ is their distribution, their prosodic properties and their meaning. In all of the examples listed under ⟨9⟩ the intensifiers immediately follow the noun phrase with which they agree,[3] i.e. they occur in an adjunct position. This means that they can be omitted without making the sentence ungrammatical, although their omission would of course slightly change the meaning of the sentence.

What do intensifiers mean? We will only summarize the most basic insights of these analyses and refer the interested reader to relevant literature (König 1991, Siemund 2000, Eckardt 2001, Hole 2002, Gast 2006b, König and Gast 2006). Note first of all that intensifiers are invariably focused, i.e. they always carry a **sentential stress**. Such focusing and stressing is generally associated with the semantic effect of establishing a contrast, i.e. of bringing **alternatives** to a given value into the discussion. The alternatives evoked by intensifiers are always of a specific type: namely, they can be identified relative to the referent of the NP in question. To illustrate this with example ⟨9a⟩, the alternatives to the value of the expression

---

[3]   This use of intensifiers is therefore generally called the 'adnominal use', in contrast to two other uses to be discussed later.

preceding the intensifier (*writers*) must be identifiable in terms of writers. And such a value is actually given in the context, namely *the work of writers*. In fact, we have chosen most of our examples in such a way that the alternatives evoked by the intensifiers are given in the context and are thus easily identifiable. In ⟨9b⟩ *the artist* is opposed to *the dust produced by his activity as sculptor*, and in ⟨9c⟩ an investigation is contrasted with the paperwork and phone calls it gives rise to.

Note that whenever we identify A in terms of its relationship to B (e.g. *Bill's wife* instead of *Mary* or *Mary's husband* instead of *Bill*), we attribute a certain importance or even '**centrality**' to B. Accordingly, the alternatives to a given value evoked by an intensifier often assume the character of a 'periphery' relative to a 'centre' (= the value given). Such a stereotypical situation can be found in ⟨4a⟩, where *the rabbi's wardens* are opposed to *the rabbi* (the 'central' referent) and in ⟨4b⟩, where *sin* is opposed to what it gives rise to. Similarly in ⟨9d⟩, the essence of kindness, kindness in its pure form, is opposed to one of its manifestations.

10.3.2 The adverbial uses of intensifiers

The view presented so far – that there is only one, i.e. adnominal, use of intensifiers with a clearly definable meaning – needs to be modified now. Most analyses of intensifiers (cf. the references given above) distinguish an adverbial (or 'non-adjacent') use in addition to the adnominal one, on the basis of both syntactic and semantic criteria. As is shown by the following examples, intensifiers are not always adjacent to the noun phrase they agree with but seem to be part of the verb phrase in these cases, occurring either on its left or its right periphery:

⟨10⟩ a. As for her little bag, might he not carry that? No, no, she said, she always carried that herself. [LH 17]

b. "Because I am an orphan," Doctor Aziz said, "I must come myself in place of my family members." [LLELC]

c. And if one started to lust after it oneself, as much as the men – and let them see that one lusted – then what weapon had one left? [LLELC]

d. "Well, I teach in a theological college." – "Ideal," said Sheldrake. "I am interested in religion myself, obliquely," he continued. [PN 75]

In all of the examples given above the intensifier is not adjacent to the noun phrase it agrees with but follows it at some distance. Moreover, in each case the intensifier follows the predicate and seems to be in the final position of the verb phrase. The term 'adverbial' (or 'adverbal') therefore seems to be the appropriate terminological choice for this use of *self*-forms. If in addition to syntactic criteria we also consider semantic ones, a further distinction seems to be required. Note that the paraphrase required for the intensifiers in ⟨10a⟩ and ⟨10b⟩ is quite different from the one required for ⟨10c⟩ and ⟨10d⟩. In the first three cases, the uses of the intensifier raises and excludes the question of delegation, help or joint action. The use of the adverbial intensifier implies that the person interested in the action is also the direct agent. Suitable paraphrases for this use are expressions like *alone* or *without assistance*. In ⟨10c⟩ and ⟨10d⟩, by contrast, expressions like *also, too* rather than *alone* provide a reasonable paraphrase for the intensifier. Accordingly, a distinction between an '**exclusive adverbial**' use and an '**inclusive adverbial**' use is often drawn in studies on intensifiers (e.g. König 1991, Siemund 2000, Gast 2006b). The following sentences do not only provide further exemplification of this distinction, but also reveal certain characteristic properties of the two uses of adverbial intensifiers. There is a clear tendency for the exclusive use to show up in connection with event predicates, whereas the inclusive use is typically found in connection with states:

⟨11⟩ Exclusive adverbial intensifiers
  a. John always repairs his car himself.
  b. To her surprise he had answered the telephone himself.

⟨12⟩ Inclusive adverbial intensifiers
  a. If he's busy breaking the rules himself, he could hardly demand that they do otherwise. [WSM 386]
  b. I was not in a terrific shape myself and I had a hard time hauling him up the stairs.

Another clear difference is that an exclusively used adverbial intensifier can be in the scope of negation, whereas an inclusively used intensifier always takes wide scope over negation (cf. also Huddleston and Pullum 2002: 1498):

⟨13⟩ a. John certainly did not repair the car himself. (exclusive)
  b. I can't blame her for not buying the picture. I don't particularly like it myself. (inclusive)

Given this complementarity in the use of the two types of adverbial intensifiers, it is of course arguable that the two different uses are the result of one general meaning interacting with different contextual factors, rather than manifestations of two different meanings. At the current state of our knowledge there is no clear evidence for deciding this controversy in one way or another.

10.4 Reflexive use of *sich* in German

Having now clearly established the necessity of drawing a distinction between reflexive pronouns and intensifiers in English despite their formal identity and, in the process, more clearly delimited the domain of reflexivity, we can now turn to German. In examining the various uses of *sich* in German we will also note that only some of these meet the criteria specified in D1 above, even though the term 'reflexive pronoun' is used much more comprehensively in the tradition of German grammar writing, quite analogously to what we found for English. Only in the examples given in ⟨14⟩ do we find a genuine reflexive use of *sich* that indicates co-reference (*sich* could be replaced by the antecedent, e.g. *Van Gogh hat van Gogh oft gemalt*), whereas the examples in ⟨15⟩ are clearly different (cf. also Chapter 9 on middle uses of *sich*):

⟨14⟩   a.   Van Gogh hat sich oft gemalt.

        b.   Manche Politiker verkaufen sich schlecht.

        c.   Viele Menschen konnten sich in Sicherheit bringen.

        d.   Diesmal hat sich Karl gründlich blamiert.

⟨15⟩   a.   Die Studierenden helfen sich (gegenseitig).
            (reciprocity: A→B and B→A)

        b.   Die Tür öffnete sich. (anticausatives)

        c.   Dieses Buch liest sich gut. (modal passive, middle voice)

        d.   Karl streckte sich und setzte sich hin. (body motion)

        e.   Karl ärgerte sich über seine Noten. (inherent reflexivity)

It is obviously the case and very much in line with our intuition that an identity of Agents and Patients (i.e. **co-reference**) is only found in ⟨14⟩: in ⟨14a⟩ the painter and the object painted is the same person and in ⟨14c⟩ the rescuers and the people saved are identical. In both cases this fact is signalled by the reflexive pronoun *sich*. In addition to these semantic intuitions we can also use specific tests to differentiate between the uses of *sich* in ⟨14⟩ and ⟨15⟩. The following tests are only applicable to examples like ⟨14⟩:

⟨16⟩   Criteria distinguishing reflexive uses of *sich* from other uses:

        a.   Reflexive *sich* can be replaced by another noun phrase.

        b.   Reflexive *sich* can be questioned. (*Wen/wem ... ?*)

        c.   Reflexive *sich* can be coordinated. (*... sich und Hans ...*)

        d.   Reflexive *sich* can be negated. (*... nicht sich, sondern ...*)

        e.   Reflexive *sich* can be stressed. (*... mag nur* SICH.)

        f.   Reflexive *sich* can be combined with *selbst*. (*sich selbst*)

        g.   Reflexive *sich* can be shifted to the Forefield. (*Sich sah er.*)

None of these tests is applicable to the examples in ⟨15⟩, which can be grouped into certain subtypes that are also distinguishable in Romance and Slavic languages. The labels added in parentheses are frequently used for these subtypes. There is also a label sometimes used for the whole class, or at least the last four examples, viz. 'the **middle voice**' (cf. Section 9.4).

One common denominator of middle constructions is that they are not transitive. Several of them can be considered as instantiating **derived intransitivity**, since their subjects are usually used as objects in the corresponding transitive construction (*Das Buch liest sich gut/Ich lese ein Buch, Die Tür öffnet sich/Ich öffne die Tür*). Another shared feature of these constructions is that *sich* does not make any contribution to the meaning of these sentences: in ⟨15e⟩ *sich* is the only possible object of the verb and part of the lexical entry for *ärgern* (*sich ärgern*). In ⟨15b⟩–⟨15d⟩ *sich* could be analyzed as a marker of derived intransitivity. The relevant verbs normally have a second argument position, which in the intransitive use is filled by *sich*. The only case where *sich* is meaningful is ⟨15a⟩. Here it has the interpretation of a **reciprocal** marker. Whether or not the construction types can all be subsumed under a single category ('middle voice') on the basis of clear criteria will not be discussed any further at this point. Suffice it to say that we find so-called 'reflexive pronouns' in such constructions in many languages besides German. Moreover, many other derived intransitive constructions, like passives (*Hier werden Gebrauchtwagen verkauft*) or sentences with understood generic objects (*Dieser Hund beißt*) are characterized by the same markers in Slavic languages. The main result of our discussion at this point is that in German, too, the same expressions are used in two very different ways, viz. for reflexivity and for what we have called the 'middle voice'. The relationship between the middle voice and reflexive pronouns in English and German is summarized in Table 10.2.

	MIDDLE VOICE	REFLEXIVE PRONOUNS
German	*Die Tür öffnet sich.*	*Karl hasst sich.*
English	*The door opens.*	*Carl hates himself.*

Table 10.2 The middle voice and reflexive pronouns

Note furthermore that English does not use *self*-forms in any of the examples listed in ⟨15⟩. Reciprocity is expressed by *each other* or *one another* and in all other cases one would simply find an intransitive verb in English (cf. Chapter 9):

⟨17⟩ a. The students help each other.

b. The door opened.

c. This book reads well.

d. John stretched and sat down.

e. John grumbled over his bad grades.

The different uses and polysemies of *self*-forms in English and *sich* in German can now be summarized as shown in Figure 10.1. on p. 177. As this diagram illustrates, both *self*-forms and *sich* are used as reflexive pronouns, but in addition to this use they have other uses, which are totally different in the two languages. Note that the two situations found in English and German are by no means unique among the languages of the world. Many languages of Continental Europe (Romance, Slavic) are like German, whereas Finno-Ugric, Indic, Celtic and many other languages manifest exactly the same polysemy as English.

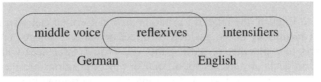

Figure 10.1 Middle voice, reflexivity and intensifiers

10.5 Some further English-German contrasts

Having identified the contexts where *self*-forms and *sich* overlap in their use and thus the domain of reflexivity in the proper sense of the word, we are now in a position to discuss the German-English contrasts in this domain.

10.5.1 Inventory of forms

The most obvious contrast concerns the formal inventory of reflexive pronouns. German only has a reflexive pronoun for the third person (*sich*). For the 1st and the 2nd person the personal pronouns are used. Moreover, *sich* is an invariant particle and does not inflect, whereas reflexive pronouns in English inflect for person (*myself, yourself, himself*), for number (*herself* vs. *themselves*) and, in the third person singular, for gender (*himself, herself, itself*). In German, personal pronouns (*mich, dich,* etc.) fill the gap of a non-existing counterpart of *sich* in the 1st or 2nd person. In most German grammars they are therefore considered as forms of the reflexive pronoun, which – strictly speaking – is not correct in spite of the formal parallelism.

⟨18⟩ a. Ich kenne mich / du kennst dich / er kennt sich / wir kennen uns / ihr kennt euch / sie kennen sich.

b. I know myself / you know yourself / he knows himself / we know ourselves / you know yourselves / they know themselves.

10.5.2 'Non-reflexive' uses of reflexive pronouns

German In the two preceding sections a use of *sich* and a use of *self*-forms were discussed which cannot be called 'reflexive' in the strict sense of the word. In German and in many other languages of the European continent the reflexive pronoun is also used as a middle marker, i.e. in anti-causative, facilitative, auto-causative and anti-passive constructions as well as in the expression of bodily motion (cf. ⟨15⟩). As has been seen, the corresponding constructions in English simply use intransitive verbs.

In contrast to English, the reflexive pronoun *sich* in German can also be used as a marker of **reciprocity** in the position of direct or indirect objects, provided the subject refers to a plurality of participants (cf. ⟨15a⟩). Sentences with plural or coordinated subjects as antecedents of *sich* in object positions are therefore generally ambiguous in German – even if one interpretation is more plausible than the other in specific contexts – but can be disambiguated with the help of the adverb *gegenseitig* (reciprocal) and the intensifier *selbst* (reflexive):

⟨19⟩ a. Die meisten Studierenden helfen sich.
       (reciprocal or reflexive)
    b. Die meisten Studierenden helfen sich selbst. (reflexive)
    c. Die meisten Studierenden helfen sich gegenseitig.
       (reciprocal)

Interestingly, *sich* does not have reciprocal readings when it occurs in a prepositional phrase (cf. ⟨20a⟩). Moreover, reciprocal readings are hardly, if at all, available when *sich* is stressed or moved to the Forefield (cf. ⟨20b⟩ and ⟨20c⟩).

⟨20⟩ a. Die Spieler vertrauten auf sich.
    b. Die Spieler beschuldigten SICH und nicht die Gegner.
    c. Sich beschuldigten sie nicht, wohl aber die Gegner.

In Modern English there is no overlap between reflexivity and reciprocity. In Early Modern English, however, *self*-forms could still be used with a reciprocal interpretation, as the following example shows:

⟨21⟩ For a toy, a thing of no regard, King Henry's peers and chief nobility Destroi'd themselves, and lost the realm of France. [Henry VI 4,1]

There is also a clear difference in the inventory of 'inherently reflexive verbs' (*reflexiva tantum*) in the two languages. In such cases the reflexive pronoun is the only possible object of a verb; it has no referent and is thus basically meaningless. There is a large number of such verbs in German (*sich beeilen, sich wundern, sich schämen, sich ereignen, sich erholen, sich weigern, sich verlassen auf*, etc.) and other Continental European languages. English, by contrast, has only a few such verbs (*to pride oneself, to absent oneself from, to avail oneself of, to perjure oneself*, etc.). This contrast is clearly connected with the fact that reflexive pronouns in English have more semantic substance and a more emphatic quality than their German counterparts, and are thus less likely to be used in purely grammatical functions. Moreover, they are much younger and thus unlikely to have undergone the relevant historical changes (cf. Geniušienė 1987: 211). The English counterparts of inherent reflexives in German are typically simple intransitive verbs (cf. ⟨22⟩), but we may also find transitive verbs with objects denoting body parts (cf. ⟨23⟩):

⟨22⟩   a. Er erholte sich / weigerte sich / beeilte sich.
        b. He recovered / refused / hurried up.
⟨23⟩   a. He blew his nose. – Er schnäuzte sich.
        b. He stood his ground. – Er behauptete sich.
        c. She cleared her throat. – Sie räusperte sich.
        d. She combed her hair. – Sie kämmte sich.
        e. Why don't you try your hand at this? –
           Warum versuchst du dich nicht mal daran?
        f. Make up your mind. – Entscheide dich!

English The most remarkable non-reflexive use of reflexive markers in English and a wide variety of other languages is the use of the relevant forms as intensifiers. In addition to the intensifiers discussed in Section 10.2, however, there is a second group of *self*-forms that is excluded from the class of reflexive pronouns by our definition (D1): '**untriggered *self*-forms**' or 'locally free *self*-forms' are among the names often given to this use of *self*-forms in English, which is exemplified in ⟨24⟩ (all examples are from the LLELC):

⟨24⟩   a. So what can a fine Tory gentleman like yourself have to do with a manufacturing Whig like Braithwaite?
        b. He told us it was asthma, and continued to arrive at Methwold's Estate once a week to sing songs which were, like himself, relics of the Methwold era.
        c. For the merest instant, some final, irreducible unit of desire, he had glimpsed a feeling, an urge within himself he had not imagined himself capable of, but now this tiny, standard piece of information, these few letters, had switched his hopes off like some cheap light-bulb.
        d. The bottom stacks were compressed but the upper layers were soft and would provide comfort for everybody soon, including myself.

The examples in ⟨24⟩ show that 'untriggered *self*-forms' share properties with both reflexive pronouns and intensifiers. Like reflexive pronouns they are found in argument positions, especially as complements of prepositions and are thus not omissible. They can, however, always be replaced by a stressed personal pronoun, and this is where the analogy ends, because such a substitution is not accompanied by a dramatic change of meaning in the case of 'untriggered reflexives'. Untriggered *self*-forms typically give us the perspective of the referent of the relevant pronoun, rather than that of an objective narrator and are therefore often called 'logophors' (lit. 'word-carriers'). Their replacement by a stressed pronoun would therefore result in a change of perspective. The replacement of a (genuine) reflexive pronoun by a simple pronoun, by contrast, completely changes the link of that expression to an antecedent and therefore its interpretation.

⟨25⟩ a. He told us it was asthma, and continued to arrive at Methwold's Estate once a week to sing songs which were, like HIM, relics of the Methwold era. (= ⟨24b⟩)

b. Fred$_i$ told Mary$_j$ that John$_k$ hates himself$_{*i/*j/k}$.

c. Fred$_i$ told Mary$_j$ that John$_k$ hates him$_{i/*j/*k}$.

In contrast to reflexive pronouns, untriggered reflexives do not find their antecedents in the same clause. In other words, these *self*-forms occupy a place in between reflexive pronouns and intensifiers in the grammar of English, since they share properties with both of these categories. In what follows we will briefly summarize those shared properties:

Properties of logophors shared with intensifiers Note first of all that untriggered reflexives typically occur in contexts in which **contrast** or **emphasis** is meant to be expressed (cf. Baker 1995: 77). This is clearly a property that they share with intensifiers, which invariably evoke alternatives to the value of the noun phrase they interact with. More often than not this evoking of alternatives is overtly indicated by the context in which untriggered *self*-forms occur (coordination, comparatives, prepositions like *including*, *apart from*, *like*, etc.). Furthermore, untriggered *self*-forms fill a gap in the distribution of intensifiers. Intensifiers combine quite freely with personal pronouns in subject positions, as one would expect:

⟨26⟩ a. He himself wanted to spring to his feet and pace the room.

b. Clive would think that he himself was responsible for the boy's death.

What is surprising, however, is the fact that such combinations are never found in other than subject positions (cf. König and Siemund 2000c: 54). In other words, combinations of object pronouns and adnominal intensifiers (like *him himself* or *her herself*) are not admissible in English. Note that this **distributional gap** cannot be the effect of a phonological constraint, since combinations like *us ourselves* are equally unattested in the major corpora of English. On the basis of such observations it is argued in Baker (1995) and König and Siemund (2000c) that untriggered reflexives are in fact fused combinations of personal pronouns and intensifiers, i.e. the personal pronoun has been incorporated into (or: omitted before) the intensifier as it were, since the latter contains a pronoun as part of its morphological make-up anyway (*him + self*). The fact that untriggered reflexives are translated by precisely such combinations of pronoun + intensifier in languages like German is an additional argument for the analysis of untriggered *self*-forms (or at least a major subclass thereof) as intensifiers with incorporated or omitted personal pronouns:

⟨27⟩ a. Jemima wasn't quite sure whether he meant Cloë or herself.
('Cloë oder sie selbst')
b. He was the kind of man whose lines of loyalty were very clear; first himself, then his family and then his friends.
('zuerst er selbst, dann seine Familie ...')

Properties shared with reflexive pronouns Unfortunately, not all instances of untriggered *self*-forms can simply be analyzed as 'fused' compounds of personal pronouns and intensifiers, reflecting synchronically the original process of combining a pronoun with the original intensifier *self*. In addition to sharing certain properties with intensifiers they also share some properties with reflexive pronouns, so that their analysis as a type of (untriggered) reflexive pronoun is understandable (cf. Zribi-Hertz 1989). The relevant properties are their exclusion from subject position (in Standard English as opposed to Irish English, cf. ⟨28a⟩) as well as their occurrence in argument position rather than adjunct position (cf. ⟨28b⟩):

⟨28⟩ a. Himself is not in his office right now. (Irish English)
b. She laughed, though even to herself the sound was high and nervous.
[PFA 165]

There is, however, also an important distinction to be drawn between the distribution of reflexive pronouns and untriggered *self*-forms. Even though the latter always occur in argument positions and are thus not omissible, these argument positions are typically not direct or indirect object positions as in the case of reflexive pronouns, but the complement positions of prepositions or the positions of conjuncts in coordinations and lists. As noted by a variety of different studies, untriggered *self*-forms in object position do occur, but are extremely rare. There are no analogous restrictions on the occurrence of personal pronouns + *selbst* in German.

10.5.3 Contextual constraints

The contrasts described in the preceding section illustrate the well-known fact that languages differ in the formal distinctions they make: distinctions made in one language may be collapsed in another. What we have also tried to show is that more often than not the relevant distinctions are by no means random and may have parallels in many other languages. Another, highly simplified, way of looking at the contrasts described above is to regard the relevant phenomena (untriggered *self*-forms) as unexpected uses of expressions also used as reflexive markers. Looking at the contrasts from this perspective, we also have to note that the relevant use types are closely related, so that the conflation (in one language) of distinctions made in the other is highly motivated and no accident. The feature that unites the contrasts to be discussed now is the fact that we find **gaps in the distribution of reflexive markers**, i.e. we do not find reflexive markers in contexts where we would expect them. Note that all of the following gaps are found in the distribution of reflexive markers (*self*-forms) in English, rather than in German.

The first of these gaps can be described in terms of predicates that manifest the relevant constraint in English. A brief look into the grammar of different languages shows that **verbs of grooming** (body care) such as *wash, shave, shower, dress*, etc. may exhibit a special syntactic behaviour. In English, they do not normally take a reflexive marker (cf. ⟨29a⟩/⟨29b⟩), unless some contrast is expressed (cf. ⟨29c⟩):

⟨29⟩   a.   John washed, showered and shaved.

b.   Mary dressed with great care.

c.   The barber always shaves himself before he shaves his customers.

Even though we can also speak of 'optional reflexives' in cases like ⟨29a⟩–⟨29b⟩, the underlying principle seems to be rooted in world knowledge. Situations of grooming are the prototypical cases of '**self-directed situations**'. The fact that Agent and Patient refer to the same person in such situations is stereotypically assumed, so that overt encoding of that fact is not necessary (cf. Kemmer 1993, König and Vezzosi 2004).[4] In German, *sich* is used in such contexts, but we would not expect to find a reinforcement of the reflexive by an intensifier in such cases (*Karl duschte sich [?selbst]*) for exactly the same reason.

The following structures totally exclude the use of a reflexive marker in English:

⟨30⟩   a.   John did not have any money on him (*himself).

b.   He likes having children around him (*himself).

c.   Mary has a whole week of travelling before her (*herself).

d.   Mary put all her problems behind her (*herself).

Note that the personal pronouns found in such sentences relate to an antecedent within the same clause, i.e. they express co-reference with the subject and thus manifest the behaviour of reflexive pronouns. A plausible explanation for the use of pronouns in these contexts is again a semantic one and thus quite similar to the one given for ⟨29⟩: co-reference between subjects and pronouns is the only semantic option here. The pronouns in ⟨30⟩ cannot be replaced by or coordinated with other noun phrases, nor can they be stressed. In other words, Mary cannot leave her problems behind somebody else and John cannot have any money on Bill (disregarding the idiomatic interpretation related to betting). In German, the reflexive marker *sich* is the only option in contexts like ⟨30⟩:

---

4   Note that in English the correlation is not a perfect one: the verb *soap* and the verb *groom* itself do require a *self*-form for the reflexive interpretation.

⟨31⟩   a. Johann hatte kein Geld bei sich/*ihm.
        b. Er hat gerne Kinder um sich/*ihn.
        c. Maria hat eine einwöchige Reise vor sich/*ihr.
        d. Maria hat alle Probleme hinter sich/*ihr gelassen.

In contexts like ⟨32⟩ – frequently discussed in the generative literature under the label '**snake sentences**' (because they are often exemplified using examples like ⟨32a⟩) – English allows the choice between simple pronouns and *self*-forms. There is a subtle but clear difference between these two options: the *self*-form indicates that the situation is looked at from the perspective of the subject referent, whereas the simple pronoun gives us the perspective of the narrator.

⟨32⟩   a. John saw a snake near him/himself.
        b. Mary pushed the brandy away from her/herself.
        c. Liz wrapped the rug around her/herself.
        d. Bill pulled the blanket over him/himself.

Examples like the following suggest that we also have a choice in German.

⟨33⟩   a. Plötzlich sah er eine Schlange neben sich/ihm.
        b. Schnell zog er die Decke über sich/ihn.

The question of what exactly the semantic contrast between reflexives and personal pronouns in examples like ⟨32⟩ is and whether the contrast is parallel for the two languages is a controversial issue that will not be pursued any further.

10.6 On the historical development of reflexives

As illustrated above, the reflexive pronoun *sich* can be combined with intensifiers for emphasis in German but not in English. This is generally possible in languages where reflexive pronouns and intensifiers differ formally. The following examples from German are cases in point:

⟨34⟩   a. Karl hat sich selbst angezeigt.
           Charles reported himSELF to the police.
        b. Wir müssen uns zunächst um uns selbst kümmern.
           First of all we have to look after ourSELVES.

Given the formal identity of the two relevant expressions, such combinations are not possible in English (*He killed himself himself*). The pattern used in English for precisely this meaning is a single *self*-form with strong stress:

⟨35⟩ a. I did not kill them, they killed themSELVES.
    b. This silver polishes itSELF.
    c. Your argument answers itSELF.

This contrast also affords a glimpse into the historical development of reflexive pronouns (and intensifiers) in English. After the loss of the counterpart of German *sich* in Old English, reflexive markers were 're-created' by combining object or possessive forms of personal pronouns with the intensifier *self-* (*him* + *self* > *himself*). The first contexts to be affected by this process were sentences with verbs denoting stereotypically '**other-directed situations**' or actions such as *give, help, kill, poison*, etc., i.e. verbs where the referential identity between subject and an object was highly remarkable. Even though the resultant forms lost some of the emphatic quality associated with the intensifier, a trace of that quality was preserved in all further uses and can be assumed to be responsible for some of the peculiar constraints of reflexives observable in English. That combinations of pronouns and intensifiers can force a reflexive reading not easily available otherwise can also be demonstrated with some structures in German. As already noted, *sich* is an invariant particle and does not inflect for case or any other category. This reflexive marker may be used in positions where an accusative or a dative object is required, but it is barred from positions where the relevant verbs govern the genitive. Since a personal pronoun clearly invites a non-reflexive interpretation in those cases, the addition of an intensifier is required to signal co-reference:

⟨36⟩ a. Eine Stadt vergewisserte sich ihrer. –
    Eine Stadt vergewisserte sich ihrer selbst.
    b. Karl gedachte seiner. – Karl gedachte seiner selbst.

This is as good a place as any to say something about the relationship between reflexive pronouns and intensifiers. So far we have insisted on drawing a distinction between these two types of *self*-forms in English on distributional, prosodic and semantic grounds. This, however, does not mean that the formal identity between members of these two classes in English is completely fortuitous and that the meanings of the two types of expressions are totally unrelated. As already mentioned, English does not at all represent a minority pattern in using exactly the same expressions both as reflexive pronouns and as intensifiers. The following facts also reveal a close semantic relatedness:

• The (original) intensifier *self* is used in **de-verbal compounds** denoting the nominal counterpart of a reflexive verb (*self-contemplation, self-disgust, self-help, self-control*, etc.). As a result of a well-known process called 'back-formation' we may also find compound verbs of this type (*This rocket self-destructs*).

• Reflexive markers are **identical** to intensifiers in a wide variety of languages and often develop from intensifiers. In English the dative forms of the personal pronouns and the possessive pronouns were combined with the originally simple intensifier *self* (*him* + *self* > *himself*) to renew a category which had disappeared before the time of our earliest written records (cf. van Gelderen 2000, König and Siemund 2000a, Keenan 2002).

- Even in languages which distinguish strictly between reflexive pronouns and intensifiers the latter are frequently used to **reinforce** the reflexive interpretation in contexts which suggest a disjoint interpretation otherwise. This is clearly illustrated by the examples in ⟨34⟩.

10.7 Summary

The preceding discussion has shown that the domain of reflexivity is structured very differently in the two languages under comparison. What are traditionally called 'reflexive pronouns' in English and in German overlap in their referential, reflexive use but have both another use that has no parallel in the other language. The other, more subtle contrasts discussed above are linked to this fundamental bifurcation. It was also shown that the contrasts identified between the two languages are by no means random: English and German exemplify two fundamentally different ways of organizing the domain of reflexivity. There are many languages that are more or less like English, and the structures of German also have many parallels inside and outside of Europe. Moreover, there are clear implicational connections between some of the contrasting properties. The explanations given for these contrasts were basically historical ones. After the loss of the old West Germanic system of reflexive-marking in Old English this system was recreated and reorganized in English with the help of intensifiers. The resultant *self*-forms were originally emphatic expressions for asserting co-reference in unexpected contexts and have preserved some of that quality to this day. Since this system had not become firmly established until Early Modern English, it should not come as a surprise that the relatively young reflexive pronouns have not been grammaticalized to the same extent as the reflexive pronoun in German or Romance languages. German *sich*, by contrast, has developed into a purely grammatical element with no semantic substance in some contexts of use.

Revision, questions and exercises

1. Given that intensifiers and reflexive pronouns cannot be distinguished in English on formal grounds, how is it possible to draw that distinction at all for such languages?

2. The possible (and impossible) translations of the following German dialogue into English show that intensifiers do not freely combine with pronouns (in contrast to nouns):

    ⟨37⟩ A: Kann ich den Chef sprechen?
         B: Sie können mit seiner Sekretärin sprechen.
         A: Nein. Ich muss mit ihm selbst sprechen.

    How could we formulate this constraint in a maximally general fashion?

3. How do the morphological properties of reflexive pronouns in English differ from their counterparts in German?

4. The following examples illustrate different uses of *sich* and *mich* in German:

    ⟨38⟩ a. Karl seifte sich ordentlich ein.
         b. Dieses Buch liest sich sehr gut.
         c. Karl beklagt sich ständig über seine Nachbarn.
         d. Nach dem Aufstehen strecke ich mich erst mal.
         e. Die Szene hat sich völlig verändert.
         f. Karl hat sich in eine schwierige Lage gebracht.
         g. Die Parteimitglieder bespitzelten sich.

    Assign these examples to one of the types differentiated in this chapter. In which cases would you also find a reflexive pronoun in English?

5. On the basis of which tests can we distinguish between inherent/obligatory reflexives and referential reflexives? Give examples!

6. How would you classify the *self*-forms in examples like the following? Would you analyze them as (i) reflexives or as (ii) intensifiers?

    ⟨39⟩ a. Fred is not himself today.
         b. According to John, the article was written by Mary and himself.
         c. Anyone but yourself would have noticed these changes.
         d. They would talk of himself, he thought fondly.

7. As has been seen, there are different uses of intensifiers in English (and German). Would you distinguish various uses in the following cases? How many would you distinguish?

    ⟨40⟩ a. Most New Yorkers want to meet Hillary Clinton herself.
         b. The evening was a disaster, although the dinner itself was quite good.
         c. I am a little short of cash myself.
         d. I certainly wrote that essay myself.
         e. You did not write the essay yourself.
         f. I have never done this myself.

8. What kind of difference between English and German is illustrated by examples like the following:

⟨41⟩   a.   John has a whole week before him.

       b.   Mary put all her problems behind her.

       c.   George pushed the brandy away from him.

       d.   He gathered all his friends around him.

       e.   Mary doesn't have any pride in her.

9.   The following examples are not acceptable in Standard English. How would you interpret them and how can we account for such usage?

     ⟨42⟩   a.   Himself is not looking too happy today.

           b.   Oh, it's David Beckham hisself.

           c.   I'm gonna get me a gun.

           d.   I'm gonna brew me a cup of tea. (vs. He is gonna brew him a cup of tea.)

           e.   Sit yourself down.

10.   What kind of difference between English and German do the following examples illustrate? You might find it helpful to translate these examples into German:

     ⟨43⟩   a.   John told Mary (a story) about herself.

           b.   Fred introduced Mary to herself.

           c.   The referee protected the enraged player from himself.

Further reading

An overview of intensifiers and reflexives in English is given by König and Gast (2002). The major reference grammars also provide comprehensive and detailed information, though most of them treat intensifiers as one type of reflexive pronoun (Quirk *et al.* 1985, Biber *et al.* 1999, Huddleston and Pullum 2002). Gast (2006b) provides an analysis of intensifiers and reflexives in Germanic languages. Studies dedicated to intensifiers exclusively include König and Siemund (1996), Siemund (1998), König and Siemund (1999) and Siemund (2000) for English and German, and König and Siemund (2000b) and König and Gast (2006) for a typological survey. Edmondson and Plank (1978), Plank (1979a) and Plank (1979b) contain interesting observations concerning adverbial intensifiers. Reflexivity has been studied extensively in the generative paradigm, for instance by Reinhart and Reuland (1993). A typological survey is offered by Faltz (1985) and Geniušienė (1987), who focuses on middle uses of reflexives. For untriggered *self*-forms see Baker (1995) and König and Siemund (2000c). The history of English reflexive pronouns is described by van Gelderen (2000), König and Siemund (2000a) and Keenan (2002).

11 Constituent order and sentence types

> The Germans have an inhuman way of cutting up their verbs.
> Now a verb has a hard time enough of it in this world when
> it's all together. It's downright inhuman to split it up. But
> that's just what those Germans do. They take part of a verb
> and put it down here, like a stake, and they take the other
> part of it and put it away over yonder like another stake, and
> between these two limits they just shovel in German.
>
> Mark Twain's Speeches, *Disappearance of Literature*

Together with morphology and intonation, word order belongs to the grammatical system of expressive devices. Learning a language also means acquiring some knowledge about permissible and non-permissible sequences of words. The term 'word order' is often used in two slightly different, though related senses. It may indeed relate to the order or **sequence of words** in statements like 'In English and German the definite article precedes the noun, whereas it follows the noun in Bulgarian and Rumanian'. More generally and more typically, though, it relates to the **sequence of constituents**, and is thus used in the sense of 'constituent order'. Even though we will deal with both types of phenomena, we use the term 'constituent order' in this chapter, as the main focus is on the ordering of major building blocks, rather than individual words.

As in most languages there are cases of strict ordering in both English and German, cases which admit of no or hardly any exceptions, and there are cases where several options are allowed with clear preferences for specific choices under certain contextual conditions. Given the close genetic relationship between English and German, it is surprising how differently the basic principles of constituent order have evolved in the two languages. As a general tendency, German constituent order is more conservative, in the sense of being more similar to older stages of Germanic. The basic intuition that German has a relatively free constituent order, whereas the order of elements in English is fixed, however, is only a partially correct summary of the relevant differences. Given the elaborate case system of German, it comes as no surprise that the order of arguments like subject and object is, on the whole, more flexible than in English, since case marking allows us to identify the grammatical relation of a constituent independently of its position in the sentence. However, constituent order in German is far from being random, and we will see that the German sentence is organized by a number of strict rules like the position of a topic or focus in main clauses, or the position of both finite and non-finite verbs, as well as various other, partially competing, principles determining the order of arguments and adjuncts.

The chapter starts with a discussion of the order of 'basic' elements (the verb and its arguments; Sections 11.1 and 11.2). In Section 11.3, four different types of inversion in English are compared to verb-first and verb-second structures in German. Sections 11.4 and 11.5 deal with the placement of adverbials and negation, and the structure of the noun phrase, respectively. Section 11.6 contains a brief summary.

11.1 The basic constituent order of English

11.1.1 Intransitive and monotransitive sentences

It is generally assumed that each language has a **basic constituent order**, a sequence which is typically the most frequent order, the order found in declarative sentences, the order from which all other patterns can easily be derived, etc. Moreover, it is usually the basic order of subject (S), verb (V) and object (O), i.e. the most central building blocks of a sentence, that is taken into consideration. In English, all criteria clearly point towards **SVO** as the basic constituent order. This sequence is found in nearly all types of declarative sentences, whether they are main clauses (cf. ⟨1a⟩) or subordinate clauses (cf. ⟨1b⟩). It is the order found in imperatives with overt subjects (cf. ⟨1c⟩), as well as in exclamative questions in which an idea is contemplated to be accepted or rejected, as illustrated in ⟨1d⟩.

⟨1⟩   a. John wrote a novel. (main clause)
      b. I know that John wrote a novel. (subordinate clause)
      c. You write a novel! (imperative)
      d. Him write a novel? Never! (exclamative question)

Describing SVO as the basic constituent order of English implies, of course, that the **subject** in English is *identified* on the basis of constituent order: It is the constituent which immediately precedes the verb phrase. Rather than saying that the subject occupies a given syntactic position, we can consequently also say that occupying the position preceding the verb phrase turns a constituent into the subject. Even adverbs and prepositional phrases may consequently function as subjects in connection with non-verbal predicates. It follows that the examples with non-verbal predications in ⟨2⟩ have peculiar subjects from the perspective of German, since none of the relevant elements is of category NP:[1]

⟨2⟩   a. Tomorrow will be cloudy in most places.
      b. Under the bed is a good place to hide.
      c. There will be no problems.

---

[1]   Note that a literal translation of ⟨2b⟩ into German is possible (with a change of meaning), but here, *ein Ort zum Verstecken* would qualify as the subject, not *unter dem Bett*.

Note that all initial constituents in ⟨2⟩ exhibit exactly the behaviour that we would expect from a subject. For example, *there* in the existential construction in ⟨2c⟩ may undergo **subject-auxiliary inversion** (cf. ⟨3a⟩), it may occur in **question tags** (cf. ⟨3b⟩), and it can even be found in raising constructions as illustrated in ⟨3c⟩.

⟨3⟩   a.   Will there be problems? (subject-auxiliary inversion)
       b.   There will be no problems, will there? (repetition of subject in tags)
       c.   I expect there to be no problems. (raising)

It also follows from the description given above that in nominal predication, it is the phrase preceding the copula (i.e. the subject) that determines the form of the verb (**subject-verb agreement**), cf. the following contrast between English and German:

⟨4⟩   a.   The problem is the students.
       b.   Das Problem sind die Studenten.

In English, singular agreement is possible in the existential construction even though the predicative noun is in the plural (this is obviously typical of spoken language). In German, such constructions are strictly ungrammatical:

⟨5⟩   a.   There are/there's five people in the room.
       b.   Es sind/*ist fünf Leute im Raum.

Identifying the order SVO as basic does not mean, of course, that the subject is invariably or even most frequently the first constituent in a sentence. There may be another constituent preceding the subject, typically an **adverbial**, but – except in cases of inversion (cf. Section 11.3 below) – the subject invariably precedes the verb (cf. ⟨6a⟩). This is also the case in those (somewhat marginal) structures in which the object has been preposed (cf. ⟨6b⟩). Note that this option is practically restricted to 'canonical' declarative sentences with pronominal subjects. A parallel structure occurs in exclamative sentences with a fronted wh-element (cf. ⟨6c⟩).

⟨6⟩   a.   Last Monday John completed his novel.
          (adverbial precedes subject)
       b.   John I quite like. (object precedes subject)
       c.   What a wonderful novel that man has written!
          (wh-phrase precedes subject)

In sentences like those in ⟨6⟩ the verb occupies the third position (counting constituents, not words). Except for cases like ⟨7a⟩ below, where two or more adverbials are combined to describe the (temporal, local, etc.) coordinates of a specific situation, it is extremely rare to find the verb in a position later than the third (note that *on Monday at nine* may also be regarded as a single, hierarchically organized, adverbial, since it refers to a single point in time). Adverbials that relate to the speech-act (cf. ⟨7b⟩), or an attitude of the speaker towards the proposition expressed (cf. ⟨7c⟩), are usually separated from the rest of the sentence by an intonational break, often represented by a comma in writing. The serialization of adverbials will be addressed in more detail in Section 11.4 below.

⟨7⟩　a.　On Monday at nine John finally posted the letter.
　　　b.　Frankly, tomorrow I might want to do something else entirely.
　　　c.　Hopefully, next year we will have more success.

Just like the subject, the object of a transitive verb is basically identified on the basis of its position. If there is only one post-verbal NP or PP, its grammatical relation can therefore be identified easily. If there is more than one object, however, the question arises which element performs which grammatical function. This brings us to sentences with ditransitive predicates.

11.1.2 Sentences with ditransitive predicates

In those cases where the verb takes two objects, 'Recipients' or 'Beneficiaries' (indirect objects) normally precede 'Themes' (direct objects) when both objects are encoded as simple noun phrases (cf. ⟨8⟩), and simple noun phrases typically precede prepositional objects (cf. ⟨9⟩):

⟨8⟩　a.　John always buys his son expensive presents.
　　　b.　John bought Mary a new hat.
⟨9⟩　a.　John blamed Bill for the accident.
　　　b.　John blamed the accident on Bill.

The sentences in ⟨8⟩ and ⟨9⟩ represent 'canonical' structures or 'default cases' that allow for exceptions. In particular, the order of nominal and prepositional objects may change if the NP in such a configuration is very complex (cf. ⟨10a⟩–⟨10c⟩), or if it contains an element that is contrastively stressed (cf. ⟨11⟩). Both of these factors are generally subsumed under the notion of '**weight**', and an NP that is either very long or contrastively stressed is called 'heavy'. If the NP is heavier than the PP, the two constituents may change places. This operation is called '**heavy NP-shift**'.

⟨10⟩　a.　John blamed [PP for the accident]
　　　　　[NP the man who had run the red light].
　　　b.　John sent [PP to Mary]
　　　　　[NP the longest letter that anyone had ever seen].
　　　c.　This irregularity in her features was not grotesque, but charming and gave [PP to Anastasia's face] [NP a humor she herself did not possess].
　　　　　(Biber *et al.* 1999: 929)

⟨11⟩   I sent [PP to Mary] [NP the [BLUE]F book] (not the [RED]F one).

It should be noted that heavy NP-shift is only possible if there is one nominal/non-prepositional and one prepositional object, but not if both objects are of category NP:

⟨12⟩   *John sent [NP a letter] [NP every musician in the orchestra].

The 'Weight Principle', which says that light constituents tend to precede heavy ones, also has an effect on constituent order in the double object construction if one or two of the objects are pronominal. Given that pronouns are the lightest elements with an argument status, pronominal objects tend to come first and precede both lexical NPs and PPs. If a pronoun functions as Recipient, the order of elements in the common double object construction is thus as expected (cf. ⟨13a⟩, from Genesis 34, 12). If, however, the Recipient is a fully fledged NP, while the Theme is a pronoun, the double object construction is ungrammatical (cf. ⟨13b⟩), and the Recipient has to be encoded by a prepositional phrase, thus conforming to the 'Weight Principle' (cf. ⟨13c⟩).

⟨13⟩   a.   Ask me a great amount for a dowry, and I will give whatever you ask of me, but give me the young lady as a wife.
        b.   *Give the young lady me as a husband.
        c.   Give me to the young lady as a husband.

In sentences with two **pronominal objects** the order of elements varies considerably across varieties of English. In the 'unmarked' case the Recipient is encoded in a PP (cf. ⟨14a⟩). In some varieties of (mostly north-western) British English, it may simply occur in its 'bare' form, following the direct object (cf. ⟨14b⟩; see Gast 2007). This order of elements corresponds to that of German (cf. ⟨15⟩). A third option is much less frequent, but can be found in north-eastern dialects of British English, as well as in spoken varieties of American and Australian English: the (pronominal) Recipient precedes the (pronominal) Theme (cf. ⟨14c⟩).

⟨14⟩   a.   I gave it to her.
        b.   I gave it her.
        c.   I gave her it.
⟨15⟩   Ich gab es ihr.

As has been shown, the order of objects in sentences with ditransitive predicates depends on three factors: (a) the participant role of the constituents, (b) their lexical or grammatical category, and (c) their discourse pragmatic status. The following '**default rules**' can be established (where '>' indicates linear precedence):

⟨16⟩   a.   Recipient > Theme

    b. pronoun > NP > PP

    c. light constituents > heavy constituents

        i. short constituents > long constituents

        ii. non-focal material > focal material

If all of the three conditions given in ⟨16⟩ are met, in a given sentence, the order of elements is fixed. For example, in ⟨17a⟩ the first element is a pronominal Recipient which is not in focus and therefore light, whereas the Theme is a heavy NP. The alternative order in example ⟨17b⟩ violates all three rules and is therefore ungrammatical.

⟨17⟩   a. John gave me the valuable book that was extremely difficult to find.

        b. *John gave the valuable book that was extremely difficult to find me.

If the Recipient is encoded by a PP, the sentence becomes much better but still sounds awkward. In this case one of the conditions is met (NP > PP), but two of them are violated (cf. ⟨18a⟩). If, however, the pronoun within the PP bears heavy stress, the sentence becomes fully acceptable. ⟨18b⟩ is in accordance with two of the rules stated in ⟨16⟩.

⟨18⟩   a. ?John gave [NP the valuable book that was extremely difficult to find] [PP to me].

        b. John gave [NP the valuable book that was extremely difficult to find] [PP to [ME]F] (not to MAry).

In some cases where two of the principles are in **competition** alternative structures are possible. For instance, in ⟨19a⟩ the Theme is of category NP, but it is heavier than the PP *to Mary*, which is why heavy NP-shift is possible but not required (cf. ⟨19b⟩).

⟨19⟩   a. John gave a very beautiful bouquet to Mary.

        b. John gave to Mary a very beautiful bouquet.

11.2 The basic constituent order of German

11.2.1 Main clauses and subordinate clauses

In German, the order of constituents in declarative sentences varies depending on whether the sentence is a main clause or a subordinate clause. While the order in main clauses seems at first sight parallel to that found in English (cf. ⟨20a⟩), the basic order in embedded clauses is clearly SOV (cf. ⟨20b⟩):

⟨20⟩   a.   Karl schreibt jetzt Romane.

        b.   Ich weiß, dass Karl jetzt Romane schreibt.

As is shown by the examples in ⟨21⟩, however, the order in main clauses cannot be completely analogous to that of English, either. In ⟨21a⟩, the first constituent is an adverbial while the subject follows the verb, and in ⟨21b⟩ it is the object that takes up a sentence-initial position:

⟨21⟩   a.   Jetzt schreibt Karl Romane. (AdvVSO)

        b.   Romane schreibt Karl jetzt. (OVSAdv)

There are consequently two problems to solve: (i) to correctly describe the constituent order in **main clauses**, and (ii) to identify the **basic constituent order**. On the basis of some ground-breaking work done in the 1960s there is now widespread agreement that it is the sequence in subordinate clauses that is basic. Among the arguments for this view the following observations are particularly important:

(i)   Infinitives used as **imperatives** have the order OV (*Bitte die Tür schließen!*). Similarly, the citation form of idioms consisting of verb and object exhibit different orders in English and German (*den Kopf verlieren* – *to lose your head*).

(ii)   **Exclamative utterances** of type ⟨1d⟩ above (*Him write a novel?*), which put up a thought for consideration and rejection, exhibit the order SOV in German – again, in contrast to English (*Er [und] einen Roman schreiben?*).

(iii)   Verbs with **separable prefixes** like *anbringen*, *ausschalten* and *einladen* leave their prefix behind in final position when they occur as finite verb in a main clause: *Ich will, dass Karl das Licht ausschaltet.* – *Karl schaltete das Licht aus.*

(iv)   Finally, it will be shown below that the order found in main clauses can easily be derived from that of subordinate clauses rather than the other way round.

Before we can discuss point (iv) in detail, some further remarks need to be made on constituent order in main clauses. Examples like ⟨21a⟩ and ⟨21b⟩ show that the subject does not always precede the verb in main clauses. Any constituent may do so. What is established as a clear anchoring point in German is the finite verb: It is always the second constituent in the main clause, hence the term '**verb-second language**'. Note furthermore that in main clauses with the so-called 'complex' or 'synthetic tenses' (*Perfekt, Plusquamperfekt, Futur II*) it is the auxiliary verb that occupies the second position, leaving the main verb in final position (cf. ⟨22⟩). It therefore seems appropriate to say that it is always the *finite* verb which takes the second position in main clauses. Accordingly, the term 'finite-second', rather than 'verb-second', has been argued to describe the basic constituent structure of German more accurately.

⟨22⟩   a. Karl hat das Licht ausgeschaltet.
      b. Karl ist sofort eingeschlafen.

After these introductory remarks we are now in a position to show how all patterns of German constituent order can be derived from the order found in subordinate clauses by two general 'transformations' or '**movement operations**'. We start from a subordinate clause like ⟨23⟩:

⟨23⟩   (Ich glaube,)
      dass Karl gestern seinem Sohn ein Fahrrad geschenkt hat.

In a first step, the finite verb (the auxiliary *hat*) is moved to the front, thus taking the position of the complementizer *dass*. The result is a **verb-first sentence**, e.g. an alternative question (or 'yes/no-question', cf. ⟨24⟩). Verb-first structures are also found in imperatives (cf. ⟨25⟩) and in narrative sentences (cf. ⟨26⟩):

⟨24⟩   Hat Karl gestern seinem Sohn ein Fahrrad geschenkt ____?

⟨25⟩   Gib (du) deinem Onkel auch einen Kuss ____!

⟨26⟩   Kommt Karl doch gestern zur Tür herein ____ und ...

In a second step, one more constituent may be moved to the initial position before the finite verb in order to form a declarative main clause, thus leaving a gap in the part of the 'basic sentence' that is enclosed by the finite verb and the non-finite verb (*hat ... geschenkt*). Given that it is generally a topical or focal constituent that is moved to the first position, this operation is often called '**topic fronting**' or '**focus fronting**'. In ⟨27⟩, it is the subject that is fronted:

⟨27⟩   Karl hat ____ gestern seinem Sohn ein Fahrrad geschenkt.

Topic fronting may apply not only to the subject, but to any constituent from the basic clause, thus deriving all the orderings that are possible in German:

⟨28⟩   Hat Karl gestern seinem Sohn ein Fahrrad geschenkt?
      Karl   hat ____ gestern seinem Sohn ein Fahrrad geschenkt.
      Gestern   hat Karl ____ seinem Sohn ein Fahrrad geschenkt.
      Seinem Sohn hat Karl gestern ____ ein Fahrrad geschenkt.
      Ein Fahrrad hat Karl gestern seinem Sohn ____ geschenkt.
      Geschenkt   hat Karl gestern seinem Sohn ein Fahrrad ____.

Examples like those in ⟨28⟩ also exhibit another important fact about the architecture of German sentence structure: its composition of three '**topological fields**'. The

FOREFIELD	V_{fin}	MIDDLE FIELD	$V_{non-fin}$	POSTFIELD
Seiner Frau	*hat*	*Karl gestern*	*gesagt*	*dass er sie liebt.*

Table 11.1 The topological fields of the German sentence

finite verb invariably occupies the second position (in main clauses) and exactly one constituent may be placed in the position before the verb. This position is traditionally called the '**Forefield**' (Germ. 'Vorfeld'). The non-finite verb, provided there is one, typically occurs in final position and the constituents enclosed by the two verbs – the 'sentence bracket', Germ. 'Satzklammer' – are called the '**Middle Field**'.

Specific types of complex or heavy constituents may or must be placed in a position behind the non-finite verb ('exbraciation' or 'extraposition'), which is called the '**Postfield**' (Germ. 'Nachfeld'). The Postfield usually contains complement clauses or adverbial clauses. The expected position for the complement clauses in ⟨29⟩ and ⟨30⟩ would be the one immediately preceding the non-finite verb, since this is the position of direct objects. Given that adverbials, too, generally occupy a position in the Middle Field, the structure in ⟨31a⟩ can likewise be regarded as being 'basic', even though the (derived) structure in ⟨31b⟩ is clearly preferred. The topological structure of the German sentence is illustrated in Table 11.1.

⟨29⟩   a. ? Die Regierung hat, was immer die Wähler verlangten, zugesagt.

   b. Die Regierung hat zugesagt, was immer die Wähler verlangten.

⟨30⟩   a. ? Die Regierung hat die Steuern zu senken zugesagt.

   b. Die Regierung hat zugesagt, die Steuern zu senken.

⟨31⟩   a. ? Fritz ging, nachdem er so wütend war, früher nach Hause.

   b. Fritz ging früher nach Hause, nachdem er so wütend war.

If we use the label '**topic**' (T) for the initial constituent in the main clause of German, its constituent order can loosely be described as $TV_{fin}X$ (Topic > finite Verb > X [the rest]). It is this freedom of selecting the so-called 'topic' that underlies the popular view that the constituent order of German is relatively free. Note, however, that this does not apply to the positions of (finite and non-finite) verbs, which provide the basic anchoring points of constituent order in German.

11.2.2   Constituent order within the German Middle Field

There is one aspect of constituent order in German which has not been discussed so far, namely the order of elements within the Middle Field in sentences like those in ⟨28⟩ above, or equivalently the order of nominal constituents between complementizer or conjunction and finite verb in subordinate clauses and related sentence types.

Here again the idea that constituent order in German is free is somewhat misguided. Sequential arrangements as found in the following sentences are felt to be odd by native speakers and will only rarely, if ever, be found in attested data:

⟨32⟩ a. ?Ich weiß, dass ein älterer Mann aus diesem Haus es sich gekauft hat.
  b. ?Ich weiß, dass mein Vater sein Geld ihm anvertraut hat.
⟨33⟩ a. ?Ich vermute, dass er einem Komplizen das Geld übergeben hat.
  b. ?Ich vermute, dass er Geld dem Komplizen übergeben hat.
⟨34⟩ a. ?...weil das Buch dem Mann Hans gegeben hat.
  b. ?...weil ihm es er gegeben hat.

Not all of the preceding sentences are equally bad, but when asked to repeat such sentences native speakers usually reorder them as follows:

⟨32'⟩ a. Ich weiß, dass es sich ein älterer Mann aus diesem Haus gekauft hat.
  b. Ich weiß, dass ihm mein Vater sein Geld anvertraut hat.
⟨33'⟩ a. Ich vermute, dass er das Geld einem Komplizen übergeben hat.
  b. Ich vermute, dass er dem Komplizen Geld übergeben hat.
⟨34'⟩ a. ...weil Hans dem Mann das Buch gegeben hat.
  b. ...weil er es ihm gegeben hat.

As is illustrated by the preceding examples, there are three principles of ordering constituents in the German Middle Field. (i) pronouns precede noun phrases (cf. ⟨32⟩/⟨32'⟩), (ii) definite noun phrases precede indefinite ones (cf. ⟨33⟩/⟨33'⟩), and (iii) there is also a specific ordering between case-marked noun phrases and case marked pronouns (cf. ⟨34⟩/⟨34'⟩): In the former case, the dative precedes the accusative (NOM > DAT > ACC), while in the latter case the accusative precedes the dative (NOM > ACC > DAT, e.g. *es ihm* vs. ?*ihm es*). These three dimensions can be summarized as shown in Table 11.2.

MIDDLE FIELD		
pronouns >	definite NPs >	indefinite NPs
NOM > ACC > DAT	NOM > DAT > ACC	NOM > DAT > ACC

Table 11.2 The order of elements in the German Middle Field

The descriptive generalizations made above do not cover all aspects of constituent order in the Middle Field, of course, nor do they offer any explanations for the attested patterns. One of the explanatory principles often found in the relevant literature is formulated in terms of information structure (cf. ⟨35a⟩). Other explanatory principles in terms of language processing are formulated in Hawkins (1994). Just like in English, there is a tendency for shorter elements to precede longer ones (the **'Weight Principle'**, cf. ⟨35b⟩).

⟨35⟩ a. Anything that is anchored (i.e. given) in the context (pronouns, definite noun phrases) occurs on the left periphery. In other words, thematic constituents precede rhematic ones.

b. Shorter elements tend to precede longer elements.

It should also be mentioned that the order of elements is sometimes sensitive to **scope relations**. While ⟨36a⟩ says that there is one bicycle that the father wants to give his two kids, in ⟨36b⟩ each of the children receives a bicycle of his/her own. Note that ⟨36a⟩ needs to be read with a rising (topic) accent on *ein Fahrrad* (here indicated by an *accent aigu*).

⟨36⟩ a. ... weil ich eín Fahrrad den zwei Kìndern schenken möchte.
(Das ándere möchte ich behàlten.)

b. ... weil ich den zwei Kindern ein Fàhrrad schenken möchte.

11.3 Inversion vs. verb-first and verb-second structures

English exhibits a number of structures – usually subsumed under the term 'inversion' – that are similar to either verb-first or verb-second structures regularly found in German. As will be seen in this section, there are important parallels but also striking differences between the relevant phenomena. Most instances of inversion in English are licensed only under very specific circumstances and are consequently severely restricted, whereas verb-first and verb-second structures in German are obligatory in many contexts and, therefore, very frequent. Four types of inversion can be distinguished for English: (i) inversion to encode mood distinctions, (ii) inversion after a specific type of adverbials commonly called 'negative adverbials', (iii) inversion in direct speech, and (iv) inversion in presentational constructions. Some of the structures to be dealt with in the following resemble verb-first sentences in German, while other types are similar to verb-second structures.

11.3.1 Inversion to encode mood distinctions

When inversion is used to encode mood distinctions, it is the subject and an auxiliary verb whose order is inverted ('**subject-auxiliary inversion**'), and the auxiliary surfaces in sentence-initial position. This type of inversion is typically used to form interrogative sentences, conditional clauses and exclamative sentences:

⟨37⟩ a. Had John known this? (interrogative)

b. Had I known this I would never have gone there. (conditional).

c. Isn't this wonderful! (exclamative)

In ⟨37a⟩, we find a regular '**polar interrogative**' ('yes/no-question'), which can simply be derived from its declarative counterpart by inverting the order between subject and auxiliary verb, if there is one to begin with (otherwise *do*-support applies). Note that **conditionals** are known to be closely related to questions in semantic terms, and the **exclamative** sentence in ⟨37c⟩ can likewise be interpreted as a (rhetorical) question, so the three structures are certainly not totally unrelated in terms of function. The sentences in ⟨37⟩ parallel verb-first structures in German not only insofar as the verb precedes the subject (cf. ⟨38⟩), but also insofar as no other constituent may precede it (cf. ⟨39⟩; the German sentence in ⟨39b⟩ can only be used as an echo question, since it manifests the order of a declarative clause).

⟨38⟩   a. Hat Hans das gewusst?

        b. Hätte ich das gewusst, wäre ich / ich wäre nicht dorthin gegangen.

        c. Ist das nicht wunderbar!

⟨39⟩   a. *Yesterday did John go to London?

        b. *Gestern fuhr Hans nach München?

An obvious difference between English and German is that in English only auxiliaries may 'participate' in such inversion processes, whereas the corresponding operation in German also applies to main verbs:

⟨40⟩   a. Kennst du Karls jüngsten Sohn?

        b. *Know you Carl's youngest son?

Not too long ago structures like those in ⟨40⟩ were of course still possible in English. Such sentences can often be found in Shakespeare's plays:

⟨41⟩   a. Comest thou again for ransom? [Henry V 4,7]

        b. Think you so? [King Lear 1,2]

Another important contrast between English and German concerns the type of sentence or speech-act such structures are associated with. Verb-initial sentences have a broader range of application in German than in English. For example, they have a narrative use (cf. ⟨42a⟩) and are also found in combination with specific particles like *doch* in a type of clause linkage that seems to be in between coordination and subordination (cf. ⟨42b⟩).

⟨42⟩   a. Kam da ein Mann auf mich zu und sprach mich an.

        b. Man konnte ihm nicht trauen; hatte er doch erst neulich wieder gelogen.

Wh-interrogatives in English (information questions) also show subject-auxiliary inversion if the wh-pronoun is not a subject. However, such sentences are always introduced by an interrogative pronoun (cf. ⟨43⟩), so the resulting sentences look like German verb-second sentences in which the interrogative pronoun has been moved to the Forefield (cf. ⟨44⟩).

⟨43⟩   a.   When will the restrictions be lifted?
       b.   Who did you take to the zoo?
       c.   Whose pencil did Jack give his sister?
⟨44⟩   a.   Wann hat der Bundestag die Gesetze erlassen?
       b.   Wer hat gestern diese Gesetze erlassen?
       c.   Welche Gesetze hat der Bundestag gestern erlassen?

Wh-interrogative elements are also used in **exclamative sentences** in both English and German, but without either inversion or verb-second ordering. The structures in ⟨45⟩ should consequently be regarded as resulting from simple leftward movement of the wh-words. In English the question word *what* is commonly used in such sentences, while in German the syntactically somewhat heterogenous expression *was für* is standardly used. A structure parallel to English *what* + NP is possible in casual speech if the whole exclamation is made up only of a noun phrase. In this case the reduced form of the article (*'n*) must be used. This structure is strictly ungrammatical in finite sentences (cf. ⟨45d⟩).

⟨45⟩   a.   What an idiot you are!
       b.   Was für ein Idiot du bist!
       c.   Was'n (?was ein) Idiot! (typical of western and northern varieties)
       d.   *Was'n Idioten du geheiratet hast!

Verb-first structures can also be found in exclamative sentences of both languages under comparison. In this case they are accompanied by specific particles like *ever* in English or *vielleicht* in German:

⟨46⟩   a.   Are you ever an idiot!
       b.   Bist du vielleicht ein Idiot!

As was mentioned in Section 11.2 above, **imperatives** in German are likewise characterized by verb-first order. Moreover, the imperative is marked by a special inflected form of the verb and a falling intonation contour (cf. ⟨47⟩). In English, second person subject or missing subjects and the base form of the verb are the only features characterizing imperative sentences, in addition to intonation, but the constituent order is exactly as in declarative sentences. The possibility of having an adverb before the verb is also found in imperatives (cf. ⟨48⟩).

⟨47⟩   Nimm (du) den Koffer!
⟨48⟩   a.   (You) take the high road!
       b.   Slowly shift into a lower gear!

11.3.2 Inversion after 'negative adverbials'

The second type of subject-auxiliary inversion is triggered by expressions like *never*, *rarely*, *no sooner*, *little*, *only* (*then*), *hardly*, *at no time*, etc. in sentence-initial position. There is no completely convincing cover term for these triggers, therefore we will use the traditional term 'negative adverbials'.

⟨49⟩   a.   Never have I seen such a sight.

b.   No sooner had I opened the door when the foul smell hit my nose.

c.   Only when he wanted to pay did he realize that his money was gone.

d.   Rarely does crime pay so well as it did in that case.

The task of giving a precise characterization of such structures is made even more difficult by the fact that 'negative adverbials' or 'determiners' do not always trigger inversion. In cases like the following both options (canonical constituent order and inversion) are possible, though they are associated with a difference in meaning. The difference is one of **scope**: only when the (explicit or implied) negation relates to the whole sentence ('takes scope over the whole sentence') do we find inversion:

⟨50⟩   a.   Not even a year ago could you get in without paying.

b.   Not even a year ago, you could get in without paying.

⟨51⟩   a.   Only yesterday did he drive into London.

b.   Only yesterday, he drove into London.

The constructions illustrated in the a-sentences of ⟨50⟩ and ⟨51⟩ above look like German verb-second structures. However, verb-second order is obligatory in German main clauses, quite independently of scope relations and negators, i.e. German does not differentiate between the a-sentences and the b-sentences on the basis of constituent order (cf. ⟨52a⟩). Still, we can distinguish between the two readings in German by either adding the adverb *noch* to the second part of the sentence (cf. ⟨52b⟩), or dissociating the 'negative' adverbial from the sentence and anaphorically picking it up with the pronoun *da* (cf. ⟨52c⟩). Both resulting sentences correspond to the 'narrow scope reading', i.e. to the reading in which the negation applies only to the adverbial. Another option available in German is to place the combination of particles *noch nicht einmal* within the prepositional phrase (cf. ⟨53⟩):

⟨52⟩   a.   (Noch) nicht einmal vor einem Jahr kam man herein, ohne zu bezahlen. (ambiguous in print; disambiguated by intonation)

b.   Noch nicht einmal vor einem Jahr kam man noch herein, ohne zu bezahlen. (narrow scope)

c.   Noch nicht einmal vor einem Jahr, da kam man (noch) herein, ohne zu bezahlen. (narrow scope, colloquial)

⟨53⟩   Vor (noch) nicht einmal einem Jahr kam man (noch) herein, ohne zu bezah-
        len. (narrow scope)

It should be mentioned that the same kind of inversion described for 'negative
adverbials' above also applies to NPs introduced by the negative determiner *no*.

⟨54⟩   a. No one have I ever despised in this way.
       b. No such thing have I ever been guilty of.
       c. The silver or gold or garments of no one did I covet. [Acts 20,3]
⟨55⟩   a. In no clothes, Charlie looks attractive.
       b. In no clothes does Charlie look attractive.
⟨56⟩   a. With no job, John would be happy.
       b. With no job would John be happy.

Note that there is another important contrast between inversion after negative adverbials in English and the corresponding verb-second structures in German: While
the latter are restricted to German main clauses, in English the relevant structures
are also found in subordinate clauses (cf. ⟨57a⟩ vs. ⟨57b⟩). In German, verb-second
order is possible only if the subordinate clause is not introduced by a conjunction
or complementizer (cf. ⟨57c⟩), i.e. if the sentence basically looks like a main clause
(recall from Section 11.2 that complementizers and verb-second structures are in
complementary distribution).

⟨57⟩   a. I was told that never had he done such a thing before.
       b. *Mir wurde gesagt, dass nie zuvor hatte er so etwas getan.
       c. Mir wurde gesagt, nie zuvor habe er so etwas getan.

11.3.3   Inversion in connection with direct speech

Instances of inversion in English can also be found in direct speech. If the verb of
speaking is *say* in the present tense or simple past, and if the subject is lexical or
a proper name, both the order 'quotation > verb of saying > subject' (i.e. OVS)
and 'quotation > subject > verb of saying' (OSV) are possible, while pronominal
subjects are not commonly found with inversion. Such sentences are not strictly
ungrammatical, but they are felt to be unusual or archaic (cf. ⟨58d⟩). In German,
verb-second order is obligatory (cf. ⟨59⟩).

⟨58⟩   a. "I hope you enjoyed the journey," said the captain.
       b. "I hope you enjoyed the journey," the captain said.
       c. "I hope you enjoyed the journey," he said.
       d. "I hope you enjoyed the journey," said he. (archaic)

⟨59⟩   "Ich hoffe, sie hatten eine angenehme Reise", sagte er/der Kapitän.

Inversion with pronouns can be found in (somewhat impolite) familiar language in the idiomatic expressions *says you* and *says he* (cf. ⟨60a⟩). Interestingly, the corresponding first person form *says I* is old-fashioned rather than impolite. It is usually found in combination with the historical present (cf. ⟨60b⟩).

⟨60⟩   a.   – I'm going to win this game!
            – Says you!

        b.   I began to see I was running the wrong trail, and so says I, "Oh! Nothing:
            I gues I was mistaken a little, that's al."
            [The Writings of Abraham Lincoln, 1842]

With some verbs of speaking other than *say* inversion is less common in English, but nevertheless possible (⟨61b⟩ is also peculiar insofar as inversion applies although the subject is pronominal).

⟨61⟩   a.   "The radio is too loud," complained Elizabeth/Elizabeth complained.

        b.   "What have you dreamt this time," asked he. (from *The devil with the golden hairs*)

We may note that inversion is not sensitive to whether the verb of speaking and the subject take up a final or a medial position in the sentence. In German, such sentences can be analyzed in terms of the common topological model: In ⟨62⟩, "*Ich frage mich*" takes up a position in the Forefield, and the rest of the quotation can be regarded as occupying the Postfield.

⟨62⟩   a.   "I wonder," John said/he said/said John, "whether I can borrow your bicycle."

        b.   "Ich frage mich," sagte John/er, "ob ich dein Fahrrad ausleihen kann."

Finally, there is a construction that exists in both English and German, but that is used in different contexts: The verb and the subject precede the quotation, even though subject-main verb inversion has taken place. In German, such sentences can be analyzed as involving an empty Forefield:

⟨63⟩   a.   Declared tall, nineteen-year-old Napier: "The show will go on."

        b.   Sagt ein Tiger zu einem Fuchs: ...

In English, constructions of the type illustrated in ⟨63⟩ are typically found in journalistic writing, whereas in German they are most commonly found in jokes.

11.3.4 Presentational constructions

In the last type of inversion to be discussed in this section it is the main verb and the subject that change places. The effect of such a **'subject-main verb inversion'** relates to information structure. These constructions introduce new discourse referents, hence the term 'presentational constructions':

⟨64⟩   a.   Here comes the Prime Minister.

         b.   Down the cobbled lane walked a scruffy looking man.

Presentational constructions seem to be even more similar to the corresponding German sentences than the other types of inversion considered above, which were either restricted to auxiliaries (inversion to encode mood distinctions and after negative adverbials), or to verbs of saying (direct speech). However, there are severe restrictions on this construction as well, most of which are not yet fully understood. As was mentioned above, one of the conditions is that a **new discourse referent** must be introduced. The semantic and syntactic class of the verb also plays a role. With a few exceptions, this kind of inversion is restricted to intransitive predicates, typically verbs of motion (cf. ⟨64⟩ above) or locative verbs like *be* or *live* (cf. ⟨65⟩). If transitive verbs undergo inversion, the relevant object NPs are usually tightly connected to the verb, i.e. verb-object combinations behave almost like intransitive verbs (*to take place*, *to play the piano*). Note that such constructions (as illustrated in ⟨66⟩) are felt to be unnatural or old-fashioned by many native speakers:

⟨65⟩   a.   An old woman lives in the woods.

         b.   In the woods lives an old woman.

⟨66⟩   a.   ?In the main square took place a violent demonstration.

         b.   Playing the piano will be Mr. Elton John.

In a closely related construction of English, locative inversion is accompanied by **there-insertion**. This construction is generally possible with verbs of existence and appearance (cf. ⟨67a⟩), with verbs of spatial configuration (cf. ⟨67b⟩), and with verbs of inherently directed motion (cf. ⟨67c⟩), to name only the most important types of predicates. It is not possible if the manner, but not the direction, of motion is specified (cf. ⟨68a⟩), or with change of state verbs (cf. ⟨68b⟩):

⟨67⟩   a.   There appeared a ship on the horizon.

         b.   There stood an angel.

         c.   There darted a little boy into the room.

⟨68⟩   a.   *There ran a little boy in the yard.

         b.   *There melted a lot of snow on the streets of Chicago.

Given that the presentational construction generally requires that a new discourse participant be introduced, it follows that there is an additional constraint to the effect that the subject cannot be definite ('**definiteness constraint**', cf. ⟨69a⟩). A parallel restriction can be observed in German: presentational constructions with *es* in combination with definite subjects are not very natural (cf. ⟨69b⟩ vs. ⟨69c⟩). As is illustrated in ⟨69d⟩, the corresponding sentence with *da* is much better.

⟨69⟩ a. *There appeared the ship on the horizon.

b. Es erschien ein Schiff am Horizont.

c. ?Es erschien das Schiff am Horizont.

d. Da erschien das Schiff am Horizont.

Some subtle distinctions that can be expressed in English by presentational sentences with *there* and sentences without *there* are discussed in Bolinger (1977: 90–123).

11.4 The order of adverbials and the position of negation

11.4.1 Adverbials

The most important contrasts of constituent order between English and German in the serialization of adverbials are well known: At the end of a sentence, adverbials of '**place**' precede adverbials of '**time**' in English, while the inverse order is found in the German Middle Field:

⟨70⟩ I met him at the station yesterday.

⟨71⟩ a. Ich traf ihn gestern am Bahnhof.

b. Ich habe ihn gestern am Bahnhof getroffen.

While the position of adverbials in the German Forefield is identical to that in the Middle Field, the order of elements in English changes if adverbials precede the subject. While 'place' precedes 'time' at the end of a sentence, the reverse order is found when the two adverbials occur at the beginning of the sentence (remember that such structures are quite rare in actual discourse).

⟨72⟩ a. Yesterday in London I met my best friend.

b. I met my best friend in London yesterday.

⟨73⟩ a. Ich habe meinen besten Freund gestern in London getroffen.

b. Gestern in London habe ich meinen besten Freund getroffen.

The relevant contrasts turn out to be even more general when phrases with more than two adverbials are considered. The examples in ⟨74⟩ show that the order of adverbials in German may be the exact **mirror image** of that found in English:

⟨74⟩   a. She has worked [on her boat] [with great care] [in the garden] [the whole time] [today].

       b. Sie hat [heute] [die ganze Zeit] [im Garten] [mit großer Sorgfalt] [an ihrem Boot] gearbeitet.

In a major reference grammar of English (Quirk *et al.* 1985: §8.87), the normal order for adverbials in end position is described as follows : 'respect > process > place > time', unless there are overriding considerations of length and information structure. Accordingly, we expect the reversed order 'time > place > process > respect' in German. This systematic contrast in the **ordering of adverbials** clearly correlates with the difference in basic verb positions as described above: the verb introduces the verb phrase in English, whereas it occurs at the end of the verb phrase in German. We can consequently formulate the generalization in ⟨75⟩.[2] Some English examples with adverbials of the relevant types are given in ⟨76⟩.

⟨75⟩   The further an adverbial is located to the left of the following hierarchy, the more it interacts semantically with the verb, and the closer it will be to the verb: respect > process/manner > place > time

⟨76⟩   a. Adverbial of respect
         i. She helped him *with his research.*
        ii. They are advising me *legally.*

       b. Adverbial of process
         i. The minister explained his policy *very clearly.*
        ii. I have difficulty eating *with chopsticks.*

       c. Adverbial of place
         i. The dog was asleep *on the grass.*
        ii. They walked *down the hill.*

       d. Adverbial of time
         i. I shall be in Chicago *until Thursday.*
        ii. She was born *in 1980.*

The correlation formulated in ⟨75⟩ is confirmed by the fact that in combination with **nominalized verbs**, which are 'head-initial' in German, the serialization is exactly parallel to that found in English, and thus the mirror image to the situation found in verb phrases (the following examples are from Haider 2000):

⟨77⟩   a. im Sommer auf Golfplätzen in Shorts herumlaufen

       b. das Herumlaufen in Shorts auf Golfplätzen im Sommer

⟨78⟩   a walk in shorts on golf courses in summer

---

2   Note that this principle can also account for the fact that the order of adverbials in English changes when the adverbials precede the subject.

11.4.2 Negation

There is one domain where the characterization of English constituent order as fixed and German constituent order as free seems quite appropriate, namely the placement of the negation marker. Except for cases to be briefly discussed below, *not* is placed after the first auxiliary verb in English. If the sentence to be negated does not contain an auxiliary, the default auxiliary *do* is inserted:

⟨79⟩   a. John does not care.

b. John has not been working in the garden.

c. John may not have seen this.

The only exception is cases where the relevant sentence contains another **scope-bearing element** (e.g. a quantifier, an indefinite NP, etc.) which is in the scope of *not*. Thus, a better way of describing the relevant rule would be to say that *not* occurs after the first auxiliary at the very latest, unless there is another expression in its scope preceding the verb phrase. In the examples in ⟨80⟩ the scope of *not* is indicated by bracketing, and the scope-bearing element in the scope of *not* is italicized:

⟨80⟩   a. Not [*a mouse* was stirring].

b. Not [*everybody* was convinced of the truth].

In German, the negative particle *nicht* can be moved around relatively freely in the Middle Field, depending on its **scope**. In other words, scope relations are (more or less) clearly identified by the linear order of *nicht* and the other relevant expressions. This is illustrated by the following German sentences and their English translations:

⟨81⟩   a. Der Professor hat mit einem Studenten nicht gesprochen.

b. The professor has not talked to one student.

⟨82⟩   a. Der Professor hat mit nicht einem Studenten gesprochen.

b. The professor has not talked to a single student.

⟨83⟩   a. Der Professor hat nicht mit einem Studenten gesprochen.

b. The professor has not talked to a single student. (≡ ⟨82⟩)

The freedom of the German negator *nicht* permits a more transparent interaction with other scope-bearing elements than would be possible in English. For example, the position of *nicht* relative to intensifiers like *selbst* (cf. Ch. 10) clearly indicates whether or not *selbst* is in the scope of *nicht*. Given that such interactions are not possible in English, the negator being confined to the position following the auxiliary, the German sentences in ⟨84a⟩ and ⟨85a⟩ have the same translation in English:

⟨84⟩   a. Karl wäscht sein Auto nicht selbst.
            (Er lässt es waschen.)
        b. Charles does not wash his car himself.
⟨85⟩   a. Karl wäscht sein Auto selbst nicht.
            (Er beschwert sich aber über andere!)
        b. Charles does not wash his car himself. (= ⟨84b⟩)

11.5   The structure of the noun phrase

While the major parameters of sentence architecture discussed above have revealed
some striking contrasts between English and German, the order of constituents
within the noun phrase is by and large identical. Here constituents are generally
ordered according to increasing complexity: Det > Num > Adj > N > NP_{GEN} >
PP > Rel Cl. Two examples of complex NPs are given in ⟨86⟩:

⟨86⟩   a. die zwei intelligenten Töchter reicher Eltern mit langen Haaren, die wir
            neulich sahen
        b. the last two hectic days in Stratford which we spent together

This ordering principle, called 'Gesetz der wachsenden Glieder' ('**law of increasing
complexity**') by Behaghel (1909), is of course closely related to the 'Weight Principle', which was shown to be relevant to the serialization of major constituents
in the sentence. In both English and German, heavy constituents tend to occur on
the right margin of the sentence or noun phrase, and in Hawkins (1994) this observation provides the basis for a complete theory of constituent order and language
processing. Hawkins' theory also accounts for the fact that certain heavy attributes
are obligatorily shifted to an NP-peripheral position following the head noun in
English (cf. ⟨87a⟩ vs. ⟨87b⟩). Such constructions are somewhat marginal or archaic
in German (cf. ⟨87c⟩), and the relevant NPs would usually be split up into two parts,
as is shown in ⟨87e⟩. A parallel contrast can be observed in ⟨88⟩.

⟨87⟩   a. a man as strong as Arnold Schwarzenegger
        b. *an as strong as Arnold Schwarzenegger man
        c. ein Mann, so stark wie Arnold Schwarzenegger
        d. *ein so starker wie Arnold Schwarzenegger Mann
        e. ein so starker Mann wie Arnold Schwarzenegger
⟨88⟩   a. a different solution from the one (what) you propose
        b. eine andere Lösung als du (sie) vorschlägst

Not only heavy adjectives like those illustrated in ⟨87⟩ follow the head noun in
English. Adjectives that describe the presence of a given person, object, idea, etc. at

a specific point in time may also be right-adjoined to the head noun. Two examples of **postnominal attributes** in English are given in ⟨89⟩. Very roughly, the difference is that preposed adjectives denote permanent properties while postposed attributes describe temporal properties of the referents. Such structures are impossible in German.

⟨89⟩ a. The members present agreed that no decision should be taken.

       b. The only 4x4 transmission available was a 4 speed manual until 1982.

⟨90⟩ a. *Die Mitglieder anwesend waren sich einig, dass keine Entscheidung gefällt werden sollte.

       b. *Der einzige Allradantrieb verfügbar war bis 1982 ein Viergang-Schaltgetriebe.

The adjective *present* is translated differently into German, depending on whether it is left-adjoined or right-adjoined. In the former case it often translates as *gegenwärtig*, and in the latter case as *anwesend*:

⟨91⟩ a. the present members – die gegenwärtigen Mitglieder

       b. the members present – die anwesenden Mitglieder

Finally, we should mention that certain elements may also be '**extraposed**', i.e. moved to an NP-external position at the right periphery of the sentence, in both English and German. This phenomenon is found especially in combination with relative clauses.

⟨92⟩ a. Ich habe mit jemandem _____ über dieses Problem gesprochen,
          [der recht gut informiert war].

       b. I talked to someone _____ about this problem
          [who was quite well informed].

The German sentence in ⟨92a⟩ can be regarded as instantiating the common topological structure as described in Section 11.2 (Forefield – Middle Field – Postfield). The somewhat suboptimal structure of those sentences – suboptimal insofar as there are 'discontinuous constituents' – is counter-balanced by the fact that the order of asymmetrically branching nodes conforms to the Weight Principle.

11.6 Summary

The major English-German contrasts in the domain of constituent order are summarized in Table 11.3. The most important contrasts certainly concern the use of identical orderings in main and subordinate clauses in English (SVO) vs. the use of different constituent order configurations in German (V2/SOV), and the basic or 'underlying' orders found in each language (SVO/English vs. SOV/German). The other contrasts – including those within the NP-domain – are clearly related to the major parameter 'SVO vs. SOV', and most of them represent innovations of English that accompanied the major reorganization of syntax in the Middle English period. As has been seen, some remnants of former V2-ordering are still found in English in the form of what is today felt to be a process of 'inversion'.

	English	German
basic order	SVO	SOV
other patterns	require specific conditions (inversion)	interrogative sentences, main clauses, imperatives (are derived by two general transformations)
main clause	SVO	TVX
subordinate clause	SVO	SOV
two objects	REC > THEME	DAT > ACC (NPs)
	light > heavy	ACC > DAT (pron.)
negation	after first auxiliary	as close to basic position of verb as is permitted by the requirements of scope marking

Table 11.3 Summary of contrasts: constituent order in English and German

Revision, questions and exercises

1. The classification of English as an SVO language only says something about the position of subjects relative to the verb phrase in declarative sentences. Are there any restrictions on the number of constituents that may precede the verb? Try to back up your description by looking at a text (say: half the page of a newspaper). In how many instances did you find more than two constituents before the verb?

2. Which ordering principles of English are exhibited by structures like the following?

⟨93⟩   a. The traders provided the Eskimos with refrigerators.

       b. The traders provided refrigerators to the Eskimos.

       c. These organizations supplied food to the refugees.

       d. These organizations supplied the refugees with food.

3. Why is the constituent order found in sentences like the following somewhat deviant?

     ⟨94⟩   a. ?I gave the valuable book that was extremely difficult to find to Mary.

            b. ?Did that John failed his exam surprise Mary?

            c. ?Finally, John looked the word he could never remember up.

What is the relevant factor that makes a different order much more acceptable or even the only option?

4. Describe the basic pattern of constituent order in main clauses and subordinate clauses in German.

5. Constituent order in German is often said to be freer compared to that in English. To what extent is this true?

6. How can changes of constituent order (fronting of constituents) contribute to the disambiguation of the following sentence:

     ⟨95⟩   Sie fahren mit Abstand am besten.

7. What types of elements can be moved to the Forefield in German? Try to find an appropriate generalization, considering examples like the following:

     ⟨96⟩   a. Besonders nett fand ich ihn nicht.

            b. Besonders nett finden konnte ich ihn nicht.

            c. Nett fand ich ihn nicht besonders.

            d. *Besonders fand ich ihn nicht nett.

            e. Der betrunkene Mann kam spät nach Hause.

            f. *Mann kam der betrunkene spät nach Hause.

            g. *Betrunkene Mann kam der spät nach Hause.

            h. Betrunken kam der Mann spät nach Hause.

8. Describe the English-German contrasts illustrated by the following interrogative structures:

English		German
a. Who saw her?	–	Wer sah sie?
b. Who did she see?	–	Wen sah sie?
c. Who saw what?	–	Wer sah was?
d. *What did who see?	–	Was hat wer gesehen?

Could there be a connection between the inadmissibility of d. in English and the fact that subjects normally precede objects in that language?

9. Try to formulate a restriction which excludes double object constructions in sentences like the English examples in b., comparing these sentences to those in a.

	English	German
a. i.	He gave her a present.	Er machte ihr ein Geschenk.
ii.	He bought her a book.	Er kaufte ihr ein Buch.
iii.	He threw the monkey nuts.	Er warf dem Affen Nüsse hin.
b. i.	He stole a book from me.	Er hat mir ein Buch gestohlen.
i'.	*He stole me a book.	–
ii.	He took everything from me.	Er nahm mir alles weg.
ii'.	*He took her everything.	–

10. The basic order of pronouns in the German Middle Field was said to be different from that of full noun phrases. How would you describe the ordering principles that can be observed in the German translations of English sentences like the following?

⟨97⟩   a. I know that he introduced her to him.

         b. I know that he mentioned it to him.

         c. I know that he introduced himself to her.

11. In what respect does the type of inversion exemplified by sentences like ⟨98⟩ differ from the one found in structures like ⟨99⟩ or ⟨100⟩?

⟨98⟩   a. Here comes the Prime Minister.

         b. Looking at me was a green-eyed monster.

         c. There appeared two dangerous-looking individuals.

⟨99⟩   a. Do you know the Joneses?

         b. Will you join me?

         c. Can you hear me?

⟨100⟩   a. Little does she know how much she means to me.

         b. Only when I wanted to leave did I notice that I had lost my wallet.

         c. At no time did he offer me any help.

12. Draw a table with all instances of inversion addressed above in one column and the corresponding German structures in a second column. Differentiate between purely structural aspects of comparison (e.g. auxiliary-subject inversion vs. verb-first structures) but consider also functional aspects in your overview (what do the relevant structures express?).

13. How can we differentiate between the two readings of English sentences with negative adverbials in an initial position (wide scope vs. narrow scope) in German? Find some English pairs of examples, translate these examples into German, and provide a list of correspondences between English and German structures.

14. The following examples show that the constituent order rules for imperatives differ for English and German. What is the difference?

⟨101⟩   a.   Carefully shift into a lower gear!

        b.   Slowly add a little sugar!

⟨102⟩   a.   *Schnell ändere die Temperatur!

        b.   Mische die Zutaten sorgfältig!

15. The following sentences are examples of so-called 'exclamative sentences' in German:

⟨103⟩   a.   Du bist vielleicht gewachsen!

        b.   Du bist aber gewachsen!

        c.   Wie groß du geworden bist!

        d.   Was für einen Unsinn Sie manchmal reden, Frau Löffler!

        e.   Was reden Sie für einen Unsinn, Frau Löffler!

        f.   Was habt ihr doch für einen fiesen Charakter.

        g.   Wen die alles kennt!

        h.   Und ob ich hungrig bin!

        i.   Das Wetter ist heute so herrlich!

Translate these sentences into English. To what extent is it possible to identify a specific exclamative sentence type on the basis of formal properties, or are exclamative sentences simply based on other sentence types? Are there any striking contrasts between English and German?

16. What are the possible positions for adverbs of manner in English and in German in sentences like the following? How could the relevant constraints be formulated for each language?

⟨104⟩   a.   Karl öffnete die Tür. (schnell)

        b.   Charles opened the door. (quickly)

17. What is the basic position of the negation particle *not* in English? In what way does German differ from English? Consider sentences like the following:

⟨105⟩   a.   i.   Fred may not have seen the accident.

            ii.   John does not care.

           iii.   Mary has not been working for a while.

           iv.   *Fred may have not been doing this.

        b.   i.   Karl weiß das nicht.

            ii.   Karl hat oft nicht geredet.

           iii.   Karl hat nicht oft geredet.

Further Reading

The most important facts concerning constituent order are summarized in the major reference grammars (Quirk *et al.* 1985, Biber *et al.* 1999, Huddleston and Pullum 2002 for English and Engel 1988, Zifonun *et al.* 1997, Eisenberg 2006b, Schäfer 2016 for German; see also Lenerz 1977 for a description of German in terms of a topological model). Hawkins (1986) discusses different types of inversion. The impact of information structure and other factors on constituent order in German is described in contributions to Reis (1993) and Haftka (1994) and in Czepluch (2000). An analysis of the double object construction within the framework of generative grammar is provided in Larsson (1988), and alternations in English are summarized in Levin (1993). Büring (2001) provides an analysis of constituent order in the German Middle Field using the theoretical framework of Optimality Theory. Frey and Pittner (1999) provide a comparative overview of the placement of adverbials in English and German. A more theoretically oriented treatment of the order of adverbials is offered by Haider (2000).

12 Wh-movement and relativization

A Japanese student of German asks his teacher: "Can you use the three definite articles or relative pronouns of German in combination with a single noun?" — "Certainly not," says the teacher. "Only one can be used depending on the gender of the relevant noun. Why are you asking?" — "Well, the other day in Munich, someone said to me: 'Herrgottsakrament, das die der Deifl hol!'"

12.1 Introduction

This chapter is concerned with structures that are characterized by the presence of '**empty categories**' or '**gaps**' which are associated with (non-empty) elements at some other position in the clause, usually to the left ('extractions', 'filler-gap dependencies'). In particular, we will be dealing with 'wh-movement', where a wh-pronoun is moved to a clause-initial position (cf. ⟨1a⟩), and with relative clause formation, where analogous processes of movement can be assumed (cf. ⟨1b⟩):

⟨1⟩   a.   Wh-movement
Where did you buy that dress ____?

      b.   Relativization
The dress [which you bought ____] was expensive.

The chapter is restricted to the most central contrasts in this domain. A more comprehensive discussion can be found in Hawkins (1986). We will start with wh-movement in Section 12.2 and turn to relativization in Section 12.3. As will be seen, both types of processes can be described in terms of the same parameters and restrictions (e.g. source and target position of the moved element). The contrasts between English and German in this domain have been summarized by Hawkins (1986: 87) as follows: "whenever German can extract, so can English, but not vice versa". We will also show that the contrasts between English and German can be seen in a larger context by relating them to typological generalizations stated in the form of implicational hierarchies. A brief summary is provided in Section 12.4.

12.2 Wh-movement

In basic sentences, every **semantic argument** of a predicate corresponds to some **syntactic element** of the appropriate category, in the appropriate position. For instance, a transitive predicate requires a subject NP in subject position and an object NP in object position. Let us call these slots '**basic positions**', and let us furthermore assume that the basic position of a constituent is the position where that constituent is interpreted. In sentences which are 'derived' in a sense to be made more explicit below, syntactic elements do not occur in their basic position. For instance, the question word *what* in ⟨2a⟩ functions as an object of the predicate *buy*, but it does not occupy the object position of that predicate. This position is the one taken by *a dress* in ⟨2b⟩. Note that *what* may also occur in that position, but such configurations are found only in 'echo questions' (cf. ⟨2c⟩) and when more than one wh-pronoun is present ('multiple wh-questions', cf. ⟨2d⟩):

⟨2⟩ a. What will you buy?
   b. I will buy a dress.
   c. You will buy what? (echo question)
   d. Who bought what? (multiple wh-words)

Given the difference between the position of *what* in surface structure and the place where it is interpreted, wh-questions (or 'parametric questions') as illustrated in ⟨2a⟩ are usually regarded as resulting from a **movement operation**: the question word *what* is assumed to move from its 'basic' position to a sentence-initial position. Given that most of the relevant question words in English begin with *wh*, this type of movement is often called 'wh-movement', which is a somewhat unfortunate term for languages other than English. The operation of wh-movement is illustrated in ⟨3a⟩. Movement may also be represented by using the notational device of **indices**: the empty (basic) position is indicated by a variable t (for '**trace**'), and the moved element and the trace bear the same index (usually $i, j, \ldots$; cf. ⟨3b⟩).

⟨3⟩ a. What will you buy ____ ?

   b. What$_i$ will you buy t_i?

12.2.1 Wh-movement within clauses

In German, wh-movement is possible for both question words in argument position (*wer*, *wen*, etc.) and question words corresponding to adverbials (e.g. *wo*, *wann*, *warum*). In the examples in Table 12.1, the base position of the moved element is assumed to be located in the Middle Field (cf. Ch. 11). Except in echo questions and in multiple wh-questions, wh-pronouns are always moved to the Forefield.

FF	V_{FIN}	Middle Field				$V_{NON\text{-}FIN}$
Wer	hat	_____	gestern	am Bahnhof	einen Freund	getroffen
Wann	hat	Karl	_____	am Bahnhof	einen Freund	getroffen
Wo	hat	Karl	gestern	_____	einen Freund	getroffen
Wen	hat	Karl	gestern	am Bahnhof	_____	getroffen

Table 12.1 Wh-movement to the Forefield in German

There are two important **restrictions** on clause-internal wh-movement: first, a noun phrase may not be moved out of (the specifier position of) another noun phrase; and second, noun phrases may not be moved out of (the complement position of) prepositional phrases. This is illustrated in ⟨4⟩:

⟨4⟩   a.   *Wessen$_i$ hat Karl [$_{NP}$ t_i Auto] gekauft?
       b.   *Wen$_i$ hat Karl [$_{PP}$ für t_i] ein Geschenk gekauft?

In cases such as ⟨4a⟩ and ⟨4b⟩, only the larger constituent containing the question word can be moved to the Forefield, i.e. the whole NP *wessen Auto* in ⟨4a⟩ and the PP *für wen* in ⟨4b⟩. This type of operation is called '**pied-piping**', since the sister constituent of the question word is 'dragged along':

⟨5⟩   a.   [Wessen Auto]$_i$ hat Karl t_i gekauft?
       b.   [Für wen]$_i$ hat Karl t_i ein Geschenk gekauft?

The first of the constraints pointed out above applies to English as well: question words corresponding to genitives cannot be fronted alone (cf. ⟨6a⟩). However, the second constraint – the one on wh-movement out of PPs – does not apply in English. A relevant example is given in ⟨7⟩. The resulting sentence manifests what is called '**preposition stranding**' in traditional grammar.

⟨6⟩   a.   *Whose$_i$ did he buy [$_{NP}$ t_i car]?
       b.   [$_{NP}$ Whose car]$_i$ did he buy t_i?
⟨7⟩   Who$_i$ did he buy a present [$_{PP}$ for t_i]? (preposition stranding)

In cases such as ⟨7⟩, English allows pied-piping as well, i.e. the structure corresponding to the German sentence in ⟨5b⟩ is also possible. PP-fronting is generally considered more formal and typically found in the written language:

⟨8⟩   [For who(m)]$_i$ did he buy a present t_i?

While the restrictions on movement pointed out above clearly confirm Hawkins' claim that "whenever German can extract, so can English, but not vice versa", there is one respect in which German is more liberal than English: in **multiple wh-questions**, the choice of the element to be fronted is more fixed in English than it is in German. A clear contrast can be observed in cases of two wh-pronouns, one of which is a subject: in English, the wh-subject always comes first, while the order is not fixed in German:

⟨9⟩ a. Who bought what?
    b. *What did who buy?

⟨10⟩ a. Wer hat was gekauft?
    b. Was hat wer gekauft?

This does not mean, however, that in English wh-subjects are always in the first position. Interestingly, *who* functioning as a subject usually follows *why* and *how* (cf. ⟨11⟩ and ⟨12⟩). In German, the order of such elements is, again, free, even though there is a clear preference for the subject to precede *warum* and *wie* (cf. ⟨13⟩):

⟨11⟩ a. Why did you chose to be buried here, if it was even your choice to make. And if not, why did who ever chose to bury you here, pick this place?[1]
    b. Why did who say what? (Crystal 1989: 41)

⟨12⟩ a. Excuse me. How did *who* get away? (emphasis original)[2]
    b. How did who get into the apartment?[3]

⟨13⟩ a. Wer hat diese schwierige Aufgabe wie gelöst?
    b. Wie hat wer reagiert?
    c. Wer hat warum gewonnen?
    d. Warum hat wer dieses überflüssige Gesetz erlassen?

The order of wh-subjects and wh-words corresponding to adverbials of time and place (*when* and *where*) may vary in both English and German:

⟨14⟩ a. Who saw Mary where/when?
    b. When/where did who see Mary?

⟨15⟩ a. Wer hat Maria wo/wann gesehen?
    b. Wann/wo hat wer Maria gesehen?

To sum up, clause-internal movement is more restricted in German than it is in English if only properties of the moved element are considered (esp. its source position), but English exhibits some restrictions concerning the order of elements in

---

[1] http://www.dokuga.com/fanfiction/story/3089/1, accessed on 17/05/18
[2] https://www.salon.com/1997/06/04/clancy/, accessed on 17/05/18.
[3] https://www.law.cornell.edu/supremecourt/text/437/385, accessed on 17/05/18.

clauses with more than one wh-pronoun. The latter contrast is obviously related to the more general differences between German and English clause structure pointed out in Section 11, and also to the differences in case morphology: German is a verb-second language with a rich case morphology, and (basically) any constituent from the Middle Field can be moved to the Forefield, whereas English is an SVO-language which lacks a structural position corresponding to the German Forefield, and moreover has a highly impoverished case morphology. In particular, the distinction between subjective and objective wh-forms is (on the verge) of disappearing even for animate wh-pronouns, since *whom* is gradually being replaced by *who*.

12.2.2 Wh-movement across clause boundaries

The constraints illustrated above relate to both properties of the moved element (e.g. its grammatical relation) and properties of the 'base position' (specifier of NP, complement of PP). In this section a family of contrasts will be pointed out that relates to the '**distance**' between the source position and the target position in movement operations. Let us first distinguish three types of contexts: (i) movement within clauses ('clause-internal movement', cf. Section 12.2.1), (ii) movement out of non-finite complement clauses and (iii) movement out of finite complement clauses. Consider the examples in $\langle 16 \rangle$:

$\langle 16 \rangle$ a. [$_{+\text{FIN}}$ Wen$_i$ hat Karl in unserem Garten t_i gesehen]?
(clause-internal)

b. [$_{+\text{FIN}}$ Wen$_i$ glaubte Karl [$_{-\text{FIN}}$ in unserem Garten t_i zu sehen]]?
(out of non-finite complement clause)

c. *[$_{+\text{FIN}}$ Wen$_i$ glaubte Karl, [$_{+\text{FIN}}$ dass er im Garten t_i sah]]?
(out of finite complement clause)

In $\langle 16a \rangle$ the question word *wen* and the corresponding 'trace' are in the same clause (hence, '**clause-internal movement**'). In $\langle 16b \rangle$ the question word is moved from a lower (infinitival) complement clause (... *in unserem Garten zu sehen*) to a higher clause (*Karl glaubte* ...). The basic position of the wh-word is in the embedded infinitival clause, as is illustrated in (the echo question) $\langle 17 \rangle$:

$\langle 17 \rangle$ Karl glaubte, WEN in unserem Garten zu sehen?

Given that *wen* surfaces in the higher clause, it crosses the (non-finite) clause boundary separating the embedded infinitival clause from the matrix clause. While such movement across a non-finite clause boundary is possible in both languages under comparison, movement out of a finite clause ('**clause-external movement**') as illustrated in $\langle 16c \rangle$ leads to ungrammaticality in German. This type of operation is possible in English. Consider first the examples in $\langle 18 \rangle$, which illustrate movement out of a non-finite clause. Their German counterparts are also grammatical, though $\langle 19 \rangle$ is somewhat marginal:

$\langle 18 \rangle$ a.   [$_{+FIN}$ What$_i$ did you try [$_{-FIN}$ to repair t_i]]?

       b.   [$_{+FIN}$ What$_i$ do you request me [$_{-FIN}$ to try [$_{-FIN}$ to repair t_i]]]?

$\langle 19 \rangle$ [$_{+FIN}$ Was$_i$ batest du mich [$_{-FIN}$[t_i zu reparieren] zu versuchen]]?

Wh-movement out of a **finite subordinate clause** is illustrated in $\langle 20a \rangle$ and $\langle 20b \rangle$. The German sentences corresponding to $\langle 20a \rangle$ and $\langle 20b \rangle$ are strictly ungrammatical (cf. $\langle 21a \rangle$ and $\langle 21b \rangle$), though similar structures seem to be possible in some (especially southern) dialects of German. Note that these sentences are better if *dass* is replaced with *was* (cf. $\langle 22 \rangle$).

$\langle 20 \rangle$ a.   What$_i$ do you think [$_{FIN}$ (that) he will say t_i]?

       b.   What$_i$ do you think [$_{FIN}$ (that) he will try [$_{NON\text{-}FIN}$ to do t_i]]?

$\langle 21 \rangle$ a.   *Was$_i$ denkst du [$_{FIN}$ dass er t_i sagen wird]?

       b.   *Was$_i$ denkst du [$_{FIN}$ dass er [t_i zu tun] versuchen wird]?

$\langle 22 \rangle$ Was denkst du, was er sagen wird?

So far, we have only looked at (finite and non-finite) complement clauses. When we consider adverbial clauses, an additional contrast can be observed: In English, wh-elements can be extracted out of **non-finite adverbial clauses**. Such extractions seem to be better with infinitival clauses (cf. $\langle 23a \rangle$) than with participles (cf. $\langle 23b \rangle$; examples and grammaticality judgements have been taken from Hawkins 1986: 91). The corresponding German sentences are ungrammatical (cf. $\langle 24 \rangle$):

$\langle 23 \rangle$ a.   What$_i$ did he come [in order to pick up t_i]?

       b.   ?What$_i$ did he drive without observing t_i?

$\langle 24 \rangle$ a.   *Was$_i$ ist er gekommen, um t_i abzuholen?

       b.   *Was$_i$ ist er gefahren, ohne t_i zu beachten?

When compared to extractions out of complement clauses, the structures illustrated above (esp. $\langle 23b \rangle$) exhibit a lower degree of acceptability and are even considered ungrammatical by some native speakers. Total ungrammaticality results when a wh-element is extracted from a **finite adverbial clause**. This is shown in the following example (from Hawkins 1986: 92), whose *in situ*-variant (echo question) is given in $\langle 25b \rangle$):

$\langle 25 \rangle$ a.   *[Which film]$_i$ did you go to the movies
           [even though you did not want to see t_i]?

       b.   You went to the movies
           [even though you did not want to see [which film]]?

The contrasts pointed out above can be summarized in the form of the **implicational hierarchy** given in $\langle 26 \rangle$, and the following cross-linguistic generalization can be made: If a language allows extractions out of a clause type at some point in the hierarchy, it will also allow extractions out of all clause types further to the left:

$\langle 26 \rangle$

clause-internal	>	complement clauses	>	adverbial clauses
		(non-finite > finite)		(non-finite > finite)

As will be seen in Section 12.3, a parallel generalization can be made with respect to relativization. Accordingly, the rules and constraints governing wh-movement and relativization are regarded as instances of more general syntactic principles, namely, principles relating to 'filler-gap dependencies' (cf. Hawkins 1999), rather than to wh movement or relativization in particular.

We will conclude this chapter with a remark on a type of syntactic configuration which can be observed in English and which does not have a counterpart in German. In English, one overt wh-element (filler) may correspond to more than one gap or trace. Given that there is usually a one-to-one correspondence between fillers and gaps, such slots which are not associated with an overt element of their own are called **'parasitic gaps'**. A standard example of this configuration is given in $\langle 27 \rangle$:

$\langle 27 \rangle$ [Which book]$_i$ did John read t$_i$ without understanding t$_i$?

As mentioned above, parasitic gaps are not allowed in Standard German (in contrast to Bavarian). This is not easy to illustrate, however, since the unacceptability of the relevant sentences is often due to other (independent) reasons. For instance, example $\langle 27 \rangle$ cannot be translated into German because it involves extraction out of a non-finite adverbial clause, which is ungrammatical in German anyway. In many cases, there is also a case conflict which would not arise in English. For instance, *wem* in $\langle 28 \rangle$ is supposed to function as an argument of both *ankündigen* and *befördern*. But this is impossible anyway because *ankündigen* requires a dative object and *befördern* an accusative object. For this reason, both $\langle 28a \rangle$ and $\langle 28b \rangle$ are ungrammatical in the intended reading (i.e. in a question corresponding to $\langle 29 \rangle$).

$\langle 28 \rangle$ a. *Wem$_i$ hast du t$_i$ angekündigt, t$_i$ zu befördern?

   b. *Wen$_i$ hast du t$_i$ angekündigt, t$_i$ zu befördern?

$\langle 29 \rangle$ Ich habe Karl$_i$ angekündigt, ihn$_i$ zu befördern.

Note that $\langle 28b \rangle$ is, of course, grammatical if *wen* is only interpreted as an object of *befördern* but not of *angekündigt*, i.e. when the question corresponds to a sentence of the form *Ich habe angekündigt, ihn zu befördern* ($\rightarrow$ *Wen hast du zu befördern angekündigt?*), but the corresponding wh-question would not contain a parasitic gap.

If we want to show that parasitic gaps are really ungrammatical in German, we thus have to find a sentence in which two gaps have identical case specifications.

Such a sentence is given in ⟨30a⟩, with the corresponding declarative clause in ⟨30b⟩. Given that ⟨30a⟩ is just as ungrammatical as ⟨28a⟩ and ⟨28b⟩ above, we can conclude that parasitic gaps are in fact not allowed in German:

⟨30⟩   a. *Wem$_i$ hast du t$_i$ auf den Kopf zugesagt,
            t$_i$ kein Wort zu glauben?

        b. Ich habe ihm$_i$ auf den Kopf zugesagt,
            ihm$_i$ kein Wort zu glauben.

12.2.3 Summary: Wh-movement in English and German

There are three major contrasts between English and German in the domain of wh-movement: (i) wh-movement is not possible out of PPs in German while this is perfectly acceptable in English (leading to 'preposition stranding'); (ii) wh-movement is not generally allowed out of finite complement clauses and out of non-finite adverbial clauses, whereas this is usually possible in English; and (iii) only English allows parasitic gaps. Moreover, it has been pointed out that the order of elements in the case of multiple wh-questions is more fixed in English than it is in German, which can be related to the more general tendency for German to exhibit freer word order.

12.3 Relative clause formation

Filler-gap dependencies as described in the previous section can also be observed in relative clauses. The parallelism between wh-movement and relative clause formation is most obvious in those cases where the relative pronoun is also a wh-element, i.e. in the case of Engl. *who/which* and Germ. *welche/r/s* ('**w[h]-relatives**'). As in wh-movement, the relevant elements are moved to a clause-initial position. The only difference is that there is no subject-auxiliary inversion in English, and no verb-second ordering in German (cf. Section 11.1):

⟨31⟩   a. The man [who$_i$ you saw t$_i$ in my house] is my uncle.

        b. Der Mann, [welchen$_i$ du gerade t$_i$ erwähntest], ist unser Präsident.

Obviously, wh-pronouns such as *who* and *welcher* are not the only relativizers of English and German, nor are they the ones most frequently used. English often uses the relativizer *that* to mark relative clauses ('***that*-relatives**', cf. ⟨32a⟩), or simply leaves a gap in the position of the relevant element ('**bare relatives**', cf. ⟨32b⟩). German uses relative pronouns that derive from determiners or demonstratives in the majority of cases ('**d-relatives**', cf. ⟨33⟩).

⟨32⟩   a. This is the man [that will lead us to glory].

       b. There's something [I've always wanted to tell you].

⟨33⟩   Dies ist der Mann, [der uns aus der Krise führen wird].

Before turning to the differences in the inventories of English and German relativizers in Section 12.3.2, we will consider contrasts relating to restrictions on movement parallel to those described for wh-movement in Section 12.2 above.

12.3.1 Relativization and movement

As has been seen, there are **restrictions** on intra-clausal wh-movement in both English and German, with the latter language being more restrictive than the former (no wh-movement out of either NPs or PPs). A completely parallel situation obtains in relative clause formation. German does not allow relativization out of either NPs or PPs and requires pied-piping in both cases. By contrast, English does allow relativization of a PP-internal NP (preposition stranding), though not of an NP-internal one:

⟨34⟩   Relativization out of NP

       a. *The man [whose$_i$ you bought [$_{NP}$ t_i car]] is a crook.

       b. *Der Mann, [dessen$_i$ du [$_{NP}$ t_i Auto] gekauft hast]], ist ein Gauner.

⟨35⟩   Relativization out of prepositional phrase

       a. The man [who$_i$ you pointed [at t_i]] is my uncle.

       b. The man [at who(m)$_i$ you pointed t$_i$] is my uncle.

       c. *Der Mann, [welchen$_i$ du [auf t_i] gezeigt hast], ist mein Onkel.

       d. Der Mann, [[auf welchen]$_i$ du t_i gezeigt hast], ist mein Onkel.

Constraints on relativization across clause boundaries are also completely analogous: movement out of finite complement clauses is possible in English while it is impossible in (Standard) German:

⟨36⟩   a. The man [$_{REL}$who$_i$ you think [$_{FIN}$ you saw t_i]] . . .

       b. *Der Mann, [$_{REL}$ welchen$_i$ du glaubst, [$_{FIN}$dass du t_i sahst]] . . .

As pointed out in the previous section, cross-linguistic generalizations can be made on the basis of a 'hierarchy' of clause types, or, alternatively, a hierarchy of structural relationships relating to the **'distance'** between the filler and the gap. This hierarchy is repeated in Table 12.2. It applies to wh-movement and relativization alike. The range of extractions allowed by English and German can now be determined on the basis of that hierarchy, which thus also provides a means of comparison.

filler-gap dependencies				
within clauses	across clauses			
	complement clauses		adverbial clauses	
	non-finite	finite	non-finite	finite
German				
English				

Table 12.2 Wh-movement and relativization within and across clauses

Table 12.2 predicts that English will allow relativization out of non-finite adverbial clauses but not out of finite ones. This is illustrated in ⟨37⟩ (cf. Hawkins 1986: 91):

⟨37⟩   a.   The speed limit which he drove without observing is 50 mph.

        b.   *[The film]$_i$ [which$_i$ you went to the movies [even though you didn't want to see t_i]] was very interesting.

Finally, the contrast concerning parasitic gaps in wh-movement operations pointed out at the end of Section 12.2 likewise has a clear counterpart in the domain of relativization. Such operations are only possible in English:

⟨38⟩   This is [the first pub]$_i$ [(that) I was ever thrown out of $\emptyset_i$] [for wearing jeans in t_i].

12.3.2   Inventories of relative markers

So far, we have been dealing with relative clauses formed by using the relative pronouns *who/which* in English and *welche/r/s* in German. As mentioned above, these elements are not the only relativizers of English and German and are not even particularly frequent or typical. In this section, some differences between the various strategies available in the languages under comparison will be pointed out.

English *that*-relatives are not commonly analyzed as resulting from an overt movement operation. The main reason is that relativizing *that* (unlike *who*) cannot occur *in situ* (cf. ⟨39⟩ vs. ⟨40⟩). Moreover, *that* does not show agreement with the head noun (wh-relatives agree in animacy with their head nouns), thus looking more like a particle than like a pronoun.

⟨39⟩   a.   The man [who(m)$_i$ you mentioned t$_i$] is my friend.

        b.   You mentioned who(m)?

⟨40⟩   a.   The man that you mentioned is my friend.

        b.   You mentioned that. (different meaning)

That-relatives are typically treated on a par with '**bare relatives**', where the relative clause is merely indicated by a gap in the relevant position. The difference between the two types of relative clauses is, thus, that in one case there is an explicit indicator of subordination (*that*, cf. ⟨41a⟩) while in the other case the subordinate status of relative clauses needs to be inferred from the overall structural configuration. In particular, the immediate sequence of two NPs (head noun and subject of relative clause) is otherwise found only in double object constructions, and is thus a good indicator of subordination or relativization (cf. ⟨41b⟩):

⟨41⟩ a. The man [that [$_S$ you mentioned Ø]] is my friend.

b. [$_{NP}$ The man] [$_S$[[$_{NP}$ you] mentioned Ø]] is my friend.

One way of looking at *that*-relatives and bare relatives thus is to regard the latter as elliptical versions of the former. *That*-ellipsis can be assumed to be possible because the subordinate status of the relative clause can also be inferred from other structural properties of the clause. This hypothesis is supported by the fact that bare relatives are subject to certain restrictions. First, this type of structure is not possible (in Standard English) when the relativized element has the function of a subject within the relative clause. Such structures would give rise to '**garden-path sentences**', i.e. a non-intended interpretation would (temporarily) be evoked during the process of parsing. In ⟨42⟩, for instance, the hearer would first think that *stands* is the predicate of the matrix sentence, thus failing to recognize the relative clause:

⟨42⟩ *[The table]$_i$ [Ø$_i$ stands in the corner] has a broken leg.

Instances of bare relativization of the type illustrated in ⟨42⟩ are only possible (though colloquial) in presentational constructions as in ⟨43a⟩ and ⟨43b⟩. Note that no 'garden-path' effect arises because in each case the valency of the existential predicate is saturated at the time the bare relative clause begins:

⟨43⟩ a. There's [a man]$_i$ [Ø$_i$ wants to see you].

b. I have [a friend]$_i$ [Ø$_i$ lives in Canada].

So far, we have focused on the difference between *that*-relatives and bare relatives, showing that the latter are generally restricted to relative clauses in which non-subjects are relativized. The question now arises what distinguishes bare relatives and *that*-relatives from **wh-relatives**. In general, wh-relatives have a rather wide distribution which covers most of the contexts licensing either *that*-relatives or bare relatives. In other words, in most contexts where a *that*-relative or a bare relative clause can be used, a wh-relative is also possible, though it is associated with a more formal context. As will be seen below, there are moreover contexts where only wh-relatives are allowed. However, under specific circumstances wh-relatives are either awkward or ungrammatical where one of the other types would be fine. One such context is the relativization of PP-internal NPs. Note first that wh-relatives do not normally allow preposition stranding:

⟨44⟩   a. Can you tell me the time at which he arrives?

        b. ??Can you tell me the time which he arrives at?

As was mentioned in Section 12.2, however, pied-piping as in ⟨44a⟩ is rather rare in the spoken language and sounds somewhat clumsy. A much more natural way of conveying the meaning of ⟨44a⟩ would thus be to use either a bare relative (*Can you tell me the time he arrives* [*at*]) or a temporal relative pronoun (. . . *the time when he arrives*). The difference is even more clearly visible in the following examples:

⟨45⟩   a. ??This is the reason which he came for.

        b. ?This is the reason for which he came.

        c. This is the reason (that) he came.

        d. This is the reason why he came.

⟨46⟩   a. *This is the way which he did it in.

        b. ?This is the way in which he did it.

        c. This is the way (that) he did it.

Another context where wh-relatives are awkward or even ungrammatical is relative clauses of the type illustrated in ⟨47⟩:

⟨47⟩   a. I am not the man (*who) I used to be.

        b. The Reichstag is not the same building (*which) it was twenty years ago.

In spite of examples like those in ⟨45⟩–⟨47⟩, wh-relatives cover a wider range of contexts than do either *that*-relatives or bare relatives, putting stylistic preferences aside. There is one context which systematically licenses only wh-relatives, namely **non-restrictive relative clauses** as illustrated in ⟨48⟩:

⟨48⟩   a. Shakespeare, who/*that wrote many important plays . . .

        b. Jane wants to marry that old man, which/*that surprises me.

Non-restrictive (or 'appositive') relative clauses do not provide information enabling the hearer to identify the referent in question, but presuppose that the referent is identifiable to the hearer, and provide additional information about that referent. Therefore, they often correspond to separate declarative main clauses. ⟨49a⟩, for instance, has similar pragmatic implications as ⟨48b⟩, while the (restrictive) relative clause in ⟨41b⟩ above cannot be paraphrased by two main clauses, as in ⟨49b⟩:

⟨49⟩   a. Jane wants to marry that old man. That surprises me.

        b. #The man is my friend. You mentioned him.

Non-restrictive relative clauses are also distinguished from restrictive ones by some further formal properties, e.g. by an intonational break (usually marked by a comma in orthography) and by the impossibility of right-dislocation (extraposition):

⟨50⟩   a.   A man who was dressed in black walked in.

        b.   A man walked in who was dressed in black.

⟨51⟩   a.   Marcia, who you wanted to meet, has just arrived.

        b.   *Marcia has just arrived, who you wanted to meet.

We have started with relativization in English because this language makes more formal and distributional distinctions in its inventory of relative clause formation than does German. German only has two sets of relative pronouns, namely *welche/r/s* ('**w-relatives**') and *der/die/das* ('**d-relatives**'). The difference between the two strategies is basically one of style: German w-relatives usually sound bookish and are hardly ever used in the spoken language except perhaps when the co-occurrence of two identical elements is to be avoided (*horror aequi*):

⟨52⟩   a.   Ich meine den, den du mir gestern gezeigt hast.

        b.   Ich meine den, welchen du mir gestern gezeigt hast.

Like w-relatives, d-relatives cover the whole range of functions distinguished for English relative clauses above: they are not constrained in terms of the syntactic function of the relevant noun in either the matrix clause or the relative clause, and they are used in restrictive and non-restrictive relative clauses alike. When comparing English and German, we are thus faced with a situation of **underspecification** in German relative to English: English simply makes more grammatical distinctions in that domain. The distribution of relative pronouns in English and German is summarized in Table 12.3. While the difference between d-relatives and w-relatives in German is merely one of style, in English there are also grammatical or structural differences between the strategies available. In those cases where speakers of English have a choice, stylistic factors obviously also play a role. As a rule of thumb, wh-relativization is more formal than *that*-relativization, which in turn is more formal than bare relativization.

	non-restrictive	restrictive	
		subject in relative clause	non-subject in relative clause
G	*der/die/das* (unmarked) *welcher/welche/welches* (formal)		
E	*who/which*		
	that		
	∅		

Table 12.3 Relativization strategies in English and German

12.4 Summary

As has been seen, the English-German contrasts in the domains of wh-movement and relativization are largely parallel. Both operations exhibit the same types of restrictions in each language, so that we can generalize over them by regarding them as different instantiations of a single operation, i.e. 'movement'. Put differently, we can say that 'filler-gap dependencies' obey the same restrictions in English and German. Most importantly, such dependencies are more restricted across clauses in German than they are in English. Moreover, German does not allow extractions out of prepositional phrases while this is possible in English. Filler-gap dependencies of the type discussed in this section have been extensively studied by John Hawkins, and in fact, the contrastive investigations conducted by Hawkins have given rise to one of the most influential theories of language processing, developed in Hawkins (1992), Hawkins (1994) and Hawkins (2004). Filler-gap dependencies thus provide an example of the benefit that general linguistics can draw from detailed pairwise language comparison as envisaged in contrastive linguistics.

Revision, questions and exercises

1. Summarize three central contrasts between English and German in the domain of extractions and illustrate them with examples.
2. Describe the difference illustrated by the following pair of sentences in English and German.

    ⟨53⟩   a. Who did you talk to? To whom did you talk?

    b. Mit wem hast du gesprochen?

3. Consider the parallels between contrasts in the domains of wh-movement and relative clause formation. To what extent is it possible to generalize over both areas of grammar, as far as English-German contrasts are concerned?
4. Of the three following relative clauses only the first has a parallel in German. How can we describe the difference in a maximally general way? (Consider the position of the clause with the gap that is created by relative clause formation relative to the head noun.)

    ⟨54⟩   a. The solution$_i$ which Bill found t$_i$ is great.

    b. This is a problem$_i$ which I know t$_i$ has never been solved.

    c. This is a problem$_i$ that I don't know how to explain t$_i$.

    ⟨55⟩   a. Die Lösung$_i$, die Karl t$_i$ gefunden hat, gefällt mir.

    b. Das ist ein Problem$_i$, von dem$_i$ ich weiß, dass es$_i$ nie gelöst wurde.

5. Which relative pronouns are possible (and which are excluded) in relative clauses like the following:

⟨56⟩   a.   John is not the man _____ he used to be.

        b.   I remember the beautiful girl _____ Mary had been in her youth.

6.   Do you see a contrast in meaning in the following minimal pair of sentences and what is it due to?

⟨57⟩   a.   Tom has a violin which once belonged to Heifetz, and Jane has one, too.

        b.   Tom has a violin, which once belonged to Heifetz, and Jane has one, too.

7.   The following infinitive constructions could also be analyzed as instances of relative clauses. What is the difference between the two types? Look at the role the subject plays in the relative clause.

⟨58⟩   a.   The next train to arrive is the express train from Glasgow.

        b.   The first man to set foot on the moon was Neil Armstrong.

        c.   The only student to get an A was Jim Smith.

⟨59⟩   a.   The best person to send is Fred.

        b.   The place for you to stay is the Hilton.

        c.   The man for John to consult is Bill Gates.

8.   What is meant by 'free' or 'headless' relative clauses in grammars of English? Give examples.

9.   Relative clauses may not only modify noun phrases but may also relate to sentences ('relativ[isch]er Satzanschluss'), as in the following example from German: *Karl treibt überhaupt keinen Sport, was mich sehr überrascht.*

(i)   How are such relative clauses translated into English?

(ii)   How would you analyze a German sentence like *Karin hat mir geholfen, wofür ich ihr sehr dankbar bin.*

10.   In non-standard dialects of both English and German relative pronouns can be found that are inadmissible in the standard varieties: *as*, *what* (English); *wo*, *was* (German). There is, however, also one context where *as* is the best choice in an English relative clause. Which context is that?

Further reading

Much of the material used in this chapter is based on Hawkins (1986), to which the reader is referred for more information. Some of the claims made by Hawkins have been relativized by Rohdenburg (1990, 1992, 1996, 2000, 2016), who has contributed a number of interesting observations and generalizations to the discussion. For a critical treatment of Hawkins' claims see also Fischer (2013). The discussion of English relative clauses is largely based on Quirk *et al.* (1985).

13   Non-finite subordination

> "I just met the old Irishman and his son,
> coming out of the toilet."
> "I wouldn't have thought there was room
> for the two of them."
> "No, silly, I mean *I* was coming out of the
> toilet. They were waiting ... "
>
> (from *Paradise News*, by David Lodge)[1]

13.1   Introduction

In this chapter non-finite subordination will be discussed, i.e. complement clauses and adverbial clauses without finite verbs. The structures to be analyzed and compared with their counterparts and translations into German include the following:

⟨1⟩   a.   I happen to have written that book.
      b.   This is guaranteed to be pure malt whiskey.
      c.   England expects every man to do his duty.

⟨2⟩   a.   Mary hopes to meet the man of her dreams one day.
      b.   Bill promised Hillary to help her.
      c.   Hillary asked Bill to help her.

⟨3⟩   a.   Looking at the election results, Hillary was very pleased.
      b.   Hillary risked losing the elections.
      c.   Knowing me, knowing you, it's the best we can do. (song by ABBA)

Some of these structures look very similar and seem to only differ in slight, insignificant details. In spite of this superficial similarity there are striking differences, however, in the way these structures are analyzed, interpreted and translated into German. These differences are clearly revealed when we apply certain tests to these structures and try to identify the expression that also functions as the understood or **implicit subject** of the non-finite verb forms. In ⟨1a⟩ and ⟨1b⟩, for instance, the subject of the whole sentence is also the understood subject of the non-finite verb form ([*It so happens that*] *I have written that book*, [*It is guaranteed that*] *this is pure malt whiskey*), whereas in ⟨1c⟩ it is the (syntactic) object of the main sentence

---

[1]   Penguin Books, 1991, p. 65.

every man that functions as a (semantic) subject of the subordinate clause (*[England expects that] every man does his duty*).

The same difference can be observed between ⟨2a⟩ and ⟨2b⟩, on the one hand, and ⟨2c⟩, on the other: In the former two example sentences, the subject of the main clause is also the (understood) subject of the subordinate clause (*[Mary hopes that] she will meet the man of her dreams, [Bill promises that] he will help Hillary*), while in the latter sentence it is the object of the matrix clause that functions as a subject of the embedded clause (*[Hillary asked Bill] whether he could help her*). ⟨3a⟩ and ⟨3b⟩ are analogous to ⟨2a⟩ and ⟨2b⟩ insofar as the understood subject of the non-finite clause is also the subject of the main clause (*Hillary looks at the election results, Hillary loses the elections*). In ⟨3c⟩, by contrast, the implied subject of the two *ing* forms (*knowing me, knowing you*) is not even syntactically encoded and needs to be inferred from the context. In this particular case, it is the speaker.

A second systematic distinction that can be observed in the examples given above concerns the semantic relationship holding between the predicates and their arguments. The subject of ⟨1a⟩ is not really a **semantic argument** of the predicate *happen* in the main clause (the sentence does not say 'I happen'), *malt whiskey* is not a semantic argument of the main predicate *guarantee* in ⟨1b⟩ (which does not imply that 'malt whiskey is guaranteed'), and ⟨1c⟩ does not say that 'England expects every man'. Predicates used in structures like those illustrated in ⟨1⟩ are called **'raising verbs'**, since the relevant sentences are assumed to result from an operation of 'raising' an NP from a lower clause to a higher clause. This type of operation will be explained in Section 13.2.

In contrast to ⟨1a⟩–⟨1c⟩, a semantic predicate-argument relation between the syntactic subject and the predicate can be recovered for the examples given in ⟨2⟩, i.e. Mary is the one who hopes in ⟨2a⟩, Bill is the one who promises in ⟨2b⟩ and Hillary is the one who asks in ⟨2c⟩. In these examples there are thus no 'unexpected' (i.e. semantically odd) subjects as in ⟨1a⟩–⟨1c⟩. What characterizes these structures is that some NP of the main clause in some way 'controls' the interpretation of the empty subject position of the non-finite verb in the subordinate clause. The relevant verbs (*promise, hope, threaten, try, manage, learn, demand, ask, tell, urge, command, advise*, etc.) are therefore called **'control verbs'**. As pointed out above, it is the main clause subject that controls the empty subject position of the infinitive with verbs like *promise, hope, threaten, try* and the object of the main clause that functions as controller after verbs like *ask, beg, tell, urge*, etc. We can therefore make a distinction between 'subject control verbs' (*promise*) and 'object control verbs' (*urge*).

The examples in ⟨3⟩, finally, contain *ing*-forms. These forms are called **'gerunds'** if they occur in an argument position, and **'participles'** when they function as adjuncts. They share with the other types of structures illustrated above the property that an argument is not realized overtly, and that the interpretation of that argument depends on a variety of semantic, syntactic and also pragmatic factors.

Our comparison of these structures with German depends to a large extent on such questions and tests as the identity of the implied subject or the presence or absence of semantic predicate-argument relations. We will therefore base our comparison on analyses which characterize the relevant semantic facts precisely in terms of the underlying (syntactic) representations of the corresponding sentences. We will say, for example, that in ⟨1a⟩ the subject of the predicate *have written* of the embedded clause is 'raised' to the subject position of the main clause and that in ⟨1c⟩ the subject of the subordinate clause is 'raised' into the main clause, so that it looks like an object of the main predicate *expect*.

The chapter is organized in accordance with the order of the examples given in ⟨1⟩–⟨3⟩: We will start with raising structures in Section 13.2. Section 13.3 contains a discussion of control phenomena as exemplified in ⟨2⟩ and Section 13.4 deals with other types of non-finite subordination, focusing on adverbial participles. A brief summary is provided in Section 13.5.

13.2 Raising

13.2.1 Raising in English

S-S raising Different types of raising can be distinguished, according to the syntactic relation of the source position and that of the target position. When both the source and the target position are subject positions, we speak of 'S-to-S raising' (or simply 'S-S raising'). Examples of this syntactic operation are given in ⟨4⟩ and ⟨5⟩. An additional difference can be made between cases like those in ⟨4⟩, where the superordinate predicate, typically an epistemic one, is in the active voice, and cases like ⟨5⟩, where the superordinate verb is in the passive voice (typically in combination with verbs of communication). Let us refer to the first type as '**modal S-S raising**' and to the second as '**reportive S-S raising**'. Reportive S-S raising corresponds to what is referred to as *nominativus cum infinitivo* in Latin grammar:

⟨4⟩ Modal S-S raising
  a. John$_i$ seems [t_i to be ill]. (verbal predicate)
  b. John$_i$ is likely [t_i to turn up late]. (adjectival predicate)
⟨5⟩ Reportive S-S raising
  John$_i$ is said [t_i to be a liar].

In the examples given above, the representational devices of 'traces' and '(referential) indices', which were introduced in Section 12, are used to symbolize the operation of raising. As pointed out in the introductory remarks to this chapter, it is assumed that the subject of the lower clause is 'raised' to the higher clause in such structures. The plausibility of such an analysis is clearly revealed if we apply certain tests to these examples. Let us take ⟨1a⟩ and ⟨4a⟩ for example. In these sentences, the whole rest of the sentence rather than a person-denoting expression is the underlying subject of verbs like *happen* or *seem*. This is clearly shown by the following paraphrases of ⟨1a⟩ and ⟨4a⟩:

⟨6⟩   a. It so happens that [I wrote that book]. (cf. ⟨1a⟩)
      b. It seems that [John is ill]. (cf. ⟨4a⟩)

Note furthermore that the following passive version of ⟨1a⟩ is equivalent to ⟨1a⟩, i.e. verbs like *happen, seem*, etc. are totally insensitive to the accompanying change in subject selection ('**voice neutrality**'), in contrast to infinitives like *John intends to write this book* (?*This book intends to be written by John*):

⟨7⟩   This book happens to have been written by me. (cf. ⟨1a⟩)

Analogous tests can be used to show that *John* is not a semantic argument or underlying syntactic argument of *said* in ⟨5⟩. While the sentence clearly does not express that 'John is said anything', the following paraphrase matches the meaning of ⟨5⟩ quite closely:

⟨8⟩   They say that [John is a liar].

The operation of 'raising' is illustrated in the form of a tree diagram in Figure 13.1.

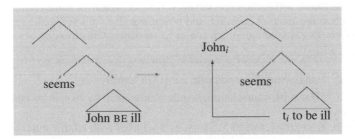

Figure 13.1 The syntactic operation of raising

S-O raising   When the source position of the raised element is that of a subject and the target position that of an object, this operation is called 'S-O raising'. These cases correspond to what is traditionally called *accusativus cum infinitivo* in the Latin grammar tradition. The class of verbs licensing S-O-raising overlaps with, but is not identical to, the one allowing reportive S-S raising:

⟨9⟩   I guarantee this$_i$ [t$_i$ to be pure malt whiskey].

A partial justification for this analysis is, again, that predicates like *expect, guarantee, believe, assume, know, understand,* etc. only take two arguments (one subject and one object) and that these underlying objects are clauses rather than simple noun phrases, as is shown by paraphrases and by translations like the following:

⟨10⟩ a. I guarantee that this is pure malt whiskey.

b. Ich garantiere, dass dies reiner Malt Whiskey ist.

O-S raising In yet another type of raising the source element is an object and the target position that of a subject. This operation is, accordingly, called '**O-S raising**' (also 'Tough Movement'), and is commonly found in the context of evaluative adjectives such as *tough, easy, difficult, boring, hard, useful, dangerous,* etc.

⟨11⟩ [This route]$_i$ is tough [to follow t_i].

Again, the syntactic subject (*this route* in ⟨11⟩) is not a semantic argument of the verb, i.e. ⟨11⟩ does not imply that 'this route is tough'.

13.2.2 A comparison of English and German

So far, we have only given examples from English. In German not all types of raising distinguished above are possible. **Modal S-S raising** is severely restricted and can be found only with a few modal verbs like *scheinen,* some change-of-state verbs such as *beginnen* or *aufhören* and nowadays also with verbs like *versprechen* and *drohen* (*Der Abend versprach schön zu werden*). Adjectives do not allow S-S raising at all:

⟨12⟩ a. Hans$_i$ schien/begann/hörte auf [t_i zu schnarchen].

b. *Hans$_i$ ist wahrscheinlich/sicher/unmöglich [t_i zu spät zu kommen].

In English, by contrast, modal S-S raising is allowed with a large number of verbs (e.g. *appear, come about, tend, fail, begin, continue*) and also with some adjectives (e.g. *likely, sure, certain,* etc.). Some English examples of S-S raising that do not have a counterpart in German are given in ⟨13⟩. Note that the correct German translations often use an adverb:

⟨13⟩ a. John happens to be my brother. ('... ist zufällig mein Bruder.')

b. 2005 proved to be a good year. ('... hat sich als gutes Jahr erwiesen.')

c. He turned out to be a liar. ('Es stellte sich heraus, dass er ...')

d. John is likely to turn up late. ('Johann kommt wahrscheinlich zu spät.')

e. This failed to convince me. ('Das hat mich nicht überzeugt.')

Reportive S-S raising is completely absent from German, while it is rather common in English and occurs with a large number of verbs of communication and cognition. The German translations of these sentences typically use a finite clause with an impersonal subject like *man* (cf. the translations in ⟨14a⟩), a paraphrase in the passive voice (cf. ⟨14b⟩) or a form of the modal verb *sollen* (cf. ⟨14c⟩):

⟨14⟩ a. John is assumed/known/believed to be a swindler.
('Man nimmt an/weiß/glaubt, dass ...')

b. John has been shown to be a swindler.
('Es ist gezeigt worden, dass ...')

c. John is said/reputed to be a swindler.
('Johann soll ein Schwindler sein.')

The structures involving **S-O raising** (*accusativus cum infinitivo*) are also absent in German while being very common in written English. In order to translate English sentences like those in ⟨15⟩ below into German, it is therefore necessary to use completely different paraphrases, usually a finite subordinate clause. The structures in ⟨16⟩, which are commonly found with verbs of perception in the two languages under consideration, are not genuine instances of raising, since the objects are also arguments of the relevant higher verbs in semantic terms, thus filling two (semantic) argument positions, as it were. For instance, *I saw him enter the room* implies both *I saw him* and (*I saw him while*) *he entered the room*, whereas *I want you to do this* does not imply *I want you*.

⟨15⟩ a. England expects every man to do his duty.

b. I find this solution to be perfectly acceptable.

c. We intend this diagram to be a summary of our main ideas.

d. I want you to do this immediately.

⟨16⟩ a. Ich sah sie kommen.

b. Ich hörte ihn kommen.

O-S raising seems to be possible in German, but it is certainly much less common than in English. It is basically restricted to the adjectives *leicht*, *schwierig/schwer*, *einfach* (cf. ⟨17a⟩) and maybe *interessant* (cf. ⟨17b⟩). But note that the following sentences could also be expansions of so-called 'modal passives' as in ⟨18⟩, as was pointed out in the introduction:

⟨17⟩ a. Das ist einfach/schwer/leicht zu verstehen.

b. Das ist interessant zu beobachten.

⟨18⟩ a. Das ist (durchaus) zu verstehen.

b. Das ist an diesem Beispiel zu beobachten.

Summary The contrasts in raising constructions between English and German are summarized in Table 13.1.

SOURCE TARGET		SUBJECT	OBJECT
SUBJ	E	modal: YES *He seems to be ill.* reportive: YES *He is said to be a drinker.*	YES *He is easy to please.*
	G	modal: YES (only few verbs) *Er scheint krank zu sein.* reportive: NO **Er wird gesagt, ein Trinker zu sein.*	YES (few adjectives) *Er ist leicht zu erfreuen.*
OBJ	E	YES *I knew him to be a liar.*	YES *I thought him easy to please.*
	G	NO **Ich wusste ihn einen Lügner zu sein.*	NO **Ich dachte ihn leicht zu erfreuen.*

Table 13.1 Raising in English and German

13.3   Control verbs and non-finite complements

As pointed out in Section 13.1, two types of control verbs can be distinguished: 'subject control verbs' and 'object control verbs'. In subject control verbs, the subject of the control verb is also the understood subject of the embedded verb, whereas in object control verbs the higher object functions as the (understood) subject of the lower verb. As ⟨19⟩ and ⟨20⟩ show, English and German exhibit completely parallel structures for both types of control. In the following examples, the (empty, understood) subject of the infinitival clause is indicated by 'PRO', which is to be distinguished from the traces ('t') used in the previous section: While 't' indicates an empty position corresponding to an element that has been moved away, no movement is assumed in control structures:

⟨19⟩   Subject control

   a. John$_i$ tried [PRO$_i$ to repair his computer].

   b. Hans$_i$ versuchte, [PRO$_i$ seinen Computer zu reparieren].

⟨20⟩   Object control

   a. John asked Fred$_i$ [PRO$_i$ to take a seat].

   b. Hans bat Fritz$_i$ [PRO$_i$ Platz zu nehmen].

13.3.1 Subject control verbs

In spite of the overall similarity between English and German in this domain, there still are some important contrasts in the behaviour of control verbs in combination with non-finite complementation (cf. Panther and Köpcke 1991, 1993, Rohdenburg 1992, among others). As far as subject control is concerned, important differences can be found in the domain of **verbs of communication and cognition**. In German, these verbs generally allow subject control, whereas most of the corresponding verbs in English cannot be complemented by infinitives (cf. ⟨21b⟩). Parallel structures are found in combination with the verbs *claim* and *profess* (cf. ⟨22⟩). Moreover, specific verbs (e.g. *think* and *presume*) may take infinitival complements when functioning as an adverbial participle, even though they may not do so when used as a main verb (cf. ⟨23⟩, from Rohdenburg 1992).

⟨21⟩   a.   Er behauptet / erklärt / bestätigt / sagt aus / vermutet / denkt / meint die Antwort zu kennen.

   b.   ??He alleges / asserts / confirms / states / supposes / suspects / thinks to know the answer.

⟨22⟩   a.   He claims to know the answer.

   b.   He professed to be a materialist.

⟨23⟩   a.   Thinking to be well-prepared for the task he asked ...

   b.   *He thought to be well-prepared for the task.

In some cases, English uses gerunds after verbs whose German counterparts take infinitival complements (cf. Rohdenburg 1992). This is particularly common in combination with **'retrospective' verbs** such as *remember, recollect, acknowledge, disclaim*, etc. and **factive verbs** like *regret, legalize, welcome*, etc. (cf. ⟨24⟩). Note that the use of a gerund is not permitted in examples such as ⟨21a⟩ above, where finite complementation is the only choice (cf. ⟨25⟩).

⟨24⟩   a.   I remember meeting you when I was a child.

   b.   I acknowledge having read and understood the information above.

   c.   I recollect wanting to cry.

⟨25⟩   a.   *He alleges / ... / thinks knowing the answer.

   b.   He alleges / ... / thinks that he knows the answer.

What these examples suggest is that English infinitives show an affinity to futurity, whereas gerunds are more strongly associated with (real) events in the past. This is not the only difference, however. As Rohdenburg (1992) has shown, infinitives are often used with positive verbs while gerunds are used with the corresponding negative verbs. This is here illustrated for the pairs *claim/disclaim* and *trust/distrust*:

⟨26⟩ a. I claim to have seen this conflict at closer range than anyone.
      (* ... having seen ...) [BNC]

   b. I disclaim having done anything of the kind.
      (*... to have done ...)

⟨27⟩ a. I trust to bring you off happily ... [BNC]

   b. I distrust being part of a self-conscious group.

13.3.2 Object control verbs

A quantitative contrast between English and German can also be observed in cases of object control. In English, object control is basically restricted to '**verbs of manipulation**' (e.g. *to ask s.o. to take a seat*), whereas in German a large number of other verbs are used with infinitival complements as well, some of which are listed in ⟨28⟩ (from Rohdenburg 1992):

⟨28⟩ *anklagen, ankreiden, beglückwünschen, benachrichtigen, bescheinigen, beschuldigen, bestätigen, bezichtigen, einreden, erklären, entschuldigen, erinnern, erzählen,* etc.

Again, the corresponding verbs of English take either gerunds or finite clauses as their complements. In combinations with gerunds there is often an additional preposition such as *of* (*accuse of -ing*) or *from* (*restrain/keep from -ing*) in ⟨29a⟩ and ⟨30a⟩:

⟨29⟩ a. They accused him of having burgled the house.

   b. Sie klagten ihn an, in das Haus eingebrochen zu sein.

⟨30⟩ a. This restrained/kept me from taking any further measures.

   b. Das hielt mich davon ab, weitere Maßnahmen zu ergreifen.

Another important contrast can be observed in the domain of 'verbs of manipulation' such as *allow* or *urge*: in German the addressee of the order or request and thus the understood subject of the embedded clause may be implicit ('**implicit controller**') while it is always expressed overtly in English (cf. ⟨31⟩ and ⟨32⟩). Such empty elements (represented as 'PRO' without an index in ⟨31a⟩) usually have an interpretation that is provided by the context. An exception to this generalization, i.e. a verb of English that does allow implicit controllers, is *help* (cf. ⟨33⟩). A list of German verbs that allow unspecified indirect objects and thus unspecified (understood) subjects in object control sentences is given in ⟨34⟩ (cf. Rohdenburg 1992). Note that in all of these examples an addressee has to be specified in English if the infinitival construction is to be used. Such specification is not necessary if noun phrases or finite clauses follow the verb:

⟨31⟩ a. Wer hat PRO erlaubt, [PRO im Haus zu rauchen]?
     b. *Who has allowed to smoke indoors? (ok: … smoking indoors?)

⟨32⟩ a. Er drängte PRO, [PRO den Gefangenen freizulassen].
     b. *He urged to free the prisoners. (ok: … that the prisoners be freed.)

⟨33⟩ Bill Clinton helped to negotiate a peace agreement for Northern Ireland.

⟨34⟩ *abhalten, abraten, anhalten, anheimstellen, anleiten, animieren, anraten, anreizen, anspornen, anstacheln, anstiften, auffordern, bewegen, bitten, drängen, einladen, empfehlen, (von der Pflicht) entbinden, erlauben,* etc.

Especially the verb *allow* is a frequent source of errors for Germans, who tend to use it in control sentences with an implicit object. In such sentences, a generic pronoun like *one* or *you* must be used in English:

⟨35⟩ a. Das neue Gesetz erlaubt PRO,
        [PRO lebensverlängernde Maßnahmen abzulehnen].
     b. The new law allows one
        [PRO to refuse life-supporting treatment].

The restrictions on implicit control are loosened somewhat in specific syntactic configurations. This situation is reminiscent of the one observed at the end of Section 13.1. For instance, the verb *advise* usually behaves like *allow* insofar as it does not permit the use of an implicit object. ⟨36a⟩ is therefore unusual, though probably not ungrammatical. However, when the NP *life jackets* is relativized, object omission becomes acceptable (cf. ⟨36b⟩). Such asymmetries have been explained in terms of the **'Complexity Principle'** by Rohdenburg (1996, 2000, 2016).

⟨36⟩ a. (?) We advise to bring life jackets along.
     b. Life jackets are included among the items (which) we advise to bring along.

13.3.3 Control shift

Verbs taking infinitival complements are not always entirely rigid with regard to their control properties. In some cases, the usual configurations are reversed, i.e. subject control verbs behave like object control verbs and vice versa. Such cases of 'control shift' are triggered by contextual information and can be found in both English and German. For instance, *promise* usually behaves like a subject control verb, but in combination with passives it may also trigger object control, and *persuade* is basically an object control verb but can also be found with subject control. Thus, ⟨37a⟩ and ⟨37b⟩ are accepted by at least some native speakers of English (cf. Panther and Köpcke 1991). Parallel German examples are given in ⟨38⟩:

⟨37⟩   a.   Bill promised Brian$_i$ [PRO$_i$ to be promoted].

         b.   Judy$_i$ persuaded Joan [PRO$_i$ to be considered for promotion].

⟨38⟩   a.   Hans verspricht Peter$_i$, [PRO$_i$ das Buch kaufen zu dürfen].

         b.   Hans$_i$ beschwört Peter, [PRO$_i$ das Buch kaufen zu dürfen].

Control shift is sensitive to semantic and structural properties of the predicates involved. As a general tendency, it is more easily allowed in German than in English. For instance, the subject control verb *versprechen* allows control shift with *bekommen* in the subordinate clause, whereas the corresponding English construction only allows the canonical control configuration (cf. ⟨39⟩). Similarly, the combination of *bitten* and *bekommen* in German allows a shift from object control to subject control, while the corresponding English structure only allows object control (cf. ⟨40⟩; see Panther and Köpcke 1991).

⟨39⟩   a.   Jürgen verspricht Harry, ein Geschenk zu bekommen.

         b.   ??John promises Harry to receive a present.

⟨40⟩   a.   Paul bittet Egon, für den Ball eine Einladung zu bekommen.

         b.   ??Paul asks Egon to receive an invitation for the ball.

Note that German has some verbs that allow both subject and object control, for instance *bestätigen*. English uses a finite complementation strategy in each case.

⟨41⟩   a.   Der Gast bestätigte dem Ober, sehr gut gegessen zu haben.
            'The guest confirmed the waiter's impression that he had eaten very well.'

         b.   Der Gast bestätigte dem Ober, ihn gut bedient zu haben.
            'The guest confirmed the waiter's impression that he had provided excellent service.'

13.3.4 Summary

To sum up this section, there are three types of contrasts between English and German in the domain of control verbs. First, in many cases German allows control structures with an infinitival complement where a gerund or finite clause has to be used in English, for instance in the case of verbs of communication and cognition (subject control) and with verbs of manipulation (object control). Secondly, in German the controller can be left implicit while this is possible only with the verb *help* in English and in specific syntactic configurations, e.g. in relative clause formation. Finally, it has been shown by Panther and Köpcke (1991) that control shift is overall more common in German than in English.

13.4 Adverbial participles and absolute participles

The preceding section was concerned with non-finite predications in specific types of complementation, i.e. with infinitives and *ing*-forms that occur in argument (valency) positions and that cannot be left out without making the sentence ungrammatical. *To know the answer* in ⟨22a⟩ and *meeting you when I was a child* in ⟨24a⟩, for example, cannot be omitted without making the sentence incomplete:

(22a) He claims to know the answer.

(24a) I remember meeting you when I was a child.

Both *ing*-forms and infinitives are also used as adjuncts, i.e. as optional constituents that can be omitted without making a sentence ungrammatical (cf. also Ch. 4). Such predications are usually referred to as '**adverbial participles**' (also 'free adjuncts', cf. ⟨35a⟩) or '**adverbial infinitives**' (cf. ⟨42b⟩). Examples of such free adjuncts are given in ⟨42⟩:

⟨42⟩ a. Coming home, John noticed that his car had been stolen.

b. I went home to make some tea.

In contrast to gerunds (cf. ⟨43a⟩), adverbial participles can also be found in German (cf. ⟨43b⟩):

⟨43⟩ a. He risked getting caught.
'Er riskierte (es), erwischt zu werden.'

b. He came into the room singing.
'Singend betrat er das Zimmer.'

In adverbial participles such as ⟨42a⟩ and ⟨43b⟩ the understood subject of the participle is again the subject of the main clause. Only in rare cases do we also find a non-subject noun phrase as the understood subject of an adverbial participle (cf. Kortmann 1991):

⟨44⟩ a. ... the Yard told them to apply to me, knowing the place and being on the spot.

b. Walking down the boardwalk, a tall building came into view.

As the examples in ⟨44⟩ show, the interpretation of the implicit subject is not always entirely fixed and needs to be inferred on the basis of contextual information. In ⟨45a⟩, for instance, the understood subject is the speakers (or more precisely, the singers), and in ⟨45b⟩ it is the whole main clause:

⟨45⟩   a. Knowing me, knowing you, it's the best we can do. (Song by Abba)

        b. Following a sharp rise last year, prices have dropped again this year.

Unlike free adjuncts, **absolute participles** always have an **overt subject** of their own. This construction is also possible in German (cf. ⟨46⟩ from Kortmann 1988), though it is certainly marginal and archaic. The same goes for the so-called *genitivus absolutus*, which is, moreover, restricted to a handful of fixed expressions (cf. ⟨47⟩).

⟨46⟩   a. (With) John driving the car, there was no need to worry.

        b. Die beiden Verliebten saßen am Caféhaustisch, ihre Hände sich sanft berührend. (Kortmann 1988: 61)

⟨47⟩   a. Wehenden Haares ritt er durch die Prärie. (*genitivus absolutus*)

        b. Erhobenen Hauptes verließ er den Raum.

Although mainly restricted to narrative fiction, **adverbial participles** are much more common in English than in German, where they are hardly used any more even in the written language. Moreover, they are by far less constrained in English if one considers the syntactic contexts licensing them (cf. Kortmann 1988). In English they are found in the active and in the passive voice, in present and in past forms, with verbal and nominal predication, with positive and negative polarity, with main verbs and auxiliary verbs, etc., whereas in German they are basically restricted to simple, unexpanded main verbal predicates, either active/present or passive/past (cf. ⟨49⟩). In German, finite adverbial clauses introduced by conjunctions are generally preferred even in those cases where adverbial participles meet the constraints mentioned above:

⟨48⟩   a. Being watched by his neighbour he decided to get dressed.
          (??'Von seinem Nachbarn beobachtet werdend ...')

        b. Having seen the great mess she was making, ...
          (??'Die große Unordnung gesehen habend ...')

        c. Being one of the oldest players of the team, he suffers injuries more often than the others.
          (??'Einer der ältesten Spieler seiend, ...')

⟨49⟩   a. Im Heuberg schlafend, wurde Karl von einer Mücke gestochen.
          (??'... geschlafen habend ...')

        b. Von seinem besten Freund verraten, verließ Alfred die Versammlung unter Protest. (??'... verraten werdend ...')

Unlike their counterparts in German, adverbial participles in English may be accompanied by a subordinating conjunction such as *while* in ⟨50b⟩:

⟨50⟩   a. I heard the children at play while watching the birds in the sky.

        b. *Ich hörte die Kinder beim Spielen während die Vögel am Himmel
            beobachtend.

Absolute participles are also extremely rare in German and even more bookish than
their English counterparts. In English both present participles and past participles
are possible, whereas only the latter are found in German:

⟨51⟩   Totenbleich lag er auf dem Bett, sein Gesicht wie zu Gips geworden.

In English, overt subjects in such constructions may be introduced by the preposition *with*, and in dialects by *what with*. In German, prepositions are neither admissible in adverbial participles nor in absolutes:

⟨52⟩   a. With Fred helping out, the party turned out to be a success.

        b. *Mit Fritz aushelfend wurde die Party ein großer Erfolg.

It is a well-known fact that, in contrast to German, present participles are not only
used in an adverbial function in English but also in a modifying function, i.e. as
reduced relative clauses:

⟨53⟩   a. The man standing over there is my father.

        b. I would like to meet the woman wearing that red dress.

In this function they often correspond to prepositions in German, as is shown by the
following examples (cf. Rohdenburg 1990):

⟨54⟩   a. . . . für Reisende mit Bahn Card
            '. . . for travellers holding Rail Cards . . . '

        b. ein Film mit Bruce Lee
            'a movie featuring/starring Bruce Lee'

        c. Mit ihm sind es sechs. 'That makes (it) six, including him.'

        d. . . . die Antwort auf die Frage an den Menschen von heute . . .
            'the answer to the question facing modern man . . . '

By using present participles in this way it is often possible to avoid the embedding
of several PPs ('**preposition stacking**'), which seems to be far less acceptable in
English than in German:

⟨55⟩   ein Buch von Professor Miller über Löwen in Afrika
        'a book written by Professor Miller on lions living in Africa'

13.5 Summary

The major contrasts pointed out in this chapter can be summarized as follows:

- Raising constructions are much more widely distributed in English than in German; English has types of raising constructions that are absent from German (reportive S-S raising, O-S raising), and those constructions that can be found in both languages (e.g. modal S-S raising, S-O raising) occur with a broader range of predicates.

- Control is more widely distributed in German than in English. In many cases, English uses finite subordinate clauses where German has a raising structure. This tendency runs counter to the general tendency of German to use more 'explicit' structures than English and has been used as a counterexample to overarching generalizations like those made by Hawkins (1986) (cf. Mair 1992, Rohdenburg 1992).

- English makes wide use of (adjunct and absolute) participles, while German prefers finite subordinate clauses in most cases. This is yet another respect in which English patterns with the Romance languages, where such structures are also frequently used.

Revision, questions and exercises

1. Discuss three central contrasts between English and German in terms of non-finite subordination and illustrate them with examples.
2. Adverbial participles may develop into prepositions. Which of the following examples are close to this use as a preposition? What are the crucial properties?

   ⟨56⟩ Ihren Wünschen entsprechend trank Karl nur noch alkoholfreies Bier.

   ⟨57⟩ Entsprechend ihren Wünschen trank Karl nur noch alkoholfreies Bier.

   ⟨58⟩ We did it, his objections notwithstanding.

   ⟨59⟩ We did it, notwithstanding his objections.

3. Do we find gerunds in German? Is it possible to predict on the basis of meaning which verbs take gerunds as objects in English and which do not?
4. On the basis of which tests can we establish that a predicate in an infinitive construction takes the whole sentence as an underlying subject?
5. What does the following pair of sentences show? Why is it remarkable?

   ⟨60⟩ a. *They alleged the president to be a liar.

         b. This is the man they alleged to be a liar.

6. Translate the following sentences into English. Which general contrast do these translations reveal?

⟨61⟩ a. Wer gab den Auftrag, den Firmenwagen zu benutzen?

b. Sie drängte, die Gefangenen zu befreien.

c. Sie verlangten, die Pressefreiheit einzuschränken.

7. Compare the distribution of infinitives in complement function in English and German. In which language are control infinitives more common? What types of structures are used in the other language to translate control infinitives?

8. Translate the following sentence into English and compare the structures used in the two languages. What type of contrast do these sentences illustrate?

⟨62⟩ Hans versprach seinem Freund, zur Abschlussfeier eingeladen zu werden.

9. What are the possible interpretations of examples like the following:

⟨63⟩ a. Tom bought the painting, not having seen it.

b. You are better off not listening to his advice.

c. He refused to stay in his office, going to the library instead.

d. Crossing the street, John entered a different country.

10. Which property is it that makes the following sentences unacceptable and deviant in the eyes of prescriptive grammarians?

⟨64⟩ a. Coming home last night, it was pouring down.

b. Watching television, the telephone rang.

c. Crossing the road, a car almost crashed into my wheel-barrow.

The following examples manifest similar problems, but are not regarded as deviant. What is the difference?

⟨65⟩ a. Following a sharp decline last year, prices have risen again this year.

b. Considering his age, Fred is still very active.

c. Even allowing for fast driving, twenty minutes was optimistic.

Further reading

Contrasts in raising constructions are discussed in some detail by Hawkins (1986). Our comparison of control phenomena is largely based on Mair (1992), Rohdenburg (1992) and Panther and Köpcke (1991, 1993). Kortmann (1991) provides an overview of non-finite subordination in English. In Kortmann (1988) the major contrasts between English and German are summarized. Contrasts in the form and interpretation of adverbial participles, absolutes and gerunds are discussed in Haspelmath and König (1995).

14 The lexicon: Content words

14.1 Problems of translation

Among the most common questions asked by beginning learners of any language is: "What does that word mean?". This question can be answered relatively easily for words like *apple*, *hammer*, or *table*, that is, for lexical items with highly specific (concrete and referential) meanings. However, such a question is more difficult to answer for words with a more general or abstract meaning. For instance, a word like *top* does not correspond to any specific German word and requires different translations according to the noun it combines with (e.g. *top of the hill*, *top of the list*, etc.). The following generalization is relatively robust: the more **general** the meaning of a word is, the more **polysemous** that word will be, and the more translational equivalents it will have in other languages. Accordingly, it is to be expected that the most striking lexical contrasts between any pair of languages will be found among words with more general meanings.

While the distinction between more specific and more general meanings – which, incidentally, needs to be kept apart from the one between abstract and concrete meanings – is gradual, a second parameter of classification allows for more categorical distinctions: we can differentiate between 'relational' and 'non-relational' (or 'absolute') meanings. The denotation of *apple*, for instance, is absolute insofar as an object can be identified as an apple without making reference to any other object. A noun like *top* on the other hand only makes sense if it is associated with another noun. Quite obviously, we expect to find more striking contrasts among the relational meanings than among the non-relational ones. What is more, some of the contrasts to be discussed in this chapter refer *primarily* to relations between elements. Some words with similar denotations basically differ in their combinatorial restrictions – which, of course, has repercussions on their 'meaning potential' as well. To illustrate this with one example, the German verb *begraben* is restricted to dead bodies, while the English verb *bury* may also be used with other types of objects (e.g. *to bury a treasure*). Consequently, the meaning of *begraben* is more specific than that of *bury* and is moreover associated with a number of connotations that *bury* lacks, for instance a coffin and a grave yard.

Let us now consider what types of difficulties may arise when we translate a given word into another language. First, there is the problem that languages use notions with different degrees of **specificity** to refer to a given object or event. In that case, we speak of '**underspecification**' in the language that uses a more general expression. Underspecification is of course a relative notion, i.e. one word is always underspecified relative to another word. For instance, German makes a distinction

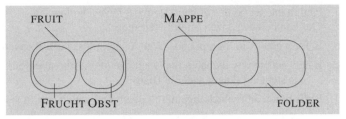

Figure 14.1 The problem of underspecification and intersection

between the count noun *Frucht* and the mass noun *Obst* which is not made in English (*fruit*). In such cases, the distribution of one word (*Obst, Frucht*) is 'a subset of' the distribution of another word (*fruit*), and we can say that *fruit* is 'underspecified relative to' both *Obst* and *Frucht*.

More typically, though, the denotations of two words from English and German '**intersect**'. For instance, the English noun *folder* translates into German as either *Mappe* or *Schnellhefter*. *Mappe*, in turn, is also used for Engl. *briefcase*. Given that there are hardly any words with exactly the same range of meaning in English and German, intersection is the situation most commonly found. The problems of underspecification and intersection are illustrated in Figure 14.1.

Closely related to the problems illustrated in Figure 14.1 is a third one which concerns **metonymical** and **metaphorical extensions** of a given meaning. Such extensions are often available in only one of the two languages. For example, *guts* is used metaphorically for 'courage' in English but not in German:

⟨1⟩   a. No team-owner had the guts to belittle a Clark or a Fangio. [BNC]
       b. He is the perfect example of what guts, honesty and tenacity get you. [BNC]

In many cases, metaphorical extensions as illustrated in ⟨1⟩ have been conventionalized, thus developing into **frozen metaphors**. For instance, *cheek* is used metaphorically with the meaning 'lack of respect', but it is more often than not used with that meaning in idiomatic expressions like *give somebody cheek* or *to have the cheek to do sth*. Moreover, there is an adjective *cheeky* which is derived from those metaphorical uses of *cheek*. Comparable idiomatic expressions can be found in German with *Stirn* (*die Stirn haben, etwas zu tun*; note, however, that *die Stirn haben* refers to a more severe offense than *have the cheek to do sth*.; cf. the difference between *frech* and *unverschämt* in German).

While in the example considered above (*cheek* vs. *Stirn*) there is still a common denominator – the use of a prominent part of the face standing for 'impertinence' – **idiomatic expressions** and **proverbs** often have to be translated by using completely different paraphrases, if they are translatable at all. Some examples are given in ⟨2⟩:

⟨2⟩   a. Paul drank six bottles of beer. He must have a hollow leg.
          'Der kann einen ganzen Stiefel vertragen.'

      b. In for a penny, in for a pound. 'Wer A sagt, muss auch B sagen.'

      c. If he wants to buy the land, that's a horse of a different colour.
          '...das steht auf einem anderen Blatt.'

      d. Birds of a feather flock together. 'Gleich und gleich gesellt sich gern.'

Problems like those pointed out above arise for any pair of languages. When we are concerned with two closely related languages like English and German, there is an additional difficulty, namely the one of '**false friends**', i.e. words that have a similar phonological make-up and typically a common etymology, but have come to differ in meaning. Notorious examples are *become* vs. *bekommen*, *stool* vs. *Stuhl*, *warehouse* vs. *Warenhaus*, *sea* vs. *See*, etc. The same problem arises in specific domains of grammar such as the use of tense forms. In particular, the English Present Perfect is very similar to the German *Perfekt*, as far as its formal make-up is concerned, but it is used in a very different way (cf. Chapter 5).

As mentioned above, interesting contrasts between English and German can be expected among meanings that are (i) relatively general, and (ii) relational rather than non-relational. The section on nouns (Section 14.2) focuses on 'classificatory' and 'partitive' nouns, both of which are relational. Some cases of underspecification and intersection will be pointed out, but no major tendencies can be identified. In other words, real world objects are structured and classified differently, but, on the whole, at more or less the same level of differentiation. The same applies to adjectives (cf. Section 14.3), even though in the domain of measure terms English has a higher number of lexical items than does German. From a historical point of view, one of the most important sources of divergence in the domain of adjectives is the development of different metaphorical extensions of identical basic meanings.

While nominal and adjectival denotations in English and German do not exhibit any major asymmetries, a relatively clear-cut contrast has been pointed out for verbs. Plank (1984) has argued that German exhibits tighter selectional restrictions and, hence, more specific meanings in some lexical fields than English. Alternatively, we could say that in German one *has to* choose a more specific meaning since no general expressions are available, whereas in English one has the choice between a highly general verb (e.g. *put*) and a set of more specific ones (*set*, *lay*, *stand*, etc.). A comparison of some English and German verbs is provided in Section 14.4.

14.2 Nouns

Given the large number of nouns in the lexicons of both German and English, it is necessary to classify these nouns in order to make more or less general comparative statements. One important parameter of classification concerns the type of entity denoted by a noun. In his work on word meanings, Leisi (1975) distinguishes five major classes of nouns: (i) abstract nouns (*peace, journey, love*, etc.); (ii) individual nouns (*man, pot, book*); (iii) collective nouns (*team, staff, fowl*); (iv) partitive nouns (*cheek, arm, rim*); and (v) privative nouns (*hole, ignorance, bareness*). These classes can, obviously, be subclassified further by refining the criteria. For instance, we can distinguish at least three types of abstract nouns (events, properties, relations), and several types of individual terms according to their form, substance, degree of specification, etc. One type of individual noun that will be relevant below is that of 'classificatory' nouns, which provide only partial descriptions of an object and generally co-occur with other nouns, in particular mass nouns. The second class of nouns that we will consider in some detail is the one of 'partitive' nouns.

Classificatory nouns describe (or 'classify') objects in terms of specific parameters like 'shape', 'consistency' or 'size' without providing a fully explicit description (*lump, heap*, etc.). They are usually used in combination with other nouns – in particular, mass nouns denoting 'material' – but may also stand by themselves. Given that objects can be classified along a great number of independent

Klumpen		
Gold	Lehm/clay	
Blut	Teig/dough	sugar
	Butter/butter	wood
	Eisen/iron	coal
lump		

Table 14.1 *Lump* vs. *Klumpen*

dimensions (the world can be 'cognitively structured' in a theoretically infinite way), it comes as no surprise that there is often a one-to-many correspondence between English and German in this domain. For instance, *Zapfen* has at least the following English translations: *cone, icicle, cork, tap, plug, faucet, bung, tenon, pin, peg, pivot, spigot, spile*, and *gudgeon* (cf. Leisi 1975: 30). One may add even more possible translations, e.g. *stud* and *journal*. Given that most of the English terms, in turn, correspond to several German words, it follows that most of the classificatory nouns of English and German have (WEAKLY) INTERSECTING denotations.

Another example discussed by Leisi is the pair of cognates *lump* and *Klumpen*, whose range of meanings is illustrated in Table 14.1 (cf. Leisi 1975: 29). As a general tendency, *Klumpen* is associated with soft, malleable substances, whereas *lump* can also be used for objects consisting of hard material (*wood, coal*). However, this example also shows that many

English → German		
pad	Bausch, Block, Ballen, Pad	
cone	Kegel, Zapfen, Tüte, Hörnchen	
pole	Stange, Pfahl, Mast, Rute	
German → English		
Ballen	bale, ball, pad	
Zapfen	cone, icicle, spigot, bung	
Stange	pole, rod, bar, stick	

Table 14.2 Classificatory nouns

classificatory nouns come with a certain, partly idiosyncratic, 'inventory' of collocates. For instance, contrary to what one would expect, *Klumpen* can be used with *Gold*, even though this may sound a bit archaic ("Dafür hab' ich einen Klumpen Gold, so groß als mein Kopf, gegeben"). Some more examples of one-to-many relationships in the domain of classificatory nouns are given in Table 14.2.

A second major class of nouns where considerable contrasts can be observed is the one of 'partitive nouns', i.e. nouns that describe only a specific part of a person or object. Such nouns often also convey information about material or substance. For instance, while the English word *top* is indifferent to the shape or substance of the relevant object, more specific nouns have to be used to translate that word into German, for instance: *(oberes) Ende*, *Spitze*, *(Berg)gipfel*, and *Wipfel* (from the PONS dictionary). This seems to be a case of underdifferentiation in English. The converse situation can be found with the German word *Rand*, which has a very general meaning and translates as *brim*, *edge*, *top*, *border*, *margin*, or *mark* into English, depending on the material and form of the relevant object. Most of those English terms, in turn, are likewise polysemous and cannot be translated one-to-one into German (e.g. *edge*, which translates as *Rand*, *Ufer*, *Schwelle*, *Schneide*, *Kante*). Such one-to-many relationships holding between English and German are illustrated in Table 14.3.

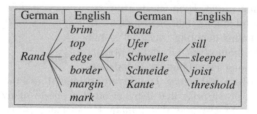

Table 14.3 Partitive nouns in English and German

14.3 Adjectives

Like nouns, adjectives can be grouped into several subclasses. First, they can be classified along the same dimensions as nouns. This parallelism follows naturally from the fact that adjectives are usually regarded as denoting sets of entities. Some adjectives describe **concrete** objects (*hard*, *tall*, *blue*, etc.), while others describe **abstract** notions (*eternal*, *interesting*, etc.), and yet others may be used with either class of noun (*long*, *nice*, *useful*, etc.). This last class of adjectives often results from a **metaphorical extension** of concrete meanings to abstract ones. For instance, *long* was first used with a physical meaning and only later acquired the temporal use. As far as parallels and contrasts between English and German are concerned, we can consequently expect to find different types of (abstract) metaphorical extensions for adjectives that have more or less the same concrete meanings.

Prima facie, the English adjective **hard** seems to correspond closely to the German adjective *hart*. On closer scrutiny, however, it turns out that Engl. *hard* exhibits a number of abstract uses which Germ. *hart* lacks. Consider the following examples:

⟨3⟩   a. This is very hard to do. ('schwer', 'schwierig')
      b. I had a very hard time. ('eine schwere/anstrengende Zeit')
      c. It was a hard blow for her. ('ein schwerer Schlag')
      d. Give it a hard push! ('einen kräftigen Stoß')
      e. Don't be so hard on him! ('streng mit')
      f. I have hard evidence for it! ('sichere Beweise')

As is illustrated in ⟨3a⟩–⟨3c⟩, *hard* often translates as *schwer* into German, which, in turn, has a number of uses that its English (physical) correlate *heavy* lacks:

⟨4⟩   a. Ich habe schwere Bedenken! ('serious concerns')
      b. Du hast einen schweren Fehler gemacht! ('a serious/big mistake')
      c. Das sind schwere Schicksale. ('Those are tragic cases.')

While the adjectives exemplified above relate to 'adversative' states of affairs, their antonyms are often used to describe 'favourable' circumstances, e.g. *leicht* in German (cf. ⟨5⟩) and *soft* in English (cf. ⟨6⟩):

⟨5⟩   a. eine leichte Aufgabe ('an easy task')
      b. eine leichte Verletzung ('a minor injury')
      c. Nichts leichter als das! ('Nothing could be simpler/easier.')

⟨6⟩   a. a soft teacher ('ein gutmütiger Lehrer')
      b. soft liberalism ('gemäßigter Liberalismus')
      c. a soft job ('ein bequemer Job')

As has been shown, the diverging metaphorical developments of originally concrete or physical notions have given rise to adjectives with intersecting denotations, the common denominator usually being the concrete uses. In one particular class of adjectives, however, there is a noticeable asymmetry between English and German even among the concrete uses: namely, in the class of '**dimensional adjectives**' or 'measure terms' like *small* or *big*. In German the typical situation is that the relevant adjectives are arranged in pairs of gradable antonyms that describe two ends of a scale, and there are only a few such pairs (cf. ⟨7⟩). Note that the terms *groß* and *klein* have a very broad range of application and can often substitute for the more specific terms. For instance, *ein hoher Leuchtturm* is also *ein großer Leuchtturm* and *eine breite Straße* is also *eine große Straße*.

⟨7⟩   a. groß – klein
      b. hoch – tief
      c. breit – schmal
      d. lang – kurz

Some such pairs of antonyms are also available in English (*long – short, broad – narrow*), but for a more general indication of the size there are more than just two adjectives, so one German word often corresponds to two or more English terms, e.g.: (i) *groß* → *big, great, large* (also *grand*, e.g. in *grand coalition*), and (ii) *klein* → *small, little*. The question arises which of these adjectives has to be chosen if one translates Germ. *groß* or *klein* into English. The *Longman Dictionary of Contemporary English* contains the following recommendations for *groß*:

- *big* and *large* are synonyms but *large* is more formal (*a big/large house*)
- *large* is used with quantity words (*a large sum, a large amount*, etc.)
- *great* is associated with a (positive) evaluation and is not usually used to refer to the mere size of an object (*a great scholar*)
- *great* is used with length, height and age (*a great height*)

According to these guidelines, a distinction can be made between the basically 'physical' adjectives *big* and *large*, on the one hand, and *great* on the other, which is often speaker-evaluative (cf. Germ. *großartig*). Moreover, *great* is sometimes semantically stronger than *big* or *large*. *A great mistake* is worse than *a big mistake*, and *a great earthquake* is more severe than *a large earthquake*. The following sentence was found on the webpage of the *California Geological Survey*:

⟨8⟩　Although the San Bernadino strand apparently did not generate ground ruptures during the 1857 earthquake ... it should be viewed as a fault capable of generating large or even great earthquakes.[1]

The difference between *big* and *large* is often said to be one of register. However, there also seem to be some purely collocational restrictions. With quantity words *large* is usually preferred: *a large number* is more natural than *a big number*, and the same asymmetry can be observed in combination with the nouns *part, proportion, amount, quantity, extent*, and *sum*. A second difference concerns uses of adjectives that we may call **'epithetic'**, where an adjective is not used to distinguish a given referent from other referents but describes a salient intrinsic attribute of a referent such as: *the big bang, the big toe, a big boy, a big freak*, or *big brother*.

A similar difficulty arises for speakers of German when referents or objects with a large **vertical extension** are described in English. In German, we can often use either *hoch* or *groß*, while in English we have to decide between *big, tall*, and *high*. The *Longman Dictionary of Contemporary English* describes the use of the English terms as follows: *tall* refers to a long vertical dimension (*a tall person, a tall tree*); *a big person* is not merely tall but also fat or strong; and *high* is used to measure the distance from the ground to the top of an object and can thus also be used to measure the distance between a hanging object and some point of reference:

⟨9⟩　The sword of Damocles is hanging high above my head.

---

[1]　https://geomaps.wr.usgs.gov/archive/scamp/html/scg_saf_sbmtns.html, acc. on 17/05/18.

14.4 Verbs

While in the two lexical classes considered above no major asymmetries between English and German could be determined – though there are some significant contrasts in particular domains of the lexicon – the class of verbs seems to exhibit more general differences. English tends to have relatively unspecific verb meanings in comparison to German. This is not to say that most of the distinctions made in German cannot be expressed in English, since English has a more specialized vocabulary as well. However, English *allows* the use of general expressions in some contexts where German *requires* the use of a more specific verb.

Some of the contrasts to be discussed in this section can be regarded as the result of **French influence**. This applies particularly to verbs of movement. As is well-known (cf. Talmy 1975, 1985), Romance languages tend to lexicalize the *direction* of movement together with the fact of motion, while Germanic languages focus on the *manner* of movement and encode the direction in prepositions or particles. Since English has lexical items from both language families, it is to be expected that we will find both 'manner of motion' and 'direction of motion' verbs, while German lexicalizes only the manner of motion in the great majority of cases.

A further striking contrast to be discussed in this section concerns the co-occurrence restrictions associated with verbs from specific classes. Many German verbs are restricted to arguments with specific inherent properties where English typically does not manifest the relevant restrictions. This, again, leads to a higher number of lexical differentiations in German.

14.4.1 Some cases of underspecification in English

English has a number of verbs that do not correspond to any particular German verb but require different translations according to the context:

⟨10⟩   a.   to put – setzen, stellen, legen

         b.   to know – kennen, wissen, können

         c.   to leave – lassen, verlassen, überlassen, abreisen, abfahren, gehen

         d.   to stop – aufhören, halten, stehen bleiben, innehalten (itr.); aufhalten, anhalten (tr.)

As far as verbs of '**change of position**' are concerned (*put*), German differentiates according to the shape and the resultant position of the object between three verbs. *Stellen* is used for objects with a prominent vertical dimension that are located upright, while *legen* is appropriate if the prominent vertical dimension is in a horizontal position. However, the difference is actually a bit more subtle than that.

Stellen is also used for 'canonical' configurations while *legen* (or the corresponding stative/intransitive verb *liegen*) indicates a non-canonical situation:

⟨11⟩ a. Er stellte (??legte) die Pfanne auf den Herd.
      b. Er legte (??stellte) die Pfanne auf den Müllhaufen.

Moreover, a distinction is made between objects that are put loosely on some other object (*legen*) as opposed to objects that are placed firmly (*setzen*):

⟨12⟩ a. das Buch ins Regal stellen/legen/??setzen
      'to put the book on the shelf'
      b. einen Legostein auf einen anderen setzen/*stellen/??legen
      'to put one piece of Lego on top of another'
      c. einen Stein auf einen anderen legen/*setzen/*stellen
      'to put one stone on top of another'

There is no denying that English has more specific verbs as well, in particular *to stand*, *to set* and *to lay*. These verbs can be used when more specificity is intended on the part of the speaker. In German, no semantically general verb like *put* is available and speakers of German always have to make a choice between *setzen*, *stellen* and *legen*. (Note that the verb *tun* is sometimes used in more informal speech in a way more or less parallel to English *put*: *Tu das mal auf den Tisch*; however, *tun* is only used for loose types of contact, so *??Tu den Legostein auf den anderen* is unacceptable in adult language.)

Similar asymmetries can be observed for the other verbs illustrated in ⟨10⟩ above. While *know* has both a modal and a non-modal use (ability vs. knowledge), German differentiates between the modal and the non-modal meanings (modal *können*[2] vs. non-modal *wissen/kennen*). Moreover, among the non-modal uses there is a selectional restriction concerning the type of the object: *wissen* is used with propositional objects, while *kennen* is used when the object denotes a person or a thing. With abstract nouns both *kennen* and *wissen um* are possible (e.g. *Ich weiß um/kenne diese Problematik*). *Leave* and *stop* are likewise verbs with highly general meanings that do not have a counterpart in German.

14.4.2 Directed motion and manner of movement

While English has both 'manner of movement' verbs and 'directed motion' verbs, the great majority of German verbs of motion are 'manner of motion' verbs. It is therefore difficult to translate verbs like the following into German: *enter*, *pass*, *raise*, and *rise*:

---

[2] *Können* is often used with ellipsis of the main verb, e.g. *Er kann English* (*sprechen*).

⟨13⟩ a. to enter the house – das Haus betreten
the bullet entered his brain – die Kugel trat in sein Gehirn ein
to enter the army – in die Armee eintreten
(from the Longman DCE)

b. We passed a group of students. – Wir liefen / fuhren / ruderten / rannten
etc. an einer Gruppe von Studenten vorbei.

c. He raised his torch. – Er hob seine Fackel höher.
They raised the prices. – Sie hoben die Preise an.
They raised their eyes. – Sie blickten nach oben.

Obviously, in English we can also use 'manner of movement' verbs or neutral verbs such as *go* to express the meanings illustrated in ⟨13⟩. For instance, we can say *go into* instead of *enter*, or *walk past* instead of *pass*. Moreover, there are also singular instances of 'directed motion' verbs in German. One such verb is *überqueren*, which corresponds quite closely to Engl. *cross* (cf. ⟨14a⟩). On the whole, however, such verbs are very rare in German (for instance, the verb *kommen* is neutral with respect to the manner of motion).

⟨14⟩ a. Sie überqueren/durchschwammen den Kanal.
('They crossed the channel.')

b. Sie überqueren/liefen über die Straße.
('They crossed the street.')

14.4.3 Co-occurrence restrictions

The co-ocurrence restrictions associated with specific verbs are the topic of a comprehensive contrastive analysis carried out by Plank (1984). In an attempt to generalize over English-German contrasts, he mentions that "some languages (such as German) have more instances of semantic agreement between verbs and objects than others (such as English)" (Plank 1984: 305). In other words, he claims that English manifests fewer distinctions in the selection of objects than does German. He points out the following contrasts, among others:

- German differentiates in the selection of verbs between **affected** and **effected** objects while English does not make any such distinction;
- among the **verbs of 'dressing'** German expresses more differentiations than English according to the piece of clothing and its position on the body;
- in some verb classes German distinguishes between **human** and **non-human objects** in its selection of verbs where English does not make any such distinction (verbs of 'killing' or 'dying', 'burying', 'teaching', 'breaking').

14.4.4 Affected vs. effected objects

It is one peculiarity of German (when compared to English) that it distinguishes between objects that come into existence as a result of an action ('effected' objects, Germ. *effiziert*) as opposed to those that exist already and are merely affected by the action ('affected' objects, Germ. *affiziert*). A relevant minimal pair is given in ⟨15⟩:

⟨15⟩   a.   Ich habe ein Bild gemalt. (effected)
           b.   Ich habe das Buch bemalt. (affected)

The differentiation between affected and effected objects is relevant to a number of rules such as, for instance, the use of 'free datives' (cf. also Chapter 8): while reflexive pronouns can be used with verbs describing effected objects, this use is often deviant with affected objects:

⟨16⟩   a.   Er hat sich eine Suppe gebraut. (effected object)
           b.   ?Er hat sich ein/sein/das Auto gewaschen. (affected object)

More often than not, the members of minimal pairs like the one illustrated in ⟨15⟩ are **derivationally related** to each other, and the affected members of the opposition are often derived from the effected ones by the addition of a prefix (cf. ⟨17⟩). In some cases, the difference is also expressed by using different lexical items (e.g. *entdecken* vs. *erfinden*, cf. ⟨18⟩).

⟨17⟩   a.   (einen Tunnel) graben – (einen Schatz) aus-graben
           b.   (ein Bild) malen – (eine Wand) be-/an-malen
           c.   (ein Loch) brennen – (ein Stück Holz) an-/ver-brennen
⟨18⟩   a.   Kolumbus hat Amerika entdeckt. (affected object)
           b.   Johannes Kunkel hat das Rubinglas erfunden. (effected object)

The difference between objects that exist independently of the action denoted by the verb and those that do not is also relevant for the distinction between *meiden* and *vermeiden* in German, in contrast to English *avoid*. *Meiden* is used for avoiding a situation that happens independently, whereas *vermeiden* describes an action that avoids the emergence of a situation in the first place:

⟨19⟩   a.   Ich habe die Schlägerei meiden können.
           b.   Ich habe die Schlägerei vermeiden können.

Thus, the general difference between English and German is that the differentiation between the two types of verbs pointed out above is not made in English. Plank provides the following examples to illustrate this point:

⟨20⟩   a.   to dig a tunnel – einen Tunnel graben

          b.   to dig potatoes – Kartoffeln aus-graben

⟨21⟩   a.   to paint a picture – ein Bild malen

          b.   to paint the wall – die Wand streichen (an-/be-malen)

⟨22⟩   a.   to burn a brick – einen Ziegel brennen

          b.   to burn coal – Kohle ver-brennen

Note finally that the contrast illustrated in this section is tightly connected to a difference in **aktionsart** ('actionality', 'mode of action'; cf. Chapter 5): while 'effected' objects are the result of an action and the relevant verbs are consequently accomplishments, in Vendler's (1967) terms, the corresponding verbs taking 'affected' objects are activities (i.e. actions without an inherent starting or end point).

14.4.5 Verbs of dressing

While English has one pair of words that may be used with virtually any type of clothes to describe an action of dressing or undressing – **put on** vs. **take off** – Standard German uses a large number of verbs for such actions, mostly particle verbs (cf. Table 14.4, with some examples from Plank 1984: 314; note that Low German has a pair of verbs parallel to those of English, i.e. *antrekken* and *uttrekken*).

German		English
verb	object	verb
anziehen	*Mantel, Handschuhe, Schuhe, Socken, Kleid, Hemd, Hose, Schürze, BH, Anzug,* etc.	*put on*
aufsetzen	*Hut, Krone, Perücke, Maske, Brille, Kapuze, Kopfhörer,* etc.	
anlegen	*Robe, Ornat, Rüstung (Panzer), Orden, Ohrringe, Schmuck,* etc.	
umbinden	*Krawatte, Kopftuch, Gürtel, Armbanduhr,* etc.	
umlegen	*Stola, Halskette,* etc.	
anstecken	*Ring, Brosche,* etc.	

Table 14.4 German verbs of dressing

The choice of the German verb depends on several factors: the type of garment, its position (*aufsetzen* for anything that 'sits on' the head, *anlegen* for things loosely attached to the body, etc.), or the type of activity (*umbinden* for pieces of clothing that need to be tied). A general verb like *put on* in English is not available, and speakers of German always have to choose one of the more specific verbs. Sometimes more than one option is possible:

⟨23⟩   Make-up auftragen/auflegen, einen Gürtel umschnallen/anlegen

14.4.6 Verbs requiring human objects

In some lexical fields German differentiates between predications with a human object and ones with a non-human object. The classes of verbs dealt with by Plank include verbs of 'killing' and 'dying', verbs of 'burying' and verbs of 'teaching'. Some relevant examples are given in Table 14.5.

German		English
human object	non-human object	
abschlachten, niedermetzeln, massakrieren	*schlachten*	*slaughter*
bestatten, beisetzen, beerdigen, begraben	*vergraben*	*bury*
ausbilden, unterrichten, anleiten	*abrichten, dressieren*	*teach, train, educate*

Table 14.5 Human vs. non-human objects in German

Note that the difference between human and non-human objects is not the only one responsible for the one-to-many relationship between the English and the corresponding German verbs. A second contrast, again, concerns *aktionsart*: many verbs listed in Table 14.5 describe telic events (e.g. *ausbilden*) while other members of the same group denote activities (*unterrichten* and *anleiten*). All these verbs translate as *teach* into English.

14.5 Summary

The 'structural organization' of the lexicon is similar in English and German. This comes as no surprise, considering the close genetic relationship between these languages. Languages may differ considerably in the number and types of parts of speech that they distinguish, in the proportion of nominal or verbal elements, the 'division of labour' between the various word classes, etc., but in general, Indo-European languages are rather similar in this respect, still reflecting the common genetic heritage. And yet, a few – relatively specific – contrasts can even be observed between such closely related languages as English and German. The information encoded in motion verbs has been shown to differ systematically between Romance and Germanic languages (Talmy 1975, 1985), and English exhibits some direction-of-motion verbs as are typically found in Romance languages, while German has preserved the Germanic pattern. In general, there seems to be a tendency for English to use more general verbs in some lexical fields, and to exhibit looser selectional restrictions than German (cf. Plank 1984), but once again it should be pointed out that such contrasts have to be taken with a grain of salt. We have furthermore tried to identify types of lexical items typically giving rise to difficulties for foreign languages learners, e.g. classificatory and partitive nouns. Moreover, different types of metaphorical extensions are often responsible for the emergence of 'false friends', and adjectives whose meanings vary with the head noun may acquire different meanings in English and German despite a basically identical content (e.g. *eine große Frau* vs. *a big woman*).

Revision, questions and exercises

1. Find three examples of classificatory nouns (not mentioned in the book) from both English and German which have at least three different translations in the other language.
2. Search for occurrences of *top* in the BNC and translate a random sample of ten occurrences into German.
3. Adjectives with concrete meanings often differ in terms of their metaphorical extensions to abstract meanings. How many abstract meanings can you distinguish for *heavy* and *schwer*? Give examples!
4. Search the BNC for *leave* and translate ten randomly chosen occurrences into German. How many different translations do you find?
5. Find five pairs of words from English and German (not mentioned in this book) that differ only in terms of the parameter 'affected' vs. 'effected' objects.

Further reading

There are very few studies dealing with contrasts in the inventory of content words of English and German. Leisi (1975) analyzes a few of such contrasts in the context of a more general discussion of word meanings. Plank (1984) has pointed out the contrasts in the domain of verb meanings discussed in Sections 14.4.3–14.4.6.

15 Compounding

15.1 Introduction

Three types of word formation are commonly distinguished, **compounding, derivation** and **conversion**. In theory, these processes are easily differentiated. In compounding, lexemes (free morphemes) are combined into new lexical items; in derivation a lexeme combines with a bound morpheme to form a new lexeme; and in conversion a lexeme is derived from another lexeme without any visible change of form. Typical examples are given in $\langle 1 \rangle$–$\langle 3 \rangle$.

$\langle 1 \rangle$ compounding
      $[\text{arm}_N \text{ chair}_N]_N$

$\langle 2 \rangle$ derivation
      $[[\text{context}_N\text{-ual}]_A\text{-ize}]_V$

$\langle 3 \rangle$ conversion
      Teacher training needs to $[\text{bridge}_N]_V$ the gap between theory and practice.

While this three-way distinction appears to be reasonably simple, it is in fact an idealization, and there are many cases which cannot easily be assigned to any of the three types. For example, so-called 'neoclassical compounds' (e.g. *bio-metry*, *Anglo-phile*, etc.) are notoriously difficult to classify, as they exhibit properties of both compounding and derivation (cf. Plag 2003: 134ff.). Similarly, the verbal particles of German – alternatively called 'separable prefixes' (cf. Chapter 16) – like *auf* and *ab* in $\langle 4 \rangle$ and $\langle 5 \rangle$ are traditionally regarded as derivational elements, and are orthographically treated as parts of their hosts, even though they behave phonologically and syntactically like words, e.g. insofar as they carry primary stress and are separated from their hosts in main clauses:

$\langle 4 \rangle$ Als der alte Mann das Buch aufschlug, ...
      (particle and verb are adjacent)

$\langle 5 \rangle$ Der alte Mann schlug nachdenklich das Buch auf.
      (particle and verb are separated)

Finally, the process of conversion is not without problems either. One of the difficulties is that in many cases it is not clear what is derived from what. While it is reasonable to assume that the verb *bridge* in $\langle 3 \rangle$ is derived from the noun *bridge* – a process that could be regarded as involving a silent derivational suffix or 'zero morpheme' (e.g. $[\text{bridge-}\emptyset_{N \to V}]_V$, cf. Marchand 1969) – in other cases the direction of conversion is more difficult to determine. For instance, if we assume that the verb *love* and the homophonous noun are related to each other via conversion, which of the words is 'basic' and which one is 'derived'? Even though several criteria have been discussed as diagnostics for the direction of derivation – for example, semantic transparency or predictability, historical developments and frequency patterns – this problem has not so far received an adequate solution (cf. Plag 2003: Sect. 5.1).

From a typological point of view, the question of what is derived from what in cases of multicategorial lexical items like *love* appears in a different light. Languages differ in the degrees to which their lexical items are specified with respect to syntactic class membership (cf. Lehmann 2008). In extreme cases, lexical items can be used in any type of syntactic environment, and their interpretation will be a function of the context. For example, Classical Chinese had many such 'precategorial' roots (cf. Bisang 2008). The word *xìn* could be interpreted as a transitive verb meaning 'believe (sth.)', as an intransitive verb with the same meaning, or as a noun 'belief', depending on whether it took up the position of an argument or of a predicate, and on whether or not there was a second argument in the latter case.

The assumption of 'precategoriality' in the lexicon, or of different degrees of 'category determinacy', 'categorial specificity', or simply **'categoriality'** (cf. Lehmann 2008), allows us to avoid the direction-of-conversion problem in our comparative study. Rather than assuming that the verb *love* is derived from the noun *love* or vice versa (cf. ⟨6⟩), we can regard both words as instantiating an underspecified root or stem, with the exact categorical features being specified syntactically (cf. ⟨7⟩).

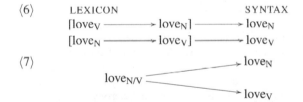

It should be mentioned, however, that from a lexical-semantic point of view the assumption of precategoriality does not solve all problems. In particular, it cannot explain why multicategorial roots like *bridge* tend to be semantically highly specialized, i.e. why their specific interpretation is relatively context invariant. When focusing on matters of morphology, the precategoriality assumption nevertheless provides a useful frame of reference. As already mentioned, the degree to which lexical roots and stems are specified with respect to syntactic class membership has been shown to be a parameter of cross-linguistic variation by Lehmann (2008). German exhibits a considerably higher degree of lexical categoriality than English. If we remove inflectional endings from German nouns, verbs or adjectives, we can, in most cases, still tell whether the relevant item is a noun or a verb. For example, the verbal stem *wüt-* ('fury') differs from the nominal stem *Wut* ('rage'). This is not of course to say that German does not have categorically underspecified lexical items. For example, the root *rauch-* ('smoke') is used both as a verb and as a noun. However, the number of such elements seems to be much lower in German than in English, according to Lehmann (2008).

As will be seen throughout this and the following chapter, the general difference with respect to the typological parameter of lexical categoriality has various consequences for the lexical-morphological properties of English and German. The relatively high frequency of conversion in English (in comparison to German) is the most obvious consequence of this difference, but it is not the only one. For example, the fact that it is very difficult to even define criteria for the distinction between compounding and the formation of syntactic phrases in English, while German differentiates relatively clearly between lexical morphology and syntax, is also due to the fact that English makes less categorical distinctions in its lexicon to begin with.

In addition to the three 'major' lexical-morphological processes mentioned above there are some 'minor' ones that will not figure prominently in our discussion. In '**incorporation**' an object is integrated morphologically into the verb. This process does not figure prominently in grammatical descriptions of English or German, even though the latter language allows it regularly. Objects like *Klavier* and *Apfel* as in ⟨8⟩ have a generic or plural interpretation. In particular, *Apfelessen* does not mean that a single apple was eaten.

⟨8⟩   a.   Beim Klavier-spiel-en schloss Helmut immer die Augen.

       b.   Beim Apfel-ess-en wurde ihm immer schlecht.

While incorporation is common in German, especially in the spoken language, there is no structural counterpart to that operation in English. Given that there is not much more we can say about this type of morphological process, we will not discuss the topic any further. Similarly, we have nothing to say about other 'minor' processes of word formation such as clippings, blends, alphabetisms, acronyms, etc. It seems to us that English and German do not exhibit any noticeable contrasts in these domains.

15.2   Types of compounds

Four major categories participate in compounding processes, i.e. verbs, nouns, adjectives and prepositions or particles, which we subsume under the more general category 'P' (cf. also Chapter 16 on the relationship between particles and prepositions). Theoretically, there are thus sixteen types of compounds. Table 15.1 shows some relevant examples from English and German (cf. Plag 2003: 143 for a similar table).

	N	A	V	P
N	air-mail	day-long	breast-feed	–
	Luft-post	tage-lang	eis-lauf-en	–
A	blue-berry	bitter-sweet	deep-freeze	–
	Blau-beere	süß-sauer	tief-kühl-en	–
V	blow-lamp	fail-safe	copy-edit	–
	Löt-lampe	brüh-heiß	bau-spar-en	–
P	after-shock	(under-researched)	over-cast	with-in
	Nach-beben	(unter-erforscht)	über-deck-en	an-bei

Table 15.1 Types of compounds in English and German

Even though most of the cells in Table 15.1 are filled, the range of common word formation processes in English and German is actually quite restricted, and many of the processes represented in Table 15.1 are marginal at best. Combinations involving prepositions are mostly unproductive and often entirely lexicalized. P-A-combinations like *under-researched* and *unter-erforscht* are put in parentheses because the adjectival components are deverbal. Note, however, that the corresponding verbs **under-research* and **unter-erforschen* do not exist, so that the assumption of P-A-compounding is not totally unwarranted.

Table 15.1 only contains **binary compounds**, i.e. compounds consisting of just two elements. The number of elements typically found in compounds represents a contrast between English and German. English compounds are mostly binary, and examples with more than two elements (like *university teaching award*) are not numerous. In German, such **recursive compounds** are rather common and cause difficulties for learners of that language. In *The Awful German Language*, Mark Twain complains about "these long things", which he considers "hardly legitimate words, but rather combinations of words", mentioning examples like *Waffenstill-standsunterhandlungen* and *Generalstaatsverordnetenversammlungen*.

Studies of compounding normally distinguish between two types of compounds that differ in their 'headednesss', i.e. endocentric and exocentric ones. **Endocentric compounds** denote subclasses of the entities denoted by their heads. In German and English, as well as in other Germanic languages, the head normally occurs in a final position. All examples given in Table 15.1 are of this type, i.e. they denote special cases of the denotation of their right members. For instance, a blueberry is a type of berry, a blow lamp is a type of lamp, etc. Under this criterion, even so-called 'copulative' compounds such as *bitter-sweet*, which denote conjunctions of properties, are endocentric, as anything that is bitter-sweet is also sweet.

Even though compounding is largely endocentric in Germanic languages, there are also examples of **exocentric compounds**. In particular, a relatively high number of V-N-compounds like *break-water* or *pick-pocket* can be found in English (cf.

Section 15.5), a type of compound which is pervasive in the Romance languages. A breakwater is not a type of water, but a device that breaks water, and a pickpocket is not a type of pocket. As will be seen, the relatively high number of such exocentric compounds in English is a consequence of language contact with French. V-N-compounds thus provide an example of contrasts between English and German that have resulted from differences in 'external' language history.

The majority of compounds found in dictionaries, databases (e.g. the CELEX-database)[1] and texts are nominal compounds, mostly of type N-N, V-N or A-N. We will therefore focus on these compounds in the following discussion, starting with A-N-compounds in Section 15.3. Section 15.4 deals with N-N-compounds, and Section 15.5 with V-N-compounds. In Section 15.6, some minor types of compounds are discussed and Section 15.7 contains some concluding remarks.

15.3 A-N-compounds

A-N-compounds represent a relatively minor pattern in both languages under consideration, and we will restrict ourselves to a few general comments on differences between English and German here. In general, A-N-compounding appears to be more productive in German than in English. German A-N-compounds often correspond to either syntactic phrases or compounds with irregular (i.e. righthand) stress in English (cf. Section 15.4). Some examples are given in ⟨9⟩.

⟨9⟩   a. [Weiß$_A$-wein$_N$]$_N$ [white$_A$ wine$_N$]$_{NP}$
       b. [Voll$_A$-mond$_N$]$_N$ [full$_A$ moon$_N$]$_{NP}$
       c. [Dick$_A$-darm$_N$]$_N$.   [large$_A$ intestine$_N$]$_{NP}$

As a general tendency, A-N-compounds appear to be more widespread in German than in English. This tendency can reasonably be explained on the basis of economy considerations. In English, there is little difference between an A-N-compound and a [A N]-phrase. In German, A-N-compounds are structurally simpler than [A N]-phrases, as the adjective does not carry inflection in the former class. For example, *Weißwein* only has four forms, i.e. *(der/den/dem)Weißwein*, *(des) Weißweins*, *(die/der) Weißweine* and *(den) Weißweinen*. By contrast, there are many possible combinations of an adjective and a noun, e.g. *(der) weiße Wein, weißer Wein, (den/dem) weißen Wein, weißem Wein, (des) weißen Weines*, to mention just the singular forms. Compounds have the structural 'advantage' of dispensing with adjectival inflection, thus providing a motivation for their use. Since in English adjectives do not inflect in attributive position, no comparable 'advantage' arises here.

---

1   Available online at http://celex.mpi.nl/.

15.4 N-N-compounds

The most important formal difference between nominal compounds in English and German has to do with the degrees of 'lexical categoriality' exhibited by the languages under investigation (cf. Section 1): in German, compounds form a natural class and are thus much more clearly identifiable as such than in English. There are two criteria for the identification of compounds in German, a morphological one and a phonological one. From a morphological point of view, German N-N-compounds are often (though not always) characterized by a specific type of 'morphological epenthesis', i.e. the insertion of a segment – a coronal consonant or schwa – between the components of a compound. We will call such segments '**compound linkers**', corresponding to the German term *Fugenlaute* (lit. 'joint-sounds') or *Fugenelemente* ('joint-elements').

As mentioned above, compound linkers occur in many, but by no means all nominal compounds. Their occurrence is (basically) phonologically conditioned, but there are also idiosyncrasies and exceptions (cf. Fuhrhop 1998, Wegener 2006). Compound linkers are often mistaken for inflectional endings of the first element of a compound, in particular for plural or genitive endings. This popular view is supported by examples where the relevant compounds can in fact be analysed in this way, as in ⟨10⟩.

⟨10⟩   a.   Studentenbude   →   die Bude [eines/von Studenten]$_{GEN.SG.PL}$

        b.   Tagesmitte   →   die Mitte [des Tages]$_{GEN}$

        c.   Geisterstunde   →   die Stunde [der Geister]$_{GEN.PL}$

However, many examples of nominal compounds cannot be so analysed. The following examples have been taken from Wegener (2006):

⟨11⟩   a.   Schokolade-n-sauce   →   Sauce von Schokoladen?

        b.   Hölle-n-tor   →   Tor der Höllen?

        c.   Erde-n-rund   →   das Runde der Erden?

Formally, the *n*-sounds in ⟨11⟩ could be regarded as plural markers, but the first elements do not allow for a plural interpretation. In ⟨12⟩, the constituents resulting from a combination of the first element with the compound linker does not even correspond to a form of the relevant noun:

⟨12⟩   a.   Aussicht-s-turm (*Aussichts)

        b.   Anstand-s-besuch (*Anstands)

        c.   Aufsicht-s-rat (*Aufsichts)

Even though compound linkers cannot simply be analyzed as inflectional endings, they are invariably made up of some consonant which is also used in nominal inflection and/or schwa. The former class comprises the coronals /n/ and /s/ as well as /r/, which is uvular in articulatory terms but behaves like a coronal distributionally. The examples in ⟨13⟩ illustrate the use of schwa in compound linkers:

⟨13⟩   a.   Kind-es-traum
       b.   Hund-e-hütte

Given that many compounds do not involve compound linkers (e.g. *Bahn-fahrt* vs. *Boot-s-fahrt*), the presence of these segments is a sufficient but not necessary condition for compound status. In this respect they differ from the second formal reflex of compound status in German, i.e. **lefthand stress**: in German, compounds are invariably stressed on the first element. In other words, lefthand stress is both a necessary and a sufficient condition for compounding. The second element of the compound retains a secondary stress. The examples given in ⟨10⟩ above are thus stressed as shown in ⟨14⟩.

⟨14⟩   a.   Stu.ˈden.ten.ˌbu.de
       b.   ˈTa.ges.ˌmit.te
       c.   ˈGeis.ter.ˌstun.de

Given the unequivocal criterion of lefthand stress and the presence of compound linkers as an additional morphological criterion, N-N-compounds form a clearly defined class in German. By contrast, in English nominal compounds are much more difficult to identify as such. Starting with the morphological properties, there are no compound linkers. The elements of a compound are simply juxtaposed. Any segment between the elements of a compound is either a genuine plural or a genitive ending, and is interpreted as such, as in ⟨15⟩.

⟨15⟩   a.   park-s_{PL} commissioner
       b.   child-ren$_{PL}$-'s$_{GEN}$ corner

Given the presence of inflectional morphology in ⟨15⟩, the question arises whether such examples should be classified as compounds at all. The answer is probably 'yes', for phonological reasons. From a phonological point of view, English compounds are also typically characterized by lefthand stress, as are their German counterparts (cf. the '**compound stress rule**' formulated by Chomsky and Halle 1968). Relevant examples are given in ⟨16⟩.

⟨16⟩   a.   ˈblack.ˌboard
       b.   ˈgreen.ˌhouse

However, unlike in German, lefthand stress is only a sufficient, but not a necessary condition for compounding in English, i.e. all N-N-combinations with lefthand stress are compounds but not all compounds have lefthand stress. Consider the examples in ⟨17⟩ (cf. Plag 2003: 138).

⟨17⟩   a. ˌapple ˈpie

         b. ˌa.pri.cot ˈcrum.ble

         c. ˌsilk ˈtie

We could argue that the examples in ⟨17⟩ are not actually compounds, and that *apple, apricot* and *silk* are here used as adjectives, in accordance with our 'precategoriality hypothesis'. However, this all too simple solution, which would rescue the 'compound stress rule', meets with other types of problems. Combinations like those in ⟨17⟩ are typically semantically specialized and form relatively clear-cut classes or even paradigms. For example, the combinations in ⟨17⟩ contain a noun denoting material and one denoting a product made of that material. Given that such semantic criteria are also normally taken to be indicative of compound status, they cannot simply be disregarded.

Morphologists have therefore tried to find regularities in the rules of stress placement in English compounds. Several factors have been explored, e.g. semantic ones, frequency, analogy and informativeness (the amount of information contributed by each member of a compound). All the generalizations made are, however, probabilistic, and a general rule for the assignment of stress in English compounds has not so far been found. English compound stress is, if not entirely random, subject to several idiosyncrasies, and second language learners of English will always have to memorize the pronunciation of specific combinations. For example, it is simply a lexical fact of English that street names ending in *Street* carry lefthand stress while those containing *Avenue* exhibit righthand stress:

⟨18⟩   a. ˈOx.ford ˌStreet, ˈFourth ˌStreet, etc.

         b. ˌMa.di.son ˈA.ven.ue, Penn.syl.ˌva.nia ˈAvenue, etc.

The facts pointed out in this section seem to indicate that nominal compounds in German are a well-defined class, while English does not make a clear-cut distinction between compounds and syntactic phrases. This might be related to the difference in lexical categoriality mentioned above: just like simple lexemes are more sharply classified into syntactic categories in German than in English, so compounds form a more clearly delimited class.

The more 'central' status of compounding in German is also reflected in the wider distribution of this class. As a general tendency, compounding is more frequent in German than in English. Moreover, the two languages under comparison differ systematically with respect to the range of semantic relations that they express in compounding. For example, English often uses relational adjectives in cases where German has nominal compounds (cf. Gunkel and Zifonun 2008). Relational adjectives are denominal adjectives that can be paraphrased by using 'with respect to N', or similarly. In English, they are typically of Latin origin. The following examples show that English often uses (relational) adjective-noun combinations where German has a nominal compound (cf. Gunkel and Zifonun 2008: 293):

⟨19⟩ a. Sonne-n-strahlung 'solar radiation' (?'solare Strahlung')

b. Körperzuckung 'bodily convulsion' (?'körperliche Zuckung')

c. Arzthelfer 'medical assistant' (?'ärztlicher/medizinischer Helfer')

d. Herzstillstand 'cardiac arrest' (*'herzlicher Stillstand')

As the above discussion has shown, English and German exhibit different difficulties for foreign language learners in the domain of nominal compounds. In German, stress is predictable, but the occurrence and form of compound linkers is not entirely systematic. Many compounds will thus have to be learned separately. In English, such morphological difficulties will not normally arise, but the placement of stress is difficult to cast into a rule. Learners of English will thus have to acquire the stress patterns of specific combinations like those in ⟨17⟩ and ⟨18⟩, which can be regarded as exceptions to the (otherwise relatively general) compound stress rule.

15.5 V-N-compounds

In this section we will consider a contrast between English and German that has resulted from differences in the historical developments of the languages under investigation. Both English and German allow verb-noun compounding. There is a crucial difference, however. In German, such combinations are invariably endocentric, in the sense that the verb modifies the noun (but see below for a complication). In most cases, some type of locative, instrumental or temporal relation between the denotation of the noun and the action denoted by the modifying verb can be recovered. Examples are given in ⟨20⟩:

⟨20⟩ a. Schlaf-sack 'Sack, in dem man schläft' (locative)

b. Wasch-maschine 'Maschine, mit der man wäscht' (instrument)

c. Lauf-zeit 'Zeit, in/während der etwas läuft' (temporal)

English also has endocentric V-N-compounds of the type illustrated in ⟨20⟩. They are not very numerous, however. Some pertinent examples are given in ⟨21⟩:

⟨21⟩ whet-stone, blow-lamp, check-list

In most cases where German uses a V-N-compound, English has a N-N-compound. The determining noun is often derived by *ing*-suffixation (e.g. *sleep-ing*):

⟨22⟩   a.   [Schlaf_V-sack_N]_N
         b.   [[sleep_V-ing]_N bag_N]_N
⟨23⟩   a.   [Wasch_V-maschine_N]_N
         b.   [[wash_V-ing]_N machine_N]_N
⟨24⟩   a.   [Park_V-ausweis_N]_N
         b.   [[park_V-ing]_N permit_N]_N

Some German V-N-compounds correspond to (derived) simple nouns in English, typically of Latinate origin. For example, V-N-compounds ending in *Mittel* are typically rendered by simple nouns in English (note that 'native' English expressions are also sometimes available, e.g. *sleeping drug* for *soporific*):

⟨25⟩   a.   Nähr-mittel 'nutriment'
         b.   Reiz-mittel 'irritant'
         c.   Schlaf-mittel 'soporific'

While endocentric V-N-compounds are thus much more numerous in German than in English, the opposite picture emerges when we consider exocentric V-N-compounds. The English lexicon contains a large number of such examples, some of which are given in ⟨26⟩:

⟨26⟩   break-water, pick-pocket, clean-all

Many of these compounds are **borrowings** or **loan translations** from French. For example, the nouns *kerchief* (< *cheuer-chef*), *passport* (< *passe-porte*) and *wardrobe* (< *guarde-robe*) are originally French. The group of loan translations comprises examples such as *cut-throat* (cf. Fr. *coupe-gorge*) and *kindle-fire* (cf. Fr. *attise-feu*). The V-N-compounding pattern ceased to be productive soon after French stopped exerting an influence on English, however. In contemporary English, many – mostly negatively connotated – examples have been preserved from Middle English times. However, new lexical items with the meaning of an agentive noun normally take the shape of a 'synthetic compound', i.e. a compound of the form [N-V-*er*]. What was called a *break-bones* in Middle English times is thus a *bone-break-er* in Modern English. In this respect, English behaves just like German (*Knochen-brech-er*).

It should be noted that exocentric V-N-compounds seem to have existed in Middle High German vernacular speech as well, but they were highly restricted in terms of register. Some of the relevant items have been preserved in non-transparent contemporary words (e.g. *Schaber-nack* < 'schabe' + 'Nacken', originally a specific type of hat) and proper names (e.g. *Störte-beker* 'stürze' + 'Becher'). A few more transparent cases have been also preserved in Modern German, but they are not very numerous (e.g. *Habe-nichts*, *Tauge-nichts* and *Störe-n-fried*).

The picture that emerges is that German has only endocentric V-N-compounding, which is fully productive, while English has both endocentric and exocentric compounding, but neither process is productive. This generalization is relatively robust. Possible cases of exocentric compounds from German are provided by examples like those in ⟨27⟩:

⟨27⟩ a. Wende-hals

  b. Plapper-maul

  c. Quatsch-kopf

Such examples typically involve body part nouns. Note that they differ from compounds of the type *pick-pocket* in that the nominal element cannot in all cases be interpreted as an object of the verbal element. While we could reasonably assume that *Wendehals* denotes persons that turn their necks, this is not possible with *Plappermaul* or *Quatschkopf*. Such combinations are better analyzed as metonymical reinterpretations of endocentric compounds (cf. also Donalies 2005: 59). For example, *Quatschkopf* can be analysed as 'a head that talks rubbish', and this denotation comes to stand metonymically for the 'owner' of the head. If this analysis is correct for all combinations of the type illustrated in ⟨27⟩ (including *Wendehals*), we can conclude that German does not have exocentric V-N-compounding at all.

15.6 Minor types of compounds

In addition to the more or less general contrasts between English and German pointed out in the preceding sections, there are of course many minor, often highly specific ones. We will use two types of compounds to illustrate what type of contrast can be observed in specific cases, i.e. reflexive compounds in Section 15.6.1 (cf. also Chapter 10 on reflexivity more generally), and adjectival compounds containing a measure phrase in Section 15.6.2.

15.6.1 Reflexive nominal compounds

Complex words exemplified by *self-determination* in English and *Selbst-bestimmung* in German provide an instance of a type of word formation on the borderline between compounding and derivation. *Self-* does not occur as a free form in Modern English in contrast to German, where the historically related form *selbst* is used as an 'intensifier' (cf. Chapter 10). That these expressions are clear instances of compounds is not only shown by the stress on the first component but also by the contrast to the corresponding nominalizations. As is illustrated by the following sentences, only the nominalizations exhibit agreement with the subject:

⟨28⟩   a. This man has great self-confidence.

        b. This man has great confidence in himself.

Note furthermore that, at least in German, **reflexive nominal compounds** (as we will call them) can enter additional processes of word formation:

⟨29⟩   a. [[Selbst-disziplin]-los]-igkeit
           'lack of self-discipline'

        b. [[Selbst-bestimm-ung]-s-[bestreb-ung]]-en
           'striving for self-determination'

In terms of their meaning, reflexive nominal compounds can be classified with the endocentric compounds: 'self-accusation' is a kind of accusation and 'self-control' is a kind of control.

The following lists of examples show that reflexive nominal compounds have a certain productivity in both English and in German. Especially in recent years the number of attested examples has greatly increased, in particular in philosophical, psychological and esoteric texts:

⟨30⟩ English
        a. self-reflections, self-abandonment, self-contemplations, self-censorship, self-accusation, self-incapacitation, self-help, self-respect

        b. self-confidence, self-control, self-fashioning, self-hate, self-pity

⟨31⟩ German
        a. Selbst-reflexionen, Selbst-aufgabe, Selbst-betrachtungen, Selbst-zensur, Selbst-bezichtigung, Selbst-entmündigung, Selbst-hilfe, Selbst-achtung

        b. Selbst-vertrauen, Selbst-kontrolle, Selbst-inszenierung, Selbst-hass, Selbst-mitleid

These lists of examples are ordered in terms of translational equivalence and divided into two groups on the basis of semantic criteria. Like all reflexive constructions, reflexive compounds express that the two arguments of a predicate refer to the same person. The compound *self-assessment* expresses that the one doing the assessment and the one being assessed are one and the same person. Such an event or situation can be remarkable for two reasons: either we find a **remarkable Agent** (referent of the subject) or a **remarkable Patient** (referent of the object). The examples listed under (a) are instances of the former situation, those under (b) exemplify the second situation. If someone is in need of help, it is remarkable that that person him/herself should provide the help (remarkable Agent, listed under a). Feelings of pity or hate are normally directed towards other persons and it is remarkable if such feelings are self-directed as in *self-pity*, *self-hate* (remarkable Patients, listed under b).

In English and German *self*-compounds are also possible for adjectives, though not for verbs:

⟨32⟩   a.   self-appointed, self-inflicted, self-supporting, self-cleaning, self-sufficient, self-reliant, self-addressed, self-respecting, self-conscious, etc.
        b.   selbst-genügsam, selbst-gerecht, selbst-bezogen, selbst-ernannt, selbst-bewusst, etc.

There is, however, one clear difference in this sub-domain of compounding: in German the adjective *eigen* can also occur as first component in reflexive compounds, in both nominal and adjectival ones:

⟨33⟩   a.   Eigen-liebe, Eigen-verantwortung, Eigen-bedarf, Eigen-lob
        b.   eigen-mächtig, eigen-händig, eigen-verantwortlich, eigen-sinnig

Given the semantic similarity between *selbst* and *eigen*, illustrated by paraphrase relations like the following, this use of *eigen* in reflexive compounds, which is also found in other Germanic languages like Dutch and Swedish, is not surprising:

⟨34⟩   a.   Karl hat sein Haus selbst gebaut.
        b.   Karl hat sein Haus mit eigenen Händen (eigenhändig) gebaut.

The use of *eigen* in reflexive compounds is less productive than that of *selbst*. *Eigen* is preferred whenever the nominal head of the compound is a basic noun and not a deverbal nominalization (*Eigen-sinn*, *Eigen-heim*, *Eigen-anteil*, *Eigen-blut*). There are, however, also a few cases where both *selbst* and *eigen* are found with subtle differences in meaning. *Selbst-ständigkeit* and *Eigen-ständigkeit* denote the same phenomenon of 'independence', but the first compound is used in economic contexts, whereas the latter is used for 'intellectual independence' or 'originality'.

15.6.2   Adjectival compounds containing measure phrases

The second 'minor' type of compound considered in this section is one involving measure phrases containing a noun and an adjective. As Rohdenburg (2008) has noticed, such compounds differ systematically in their interpretation: in German, the first element regularly receives a plural interpretation, while in English it can be interpreted as either a singular or a plural noun. Consider the examples in ⟨35⟩.

⟨35⟩   a. eine meter-dicke Mauer
       b. ein jahr-e-langer Kampf
       c. ein jahrhundert-e-altes Buch

These examples are most straightforwardly interpreted as 'a wall that is several metres thick', 'a struggle that lasted for several years' and 'a book that is many centuries old'. Consider now the apparent English counterparts to the NPs in ⟨35⟩:

⟨36⟩   a. a yard-thick wall
       b. a year-long struggle
       c. a century-old book

Unlike the German examples in ⟨35⟩, those in ⟨36⟩ invite a singular interpretation. Typically, *a yard-thick wall* would be interpreted as 'a wall that is one yard thick'. This is probably due to the fact that the nouns in such compounds may also occur in their plural forms, as in ⟨37⟩.

⟨37⟩   a. a yards-thick wall
       b. a years-long struggle
       c. a centuries-old book

When we reconsider the German examples from the perspective of English it turns out that the nominal components can also be interpreted as plural forms. Accordingly, the schwa in *jahr-e-lang* and *jahrhundert-e-alt* could be a 'genuine' plural suffix, rather than a compound linker. This would explain why a singular interpretation is unusual for the relevant compounds. This interpretation can be made explicit with phrasal prenominal modification as illustrated in ⟨38⟩:

⟨38⟩   a. eine [ein Meter] dicke Mauer
       b. ein [ein Jahr] langer/lang andauernder Kampf
       c. ein [ein Jahrhundert] altes Buch

Even though the English-German contrast concerning the interpretation of adjectives containing a measure phrase may be relatively 'minor' insofar as it does not occur very often, it is interesting to note that it often gives rise to mistranslations, as Rohdenburg (2008) has shown. For example, "erroneous renderings" like the following are often found in "authorized translations" (Rohdenburg 2008: 230).

⟨39⟩   Damit war das jahrhundertealte Duell zwischen Tibet und China wieder eröffnet. (Harrer)
       'Thus the century-old quarrel between China and Tibet broke out again.'

⟨40⟩   ... as the dark cloud of blood had settled and dispersed in the mile-deep sea.
       '..., als die dunkle Blutwolke sich gesetzt und in der meilentiefen See verteilt hatte.'

15.7 Summary

Even though there are many similarities between compounding in English and German – for instance, the categories participating in compounding processes are largely parallel (cf. Table 15.1) – a number of striking contrasts have also been identified. In general, compounding tends to involve more elements, and more levels of embedding, in German than in English, where more-than-binary compounds are rare. Moreover, we have seen that there are systematic differences in the morphological and phonological properties of compounds. In German, nominal compounds often contain 'compound linkers' (*Fugenelemente*), while no such elements can be found in English. They invariably have lefthand stress in German, whereas there are exceptions to the 'compound stress rule' in English. More generally speaking, nominal compounds appear to form a more clearly defined category in German than they do in English, where they are sometimes hard to differentiate from syntactic phrases. This contrast can be related to a general difference in the 'degrees of categoriality' in the lexicons of English and German. Another contrast has been observed in the domain of V-N-compounds: while this type constitutes a highly productive class of (endocentric) compounds in German, in English it is not productive, though it comprises endocentric as well as exocentric elements, the latter mostly as a result of language contact with French. Finally, we have considered two minor domains of compounding (reflexive compounds and adjectival measure phrases), with the intention of providing some illustration of the more subtle English-German contrasts that can be found in specific domains of lexical morphology.

Revision, questions and exercises

1. Despite their orthography and stress pattern (righthand stress), adjective-noun combinations like the following are often regarded as compounds. Can you imagine why? Find a German translation in each case!

   ⟨41⟩   a. free trade
           b. civil war
           c. new year
           d. cold war
           e. green light

2. What phonological or phonetic effect do the compound linkers in the following examples have? Consider the compounds without a compound linker given in parentheses for comparison!

   ⟨42⟩   a. Geist-er-stunde (Abend-stunde)
           b. Hühn-er-ei (Spiegel-ei)
           c. Tag-e-blatt (Abend-blatt)

3. What is the difference between the following elements of 'stress doublets'? How can they be translated into German?

⟨43⟩ a. 'toy ,factory vs. ,toy 'factory
      b. 'woman ,doctor vs. ,woman 'doctor
      c. 'glass ,case vs. ,glass 'case
      d. 'hair ,net vs. ,hair 'net

4. How are compounds with more than two components stressed in German and in English? Consider alternative stress patterns for the following English examples in your answer! Do we find similar differences between pairs of German 'ternary' compounds?

⟨44⟩ a. university teaching award
      b. kitchen towel rack
      c. government working party

5. English V-N-compounds are restricted in terms of their range of denotation. Can you make any generalizations with respect to the meanings that they typically express? Consider the following examples in your answer and provide German translations for them (consult a dictionary, ideally the OED, if you are not familiar with the terms): *shuffle-wing, eat-bee, break-bones*; *spend-all, turn-penny, break-vow*; *saw-bones, fetch-water, turn-spit*.

6. Translate the following English examples containing measure phrases (from Rohdenburg 2008: 215) into German. What types of difficulties do you encounter?

⟨45⟩ a. a four-inch round pot
      b. The river is as wide as 80m.
      c. The suitcase is ten pounds heavy.

Further reading

Some of the major reference works on word formation contain comprehensive information on compounding (e.g. Marchand 1969, Plag 2003, Schmid 2011 and Bauer *et al.* 2013 for English and Fleischer and Barz 1992, Erben 1992 and Donalies 2005 for German). The morphophonology of word formation is discussed by Giegerich (2015) for English and Fuhrhop (1998) for German. There are some (English-German) contrastive studies of compounding, e.g. Berg (2006, 2012, 2016, 2017) and Berg *et al.* (2012) on nominal compounds, Gast (2008b) on V-N-compounds, and Rohdenburg (2008) on adjectives containing a measure phrase).

16 Derivation

16.1 Introduction

By and large, English and German exhibit similar patterns of derivation. Some major types are illustrated in Table 16.1. Each row corresponds to one source category and each column to the target category of the relevant derivational process.

	N	A	V
N	ex-husband	spirit-ual	material-ize
	mis-print	fragment-ary	(de-)naz(i)-ify
	co-author	resent-ful	be-head
	Erz-feind	sünd-haft	haus-ier[en]
	Günst-ling	abenteuer-lich	be-mann[en]
	Häus-chen	hölz-ern	ver-sumpf[en]
A	sad-ness	a-symmetrical	alien-ate
	blond-ism	super-natural	white-en
	formal-ity	un-educated	solid-ify
	Blind-heit	hyper-aktiv	er-grau[en]
	Bitter-nis	über-natürlich	be-grün[en]
	Gemein-schaft	un-gebildet	ver-länger[n]
V	arriv(e)-al	do-able	de-select
	depend-ence	chang-ing	un-tie
	cancell-ation	offen(d)-sive	be-fall
	Bewerb-er	beliefer-bar	be-werf[en]
	Ge-renn-e	genüg-sam	ent-nehm[en]
	Betreu-ung	regn-erisch	auf-schreib[en]

Table 16.1 Major patterns of word formation in English and German

In addition to elements from the major categories 'noun', 'verb' and 'adjective', prepositions can also be the target of derivation in English. They are often based on verbs (e.g. *considering, according to, notwithstanding, including, owing to*, etc.). In German, such deverbal prepositions are very rare (e.g. *entsprechend, während*), but there are many prepositions based on nouns, e.g. *zeit* (*meines Lebens*), *kraft*, *laut, dank*, etc. Many such prepositions are originally genitive forms, e.g. *mangels*, *zwecks* and *betreffs*. The relevant processes of derivation are not productive, however, and such denominal prepositions are mostly relatively old.

The examples given in Table 16.1 show that both prefixes and suffixes play a role in the derivational processes of English and German. Note that many of the affixes are not fully specified with respect to their source category. For example, the English *ify*-suffix derives verbs from both adjectives (*solid-ify*) and nouns (*de-naz[i]-ify*). The same is true of the prefix *un-* in English (*un-clean* vs. *un-pack*). Those affixes for which the source and target category are different are commonly called '**transpositional**'. Such affixes are typically suffixes, and exceptions are not numerous (e.g. *be-head* and *de-flea* in English).

Table 16.1 does not contain a column or row for adverbs. German simply uses the plain adjectives as adverbs, i.e. there is no regular adverbial derivation. English, by contrast, uses the *ly*-suffix to derive adverbs from adjectives. In fact, this process is so regular that it is sometimes regarded as an instance of inflection rather than derivation (cf. Chapter 4). Given the high degree of regularity in the application of this rule, adverbial derivation does not present any major learning difficulties for advanced learners, though it is certainly a common stumbling block for beginning learners of English. We will not consider adverbial derivation any further.

Contrasts in derivational morphology rarely allow such generalizations as are found in inflectional morphology or in syntax. They relate to questions like whether or not a certain affix has a counterpart with a similar meaning in the other language, how affixes with similar meanings in the two languages overlap and differ in their use and distribution, whether one language draws a distinction which is not overtly made in the other, etc., and lead very quickly into a comparison of the inventories of lexical differentiations made by the languages under comparison. Some such specific aspects of derivation will be considered in Section 16.3, which deals with patterns of adjectival derivation. Before turning to adjectives, we will discuss some more or less systematic and general contrasts between English and German in the domain of verbs in Section 16.2. Section 16.4 contains a brief summary.

16.2 Verbal prefixes and particles

In grammars of German two classes of verb-deriving elements that precede the root in non-finite forms are usually distinguished, i.e. (i) 'separable prefixes' or 'verbal particles', and (ii) 'non-separable prefixes' or simply 'verbal prefixes'. We will use the terms 'verbal particle' and 'verbal prefix' for these expressions and 'particle verb' and 'prefix verb' for the relevant (complex) verbs. Elements of both classes are illustrated in ⟨1⟩ and ⟨2⟩ respectively. The two types of elements can be differentiated phonologically: verbal particles carry primary stress whereas verbal prefixes are unstressed.

⟨1⟩   Verbal particles and particle verbs
      ab-fahren, an-blicken, auf-steigen, aus-gehen, bei-legen, durch-steigen, ein-
      bauen, los-legen, nach-eilen, vor-fertigen, zu-lächeln

⟨2⟩   Verbal prefixes and prefix verbs
      be-laden, be-schmutzen, ent-führen, ent-mutigen, er-dolchen, er-bauen, ver-
      golden, ver-gittern, zer-kratzen, zer-stören

While the elements illustrated in ⟨1⟩ and ⟨2⟩ are used as either particles or prefixes,
those in ⟨3⟩ occur in both functions, with their stress properties varying accordingly:

⟨3⟩   a. 'durch-ˌlaufen   vs.   durch-'laufen
      b. 'über-ˌziehen   vs.   über-'ziehen
      c. 'um-ˌfahren   vs.   um-'fahren
      d. 'unter-ˌstellen   vs.   unter-'stellen
      e. 'wider-ˌhallen   vs.   wider-'setzen

In addition to functioning as prefixes and particles, the elements in ⟨3⟩ are also
used as prepositions. For examples, *durch* is found in all contexts with a more or
less invariant meaning:

⟨4⟩   a. Karl durchreiste viele Länder. (prefix)
      b. Karl wird lediglich durchreisen. (particle)
      c. Karl reiste durch viele Länder. (preposition)

The 'multiple' use of elements such as *durch* as both prepositions and derivational
verbal elements is a typical feature of Indo-European languages and is quite characteristic of older languages such as Latin and Greek:

⟨5⟩   Latin
      a. ex-cēdere 'out.of-go', i.e.'go out/away'
      b. ab-īre 'from-go', i.e. 'go away'
      c. ac-cēdere (<ad-cēdere) 'to-go', i.e. 'approach'
      d. con-cēdere 'with-go', i.e. 'join' (also 'move away, leave')
      e. in-cēdere 'in-go', i.e. 'go in'
⟨6⟩   Ancient Greek
      a. ana-bainein 'up-walk', i.e. 'walk up, climb'
      b. apo-bainein 'from-walk', i.e. 'walk away'
      c. dia-bainein 'through-walk', i.e. 'walk through/across'
      d. em-bainein 'in-walk', i.e. 'go in, get on board'
      e. epi-bainein 'on.top-walk', i.e. 'climb'

While homophony between a preposition and a prefix is thus a widespread feature among the Indo-European languages, the use of the relevant elements as particles (as in German) is a typical feature of Germanic languages and is not found in older language stages or in Romance, Celtic or other branches of Indo-European.

English behaves like German insofar as there is widespread homophony of verbal particles and prepositions. Unlike German, however, English has lost most of the 'de-prepositional' prefixes. Roughly speaking, English, German and the other Indo-European languages can thus be compared as follows: German allows the use of 'P-elements' in all contexts, most (esp. older) other Indo-European languages only have prepositional and prefixal uses, and English only has prepositional and particle uses of P-elements. This generalization obviously simplifies matters considerably, however. A more detailed discussion of P-elements and their distribution in English and German is provided in this section.

16.2.1 Verbal prefixes

German has largely retained the Indo-European pattern illustrated in ⟨5⟩ above for Latin and Greek and has many verbal prefixes that are homophonous with prepositions. We have seen that *durch* is used in both functions. Two further examples are provided in ⟨7⟩ and ⟨8⟩.

⟨7⟩ a. Er überfuhr einen Marder.

  b. Er fuhr über einen Marder.

⟨8⟩ a. Er umfuhr den Polizisten.

  b. Er fuhr um den Polizisten (herum).

The main difference between the verbal prefixes and the combinations of a verb and a prepositional phrase is that the verbal prefixes contain some additional **aspectual** (mostly perfective) information, and that the object of prefixed verbs tends to be more strongly affected than the complement of the corresponding preposition. For example, ⟨7a⟩ implies that the marten was killed or at least hurt, whereas in ⟨7b⟩ it may have remained uninjured.

The verbal prefixes discussed so far thus seem to stand in a certain relationship of '**alternation**' to prepositions and are in complementary distribution with the latter. The various elements show different degrees of semantic transparency or specialization. Note that a relationship of 'alternation' can even be recovered for elements that are completely unrelated in terms of form to near-equivalent prepositions. The prefix *ent-* often corresponds to the preposition *aus*, and the prefix *be-*, in its locative meanings, often corresponds to the particle and preposition *auf*.

⟨9⟩   a. Er entnahm dem Kühlschrank ein Bier.

       b. Er nahm ein Bier aus dem Kühlschrank (heraus).

⟨10⟩   a. Er bestieg den Berg.

       b. Er stieg auf den Berg (hinauf).

Locative uses of *be-* are actually quite rare. In most cases, this prefix has a more grammatical function and is associated with a change in argument structure. Regardless of the semantic category of the base it derives monotransitive verbs. Its basic function is to change the argument structure of a verb in such a way that it is not the Patient, i.e. the argument expressing the entity that is under control of an Agent and manipulated by him/her, that is encoded as direct object. Instead it is a Location, an Experiencer, Instrument, etc. that is encoded as object with the subsequent encoding of the Patient as an adjunct (cf. ⟨11⟩–⟨13⟩). Many of the relevant German verbs are rendered by alternations in English (cf. ⟨14⟩–⟨16⟩; see also Chapter 9).

⟨11⟩   a. Karl pflanzte Blumen in seinen Garten.

       b. Karl bepflanzte seinen Garten mit Blumen.

⟨12⟩   a. Karl sprühte Farbe auf die Wand.

       b. Karl besprühte die Wand mit Farbe.

⟨13⟩   a. Karl schmierte Butter auf die Wand.

       b. Karl beschmierte die Wand mit Butter.

⟨14⟩   a. Charles planted his garden with flowers.

       b. Charles planted flowers in his garden.

⟨15⟩   a. Charles sprayed paint on the wall.

       b. Charles sprayed the wall with paint.

⟨16⟩   a. Charles smeared butter on the wall.

       b. Charles smeared the wall with butter.

The modification of the argument structure of a verb is also the most important function of the prefixes *ver-*, *er-* and *zer-*. *Ver-* is one of a few prefixes that do not have a prepositional counterpart. Its original meaning as well as the preposition(s) that it derives from are difficult to determine (Gothic *faí*, *faúr* and *fra* are possible candidates; cf. Ancient Greek *perí*, *pará*, *pro*). Some examples of *ver-* are classified semantically in ⟨17⟩. Note that the labels assigned to the various readings are merely rough characterizations of their functions.

⟨17⟩   a. 'ornative': ver-golden

       b. 'effective': ver-filmen, ver-steinern

       c. 'terminative': ver-hungern, ver-schließen, ver-spielen

The prefix *er-* derives from Old High German ur- ('out of'), which in turn reflects Indo-European **uds* (cf. also *aus*). The original meaning is only (remotely) preserved in a few verbs, however (e.g. *er-heben, er-wachsen*). In contemporary German, *er-* is basically a marker of argument structure and often has an aspectual function. It is sometimes called 'effective' in this function (cf. ⟨18⟩.

⟨18⟩ 'effective': er-mannen, er-bauen, er-bleichen, er-klingen, etc.

Finally, *zer-* is also found only as a prefix. Its function can be described as 'destructive' (cf. ⟨19⟩). It is etymologically related to the *dis*-prefix of Latin as in *dissociate, dis-integrate*, etc., and derives from an Indo-European root **zu̯is* (cf. the German word *Zwist*).

⟨19⟩ 'destructive': zer-bröckeln, zer-knittern, zer-kratzen, etc.

Unlike German, English has lost most prefix verbs, which provided a common pattern of verbal derivation in Old English (cf. ⟨20⟩). Only a few traces have been preserved in the lexicon of Modern English, some of which are listed in ⟨21⟩.

⟨20⟩ ādruwian 'to dry up', bedrincan 'drink in or up', forðbringan 'bring forth', oftredan 'to tread down' (Brinton 1988: 202/3)

⟨21⟩ arise, bereave, forbear, outdrink, overtake, upbraid, withdraw (Brinton 1988: 187)

The verbal prefixes of Old English were gradually replaced by, or turned into, verbal particles. This process went through an intermediate stage, where particles and prefixes cooccurred. Put differently, the particles 'reinforced' the prefixes.

⟨22⟩ Gif man cealf of a-drife 'If someone drives off a calf' (lit. 'If man calf off away-drives'; Brinton 1988: 217)

The loss of prefix verbs in English and their replacement by particle verbs can be regarded as another symptom of the general tendency towards more analyticity that characterizes the historical development of that language. From a contrastive perspective, it implies that many synthetic constructions of German are rendered analytically in English. For example, the contrast between *brennen* and *ver-brennen* as in ⟨23a⟩ can be rendered by using the particle *up* (note, however, that the use of the progressive aspect provides another way of making this aspectual distinction, which runs counter to the general 'analyticity trend' of English):

⟨23⟩ a. Der Dornbusch brannte, aber er verbrannte nicht.
　　 b. The bush was burning, but it did not burn up.

The class of prefix verbs thus allows for a relatively categorical generalization. While Modern English does not have a morphological process of verbal prefixation for locative and aspectual meanings, as well as for operations on argument structure, this process still plays a prominent role in the German lexicon. As pointed out above, many of the English verbs were replaced by verbal particles, to which we turn now.

16.2.2 Verbal particles

As mentioned above, verbal particles in German are also called 'separable prefixes'. This might be due to spelling conventions – the relevant elements form part of their hosts orthographically – or perhaps to their derivational function, which is traditionally located at the level of morphology (rather than syntax). From a phonological and syntactic point of view, however, the elements in question behave like independent words. They carry main stress when they are adjacent to their verbal host, and they are separated from their verbal host when the latter occurs in the second position, as in ⟨24b⟩:

⟨24⟩　a. Während der Fahrer 'an-ˌfuhr, ...

　　　b. Der Fahrer ˌfuhr langsam 'an.

The class of 'verbal particles' or 'particle verbs' is difficult to define in German. The reason is that combinations of a verb and some other, non-inflecting element as illustrated in ⟨24⟩ and other examples given above is found with a variety of lexical classes. The syntactic and phonological properties displayed by *an* in ⟨24⟩ can also be exhibited by adjectives like *tot* and nouns like *Rad* (cf. Müller 2002: Ch. 6):

⟨25⟩　a. Er ˌschlug den Ganoven 'tot. (resultative)

　　　b. ... als er den Ganoven 'totˌschlug.

⟨26⟩　a. Er ˌfuhr lieber 'Rad. (instrumental)

　　　b. ... weil er lieber 'Rad ˌfuhr.

While combinations like those in ⟨25⟩ and ⟨26⟩ are mostly regarded as syntactic constructions, rather than instances of word formation, as the stressed elements (*tot, Rad*) have clearly definable meanings and can hardly be regarded as having a derivational function, directional adverbs like those in ⟨27⟩ appear to have more abstract meanings and are thus closer to derivational elements like *an* in ⟨24⟩.

⟨27⟩　a. Er ˌfuhr 'weg.

　　　b. Er ˌrannte da'von.

It is a matter of debate whether elements like *weg* and *davon* should be regarded as 'common' directional adverbs or as verbal particles. Given that a comprehensive comparison of the constructions illustrated by ⟨24⟩–⟨27⟩ is beyond the scope of this chapter, we will focus on those verbal particles that are homophonous with some preposition in the following discussion. Among the most important representatives of this class are elements like *an*, *ab*, *auf*, *zu*, *nach*, *vor*, *aus*, *mit*, *um*, etc. Even though these particles are independent words, rather than prefixes, we will speak of 'derivation' – 'derivation in the syntax', as it were – and particles will be assumed to derive 'phrasal verbs'. In most cases, verbal particles are non-transpositional, as is illustrated in ⟨1⟩ above: phrasal verbs are derived from simple verbs. However, there are also a few instances of particle verbs that could be regarded as being transpositional. The verbs in ⟨28⟩ do not have (transitive) verbal bases.[1]

⟨28⟩   a.   ab-fackel$_N$-n (*fackeln)

       b.   nach-besser$_A$-n (*bessern)

The various particles exhibit different degrees of semantic relatedness with the corresponding prepositions. As pointed out above, *durch* is probably one of the particles with the most transparent 'cross-categorial' meaning. In spite of their equivalence, particles and prepositional phrases may cooccur. Even though examples like those in ⟨29⟩ may have a somewhat redundant flavour, they are not at all uncommon in the spoken language:

⟨29⟩   a.   Er lief durch den Wald (hin)durch.

       b.   Er stieg aus dem Auto aus.

       c.   Er stieß an das parkende Auto an.

Like verbal prefixes, verbal particles mostly convey locative-directional and/or temporal-aspectual meanings. The locative-directional meanings are semantically closer to those of the corresponding prepositions. When conveying an aspectual function or change in aktionsart, verbal particles typically focus on the boundaries of an event (e.g. inchoative, terminative), i.e. they have a perfectivizing function:

⟨30⟩   a.   ab-fahren (directional, inchoative)

       b.   an-steuern (directional), an-brennen (inchoative)

       c.   auf-steigen (directional), auf-wachen (inchoative)

       d.   aus-steigen (directional), aus-trocknen (terminative)

       e.   ein-werfen (directional), ein-schlafen (inchoative)

       f.   nach-laufen (directional), nach-bestellen (temporal/posteriority)

       g.   vor-treten (directional), vor-kochen (temporal/anteriority)

---

[1]   Note however that *fackeln* occurs in the idiomatic negative polarity expression *nicht lange fackeln* 'not hesitate', and *bessern* occurs as a middle verb (*sich bessern* 'improve').

Homophony of prepositions and verbal particles is also widely found in English. Quirk *et al.* (1985: 1151) provide the following list of elements with both functions:

⟨31⟩ about, above, across, after, along, around, by, down, in, off, out (AmE), over, past, round, through, under, up, etc.

The verbal particles of English differ from their German counterparts syntactically in following their hosts in all contexts and not only in finite constructions. Another contrast concerns the delimitation of this class from other types of 'phrasal verbs'. In English, particle verbs are often differentiated from 'prepositional verbs' such as *look after* in grammars (e.g. Quirk *et al.* 1985). One of the differences is that particle verbs, unlike prepositional verbs (**He looked after*), may be intransitive:

⟨32⟩ a. The plane has just touched down.
 b. I hope you'll get by. (Quirk *et al.* 1985: 1152)

The position of the particle relative to an object is variable (cf. ⟨33⟩). The complements of prepositional verbs are invariable in final position (cf. ⟨34⟩). Moreover, prepositions do not carry stress. This difference can most clearly be seen when the particle or preposition is 'stranded' (cf. ⟨35⟩ vs. ⟨36⟩).

⟨33⟩ a. He turned on the light.
 b. He turned the light on.
⟨34⟩ a. He looked after the child.
 b. *He looked the child after.
⟨35⟩ a. He 'called on the dean.
 b. The dean was 'called on.
⟨36⟩ a. She switched 'on the light.
 b. The light was switched 'on. (Quirk *et al.* 1985: 1157)

As mentioned above, the verbal particles of Modern English more or less correspond to the verbal prefixes of Old English. Some of the particles seem to derive directly from such prefixes, in particular *off* (< *of-*), *over* (< *ofer-*), *forth* (< *forð*) and *through* (< *þurh-*). The change from verbal prefix to verbal particle seems to have happened in Middle English and can be illustrated with pairs of examples like those in ⟨37⟩ (cf. Brinton 1988: 205–210):

⟨37⟩ a. þurh-crēopan → creep through
 b. over-rǣdan → read over (or through)
 c. forþ-faran → 'go forth'

While some verbal prefixes of Old English have been lost (or have become non-transparent), some new particles were formed, either on the basis of prepositions (e.g. *out* < *ūt*), or of prepositional phrases (e.g. *away* < *on weg*, *down* < *of dune*). This is the reason why the inventories of particles are quite different in English and German, despite the close genetic relationship between these languages. Many of the English particles represent innovations, while the German inventory of particles is still quite similar to the original (Proto-Germanic) one.

In spite of the formal differences between English and German particles, the types of meaning covered by the relevant elements are quite similar. Like their German counterparts, many English particles have a literal **locative** use. Such examples often correspond quite closely to particle verbs in German.

⟨38⟩   get off ('aus-steigen'), climb up ('auf-steigen'), put on ('an-ziehen')

Aspectual uses of particles in English are also quite common. For example, *up* often has an aspectual function (completive) in *eat up* and *drink up* (cf. Germ. *auf-essen*, *aus-trinken*). The overlap between locative-directional and temporal-aspectual meanings that is characteristic of German can also be observed in some English particles, e.g. *stand up*. This example illustrates how a directional specification can also affect the aspectual properties of a predicate, as directionality implies movement and movement, in turn, implies a change of state, i.e. perfectivity.

A third group of verb-particle combinations is constituted by lexical items that are fully **idiomatic** in the sense that their meaning has moved away considerably from the original meaning of the verb. For example, the meaning of *figure out* is largely opaque, though it can be recovered metaphorically from the original meanings of its components. Such 'phrasal verbs' have to be learned separately and have entries of their own in dictionaries.

The following examples illustrate the three cases distinguished above – (i) locative-directional meanings, (ii) aspectual meanings, and (iii) idiomatic uses for the particles *up*, *out*, *over*, *away*, *out* and *off*:

⟨39⟩   locative-directional
      a. hang up, nail up, flare up, push up
      b. pour out, push out, reach out
      c. hand over, give over
      d. walk away, drive away, take away

⟨40⟩   aspectual
      a. mix up, shake up, cover up, break up
      b. die out, fade out, fire out, wear out, hang out
      c. work away, sing away, fire away
      d. broaden out, even out, widen out

⟨41⟩   idiomatic

    a. look up, turn up, give up, let up, bring up

    b. work out, figure out, read out

    c. show off, take off, tick off

    d. hand on, carry on

16.2.3 Summary

The present section has been concerned with three types of elements, i.e. prefixes, particles and prepositions. There are direct diachronic as well as synchronic relationships between these elements. As has been seen, many German elements are used in three functions, i.e. as prepositions, prefixes and particles. English only shows homophony of some particles and prepositions. It has lost (productive) verbal prefixes, and many of the particles represent innovations and therefore differ from their (semantic) counterparts in German. The correspondences between prefixes, particles and prepositions are summarized in Table 16.2.

	prefix	particle	preposition
German		über	
English		over	
German		unter	
English		under	
German		durch	
English	–	through	
German		wider	
English	–	–	against
German		um	
English	–	around	
German	–	an	
English	–	on	
German	–	(her)ein	in
English	–	in(to)	
German	ent-	(her)aus	
English	–	out (of)	
German	ver-	ab	von
English	–	on	
German	hinter-	nach	hinter
English	–	after	

Table 16.2 The functions of P-elements

16.3 Minor patterns of adjectival derivation

Given the close genealogical relationship between English and German it should not come as a surprise that the two languages still have derivational affixes with identical or similar form and more or less identical meaning. The affix *-er* which derives agentive or instrumental nouns from verbs (*sing-er*, *writ-er*, *build-er*, *print-er*; *Säng-er*, *Dicht-er*, *Maur-er*, *Druck-er*), or the suffix *-en*, which combines with adjectives to derive verbs (*black-en*, *schwärz-en*), are cases in point.

In spite of their formal identity, affixes from English and German may differ considerably in their use potential. The prefix *un-*, for example, is used to derive antonyms from adjectives in both English and German (*kind* – *un-kind*; *freundlich* – *un-freundlich*, etc.). In English this affix is also used, however, in combination with verbs to derive their reversive counterparts (*tie* – *un-tie*; *cover* – *un-cover*), i.e. that meaning which erases the effect denoted by the basic verb. Note also the difference in stress that we find between English and German in adjectival antonyms: *un'kind* vs. *'un freundlich*. Moreover, the *un-*prefix of German is more narrowly distributed than the one of English, as English *un-* is basically restricted to adjectives of Germanic origin, and *in-* is often (though not invariably) used with Latinate ones (e.g. *in-adequate*). For verbal predicates, the prefix *dis-* is also often found (e.g. *dis-like*). The same root may thus occur with three different types of negation, e.g. *un-able*, *in-ability*, *dis-able* (note that the use of *un-* with *able* provides a counterexample to the generalization that Latinate adjectives are negated with *in-*).

The use of negative prefixes shows how elements deriving from the same origin may be distributed differently in English and German. Another example of this type of contrast is provided by the suffix *-y* in English and its etymological German counterpart *-ig*. These suffixes derive adjectives from nouns (*foggy*, *windy*, *stormy*, *rainy*, *mousey*, *watery*, *silky*, *stubbly*, etc.). English *-y*, whose meaning can frequently be paraphrased by 'like', 'full of', 'covered with', is productively applied *inter alia* to nouns denoting body parts (cf. ⟨42⟩). Note that many of these adjectives have a non-compositional, metaphorical meaning. The adjective *cheeky* certainly implies 'a lot of cheek', but in the metaphorical sense of 'impertinence'.

⟨42⟩   throaty, hairy, nosy, cheeky, chesty, leggy, bony, bloody, hearty, skinny, etc.

The *y*-suffix contrasts systematically with the suffix *-ed*, whose meaning can roughly be paraphrased by 'equipped with'. For obvious reasons this affix only combines with body part nouns when they are accompanied by adjectival modifiers. Without these additional modifiers the derived adjective would be trivial (for example, *a faced man* for 'a man with a face'), and such derivations are only possible if they denote a remarkable, unusual aspect (*a freckled face*, *a bespectacled man*). Some common examples are given in ⟨43⟩.

⟨43⟩   blue-eyed, broad-shouldered, light-hearted, dark-haired, thick-lipped, broad-cheeked, brown-skinned, left-handed, strong-boned, etc.

In German the distinction carried by -y vs. -ed is neutralized and not overtly marked, even though the semantic distinctions just described are exactly the same:

⟨44⟩   a.   haarig, blutig, fleischig, knochig, sehnig, nervig, etc.

          b.   dünn-häutig, blau-äugig, links-händig, schwarz-haarig, stier-nackig, etc.

This example illustrates just one among many contrasts in the interpretation and distribution of specific derivational elements, whose detailed analysis and comparison would amount to an exercise in comparative lexical semantics.

16.4 Summary

A systematic contrastive investigation of derivational elements is a difficult undertaking, because derivational elements, just like lexical items, tend to exhibit highly specific semantic and distributional properties. One way of comparing genetically related languages like English and German is to consider elements that have counterparts in both languages under comparison, and to compare their semantic and distributional properties. We have focused on verbal derivation, specifically on verbal particles and verbal prefixes. More generally speaking, both types of elements can be subsumed under the label 'P-element', which also includes prepositions. German shows a characteristic three-way multifunctionality of P-elements, as many of the relevant elements function as prefixes, particles and prepositions. In English, formal identity of particles and prepositions is quite common, but the verbal prefixes of Old English have been lost. The increasing use of particle verbs, which characterizes the recent history of English, can be seen as yet another symptom of the tendency towards more analyticity exhibited by that language. In addition to the (more or less) comprehensive discussion of verbal derivation, we have presented a case study of adjectival derivation, focusing on adjectives ending in -y or -ed in English. This case study was intended to show how specific derivational meanings that are made in one language may be neutralized in another.

Revision, questions and exercises

1.   What are the differences between the following pairs of examples and how could you render these differences in English?

      ⟨45⟩   a.   Karl überschritt die Grenze.

      b. Karl schritt über die Grenze.

⟨46⟩ a. Karl durchschwamm den Kanal.

      b. Karl schwamm durch den Kanal.

⟨47⟩ a. Karl umfuhr die Unfallstelle.

      b. Karl fuhr um die Unfallstelle herum.

2.   Try to describe the function of the prefix in each of the following examples and compare it to the corresponding sentence with a prepositional phrase. How can the difference be rendered in English?

⟨48⟩ a. Karl beantwortete die Frage.

      b. Karl antwortete auf die Frage.

⟨49⟩ a. Karl zerstach seinem Nachbarn die Autoreifen.

      b. Karl stach in die Autoreifen seines Nachbarn.

⟨50⟩ a. Karl erforschte HIV-Viren.

      b. Karl forschte an HIV-Viren.

3.   How can you differentiate particle verbs from prepositional verbs in English? Provide examples not given in the book!

4.   How are locative or directional meanings (e.g. *go up*) and aspectual ones (e.g. *drink up*) related? Provide both English and German examples illustrating the connection!

5.   How would you analyse the sentence in ⟨51⟩? Consider the following options: (i) *durch ... durch* is a circumposition, (ii) *durch* is used both as a preposition and as a postposition here, and (iii) *durch* is used as a preposition and as a verbal particle with a basically derivational function.

⟨51⟩ Er ging durch den Wald durch.

6.   Find three examples of English (verbal, adjectival or nominal) roots that use different forms of negation depending on the syntactic category of the word! Provide the German translation in each case!

7.   Find three examples of German verbs derived by *be*-prefixation that correspond to alternations in English! (Do not use examples given in the book.)

8.   Most English particles have a perfectivizing function (e.g. *eat up*). How would you describe the function of the following particles?

⟨52⟩ a. *along* as in *sing along*

      b. *on* as in *babble on*

      c. *away* as in *chatter away*

Further reading

A classical reference work for word formation in English is Marchand (1969). Plag (2003) and Schmid (2011) are more recent monographs (see also Blevins 2006, Don 2014: Ch. 2). Bauer *et al.* (2013) contains comprehensive information on derivation. Several monographs deal with word formation in German, e.g. Fleischer and Barz (1992), Erben (1992) and Donalies (2005) (cf. also Szigeti 2017, with a focus on derivation).

17　The lexicon: Function words

A: LIEBST du mich auch?

B: Ja, dich AUCH.

The category of function words comprises elements that are typically simple in terms of morphological structure and that have abstract meanings or even purely grammatical functions. In this section only specific subclasses of function words will be discussed, namely those exhibiting interesting contrasts between English and German. Two such classes are those of impersonal pronouns (e.g. Germ. *man*) and indefinite pronouns (e.g. Engl. *somebody*), which are dealt with in Section 17.1. The second major class of elements discussed in this chapter is that of particles, which is a cover term for invariant elements with typically abstract functions relating to sentence or utterance meanings. The two types of particles that will be covered are 'focus particles' (Section 17.2) and 'modal particles' (Germ. *Modalpartikeln, Abtönungspartikeln*; Section 17.3). A brief summary is provided in Section 17.4.

17.1　Minor classes of pronouns

As already pointed out in Chapter 4, we can distinguish eight classes of pronouns: (i) personal pronouns (*he, she,* etc.), (ii) possessive pronouns (*my, your,* etc.), (iii) reflexive and reciprocal pronouns (*himself, herself, each other*), (iv) relative pronouns (*who, which*), (v) interrogative pronouns (*who, what,* etc.), (vi) demonstrative pronouns (*this, that,* etc.), (vii) impersonal pronouns (*one*), and (viii) indefinite pronouns (*somebody, anybody,* etc.). Since the major types of pronouns were already dealt with in Chapter 4, and a chapter of its own has been dedicated to reflexive and reciprocal pronouns (Chapter 10), it is the minor groups of pronouns that we will focus on in this section, namely impersonal pronouns and indefinite pronouns.

17.1.1　Impersonal pronouns

The term 'impersonal pronoun' is often used for elements like German *man* as exemplified in ⟨1⟩. *Man* refers to unspecific individuals or groups of individuals and is typically used in generic contexts, that is, in contexts in which no specific situation is referred to:

⟨1⟩   a. Man tut so etwas nicht.

        b. Man sagt, er sei ein Trinker gewesen.

        c. Man wird dir nicht glauben.

Impersonal pronouns are characterized by two salient features: first, even though they do not refer to any individual or group of individuals in particular, they always stand for **human referents** (cf. ⟨2⟩); and secondly, they may not be stressed, except in meta-linguistic contexts where different formulations are contrasted (e.g. 'echo contexts', as in ⟨3⟩):

⟨2⟩   ??Dein Hund ist nicht sehr gut erzogen. Man sollte Besucher nicht anbellen.

⟨3⟩   Stimmt es, dass man Ihr Auto beschädigt hat? – Nicht MAN, sondern ihr SOHN hat mein Auto beschädigt. (echo context)

Impersonal pronouns are restricted to specific sentence types and are often found in the context of **non-indicative modality**. They occur in conditional clauses (cf. ⟨4a⟩), in combination with modal predicates like *sollte*, *muss*, etc. (cf. ⟨4b⟩), or when an unspecified 'source' of information is indicated ('evidential use'; cf. ⟨4c⟩). They are often used in statements expressing a 'common sense' and stand for the 'average person':

⟨4⟩   a. Wenn man ihn kennt, weiß man, was für ein Betrüger er ist.

        b. Man soll den Tag nicht vor dem Abend loben.

        c. Heute weiß man, dass die Parkinson'sche Krankheit keine Schüttelläh-
           mung ist.

Like French *on* (< *homme*), German *man* derives historically from a noun meaning 'man, person'. In English there is no equivalent pronoun and the various uses of *man* have different translations. The closest equivalent we can get is the pronoun *one*. However, the distribution of *one* is restricted to only some of the contexts exemplified in ⟨1⟩–⟨4⟩ above. While it can be used in conditional clauses and modal contexts (cf. ⟨5a⟩ and ⟨5b⟩), it is inappropriate, or at least unusual, when the epistemic source of a proposition is indicated ('evidential use'). This is illustrated in ⟨5c⟩:

⟨5⟩   a. If one tries to understand the British Constitution simply by reference
           to case law and statute, one obtains a totally false impression. [BNC]
           (conditional)

        b. I know one shouldn't bite the hand that feeds but sometimes I feel that
           the roles are reversed: ... [BNC] (modal predication)

        c. ??Today one knows that the earth is round and not flat.
           (evidential use)

In order to indicate the epistemic source of a proposition in English in contexts like ⟨4c⟩, the pronoun *they* or the quasi-pronominal element *people* are more commonly used. First person plural pronouns (*we*) or a universal quantifier such as *everybody* are also frequently found:

⟨6⟩   a.   They say (??one says) he was a legend in the south.

b.   People say he was the illegitimate son of the chancellor.

c.   Today we / everybody know/s that the stars are objects like our sun.

Moreover, in English the second person pronoun *you* is commonly used with impersonal/generic reference. This is illustrated in ⟨7⟩. In German, such uses of second person pronouns are also possible in the spoken register. Given that a 'genuinely' impersonal pronoun (*man*) is available, however, examples such as ⟨8a⟩ and ⟨8b⟩ could be interpreted in such a way that the addressee is referred to specifically, and *man* is a more common choice here, cf. ⟨8c⟩.

⟨7⟩   I think I'll go home now. You shouldn't try to work when you're sick.

⟨8⟩   a.   ? . . . Du solltest nicht versuchen zu arbeiten, wenn du krank bist.

b.   ? . . . Sie sollten nicht versuchen zu arbeiten, wenn Sie krank sind.

c.   . . . Man sollte nicht versuchen zu arbeiten, wenn man krank ist.

Finally, specific occurrences of the impersonal pronoun *man* in German are translated into English using a passive clause:

⟨9⟩   a.   Man spricht Deutsch. – English (is) spoken.

b.   Man hat ihn verunglimpft. – He was disparaged.

The uses of the generic pronoun *man* in German and its possible translations into English are summarized in Table 17.1 on p. 294.

17.1.2 Indefinite pronouns

Like impersonal pronouns, indefinite pronouns are used to refer to some unspecific referent or group of referents. The difference is that indefinite pronouns are usually used in 'episodic' statements, that is, in propositions referring to situations that actually take place or are thought of as taking place:

⟨10⟩   a.   Someone has mown the lawn.

b.   Jemand hat den Rasen gemäht.

In both English and German indefinite pronouns stand in a paradigmatic relationship to negative pronouns (*some-body* vs. *no-body*, *je-mand* vs. *nie-mand*). However, the inventory of English pronouns is richer than the German one, since indefinite pronouns can be based on three different stems: *-body* and *-one* for human

German	English
MODAL PREDICATES: *man*	*one, you*
Man sollte ihn nicht unterschätzen.	*One/you shouldn't underestimate him.*
CONDITIONALS: *man*	*one, you*
Wenn man zu spät kommt, sollte man sich entschuldigen.	*If you are/one is late, you/one should apologize.*
GENERAL TRUTHS: *man*	*we, everybody*
Heute weiß man, dass die Sterne Objekte wie unsere Sonne sind.	*Today we know/everyone knows that the stars are objects like our sun.*
EVIDENTIAL USE: *man*	*people, they*
Man sagt, er sei ein guter Schachspieler gewesen.	*People/they say he was a good chess player.*
UNKNOWN AGENT: *man*	agentless passive
Man hat ihn wegen seiner angeblichen Arroganz verunglimpft.	*He has been disparaged for his perceived arrogance.*

Table 17.1 Impersonal pronouns in English and German

beings and *-thing* for objects. Moreover, the system is more consistent formally in English since the various elements clearly stand in a paradigmatic opposition to each other, and there is a three-way contrast between the pronouns formed with *some, any,* and *no: some-body, any-body, no-body.* These forms can be grouped into two positive (*some, any*) and a negative one (*no*). The positive members of the opposition are furthermore subdivided into '**assertive**' (*some*) and '**non-assertive**' (*any*) ones. English and German indefinite pronouns are summarized in Table 17.2.

	assertive		non-assertive		negative	
	human	objects	human	objects	human	objects
E	some-body some-one	some-thing	any-body any-one	any-thing	no-body no one	no-thing
G	je-mand	et-was	je-mand/wer	(et)was	nie-mand	nichts

Table 17.2 Indefinite pronouns

One of the most important issues from the perspective of German is the distribution and use of assertive (*some-*) as opposed to non-assertive (*any-*) indefinite pronouns in English. Among the most important questions concerning the distribution of indefinite pronouns is thus the following: When do we use (assertive) *some* and when do we use (non-assertive) *any*? A generalization frequently found in grammatical descriptions of English is that *some* is used in positive contexts and *any* in negative statements, questions, and conditionals (cf. Quirk *et al.* 1985: 83f.):

⟨11⟩   a.   Have you found anything yet?

       b.   No, I haven't found anything.

       c.   If you find anything, let me know!

⟨12⟩   Yes, I have found something.

However, the generalization made above cannot account for all occurrences of indefinite pronouns or the determiners *some* and *any*. In ⟨13a⟩ *some* is used in a question, and in ⟨13b⟩ *anybody* occurs in an assertion:

⟨13⟩   a.   Would you like some wine?

       b.   Anybody can do that.

How can we generalize over the use of *any* and *some*, then? Answering this question requires some knowledge of sentence semantics and a model of description whose elaboration would take us too far. We will therefore restrict ourselves to some basic guidelines. Note first that it is important to distinguish between stressed and unstressed occurrences of *any*. The difference is illustrated in the following pairs of examples:

⟨14⟩   a.   I DON'T think that anybody will show you the way to the station.

       b.   ANYbody will show you the way to the station.

⟨15⟩   a.   She doesn't EAT anything.

       b.   She doesn't eat (just) ANYthing.

While *anything* in ⟨14a⟩ and ⟨15a⟩ is a mechanical reflex of the preceding negation, the stressed occurrences of *anything* in ⟨14b⟩ and ⟨15b⟩ have a different meaning; here, *any* indicates 'free choice': ⟨14a⟩ says that whoever you ask will be able to show you the way, and ⟨15b⟩ means that 'She doesn't eat food which has been randomly chosen', i.e. she is a selective eater. Moreover, (stressed) *any* triggers a scalar implicature: even the most unlikely person (e.g. a stranger) is asserted to be able to show the addressee the way in ⟨14b⟩, and ⟨15b⟩ would be used if the person in question were offered food of poor quality. In the following discussion, stressed occurrences of *any* as illustrated in ⟨14b⟩ and ⟨15b⟩ will not play any role, and we will focus on unstressed occurrences of *any*, as in ⟨14a⟩ and ⟨15a⟩.

As a first rule, *any* is used in so-called '**downward entailing contexts**'. In order to understand that notion, we briefly have to consider logical relationships between sentences. We say that a sentence A 'implies' or 'entails' a sentence B whenever the following condition applies: if A is true, B is also true. For instance, ⟨16a⟩ entails ⟨16b⟩. The relationship of entailment is represented by an arrow (→):

⟨16⟩   a.   A young man came in.

       b.   A man came in.

⟨17⟩   A young man came in. → A man came in.

In most declarative sentences, substituting a more general expression (e.g. *man*) for a more specific one (*young man*) delivers a more general proposition, which means that truth is preserved: since every young man is also a man, the sentence *A man came in* will always be true if *A young man came in* is true. We can say that *A young man came in* is '**more informative**' than *A man came in*. Such contexts are called 'upward entailing' because relative to a taxonomy of the form shown in ⟨18⟩, entailment relations hold upwards:

⟨18⟩

man

young man   old man

Consider now the pair of examples in ⟨19⟩:

⟨19⟩   a. I don't like white wine.
       b. I don't like wine.

The two examples in ⟨19⟩ manifest a behaviour that is diametrically opposed to the pair of sentences in ⟨16⟩: *white wine* is more specific than *wine*. But now, the relationship of entailment is reversed: While in ⟨16⟩ the proposition containing the more specific expression (*young man*) entails the proposition containing the less specific expression (*man*), in ⟨19⟩ it is the other way around. This is illustrated in ⟨20⟩:

⟨20⟩   I don't like wine.
          ↓
       I don't like white wine.

In (downward entailing) sentences like those in ⟨19⟩ and ⟨20⟩, substituting a more specific expression for a less specific one preserves truth, while in 'upward entailing contexts' (i.e. the 'normal' or 'canonical' situation exemplified in ⟨16⟩) the opposite is true. To what extent is the distinction between 'downward entailing' and 'upward entailing' contexts relevant to the choice between *some* and *any*? We can explore the following generalization:

⟨21⟩   *Any* can only be used in downward entailing contexts.

Let us consider some examples in order to see if ⟨21⟩ holds true. First, it has been illustrated that **negated sentences** as in ⟨19⟩ license or even require *any*. Since negated sentences are generally downward entailing, this fact is clearly in accordance with the generalization made in ⟨21⟩. A second type of context where *any* is found is provided by **conditional clauses**. Since ⟨22a⟩ entails ⟨22b⟩, although *red book* is more specific than *book*, conditional clauses clearly qualify as 'downward entailing contexts' as well.

⟨22⟩   a. If you steal a book from the library you will be expelled.
             ↓
        b. If you steal a red book from the library you will be expelled.

⟨23⟩   If you steal anything from the library you will be expelled.

Of course, *some* is also a possible option in conditional clauses, with a clear difference in meaning (e.g. *If you steal something, you will be expelled.*). Note that the generalization in ⟨21⟩ does not say anything about the use of *some*. We will return to this matter below.

A third type of context where *any* is licensed is provided by certain modal environments as illustrated in ⟨24a⟩. The fact that such modal contexts are downward entailing can be shown using a simple substitution test as illustrated in ⟨24b⟩:

⟨24⟩   a. Any man should be able to do that.
        b. A man should be able to do that.
             ↓
        c. An old man should be able to do that.

Although *old man* is more specific than *man*, ⟨24b⟩ entails ⟨24c⟩. In an upward entailing context, the entailment relation would be reversed: For instance, *An old man did that* entails *A man did that* but not vice versa.

Let us finally consider **questions**. This is the most difficult part because the semantics of questions are, for several reasons, very hard to capture. 'Ordinary' yes/no-questions are downward entailing. For example, a question like ⟨25a⟩ 'includes' the question in ⟨25b⟩, even though a more general expression (*dog*) is replaced with a more specific one (*poodle*). If one asks the question in ⟨25a⟩, the question in ⟨25b⟩ constitutes a 'subquestion', and a positive answer to the former entails a positive answer to the latter. The entailment relation holding between ⟨25a⟩ and ⟨25b⟩ can be made more explicit by paraphrasing both sentences as representative speech acts as is done in ⟨26⟩: ⟨26b⟩ entails ⟨26a⟩.

⟨25⟩   a. Do you have a dog?
        b. Do you have a poodle?

⟨26⟩   a. I want you to say "yes" if you have a dog.
        b. I want you to say "yes" if you have a poodle.

We can thus conclude that the generalization in ⟨21⟩ also covers the use of *any* in yes/no-questions.

So far, it has been shown that non-assertive pronouns (as well as *any* in the function of a determiner) only occur in downward entailing contexts. But this answers only half of the question when to use *some* and when to use *any*, since the question of what determines the choice between *some* and *any* in downward entailing contexts (where both options are often available) still requires an answer. As hinted at by Quirk *et al.* (1985: 390), **presuppositions** play an important role. If a speaker holds a belief that something is true and merely asks the addressee for confirmation – i.e. if part of the utterance is presupposed – *some* is used instead of *any*. This can be seen in the pair of sentences in ⟨27⟩ (from Quirk *et al.* 1985: 390). ⟨27b⟩ could be paraphrased as in ⟨28⟩:

⟨27⟩   a. Did anybody telephone last night?
        b. Did somebody telephone last night?

⟨28⟩   I take it someone telephoned last night. Is that true?

Since the presupposition that 'someone telephoned last night' is an upward entailing context, *some* has to be used instead of *any*. This effect is commonly exploited for matters of **politeness**. Consider the contrast between ⟨29a⟩ and ⟨29b⟩:

⟨29⟩   a. Would you like some wine?
        b. Would you like any wine?

Obviously, ⟨29a⟩ sounds more polite than ⟨29b⟩. The reason is that the speech act expressed in this sentence is not a question, but an **offer**, and the positive presupposition associated with ⟨29a⟩ anticipates a positive answer, thus indicating the speaker's willingness to give away some of his/her wine. This aspect of politeness can be illustrated by paraphrasing ⟨29a⟩ as shown in ⟨30⟩:

⟨30⟩   I suppose you would like some wine?

17.2   Focus particles

The term 'focus particle' subsumes invariant elements like English *only*, *too* and *even* and German *nur*, *auch* and *sogar*. Focus particles are characterized by the following properties:

- Focus particles interact with the **focus** of a sentence, i.e. with the constituent that bears the main stress;
- focus particles are **scope-bearing elements**, i.e. they relate to a specific, often syntactically determined, part of the sentence (which may be the whole sentence). In other words, a constituent is focused against the background of the information given in the rest of the sentence (scope);

- focus particles provide information about **sets of alternatives** contrasting with the focus.

In order to illustrate the properties of the focus particles listed above, let us consider an example. The English particle *only* is among the most typical members of the class of focus particles. In ⟨31⟩, the scope is indicated by brackets bearing a subscript 'SC' and the focus by a subscript 'F':

⟨31⟩   a.   If only [[JOHN]$_F$ sends me flowers]$_{SC}$ I will be disappointed.
           ('If no one other than John ...')
        b.   Only [if [JOHN]$_F$ sends me flowers will I be disappointed]$_{SC}$.
           ('... otherwise I will not be disappointed.')

As the examples in ⟨31⟩ show, the contribution made by *only* to the sentence meaning varies with its position, and also with the syntactic structure of the whole sentence (inversion vs. no inversion). The reason is that the scope of the two occurrences of *only* is different. In ⟨31a⟩ *only* takes scope within the conditional clause, whereas it takes scope over the whole sentence in ⟨31b⟩.

The second property of *only* – its interaction with the **focus** of a sentence – can be illustrated by changing the intonation pattern of ⟨31b⟩. Consider ⟨32⟩:

⟨32⟩   Only [if John sends me [FLOWERS]$_F$ will I be disappointed]$_{SC}$.

⟨32⟩ exhibits the same word order as ⟨31b⟩ above, but the focus is different. Accordingly, the sentence has different truth conditions. While ⟨31b⟩ says that the speaker would not be disappointed if, say, Fred sent him/her flowers, ⟨32⟩ states that s/he would not be disappointed if John sent something other than flowers.

These examples can also be used to illustrate the third important property of focus particles: they provide information about **alternative values** contrasting with the focus. We can paraphrase the sentences given above by applying a simple 'algorithm': first, we replace the focus with some (contextually given) alternative value, or simply with a variable 'x'; and second, we add a negation operator saying that the resulting sentence is not true for any assignment of x other than the focus value. ⟨33⟩ corresponds to ⟨31a⟩ above and ⟨34⟩ to ⟨31b⟩:

⟨33⟩   If no x other than John sends me flowers, I will be disappointed.

⟨34⟩   If some x other than John sends me flowers, I will NOT be disappointed.

As we have seen, sentences with focus particles provide information not only about the focus referent, but also about alternative values contrasting with that focus. Moreover, we have seen that *only* **excludes** paradigmatic alternatives. There is a second group of particles which is used with quite the opposite function, namely, to indicate **inclusion** or 'addition' of alternative values with respect to the open proposition constituting the background of a sentence. Consider ⟨35a⟩ and ⟨35b⟩:

⟨35⟩   a. I only met [John]$_F$.

b. I also met [John]$_F$.

While ⟨35a⟩ expresses that the 'open proposition' 'I met x' applies to John, and to no other contextually given person, ⟨35b⟩ says that there *is* some person other than John such that the speaker met him/her. This difference between *only* and *also* can also be described as follows: both particles express quantification over a set of alternative values contrasting with the focus: *only* expresses 'negated existential quantification' ('there is no x other than the focus such that …'), whereas *also* expresses (non-negated) 'existential quantification' ('there *is* some x other than the focus …').

So far, we have established two classes of focus particles: 'exclusive' and 'additive' ones. In addition to *only*, the former class includes elements like *solely*, *merely*, *alone*, etc. and the latter class contains elements like *also*, *too* and *as well*. In addition to this first parameter of classification there is a second one which is independent of and orthogonal to the first, and which concerns the sets of alternatives under discussion: while some focus particles interact with 'unordered' sets of alternatives, others require '**ordered sets**' or '**scales**' to interact with. What does that mean? Consider the contrast betwen ⟨36a⟩ and ⟨36b⟩:

⟨36⟩   a. I also met [John]$_F$.

b. I even met [John]$_F$.

Both ⟨36a⟩ and ⟨36b⟩ say that the speaker met John, and both sentences presuppose that s/he must have met someone else in addition to John. The difference is that in ⟨36b⟩ there is an additional aspect of meaning which is not contained in ⟨36a⟩: the sentence implies that John is the most unlikely (or most remarkable) person to be met by the speaker. This fact is captured by the adjective '**scalar**': *even* is called a 'scalar (additive) particle' since the various alternative values are ordered according to some 'dimension of meaning' (here, 'probability').

Having established two independent parameters of classification we can now cross-classify focus particles according to these parameters, which gives us four types of focus particles: (i) non-scalar exclusive particles, (ii) scalar exclusive particles, (iii) non-scalar additive particles, and (iv) scalar additive particles. This cross-classification, which is illustrated in Table 17.3, will help us to carry out a more systematic comparison of the focus particles of English and German.

Note that both *only* and *nur* appear twice in Table 17.3, namely in the two rows for 'scalar' and 'non-scalar'. The reason is that those particles in fact have two uses, a scalar and a non-scalar one. Accordingly, sentences with *only* may be ambiguous. Consider ⟨37⟩, which has the two readings paraphrased in ⟨37a⟩ and ⟨37b⟩:

⟨37⟩   I only said that you were mistaken.

a. The only thing I said is that you were mistaken; I did not say anything else.

b. I merely said that you were mistaken; I did not say anything more offensive than that.

As will be seen below, the four major types of focus particles considered in this section and summarized in Table 17.3 only constitute the core of this category, and there are other, more marginal, members of this class.

		exclusive	additive
non-scalar	English	*only*	*also, too*
	German	*nur, einzig*	*auch*
scalar	English	*only, merely*	*even*
	German	*nur, lediglich*	*sogar*

Table 17.3 Exclusive and additive particles (assertive)

17.2.1 Contrasts between English and German

Two major contrasts between English and German can be observed in the domain of focus particles, which can be regarded as instantiations of a single generalization, namely that German tends to use more particles than English (cf. König 1982). First, in many cases where German uses genuine (mono-morphemic and uninflected) particles, English has a more complex syntactic construction. For instance, the (temporal) focus particle *erst* is often translated using a comparative construction of the form *as X as Y* (cf. $\langle 38a \rangle$), and Germ. *ausgerechnet* is in most contexts translated using a construction of the form *X of all Y's*, where *X* stands for the focus value and *Y* for a superset containing *X*, typically the *genus proximum*:

$\langle 38 \rangle$ a. *as* Adj/Adv *as*
This program always commands its own audience of *aficionados* even when it is on as late as midnight.
('...selbst wenn es erst um Mitternacht ausgestrahlt wird.')

b. X *of all* Y's
You don't think I want to upset you, do you, now of all times?
('...ausgerechnet jetzt?')

The second central difference between English and German is that, with the exception of non-scalar additive particles, there is often a one-to-many relationship between a given English particle and a set of German translational equivalents which are chosen depending on the context. In other words, German has overall more particles and also more semantic differentiations than English.

17.2.2 Exclusive particles

The most important contrast between *only* and *nur* is that *only* has a broader range of application. In particular, it has both a temporal and a non-temporal use, and within the temporal uses both a scalar and a non-scalar one, whereas *nur* only has a non-scalar interpretation with points-in-time as its focus. German has the specialized particle *erst* for such cases:

⟨39⟩   a. I saw Paul only yesterday.

      b. Ich habe Paul erst gestern gesehen. (nicht vorher)

Nur is not of course ungrammatical in sentences such as ⟨39a⟩ or ⟨39b⟩. However, it only has a non-scalar reading, as is illustrated in ⟨40⟩:

⟨40⟩   Ich habe Paul nur gestern gesehen (an keinem anderen Tag).

As already pointed out in Chapter 5, the translation of *only* into German also depends on the tense form: in combination with the Present Perfect it often translates as *erst* while it translates as *nur* in sentences in the Simple Past:

⟨41⟩   a. I saw him only once. ('I habe ihn nur einmal gesehen.')

      b. I've seen him only once. ('Ich habe ihn erst einmal gesehen.')

The difference between *erst* and *only* is that *erst* excludes alternatives on one side of the value given, whereas *only* can exclude values on both sides. Accordingly, *not … until* and *as late as* are often more appropriate translations of *erst*:

⟨42⟩   a. Ich werde erst morgen abreisen.

      b. I will not leave until tomorrow.

⟨43⟩   a. Das Fahrrad wurde erst im 18. Jahrhundert erfunden.

      b. The bicycle was invented as late as the 18th century.

Finally, there is a non-temporal use of *erst* which requires yet another translation. It is illustrated in ⟨44⟩ (from König 1982: 81):

⟨44⟩   a. Erst ein Professor wäre ihr als Schwiegersohn recht.

      b. Nothing less than a professor would be acceptable to her as a son-in-law.

The foregoing discussion has shown that English often uses some kind of syntactic periphrasis where German has 'genuine' focus particles (*nur*, *erst*).

17.2.3 Additive particles

As far as additive particles are concerned, there are two major contrasts between English and German: first, contrary to the overall tendency, English has more particles (or equivalent expressive devices) than German in the domain of **non-scalar additive particles**; and second, scalar additive particles provide a superb example of the general tendency for parsimony and/or polysemy in English where German makes more lexical differentiations.

As is well-known, English has two (non-scalar) additive particles *also* and *too*, whereas German only has *auch*. What is more, English has a third form, which is used only in negative sentences, namely *either*. Accordingly, the German particle *auch* corresponds to three particles of English:

⟨45⟩ a. She's here, too. ('Sie ist auch hier.')

   b. She's also here. ('Sie ist auch hier.')

   c. She isn't here either. ('Sie ist auch nicht hier.')

The difference between *also*/*too* and *either* can easily be explained: *either* is restricted to negative sentences and is used when it takes scope over sentence negation. The choice between *also* and *too* is much more subtle and depends on three factors (cf. Gast 2006a): first, *also* is more formal than *too*; second, *also* tends to be used with very long foci; and third, *also* cannot be used in some (information-structural) configurations where *too* is appropriate. The fact that *too* often sounds awkward when the foci are exceedingly long can be seen in the following pair of examples (⟨46a⟩ sounds much better than ⟨46b⟩):

⟨46⟩ a. It is almost certain that targets will be set, including efforts to reduce by a third the number of smokers by the year 2000. There will also be [targets aimed at reducing the incidence of strokes, heart disease and preventable cancers]$_F$. [BNC]

   b. It is almost certain that targets will be set, including efforts to reduce by a third the number of smokers by the year 2000. There will be targets [aimed at reducing the incidence of strokes, heart disease and preventable cancers]$_F$, too.

Irrespective of matters of style (formal vs. informal) and the length of the focus, *also* is impossible in some contexts where *too* is fine. This is particularly perspicuous in the following conversation:

⟨47⟩ – I love you.

   a. – I love you, too.

   b. – #I also love you.

A similar effect can be observed in German. Even though *auch* is the only option, a difference in meaning can correlate with the position of *auch* relative to the focus:

⟨48⟩   – Ich liebe dich.

    a. – Ich liebe dich auch.

    b. – #Auch ich liebe dich.

Without going into detail as to why ⟨47b⟩ and ⟨48b⟩ are infelicitous, the following generalization holds in most cases: whenever *also* (in a medial position) can be used, *too* (in a final position) can also be used, but not vice versa; and whenever preposed *auch* can be used in German, postposed *auch* can also be used, but not vice versa.

A second striking contrast between English and German can be observed in the domain of **scalar additive particles**. Remember that among the non-scalar additive particles English makes a difference between *also/too* and *either*, while no such differentiation is made in German. We can say that *also, too* and *either* are 'polarity sensitive', since they can only co-occur with either positive or negative polarity. Interestingly, the opposite situation is found with scalar additive particles: while English *even* is indifferent to the polarity – or, more generally, to the 'direction of entailment' – of a sentence (upward entailing vs. downward entailing; cf. Section 17.1), German *sogar* is usually used only in upward entailing contexts. In negative sentences, the particle (*nicht*) *einmal* is used, as is shown by the following example:

⟨49⟩   a. He even drank four bottles of wine.

    b. He didn't even drink a single glass of wine.

⟨50⟩   a. Er hat sogar vier Flaschen Wein getrunken.

    b. Er hat nicht einmal ein Glas Wein getrunken.

In downward entailing contexts other than negation there is another combination of particles that corresponds to Engl. *even*, i.e. *auch nur*. It occurs in questions and conditionals indicating that some value occupies a low rank on some 'natural' scale:

⟨51⟩   a. Werden wir auch nur den Hauch einer Chance haben?

    b. Will we even have a ghost of a chance?

English has a particle group which corresponds quite closely to *auch nur* as illustrated in ⟨51a⟩, and which may be used to avoid repetition of *even*, i.e. *so much as*. Consider the German sentence in ⟨52⟩ and the English translations in ⟨53⟩:

⟨52⟩   Er hat nicht einmal versucht, auch nur ein Wort zu verstehen.

⟨53⟩   a. He did not even try to understand so much as a word.

    b. ?He did not even try to understand even a word.

So far, we have seen that there are three possible translations of *even*: (i) 'sogar', (ii) 'einmal' (with negation) and (iii) 'auch nur'. However, there are actually many more (cf. König 1982):

⟨54⟩ a. Even if nobody helps us, we'll manage.
'Selbst wenn uns niemand hilft, werden wir es schaffen.'

b. Even giants started from small beginnings.
'Auch Riesen haben einmal klein angefangen.'

c. One executive of J.H.J. said that his company was hoping for arms export orders, a statement which would have been unthinkable in Japan even a year ago.
'... eine Aussage, die in Japan vor noch einem Jahr undenkbar gewesen wäre.'

d. Even before 1912 there were signs that a war had become inevitable.
'Schon vor 1912 gab es Anzeichen dafür, daß ein Krieg unvermeidbar geworden war.'

e. I'm now wondering whether this was even necessary.
'Ich frage mich jetzt, ob das überhaupt nötig war.'

König (1982: 94) identifies the following conditions for an appropriate translation of *even* into German:

⟨55⟩ *even*

a. *sogar* in affirmative contexts, if the focus is a VP, V, or Adj;

b. *selbst* in affirmative contexts, if the focus is an NP, PP, or S;

c. *auch* in affirmative contexts, if the focus is described in such a way that it suggests a scale;

d. *einmal* after an immediately preceding *nicht*;

e. *auch nur* if the scope is a nonaffirmative context and the focus value can be placed on a 'natural' scale;

f. *überhaupt* in nonaffirmative contexts, if focus value and alternatives cannot be ordered on a natural scale;

g. *schon* if the focus denotes a time interval and all alternatives under consideration follow this interval;

h. *noch* if the focus denotes a time interval and all alternatives under consideration form a continuous interval which precedes the interval denoted by the focus.

17.2.4 Other focus particles

As mentioned above, the class of focus particles is actually much larger than Table 17.3 suggests and also contains a number of elements whose meaning cannot easily be described with reference to the two parameters structuring this table (exclusive/additive, scalar/non-scalar). One such particle is English *at least* in the use illustrated in ⟨56⟩:

⟨56⟩   At least the [chairman]$_F$ was sober.

At least introduces an aspect of 'non-maximality', insofar as it points to a positive aspect of an overall negative situation. In German there are three particles conveying this function. Consider the examples in ⟨57⟩.

⟨57⟩   a.   Wenigstens war der Vorsitzende nüchtern.

       b.   Zumindest war der Vorsitzende nüchtern.

       c.   Immerhin war der Vorsitzende nüchtern.

Wenigstens corresponds quite closely to *at least* as illustrated in ⟨56⟩ above and is thus the most 'neutral' way of translating it. *Zumindest* and *immerhin* have some additional connotations. For instance, *zumindest* indicates a certain 'upward potential', insofar as it suggests that the proposition under consideration may be true for some value other than the focus as well. *Immerhin*, by contrast, does not seem to allow any stronger value from the set of alternatives, i.e. the set of entities to which the predication in the scope of the particle applies is 'exhaustive':

⟨58⟩   a.   Zumindest war der Vorsitzende nüchtern, vielleicht auch einer der anderen Teilnehmer.

       b.   #Immerhin war der Vorsitzende nüchtern, vielleicht auch noch ein anderer Teilnehmer.

Note that both *zumindest* and *immerhin* are not necessarily associated with a positive aspect of an overall negatively evaluated situation and can also be used in a more neutral way (cf. ⟨59a⟩ and ⟨59b⟩). In these examples using *wenigstens*, just like *at least* in English, would be inappropriate because this would imply that four people getting hurt is evaluated positively:

⟨59⟩   Dieser Unfall war gar nicht so schlimm.

       a.   Oh doch! Immerhin sind vier Leute verletzt worden!

       b.   Na hör mal! Zumindest sind vier Leute verletzt worden!

       c.   #Na hör mal! Wenigstens sind vier Leute verletzt worden!

17.2.5 Summary

As has been seen, it is very difficult to generalize over English-German contrasts in the domain of focus particles, but the quantitative generalization made at the beginnning of this section – the claim that German has more focus particles than English – has been confirmed. However, in the domain of non-scalar additive particles, English seems to have more particles than German (*also*, *too*, *either*). But then, the question is what exactly counts as a focus particle. If we take German particles such as *ebenso*, *gleichermaßen*, etc. into account, the overall tendency for German to have more particles than English may apply in the domain of non-scalar additive particles as well.

17.3 Modal particles

Modal particles (in German *Modalpartikeln* or *Abtönungspartikeln*) convey meta-linguistic meanings relating to aspects of the 'communicative embedding' of an utterance. For instance, *aber* in ⟨60a⟩ expresses spontaneous surprise, *vielleicht* in ⟨60b⟩ serves as a 'downtoner', and *ja* in ⟨60c⟩ indicates that common knowledge is being communicated:

⟨60⟩   a. Der ist *aber* schön!

   b. Könntest du mir *vielleicht* dreihundert Euro leihen?

   c. Pelé war *ja* einer der besten Fußballspieler aller Zeiten.

In some cases modal particles can be translated into English by using particles or particle groups as well. For instance, *vielleicht* in ⟨60b⟩ can straightforwardly be translated using *by any chance* into English:

⟨61⟩   Could you lend me three hundred Euros by any chance?

However, in most cases no such particle is available in English and other grammatical means have to be used, in particular: (i) question tags, (ii) 'verum focus' constructions, (iii) specific intonation patterns, (iv) specific sentence types (imperative, rhetorical questions, etc.), or (v) combinations of (i)–(iv). It is very hard to establish rules predicting which type of construction is used in English for which German particle. The only generalization that can be made relatively safely is that English lacks a class of modal particles comparable to the German elements considered in this section. In the following we will briefly consider some examples.

German *doch* → English question tag   The particle *doch* in the use illustrated in ⟨62a⟩ below indicates that a piece of information is being communicated which the speaker assumes to be **shared knowledge** (presupposed), but which is in **contradiction** to some presupposition or to the addressee's behaviour. A possible paraphrase of ⟨62a⟩ would be: 'I don't understand why you're acting the way you do, given that we both know that we wanted to see a play – or don't we?' Since question tags may also be used as presupposition indicators, and since they put up the opposite of a proposition for consideration, they can be used as rather close equivalents of *doch* in such cases (cf. ⟨62b⟩). If ⟨62a⟩ is uttered with some emphasis, an imperative as in ⟨62c⟩ would also be appropriate:

⟨62⟩   a.   Wir wollten doch ins Theater gehen!
         b.   We wanted to see a play, didn't we?
         c.   Don't tell me you forgot that we wanted to see a play!

German *doch* → English 'verum focus'   Since *doch* always implies a contrast between the sentence it forms part of and a contradictory statement, it sometimes corresponds to a 'verum focus' construction in English. ⟨63a⟩ could be paraphrased as 'don't act as though we didn't know that you are a drinker, since we *do* know that you drink'. This use may be exploited for the sake of **politeness** as well. When a visitor is hesitant to take a seat, s/he can be encouraged by uttering the sentence in ⟨64a⟩. A possible paraphrase would be 'you seem to be considering whether to sit down or not – *do* sit down!'.

⟨63⟩   a.   Wir wissen doch alle, dass du ein Trinker bist.
         b.   We all do know that you are a drinker.
⟨64⟩   a.   Aber setz dich doch!
         b.   Do sit down!

German *doch* → English heavy stress on main verb   In some cases, *doch* is used to remind the hearer of some shared piece of information, and the contradictory proposition is categorically and emphatically excluded. In ⟨65a⟩, the speaker does not even allow the hearer to entertain a different opinion. This aspect of assertiveness can be expressed by putting an emphatic falling accent on the main verb in English:

⟨65⟩   a.   Ich warte seit Jahren darauf. Das weißt du doch!
         b.   I've been waiting for this for years, and you KNOW it.

German *vielleicht* in questions → negated assertion in English   In its semantically most transparent use, the adverbial *vielleicht* indicates possibility. Related to this function is its use as a '**downtoner**'. A question like 'Is it possible that you ...' gives the addressee the opportunity to reject the request without too much loss of 'face' on the part of the speaker, since the issue is 'objectified' ('no, it is not possible' rather than 'no, I don't want to'). In English, such a 'modalization' of a request can be expressed using an adverbial like *by any chance* (cf. ⟨61⟩ above). Another way of toning down a request is to anticipate a negative answer as shown in ⟨66b⟩. The common denominator is that both strategies are 'face-preserving' insofar as they give the addressee room for a negative answer.

⟨66⟩   a. Könntest du mir nicht vielleicht dreitausend Euro leihen?

        b. I don't suppose you could lend me three thousand euros?

German *etwa* in questions → negated question in English Just like *vielleicht* in ⟨66⟩ and the English translation given in ⟨66b⟩, which positively seems to invite a negative reaction on the part of the addressee, the particle *etwa* as used in ⟨67⟩ anticipates a negative answer. The difference is that *etwa* clearly conveys that the speaker really hopes for a negative answer, whereas s/he only pretends to do so for the sake of politeness in the case of *vielleicht* or *by any chance*. In English, this effect can be achieved by using a negative (rhetorical) question as in ⟨67b⟩.

⟨67⟩   a. Bist du etwa verheiratet?

        b. Do you mean to tell me you are married?

Summary As the preceding discussion has shown, German modal particles relate to different aspects of utterance meaning like illocutionary force, presuppositions, speakers' expectations, matters of politeness, etc. Speakers of English have to resort to different types of strategies to express these functions, and they use 'higher-level' grammatical means like intonation or sentence types, rather than the lexical means employed by German. In most cases a one-to-one translation is not possible and 'combined' strategies have to be used in English if one wants to convey the communicative meanings of German modal particles.

17.4 Summary

The domain of function words presents some non-trivial difficulties for German learners of English and vice versa. The correct use of pronouns, especially of polarity sensitive pronouns like *someone, anyone*, etc. is not only difficult to learn for non-native speakers of English, it is also difficult to analyse from a theoretical point of view, and the generalizations made on the basis of notions such as 'downward entailingness' (Ladusaw 1979), while providing a reasonable approximation, are not totally 'waterproof' either. While German is less specific than English in the choice of pronouns (depending on the sentential context), it has a richer inventory of particles. Specifically, the class of modal particles, which play a very important role in face-to-face conversation in German, is totally absent from English. It thus comes as no surprise that these particles are among the most difficult features of German even for advanced learners of that language. Native speakers of German, in turn, need to learn the alternative 'strategies' available in English to convey the types of communicative intentions or attitudes associated with modal particles.

Revision, questions and exercises

1. Find ten occurrences of *anybody* or *anything* in the a corpus (e.g. the BNC) and determine whether they occur in downward entailing contexts. Apply substitution tests!
2. How many possible translations of Engl. *even* are there in German? Find two examples for each possible translation.
3. Try to find translational equivalents for *schon* in the following German examples. (You may want to use a dictionary):

   ⟨68⟩　a. Schon seine Stimme regt mich auf.

   　　　b. Schon vor dem Zweiten Weltkrieg hatte Europa seine zentrale Stellung verloren.

   　　　c. Wir schaffen das schon.

   　　　d. Karl bereitet sich schon auf das Examen vor.

   　　　e. Es war schon dunkel, als wir in London ankamen.

4. How does one translate the focus particle *ausgerechnet* in sentences like the following into English?

   ⟨69⟩　a. Ausgerechnet mein Chef musste mir damals über den Weg laufen.

   　　　b. Karl will ausgerechnet morgen vorbei kommen.

   　　　c. Plötzlich begann mein Prüfer mich ausgerechnet über Shakespeare zu befragen.

5. Translate the following sentences into English:

   ⟨70⟩　a. Bist du etwa schon wieder hungrig?

   　　　b. Es gefällt dir doch, oder etwa nicht?

   　　　c. Er soll nicht etwa glauben, dass ich auf ihn warte!

6. How would you characterize the meaning of German *überhaupt* in the context of superlatives? How do you translate sentences like the following into English? You can test the contribution made by *überhaupt* to the meaning of these sentences by leaving it out and comparing the result to the original sentence.

⟨71⟩   a. Das war das erste Treffen zwischen einem irakischen und einem albanischen Präsidenten überhaupt.

b. Das älteste menschliche Skelett überhaupt stammt aus Afrika.

c. Wir verwenden die beste Reinigungsmethode überhaupt.

Further reading

Given the heterogeneity of the class of function words, there are no specific reference works or comparative surveys. The most important properties of indefinite and impersonal pronouns are described in the relevant reference grammars (e.g. Quirk *et al.* 1985, Huddleston and Pullum 2002, Zifonun *et al.* 1997). Gast (2015) provides a comparison of impersonal pronouns in English and German (cf. also van der Auwera *et al.* 2012 on English, German and Dutch). A systematic survey of focus particles can be found in König (1991), and a comparison of English and German is given in König (1982). Gast (2017) compares Engl. *even* to some German equivalents. There is a large body of studies dealing with modal particles in German, largely inspired by some earlier work of H. Weydt. Modal particles and their translations into English are studied in Bublitz (1978) (cf. also Gast 2008a). König *et al.* (1990) is a comprehensive lexicographic study of particles in German and in English, and Rinas (2006) is a monograph dealing with *ja* and *doch* (and their Czech equivalents).

18 Generalizations and explanations

18.1 Two questions

Our concluding remarks will take the form of two questions and their possible answers:

- Is it possible to unify two or more observations about contrasts under a more pervasive generalization? Are the contrasts discussed in the preceding chapters linked to or even derivable from a limited number of basic contrasts between the two languages which led to some profound readjustments across all major areas of the linguistic systems?
- How can we explain the fact that the structures of English and German differ in the way they do?

Obviously, these two questions are closely linked. Answers to questions of explanation presuppose the exploration of **implicational connections** between contrasting principles or rules and may often simply take the form of such implicational connections as a first approximation. That there are regularities in the way languages differ from each other has been clearly established by language typology, i.e. by large-scale comparisons of languages (cf. Comrie 1989, Croft 2003, Song 2010, Moravcsik 2013, Aikhenvald and Dixon 2017). The view that all or at least most of the differences between two languages are connected in some way underlies the famous structuralist credo that "chaque langue forme un système où tout se tient" (Meillet 1903: 407) as well as all attempts to develop a holistic typology (or 'characterology') for a language. Older as well as more recent discussions of these issues (e.g. von der Gabelentz 1901, Plank 1984, Hawkins 1986, König 1987, 1996, Rohdenburg 1990, Fischer 2013, etc.) have shown that the strongest hypothesis of a holistic typology, i.e. the view that all properties of a language are connected in some way, is difficult to maintain and to justify. We will therefore take a weaker and more modest version as our starting point and simply assume that there are implicational connections between at least some of the major contrasts discussed above.

Our second question concerns one of the most difficult problems of any scientific inquiry. How can we explain the contrasts observed above, and the divergences in the historical development of the two languages underlying them? Reduced to its basic core, explanations are answers to *why*-questions about certain phenomena in need of explanation (the *explananda*). Any explanation (or *explanans*) must meet certain conditions. Among other things explanations must be more basic and more clearly established than the phenomena they are meant to explain. Moreover, *why*-questions can be iterated, i.e. any answer given to such a question may be in need of further explanation. So ideally we would need criteria establishing beyond any doubt that we have reached a final explanation. In Generative Grammar such criteria are discussed under the heading 'explanatory adequacy'. Again, we will not enter into a discussion of such fundamental philosophical problems, but simply try to find plausible and reasonably convincing answers to our second question. Right from the start our basic assumption will be that the different contrasts discussed in this book may require different explanations. We will chiefly refer to the following three factors: (i) dependencies between grammatical subsystems, (ii) properties of the human perceptual and articulatory system, and (iii) external language history, including language contact.

18.2 Towards some generalizations

Phonology There is no general explanation for the wealth of contrasts between the phoneme inventories of English and German. There is, however, a possible (historical) explanation for the loss of symmetry that was pointed out in Chapter 2 as a characteristic feature of the English system, in comparison to the German one. Remember that Modern English differs from both Old English and Modern German in not having rounded front vowels, and in not distinguishing systematically between tense and lax vowels. The disappearance of these features in Middle and Early Modern English may be due to language contact of various types, most importantly with Anglo-Norman (cf. Ingham 2010, 2012) and Scandinavian (cf. Emonds and Faarlund 2014), as well as potentially Celtic varieties (cf. Hickey 2012). Anglo-Norman seems to have lost its close rounded front vowel at an early stage, and the mid-close rounded front vowel does not seem to have developed in the first place (cf. Ingham 2012: Sect. 5.4). Insular Celtic languages do not have the rounding parameter as a distinctive phonological feature. It thus seems that the absence of rounded front vowels is, to some extent, an areal feature of the British Isles.

Given the various types of high-intensity language contact situations during great parts of British history – with a strong influence of Old Norse in the region corresponding to the Danelaw, with a French-speaking nobility in Early Middle English times, and potentially with some influence from Celtic – the '**destabilization**' of a phoneme system as complex as the Old English one does not come as a great surprise. Under the structuralist assumption that each language forms "un système où tout se tient", it is, moreover, to be expected that neutralizing two central features of vowel classification will lead to a considerable reorganization of the whole system. The relative 'instability' of the vowel system, which characterizes English up to the present day, is manifested by the fact that many varieties of English have reorganized their vowels differently from the major standard varieties and have developed more symmetric systems (cf. the discussion of Scottish English in Chapter 2 and, more generally, various descriptions given in Kortmann *et al.* 2004).

Note furthermore that the phonology of Modern English, much more than that of German, suffers from being poorly reflected in the **orthography**. The greater distance between spelling and pronunciation in English is mainly due to the fact that English orthography still represents, to some extent, Middle English pronunciation. Some major sound changes (e.g. the Great Vowel Shift, the loss of nasals after plosives, etc.) have found no representation in the writing system. The sound changes taking place in the earlier periods of Modern German were less dramatic and German orthography has been somewhat more flexible in adapting these changes.

In some subdomains of phonology, it is possible to relate contrasts between English and German to cross-linguistic findings and (supposedly) universal principles which are ultimately based on properties of the human articulatory and perceptual system. Phonotactic constraints are a case in point. As pointed out in Chapter 3, many cross-linguistic rules can be formulated in terms of the '**Sonority Hierarchy**', which is represented in ⟨1⟩ on page 36. One such constraint concerns the formation of consonant clusters in the onset. As pointed out in Chapter 3, consonant clusters generally conform to the '**Sonority Principle**' in this position, i.e. the first consonant is always less sonorous than the second. However, there are further predictions that can be derived from the Sonority Hierarchy. For instance, members of consonant clusters in the onset tend to be maximally distant on that hierarchy. Therefore, /pr/ is cross-linguistically more common than /pn/, which in turn is more common than /ps/. The range of cross-linguistic variation with respect to structural constraints on onset formation can therefore be described with reference to the Sonority Hierarchy, and the following prediction can be made: If a language allows the combination of a plosive and some other consonant C, then all (types of) consonants that range higher on the Sonority Hierarchy than C can also form a consonant cluster in the onset together with a plosive. English and German can now be characterized with respect to the cut-off points that they define on the Sonority Hierarchy with regard to the formation of consonant clusters (note that in neither of the two languages can plosives combine with other plosives, as in the Egyptian proper name *Ptolemeus*):

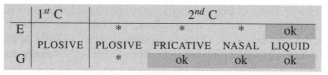

	1st C	2nd C			
E		*	*	*	ok
	PLOSIVE	PLOSIVE	FRICATIVE	NASAL	LIQUID
G		*	ok	ok	ok

Table 18.1 The Sonority Hierarchy and syllable onsets

Morphology and constituent order As pointed out in Chapter 4, the inflectional distinctions found in English are not simply a subset of those found in German, even though the inventory of inflectional categories found in English is much poorer than that of German, in particular in the nominal domain. Overall, English has moved further away from Proto-Germanic than has German. English is therefore often described as an **isolating** (or **analytic**) language, while German can still be said to manifest many properties of an inflecting language. As in the case of phonology, the reason and explanation for this difference in the degree of morphological simplification is often seen in the exposure of English to massive language contact. Language contact and the need to communicate across languages may often lead to simplification, e.g. the loss of case (cf. Bentz and Winter 2013). In fact, the transition from Old to Middle English has been compared to a process of creolization (e.g. Poussa 1982, Allen 1997). This view might be a bit extreme and it cannot explain all the details, but the assumption that language contact had a role to play in the structural simplification of English is certainly not unreasonable.

While the simplification or even loss of some morphological distinctions in English such as gender or mood (indicative vs. subjunctive) do not seem to have any repercussions on the rest of the system, the loss of case distinctions clearly does. One example of a minor consequence of this development is the absence of **external possessor constructions** as in the German sentence *Karl hat sich den Fuß verstaucht* 'Charles sprained his ankle' (cf. Chapter 8). This construction crucially involves a noun phrase or pronoun in the dative case, and since English has lost the dative case together with the other case distinctions it is not surprising that this construction is no longer available, except in some formulaic expressions such as *He looked her in the eyes*. A more dramatic consequence concerns the marking of **grammatical relations**: Constituent order took over the function of identifying subject and object, which was signalled by case marking in Old English, and still is in Modern German.

The loss of freedom in the permissible orderings of verbs and their arguments (subjects, objects) is widely assumed to be causally linked to this type of morphological change. As pointed out in Chapter 11, it would be a simplification to say that English constituent order is fixed, whereas German constituent order is free. Remember that German sentence structure is quite rigid with regard to the position of the verb(s), that there is always a topical or focal constituent in main clauses, etc. A more appropriate way of describing the difference between English and German is to say that constituent order in German depends on more factors than it does in English. While the ordering of elements is almost exclusively determined by grammatical relations in English, further aspects play a role in German, such as information structure (topicality and focusing), pronominal vs. non-pronominal status and definiteness. What we can say, therefore, is that constituent order in German is more 'multi-factorial' than in English, where it basically (though not exclusively) depends on the grammatical relations involved.

It has also been claimed that the placement of finite verbs in English (in front of the object) is also a consequence of the loss of case marking, but this has not been clearly established so far (cf. Hawkins 1992, 1999). The relevant change cannot simply be described as a change from SOV to SVO, but it certainly led to predominant

SVO-ordering in English. The hypothesis that there is an implicational relationship between the relative ordering of verb and object, and the presence or absence of case morphology, is, to some extent, supported by cross-linguistic evidence: SOV languages such as Turkish or Japanese typically have case distinctions, whereas languages without case systems are typically SVO. A correlation has also been claimed to hold between the VO/OV-parameter and what was called '**multi-factorial**' vs. '**mono-factorial**' ordering principles above (cf. Koster 1999, 2000): among the Germanic languages, only OV-languages (e.g. Dutch, German) allow 'scrambling', i.e. the optional reordering of constituents within the Middle Field, while the order of elements is more fixed in VO-languages (English, Scandinavian). One possible explanation for this tendency is to say that in (Germanic) VO-languages, case is assigned in specific structural configurations ('structural case'), whereas it is assigned to specific functional roles of arguments (recipient, goal, etc.) in OV-languages ('inherent case'). It should be mentioned, however, that such generalizations are rather specific and cannot easily be extended beyond the Germanic family.

The greater freedom of English in mapping participant relations unto grammatical relations in comparison to German, especially the greater freedom of encoding participants as **subjects**, can also be linked to the loss of case marking. Many of the relevant structures can be seen as the result of reanalyzing initial objects as subjects. For instance, in examples like the following, the constituent preceding *lyketh* was originally a dative NP:

⟨1⟩ a. And these be the poyntes of wedlocke, whiche god lyketh beste in a maried woman. [Juan Luis Vives, Instruction of a Christen woman]

b. ...that every wight may entre whan him lyketh ...
'...that everyone may enter when he likes ...'
[Chaucer, Canterbury Tales, Tale of Melibeus, §12]

As case marking was lost, the argument structure of the whole sentence was consequently reanalyzed. The sole argument of a clause was regarded as a subject and as a consequence subjectless sentences are no longer part of English grammar. A similar explanation can be given for locative subjects. Note first the apparent parallelism between the two sentences in ⟨2⟩:

⟨2⟩ a. Hans wuchs ein Bart.

b. John grew a beard.

A similar parallelism can be observed in ⟨3⟩, even though sentences such as ⟨3a⟩ are awkward in contemporary German, due to the fact that external possession is basically restricted to animate possessors.

⟨3⟩ a. Der Maschine ist eine Sicherung durchgebrannt.

b. The machine blew a fuse.

While such connections between case marking and argument structure seem to be relatively obvious, it has to be pointed out that the exact chronologies and causalities in this process are a complex matter. In particular, it would be simplistic to assume that the broader range of thematic roles covered by subjects in English is solely a consequence of the loss of case in that language.

Finally, without a system of clearly expressed case distinctions there are no case-dependent rules. The derivation of passive structures from active ones described in Chapter 9 is such a case-dependent rule in German which does not exist in English. Remember that the German *werden*-Passiv allows the promotion of the accusative argument to subject status. The English *be*-passive, by contrast, allows the promotion of the first post-verbal element. Given that both the direct and the indirect object may occur in that position, both types of constituents can be promoted to subject function (*I gave him a book* ⟶ *He was given a book by me*; *I gave a book to him* ⟶ *A book was given to him by me*). Moreover, as shown in Chapter 9, passive sentences may even be derived from basic structures with prepositional objects and from structures with adjuncts in English, whereas we find a clearly case-dependent rule in German.

Tense and aspect The formal parallels in the tense systems of the two languages – e.g. the formation of the past tense through vowel gradation as in *sing/sang*, and the competition of these 'strong' forms with a larger set of weak verbs – are due to the common genealogical origin of English and German. However, both English and German have undergone considerable changes in their systems, in particular by adding new formal means to the basically two-term system of past vs. non-past. While the relevant categories are often parallel in formal terms – e.g. the *have*-perfect – they differ in terms of the functions that these parallel forms have, since their developments were accompanied by different extensions in the use of these tenses. The semantic change from a genuine perfect to a narrative tense that took place in in German is widely attested in the languages of Europe and becomes more and more prevalent as we move from the north to the south of Europe. If this change is regarded as a result of language contact, the geographical distance between English and German can be regarded as being responsible for the diverging developments in this domain. As far as the development of the Progressive aspect in English is concerned, it has been hypothesized that contact with Celtic may have played a certain role (Hickey 2012).

Extraction and non-finite subordination The most general distinction between English and German in the domain of subordinate structures concerns extraction phenomena. There is much more freedom in the movement of constituents across clause boundaries in English than there is in German. Alternatively, we can say that the distance between a gap in clause structure and its filler can be much greater in English. Hawkins (1992, 1999) has proposed an explanation of this contrast in terms of processing and constituent order (cf. the above discussion of case morphology and constituent order). In German the basic position of the finite verb is the one following all arguments (SOV), whereas English is SVO. In processing an English sentence, the early occurrence of the verb will provide early information on the interpretation of the relevant structures even if one argument has been extracted. In German, by contrast, a complete interpretation is only possible once we have processed all the arguments and finally get to the verb. Empty argument positions and a long distance between these positions, i.e. a filler higher up in the sentence associated with a gap further down, will thus be more misleading in SOV-languages (like German) than in SVO-languages (like English).

Reflexivity The most convincing explanation for the contrasts between English and German in the domain of reflexivity is certainly a historical one. The counterpart of the reflexive pronoun *sich* in German was lost in the other West Germanic languages. While Dutch (re)borrowed *zich* from German, the system of reflexivity was completely renewed in English with the help of the intensifier *self*. The resultant complex forms (pronoun + *self*) were used both as intensifiers and as markers of reflexivity. The fact that these forms are not used in certain contexts where we find *sich* in German (verbs of grooming, locative adjuncts) is due to the low time depth of the relevant change, as well as the fact that the complex reflexives of English have not completely lost their basic emphatic quality. It is also for these reasons that the complex *self*-forms are not productively used as middle markers in English, in contrast to German. The German reflexive marker *sich* has been grammaticalized to such an extent that it can be used as a purely grammatical marker of derived intransitivity (*Meine Vermutung hat sich bestätigt. — My assumption turned out to be true.*). The identity of intensifiers and reflexive markers in English – in contrast to German – is the concomitant result of the renewal of the system of reflexivity in English, which is a frequently attested situation in the languages of the world.

The lexicon There are no pervasive generalizations to be made in the distinctions expressed by the lexical inventories of two languages, even though there may be systematic contrasts in specific subsystems of the lexicon. There are numerous contrasts and these contrasts are typically random and difficult to systematize, with the possible exception of contrasts due to contact with and borrowing from different neighboring languages. In the lexical domain we generally expect contrasts rather than parallels and the more interesting question is why we still find so many similar or even parallel lexical differentiations and polysemies between two languages that have taken such strikingly different paths in their grammatical developments.

Summary In our brief explanatory survey of the individual chapters and individual contrasts we have already linked several contrasts to one trigger or cause and in doing so we have subsumed several contrasts under one generalization. Another

	German	English
morphology	(more) inflecting	(more) isolating
case marking	rich	loss of case distinctions
basic constituent order	SOV	SVO
freedom of const. order	freer const. order (multi-factorial)	(more) fixed const. order (mono-factorial)
encoding of grammatical relations	paradigmatic	syntagmatic

Table 18.2 English and German: Major parameters of variation

way of making such generalizations is to take well-known parameters of variation, i.e. dimensions along which languages are known to typically differ and which are also known to correlate with other parameters, and then characterize the two languages under comparison in terms of a list of such parameters of variation. In our particular case such a confrontation of English and German could take the form shown in Table 18.2.

Note that summaries as shown in Table 18.2 invariably involve simplifications and overstatements. For instance, saying that constituent order in German is 'multi-factorial' while it is 'mono-factorial' in English is such a simplification, since objects may also be preposed under specific circumstances in English (*John I quite like*). Comparisons of this type can obviously only be rough approximations and have to be taken *cum grano salis*.

Even more ambitious attempts at unifying the contrasts between English and German, thus approaching a holistic typology, have been made in Hawkins (1986), in Berg (2014) and in Hawkins (2018). Hawkins (1986) argues that the major contrast between English and German can be stated as proper **subset relations** between the contrasting structures. The unifying generalization which summarizes all of the differences identified in his book is formulated by Hawkins as follows: "Where the grammars of English and German contrast, the surface forms [...] of German are in closer correspondence with their associated meanings". In English we find "greater ambiguity and/or vagueness [...] i.e. greater collapsing of semantic distinctions and of different semantic types onto common surface forms" (Hawkins 1986: 121f.). This characterization of English as a language with a '**loose fit**' between form and meaning – as against the '**tight fit**' language German – has been criticized as applying only to (some of) the contrasts investigated in Hawkins (1986). In other domains of grammatical organization the more explicit semantic information and the relevant grammatical differentiations are found in English and not in German (cf. Rohdenburg 1990, Kortmann and Meyer 1992).

In Berg (2014) an attempt is made to subsume a variety of contrasts between English and German under a general parameter proposed for languages typology called 'boundary permeability'. Languages in general – English and German being a case in point – may differ in how they draw boundaries between categories, establishing either soft boundaries (English) or sharp and strict ones (German). This greater permeability between boundaries in English is illustrated by looking at the boundaries between word classes, between the voice system 'active' vs. 'passive', between the count-mass distinction, between nominal and verbal constructions, etc. For many of the case studies presented it is shown that German draws stricter distinctions between the relevant categories.

In a more recent version of general developments and characteristics of English as opposed to German and other West Germanic languages, Hawkins (2018) draws a fundamental distinction between word-internal and word-external information provided by a language for the interpretation of its sentences. While the identification of a lexical element as a noun or the subject of a sentence, for example, is provided word-internally through inflection in German, the relevant information has to be retrieved from the linguistic environment in English and other languages, which rely more on co-occurrence relations. Another clear example of this contrast can be found in our discussion of the multiple uses of the *ing*-suffix in English (Sect. 4.4). It is only by looking at the syntactic environment of the relevant form that we arrive at its interpretation. According to Hawkins, it is the frequency of such minimal surface forms in English, and the resulting need of their word-external processing, that manifest particularly clear cases of pervasive contrasts between English and German.

18.3 Concluding remarks

What the controversial discussions summarized in Section 18.2 ultimately show is that a strictly holistic typology is not feasible at the moment. At least at the present state of our knowledge, the large number and wide variety of contrasts between two languages cannot be reduced to different values on one or a few fundamental parameters, from which everything else follows. Many of the structures analyzed and compared above give us the impression that a language is in fact "un système où tout se tient" (Meillet 1903: 407). However, there are many aspects for which Wittgenstein's simile seems to be more appropriate: A language is like on old town with narrow, winding streets, lanes and alleyways in the old centre, as well as well-organized and symmetric suburbs surrounding this centre.[1]

---

[1] "Unsere Sprache kann man ansehen als eine alte Stadt: Ein Gewinkel von Gässchen und Plätzen, alten und neuen Häusern, und Häusern mit Zubauten aus verschiedenen Zeiten; und dies umgeben von einer Menge neuer Vororte mit geraden und regelmässigen Strassen und mit einförmigen Häusern." (Wittgenstein 1953: Part 1, No 18)

Answers and solutions

(Note that only the general direction of the correct answer or solution will be indicated on the following pages.)

Chapter 2

1. (i) [g] initially (*ghost*); (ii) [f] after open vowels (*rough, laugh*); (iii) silent after close vowels (*though, plough, high*); (iv) [ə] in *Edinburgh*.

3. /θ/ and /ð/ contrast only in a final position, e.g. *teeth* vs. *teethe*. /θ/ is found initially in content words (e.g. *thing, throw*) and /ð/ in function words (*the, though*). In a medial position, only /ð/ is regularly found (*father, hither*), with very few exceptions (e.g. *author*).

4. Most speakers pronounce *Lügner* and *Stieglitz* without devoicing the /g/, whereas /g/ is devoiced in *Bagdad* and *Magdalena*. In the first two words the plosive is regarded as forming part of the second syllable ('resyllabification'), so the rule of final devoicing does not apply (*Lü.gner, Stie.glitz*).

5. Final devoicing in English → potential misunderstandings (*My bag is broken* vs. *My back is broken*); no final devoicing in German → accent, but no misunderstandings.

6. Voiceless plosives are unaspirated in Austrian German, which makes them very similar to voiced plosives for speakers of Standard German.

7. /ɜː/ → /øː/ or /œ/ (e.g. [hepi bœʁsdeɪ]); /ɒ/ → /ɔ/ ([pɔpmusiːk]).

8. /eː/ → /eɪ/; /oː/ → /əʊ/ or /oʊ/. The English vowels are not only phonetically, but also distributionally, similar to the German ones: they are produced with a similar tongue position and can occur in stressed open syllables (i.e. they are tense).

9. There is only one lax unrounded (mid-)open front vowel in German while there are two such vowels in English (underdifferentiation in German → source of interference).

10. In English, tense/long vowels are shortened before voiceless obstruents. There is no such rule in German.

Chapter 3

1. Specific homorganic combinations of a plosive and a liquid or glide are not allowed in the onset. There is a certain tendency to avoid homorganic formations in this part of the syllable.

2. In contrast to the onset, articulatory similarity of adjacent sounds is preferred in the coda.

3. A vowel is inserted, usually an /e/, thus allowing resyllabification ([es.peɪn], [es.troŋ]).

4. Contra: They are morphologically dependent on a verb. Pro: they have a stress position and regularly carry primary stress; they can be coordinated (*Er fuhr herauf und herab*). From a phonological point of view, they consequently behave like words. The resultant verbs are similar to compounds in phonological terms (i.e. *ab-warten* behaves like *Haus-meister*).

Chapter 4

1. English is developing into an isolating (analytic) language. The following inflectional categories of Old English have disappeared or are disappearing in Modern English: (a) nouns: case, gender; (b) verbs: mood, person (except for 3rd person, marked by SG *-s* in the present tense); (c) adjectives: strong vs. weak inflection; (d) pronouns: case.

2. The so-called 'Saxon' genitive *-s* (*the man's*) combines with both nouns and phrases (*someone else's car*) and is therefore often described as a phrasal adposition.

3. At first sight we can say that all inflectional categories found in English are also found in German, but not the other way round. But if we regard the adverbial ending *-ly*, the Progressive *be* + *-ing* and the gerund affix *-ing* as inflectional markers, we have to admit that these markers have no counterpart in German. Moreover, reflexive pronouns only inflect in English.

4. An adjective combines with the affix *-ly* if it is in construction with a verb (manner adverb), an adjective (degree adverb) or a sentence (sentence adverb). In view of the regularity, productivity and generality of this morphological process, there are good reasons for regarding it as an example of inflectional morphology. However, unlike all other instances of inflectional morphology, suffixation of *-ly* usually changes the word class.

5. The use of the comparative markers *-er* and *more* depends mainly on prosodic properties of the adjectives: its number of syllables, its stress and syllable structure

(in the case of disyllabic adjectives). Frequency of use also plays a role, and there are some idiosyncratic restrictions.

6. Reduced relatives with non-finite *ing*-forms are parts of noun phrases, in contrast to adverbial participles like those in ⟨54b⟩ and ⟨54c⟩. None of these *-ing*-forms can be regarded as reduced Progressive forms, since there are no restrictions on possible verbs in these non-finite constructions, in contrast to the Progressive (**He is owning a dog*). Note furthermore that adverbial participles may neutralize the distinction between the Progressive and the Non-Progressive aspect:

(i) Living, as he did, in Canada, he caught his own fish.
(ii) Living, as he was, in Canada, he caught his own fish.

7. The relevant distinction is that between mass and count nouns.

Chapter 5

1. The two systems are more or less parallel in their formal make-up, but parallel forms are used quite differently (especially the *Perfekt* and the Present Perfect).

2. German has the choice between the simple *Präsens* and the *werden*-future. In English, there are at least four different ways of referring to future time: *will* (*shall*), *going to*, the Progressive in the Present tense and the Simple Present, with subtle but clear contrasts in meaning:

(i) Will you play tennis tomorrow?
(ii) We shall find a solution.
(iii) Are you going to play tennis tomorrow?
(iv) Are you playing tennis tomorrow?
(v) When does the first train leave tomorrow?

3. (i) *will* expresses a contingent (sometimes also a distant) future, and there is often a hidden conditional; (ii) *going to* is used for a future fulfilment of present intention or of present cause; (iii) the Present Progressive is used for future realizations of present arrangements; (iv) the Simple Present is used for future events based on general regulations and laws.

4. Conditionals denoting future actions require a future marker (typically *will*) in the main clause.

5. The use illustrated in ⟨54⟩ is the 'universal' use. The verbs in these sentences denote states rather than processes or events.

6. The German *Perfekt* has a resultative use, but is also taking over the narrative use of the *Präteritum*.

7. The Simple Present relates to a stretch of time around the moment of utterance. The Present Perfect has several interpretations, the most important of which are

(i) the universal use, which relates to an interval beginning before the moment of utterance and reaching up to and including the moment of utterance, and (ii) the existential use, which indicates an event in the indefinite past which has consequences for the moment of utterance.

8. The Present Perfect in English can only be used whenever stretches of time are considered that begin before the moment of utterance and lead right up to it. In contrast to German, it cannot be used in combination with definite time adverbials in the past and thus not for narration.

9. In combination with event verbs the Present Perfect typically has a resultative meaning. In combination with states it describes a continuous state up to the moment of utterance. In combination with process verbs and event verbs it may identify an indefinite time in the past.

10. (a) Current happenings, (b) temporal frame, (c) the backgrounding use, (d) the futurate use.

11. There are modest beginnings of an aspectual differentiation in German. A kind of progressive aspect can be expressed by the following markers: *dabei sein zu V, beim V-en sein, am V-en sein, im V-en sein*, etc.

12. This term is normally not used for English, since the absence of the agent from the place of the speaker has to be overtly expressed in English:
   (a) Karl ist einkaufen.
   (b) Charles is off shopping / Charles has gone shopping.

13. The a-example is often considered as a dialectal form.

14. It is the tense (future vs. past) which requires a different translation for the two cases:
   (i) In time he will become a valuable colleague.
   (ii) As time went on the suspicion became stronger.

15. These are all cases of the interpretative use of the Progressive.

16. Yes. The following example is a case in point: *For goodness sake, be working when the boss comes in!*

Chapter 6

1. *Need* is used as main verb in ⟨99a⟩ and ⟨99d⟩ and as auxiliary verb in ⟨99b⟩ and ⟨99c⟩. *Dare* is used as main verb in ⟨99e⟩.

2. *Used to* is treated as a main verb in ⟨100a⟩, while it can be regarded as an auxiliary verb in ⟨100b⟩.

3. In all of these cases we find circumstantial modality.

4. *Will* is a main verb in ⟨102a⟩ and an auxiliary verb, expressing a habit, in ⟨102b⟩.

5. The first sentence could only be used if the speaker repeats and rejects a claim made by somebody else. Quotative *wollen* cannot easily be used with a first person subject, since the verb is used to attribute a claim to somebody else. Concessive *mögen* is used if a speaker concedes a claim made by others, but not for the speaker's own claims.

6. External: a, b, c; internal: d, f: e could be internal as well as external.

7. ⟨105a⟩: epistemic; ⟨105b⟩: epistemic; ⟨105c⟩: epistemic; ⟨105d⟩: circumstantial (deontic); ⟨105e⟩: dispositional; ⟨105f⟩: circumstantial (existential).

8. Tag questions do not always repeat the modal of the preceding sentence or insert the auxiliary *do*. In ⟨107⟩ we find tags as reduced sentences which would also express the same function (speech act) as the preceding sentence: *Shall we (go to see a movie)?*, *Will you (stay on the pavement)!*

9. This distinction is drawn on the basis of the NICE properties (placement of negation, inversion, *verum focus* (code) and post-verbal ellipsis). In German, modal verbs have some special properties, but they are less clearly distinguished from the other verbs.

10. There are only three auxiliary verbs found at the beginning of conditionals (*should, were, had*):

(i) Should he not come in time, we could always postpone our meeting.

(ii) Had I known this, I would not have come.

(iii) Were they to reveal their secrets, there would be several arrests.

Chapter 7

1. English: The subject precedes the verb in declarative sentences, the objects follow. The distinction between direct and indirect objects is only made for sentences with two objects: indirect objects precede direct objects and typically denote human beings. German: Grammatical relations are identified by cases: nominative → subject; accusative → direct object; dative → indirect object. Criteria for the identification of subjects in both English and German include: (i) the omission of subjects in imperatives, coordinations and embedded clauses, and (ii) the encoding of the Agent as a subject.

2. ⟨64a⟩: *der König*; ⟨64b⟩: no subject; ⟨64c⟩: *es*. Existential *there* is typically used to translate *es*.

3. All examples in ⟨65⟩ are subjectless sentences.

4. Like *George*, *there* can be the subject of an object clause; and, like *George*, *there* can be raised to the object position of *expect*; or, put differently, *there* can be the object in an a.c.i.-construction.

5. In English, we cannot use double object constructions for these cases and prepositional objects are used instead.

6. German always distinguishes location from direction. In English, disambiguation may be achieved by using different preposition in some cases (*on/onto*, *in/into*), or by using specific verbs.

7. a. Fred's car broke a piston.; b. Suddenly the machine blew a fuse.; c. In the third curve the car burst a tire. The general contrast illustrated by these examples is that English, unlike German, allows instrumental and locative subjects.

Chapter 8

1. Constructions with internal possessors in English typically correspond to constructions with external possessors in German. The notion of possession involved is that of 'inalienable possession'. The syntactic phenomenon illustrated by the German examples is the increase in valency, i.e. in the number of arguments that the relevant verbs have in these constructions (intransitive → transitive; transitive → di-transitive).

2. External possessors are possible in English if the possessum (typically a body part) is expressed within a prepositional phrase which can be omitted without rendering the sentence ungrammatical (e.g. *He hit me on the head*).

3. Sentence ⟨36a⟩ suggests that the speaker is in the relevant room and feels bothered by a neighbour, whereas the b-sentence does not imply such 'affectedness'. The a-sentence of ⟨37⟩ is used in a non-literal sense: 'We have to keep an eye on the pianist.' In ⟨37b⟩ we find the literal interpretation, a recommendation to watch the fingers of the pianist, e.g. with the intention of learning something.

4. You can simply look for a metaphorical expression with a dative object and a body part, like for instance: *Du raubst mir den letzten Nerv. Das geht mir nicht aus dem Sinn.*

5. In English, we find transitive constructions with the possessive pronoun in front of the expression denoting a body part (internal possessors). In German, an implicit possessor construction is used, i.e. there is only a definite article and the possessor is not encoded overtly.

Chapter 9

1. Both direct and indirect objects can be promoted to subjects in English using the *be*-passive. In German, a special auxiliary (*bekommen*) is used to promote indirect objects, which is moreover regionally restricted; the common *werden*-passive can only be used to promote direct objects. In English, a prepositional object and the noun phrases of locative and directional phrases can also be promoted to subjects, provided a general semantic condition on the meaning of the resultant sentences is met. This is not possible in German.

2. The most general concept of voice (diathesis) relates to the mapping of participant roles (Agent, Patient, Instrument, etc.) onto grammatical relations. Under a more narrow definition, the term *voice* refers to the opposition between active and passive (and possibly also the middle voice), where the active is normally taken as basic.

3. The *get*-passive is more colloquial than the *be*-passive and expresses the personal involvement of the subject and/or his/her partial responsibility for the event. Unlike the *be*-passive, it can only be used with monotransitive predicates.

4. The auxiliary *werden* is used in German whenever an accusative object is promoted to subject. *Bekommen* or *kriegen* are used when a dative (indirect) object is promoted to subject. *Gehören* is also developing into a passive auxiliary, but is even more restricted in its use than *bekommen* and *kriegen*.

5. The sentence does not meet the general semantic condition that the subject of a passive sentence must be a real Patient. The house can hardly be affected (become famous, important, etc.) as a result of a look by the Duke of Edinburgh.

6. Noun phrases which are part of prepositional phrases can never be promoted to subject in German.

7. Either the light verb *make* alone or the complex verbal form *make a fool of* can be analyzed as the predicate of the relevant construction.

8. ⟨70a⟩: *Ich mag es nicht, wenn im Kino Leute vor mir sitzen.* An active sentence would also be used as a translation for ⟨70b⟩.

9. As a result of the general suppression of an Agent in passive sentences, passives that are derived from intransitive verbs are subjectless. They denote events without identifying the participants and often have generic time reference (*Hier wird nicht geraucht.*).

10. Middle constructions are intransitive constructions with basically transitive verbs ('derived intransitivity'). Their subjects correspond to the objects in the relevant transitive constructions. They denote properties rather than actions or events.

11. The two affixes can be analyzed in terms of a voice opposition (the employer = the one who employs people; the employee = the one who is employed by someone). An analogous analysis is possible for such contrasts as *in* vs. *under*: *John is in control* vs. *The situation is under control.*

Chapter 10

1. Intensifiers and reflexive pronouns in English can be distinguished on the basis of their distribution (adjunct vs. argument positions), their prosodic properties, their meaning and their translations into languages like German.

2. In English, intensifiers only combine with personal pronouns in subject position.

3. Reflexive pronouns in English are complex expressions, i.e. combinations of a (personal or possessive) pronoun and the intensifier *self* found in older stages of the language. In contrast to German *sich*, they inflect for person, number and in the third person singular also for gender.

4. ⟨38a⟩: reflexive use; ⟨38b⟩: modal passive/middle voice; ⟨38c⟩: inherent (obligatory) reflexive; ⟨38d⟩: so-called 'auto-causative' use/bodily motion; ⟨38e⟩: anti-causative use/change of state; ⟨38f⟩: reflexive use; ⟨38g⟩: reciprocal use. English only uses a reflexive pronoun for ⟨38a⟩ and ⟨38f⟩.

5. An instance of German *sich* that is part of an inherently reflexive use of a verb cannot be replaced by another noun phrase, cannot be questioned, cannot be stressed, cannot be moved to the initial position in a sentence, and is meaningless.

6. The *self*-forms in ⟨39⟩ are neither clear instances of reflexive pronouns nor are they instances of intensifiers. ⟨39b⟩–⟨39d⟩ are best analyzed as instances of the logophoric use of these forms, and *himself* in ⟨39a⟩ can be analyzed as an intensifier without accompanying pronoun.

7. The *self*-forms in ⟨40a⟩–⟨40b⟩ are adnominal intensifiers, all the others exemplify the adverbial use. The inclusive adverbial use is found in ⟨40c⟩, and ⟨40f⟩ is ambiguous. ⟨40d⟩ and ⟨40e⟩ illustrate the exclusive use.

8. The prepositional phrases containing the pronouns are not arguments (complements) of the relevant verbs. That the 3rd person pronoun is co-referent with the subject is predictable in these cases. In German, we find *sich* in all cases.

9. The examples in ⟨42⟩ are all dialectal and slightly archaic forms. ⟨42a⟩ and ⟨42b⟩ are intensifiers as used in non-standard varieties of English. ⟨42c⟩ and ⟨42d⟩ are instances of locally bound non-reflexive pronouns, which reflect the situation in Old and Middle English. *Yourself* in ⟨42e⟩ is a reflexive pronoun which could be omitted without making the sentence ungrammatical.

10. In these three cases the reflexive pronoun is co-referent with the object rather than with the subject. In German, the intensifier *selbst* is typically added to the reflexive pronoun in such cases.

Chapter 11

1. The finite verb is rarely preceded by more than two constituents.

2. NPs precede PPs.

3. Complex constituents typically occur towards the end of a sentence.

4. Subordinate clauses: SOV; main clauses: TVX. In the Middle Field, pronouns precede lexical noun phrases.

5. This statement does not apply to the placement of verbs in German. In English, a change in the basic constituent order is often accompanied by a change in the construction (cf. *It's a free constituent order language is English*).

6. a) Mit Abstand fahren Sie am besten. – b) Mit Abstand am besten fahren Sie!

7. Only one constituent can occur in the Forefield.

8. In both languages interrogative pronouns are fronted. If there are several, one of them being the subject, the subject has to be fronted in English. In German, any interrogative pronoun can be fronted even if there are several of them.

9. In contrast to German, an indirect object cannot denote the Source of an action in English.

10. (Nominative >) accusative > dative.

11. In ⟨98⟩ the subject and the main verb are inverted. The sentences in ⟨99⟩ and ⟨100⟩ exemplify the more common inversion of subject and auxiliary.

13. In German, we can often use constituent order or different types of particles (*noch, da*) to distinguish the two readings.

14. Only verb-initial structures are used as imperatives in German. If an adverb is shifted into the topic position, the resultant structure could be a declarative sentence (with the right verbal form).

15. Not all of these patterns have a clear counterpart in English. ⟨103b⟩, ⟨103g⟩ and ⟨103h⟩ cannot be translated literally and different sentence types have to be used (e.g. rhetorical questions).

16. In German the position between the subject and the following verb is excluded, since only one constituent can be fronted. In English the position between verb and object is included.

17. The typical position of *not* in English is the one behind the first auxiliary verb. The position of *nicht* in German depends on its scope.

Chapter 12

1. The following table summarizes the most important contrasts:

		E	G
(a)	NP-movement out of PP	yes	no
(b)	extraction across finite clause boundaries	yes	no
(c)	parasitic gaps	yes	no
(d)	order of wh-pronouns	fixed	free

2. Extraction out of prepositional phrases and the resultant preposition stranding are admissible in English but not in German.

3. The restrictions are more or less parallel, even if the relevant structures may differ.

4. Extraction out of finite complement clauses and out of non-finite adverbial clauses is possible in English but not in German.

5. Only *that*-relatives or bare relatives are possible.

6. The first sentence asserts that Jane also has a violin which once belonged to Heifetz. This is not implied in the second sentence.

7. The head noun of the non-finite relative clause functions as understood subject in the first three sentences and as object in the others.

8. Headless relatives do not have a head noun before the relative pronoun:

⟨4⟩   a.   I will follow you wherever you go.

     b.   I did not like what I saw.

⟨5⟩   a.   Wer immer das gesagt hat, lügt.

     b.   Was du kochst, macht mich krank.

9. If the relative clause relates to the whole preceding sentence, only *which* can be used as relative pronoun in English.

10. *As* is used after *such*: *Such people as he knew were not of much use.*

Chapter 13

1. (i) Raising operations are much more restricted in German than in English (no reportive S-S raising, no S-S raising with adjectives, no S-O raising in German, etc.); (ii) control structures are more restricted in English than in German (more control verbs in German, no explicit controllers in English, more control shift in German); (iii) adverbial participles (free adjuncts and absolute participles) are more widespread in English (found in all tenses, in the active and passive, etc.; absolute participles are almost non-existent in German).

2. *Entsprechend* in ⟨57⟩ and *notwithstanding* ⟨59⟩ cannot simply be analyzed as participles because in that case both elements would have to follow the relevant NP (*ihren Wünschen* as an object of *entsprechend* and *his objections* as a subject of *notwithstanding*). Therefore, these structures are best analyzed as prepositional phrases.

3. There are no gerunds in German. English gerunds usually correspond either to *zu*-infinitives (*Reading poetry is fun* 'Es macht Spaß, Lyrik zu lesen', *He risked getting caught* 'Er riskierte [es], erwischt zu werden'), or to nominalized infinitives (*Das Betreten des Rasens ist verboten.*). Even though it is not always possible to predict which verbs take infinitives and which verbs require a gerund, there are certain tendencies: (i) 'retrospective' and factive verbs (*remember, recollect*; *enjoy, regret, welcome*, etc.) usually take a gerund; (ii) in some cases, 'positive' verbs take infinitives while 'negative' verbs take gerunds (*I claim to have seen . . . , I disclaim having done . . .*). German object control verbs usually correspond to English verbs requiring a gerund, with the exception of 'verbs of manipulation' such as *to ask s.o. to do sth.*

4. (i) The (matrix) subject is not a semantic argument of the (matrix) verb; (ii) a paraphrase with *it . . . that* is usually possible; (iii) active-passive pairs of type ⟨1a⟩/⟨7⟩ are equivalent ('voice neutrality').

5. This pair of sentences shows that certain raising operations are possible only if there are also extractions.

6. The following sentences are possible translations:

⟨61a⟩ Who ordered that the company car be used?

⟨61b⟩ She urged that the prisoners be freed.

⟨61c⟩ They demanded that the freedom of the press be restricted.

The general contrast illustrated by these examples is that German but not English allows implicit controllers. Moreover, English often uses finite complementation strategies where German uses control structures.

7. Control infinitives are more common in German than in English. English often uses either finite complement clauses or gerunds corresponding to German control infinitives.

8. The sentence could be translated as in ⟨62⟩:

⟨62⟩ John promised his friend that he would be invited to the graduation ceremony.

Control shift is more restricted in English than it is in German.

9. ⟨63a⟩: concessive; ⟨63b⟩: conditional; ⟨63c⟩: temporal/substitutive; ⟨63d⟩: manner ('indem').

10. In the sentences in ⟨64⟩, the understood subject of the absolute participle is not part of the main clause ('dangling participles'). In ⟨65a⟩, the whole sentence functions as a subject of the participle, and in ⟨65b⟩ and ⟨65c⟩ there is a generic understood subject (*one*).

Chapter 14

3. The Longman Dictionary of Contemporary English distinguishes 28 different meanings, 25 of which represent metaphorical extensions of the basic (physical) meaning. A similar number of possible readings can be assumed for German *schwer*.

Chapter 15

1. These combinations are semantically highly specialized (lexicalized). This is also reflected in their German translations. *Free trade* is normally translated as *freier Handel* when occurring in isolation, but the compound *Freihandel* is commonly used as a part of other compounds, e.g. *Freihandelsabkommen*. *Civil war* and *new year* translate as compounds into German (*Bürgerkrieg* and *Neujahr*). *Cold war* and *green light* are rendered as syntactic phrases in German, but they exhibit indications of lexicalization insofar as no modifier can intervene between the adjective and the noun, e.g. *kalter zehnjähriger Krieg*, *grünes helles Licht* (in both cases the specific [idiomatic] reading is lost).

2. These examples show that compound linkers often prevent adjacency of two stressed syllables leading to sub-optimal phonotactic configurations. The examples with compound linkers contain only monosyllabic words. This may give rise to complex consonant clusters such as [stʃt] in **Geist-stunde* and [gbl] in **Tag-blatt*. As both elements carry stress, they are not normally reduced phonetically. In some cases, compounding without a compound linker obscures the morphological structure of the word, as in **Hühn-ei* ([hyː.naɪ]).

3. These doublets differ in terms of the semantic relation holding between their components. Those expressions with phrasal stress are typically 'ascriptive' (*x* is [made of] *y*). Compounds with lefthand stress imply a broader range of semantic relations, e.g. a purpose or benefit: *toy factory* (factory is a toy or produces toys), *woman doctor* (female doctor or doctor for women/gynaecologist), *glass case* (case made of glass vs. case for [the storage of] glass), *hair net* (net made of hair vs. net for hair).

4. German invariably has lefthand stress, e.g. 'Ba.de.la.tschen.fabri.kant. The rule of English is different: stress falls on the lefthand member of the compound within the compound, e.g. [*university* ['*teaching award*]] vs. [[*uni'versity teaching*] *award*] (cf. Plag 2003).

5. When denoting human referents, English V-N-compounds normally carry a negative connotation. They often express 'lower' professions (e.g. *turn-spit*) or negative character traits (*break-vow*). They are neutral when they denote animals (*break-bones*) and plants (*heal-all*). The majority of English V-N-compounds in use today denote animals or plants, but most of the relevant items are very rare because of the highly specific meanings (often there are also alternative [Latin or Greek] names for the relevant animals or plants).

6. In a) *four-inch* and *round* modify the noun independently (i.e. *four-inch* is not a modifier of *round* but provides a measure specification by itself). *As wide as* in b) is not a comparison but a scalar expression that could be rendered in German by using a particle such as *immerhin* or (less natural in that context) *sogar*. Finally, c) does not say that the suitcase weighs ten pounds; it indicates that its weight exceeds the weight allowed for suitcases by ten pounds (Germ. *zu schwer*).

Chapter 16

1. The verbs with prefixes describe the action as a whole and are thus 'more perfective' than their simple counterparts. They focus on the result more than the action itself. In English, a similar effect can be achieved by using a Latinate verb for the 'perfective' version and a native, simple verb – sometimes combined with a particle – for the 'more imperfect' situation: *cross/transgress* vs. *walk across*, *cross* vs. *swim across*, *circumvent* vs. *make a detour around* (or similar).

2. The prefix verbs imply that the action was carried out completely and (typically) successfully, while verb-PP combinations are more neutral in this respect (e.g. *antworten auf* vs. *beantworten*, *zerstechen* vs. *stechen in*, *erforschen* vs. *forschen an*). In English we often have to use an adverb to make that distinction, e.g. *answer (completely)*. In other cases, a transitive verb alternates with a verb-PP combination, e.g. [*stab* NP] vs. [*stab* [*at* NP]]. When no such alternation is available, different lexical items have to be used, e.g. *investigate* vs. *study*.

3. The main criterion concerns the placement of pronominal objects, which precede the particle but not the preposition (*switched it off* vs. **look him after*). Moreover, particles (unlike prepositions) carry main stress when occurring in a final position.

4. Directional elements (which are closely related to locative ones) imply a change of state; a change of state, in turn, often implies perfectivity (depending on the predicate). The historical development often proceeds along the path 'location > direction > aspect' (e.g. *up* 'on top' > 'upwards' > 'perfective').

5. The most natural analysis is to regard *durch den Wald* as a PP and the second occurrence of *durch* as a particle. An analysis of *durch ... durch* as a circumposition has been proposed because the entire constituent *durch den Wald durch* can occur in the Forefield (*Durch den Wald durch gehe ich nicht*). An analysis of *durch* as a postposition does not make sense. The problem with the analysis of *durch ... durch* as a circumposition is that it is based on a rule with does not seem to be without exceptions, as it is not uncommon for more than one constituent to occur in the Forefield (cf. Müller 2005).

8. These particles represent systematic exceptions to the generalization that particles have a perfectivizing function. They express duration or continuation of an activity, sometimes with additional meaning components like the 'comitative' meaning expressed by *sing along*.

Chapter 17

2. Cf. the translations given on page 305.

3. ⟨68a⟩: *His voice alone ... / His very voice ... / merely his voice*; ⟨68b⟩: *Even before World War II ...* ; ⟨68c⟩: *We'll manage all right*; ⟨68d⟩: *already*; ⟨68e⟩: *... by the time ....*

4. *... of all X's*, where X is a superordinate term of the focus referent: ⟨69a⟩ and ⟨69b⟩: *of all persons*; ⟨69c⟩: *of all poets*.

5. ⟨70a⟩: *Do you mean to tell me ... ?*; ⟨70b⟩: question tag; ⟨70c⟩: paraphrase, e.g. *He shouldn't be led to believe ....*

6. *Überhaupt* widens the scope of possible referents.

List of references

Aarts, Flor (1982): The contrastive analysis debate: Problems and solutions. *Studia Anglica Posnanensia* 14, 47–68.

Abraham, Werner (1991): Modalverben in der Germania. In **Iwasaki, E.** (ed.), *Begegnungen mit dem 'Fremden': Grenzen – Traditionen – Vergleiche. Akten des VIII. Internationalen Germanistenkongresses, Tokyo, 1990*, Vol. 4. München: Iudicium, pp. 109–118.

Abraham, Werner (2002): Modal verbs: Epistemics in German and English. In **Barbiers, S. / F. H. Beukema / W. van der Wurff** (eds.), *Modality and its Interaction with the Verbal System*. Amsterdam: Benjamins, pp. 19–50.

Abraham, Werner / Theo Janssen (eds.) (1989): *Tempus – Aspekt – Modus. Die lexikalischen und grammatischen Formen in den germanischen Sprachen*. Tübingen: Niemeyer.

Abraham, Werner / Larisa Leisiö (eds.) (2006): *Passivization and Typology: Form and Function*. Amsterdam: Benjamins.

Abraham, Werner / Elisabeth Leiss (eds.) (2013): *Funktionen von Modalität*. Berlin: de Gruyter Mouton.

Aijmer, Karin / Bengt Altenberg (eds.) (2013): *Advances in Corpus-Based Contrastive Linguistics. Studies in Honour of Stig Johansson*. Amsterdam: Benjamins.

Aikhenvald, Alexandra Y. / R.M.W. Dixon (eds.) (2017): *The Cambridge Handbook of Linguistic Typology*. Cambridge: Cambridge University Press.

Alatis, James E. (ed.) (1968): *Contrastive Linguistics and its Pedagogical Implications*. Washington: Georgetown University Press.

Allen, Cynthia (1997): Middle English case loss and the 'creolization' hypothesis. *English Language and Linguistics* 1(1), 63–90.

Altenberg, Bengt / Sylviane Granger (eds.) (2002): *Lexis in Contrast. Corpus-Based Approaches*. Amsterdam & Philadelphia: Benjamins.

Aston, Guy (1999): Corpus use and learning to translate. *Textus* 12(2), 289–314.

Baker, Carl L. (1995): Contrast, discourse prominence, and intensification, with special reference to locally free reflexives in British English. *Language* 71(1), 63–101.

Bauer, Laurie / Rochelle Lieber / Ingo Plag (2013): *The Oxford Reference Guide to English Morphology*. Oxford: Oxford University Press.

Beck, Sigrid / Remus Gergel (2014): *Contrasting English and German Grammar: An Introduction to Syntax and Semantics*. Berlin: de Gruyter Mouton.

Behaghel, Otto (1909): Beziehungen zwischen Umfang und Reihenfolge von Satzgliedern. *Indogermanische Forschungen* 25, 110–42.

Bentz, Christian / Bodo Winter (2013): Languages with more second language learners tend to lose nominal case. *Language Dynamics and Change* 3, 1–27.

References

Berg, Thomas (1997): Lexical-stress differences in English and German: The special status of proper names. *Linguistische Berichte* 167, 3–22.

Berg, Thomas (2006): The internal structure of four-noun compounds in English and German. *Corpus Linguistics and Linguistic Theory* 2, 197–231.

Berg, Thomas (2012): The cohesiveness of English and German compounds. *The Mental Lexicon* 7, 1–33.

Berg, Thomas (2014): Boundary permeability: A parameter for linguistic typology. *Linguistic Typology* 18(3), 489–531.

Berg, Thomas (2016): The semantic structure of English and German compounds: Same or different. *Studia Neophilologica* 88, 148–164.

Berg, Thomas (2017): Compounding in German and English: A Quantitative translation study. *Languages in Contrast* 17, 43–68.

Berg, Thomas / Sabine Helmer / Marion Neubauer / Arne Lohmann (2012): Determinants of the extent of compound use: A contrastive analysis. *Linguistics* 50, 269–303.

Berlage, Eva (2009): Prepositions and postpositions. In **Rohdenburg, G. / J. Schlüter** (eds.), *One Language – Two Grammars? Differences between British and American English*. Cambridge: Cambridge University Press, pp. 130–148.

Biber, Douglas / Stig Johansson / Geoffrey Leech / Susan Conrad / Edward Finegan (1999): *The Longman Grammar of Spoken and Written English*. London: Longman.

Bisang, Walter (2008): Precategoriality and syntax-based parts of speech: The case of Late Archaic Chinese. *Studies in Language* 32, 568–589.

Blevins, James P. (1994): A lexicalist analysis of gerundive nominals in English. *Australian Journal of Linguistics* 14(1), 1–38.

Blevins, James P. (2005): Remarks on gerunds. In **Orgun, C.O. / P. Sells** (eds.), *Morphology and the Web of Grammar – Essays in Memory of Steven G. Lapointe*. Stanford: CSLI Publications, pp. 25–47.

Blevins, James P. (2006): English inflection and derivation. In **Aarts, B. / A. McMahon** (eds.), *The Handbook of English Linguistics*. London: Blackwell, pp. 507–536.

Bolinger, Dwight (1977): Transitivity and spatiality: The passive of prepositional verbs. In **Makkai, A. / V. Becker Makkai / L. Heilmann** (eds.), *Linguistics at the Crossroads*. Lake Bluff: Jupiter Press, pp. 57–78.

Brdar, Mario / Szabó Brdar (1992): How tough is tough movement to typologize? In **Mair, Ch. / M. Markus** (eds.), *New Departures in Contrastive Linguistics*. Universität Innsbruck, pp. 105–114.

Brinton, Laurel (1988): *The Development of the English Aspectual System*. New York: Cambridge University Press.

Bublitz, Wolfram (1978): *Ausdrucksweisen der Sprechereinstellung im Deutschen und Englischen. Untersuchungen zur Syntax, Semantik und Pragmatik der deutschen Modalpartikeln und Vergewisserungsfragen und ihrer englischen Entsprechungen*. Tübingen: Niemeyer.

Bühler, Karl (1934): *Sprachtheorie. Die Darstellungsfunktion der Sprache.* Frankfurt/Berlin/Wien: Ullstein.

Burgschmidt, Ernst / Dieter Götz (1974): *Kontrastive Linguistik Deutsch / Englisch.* München: Hueber.

Büring, Daniel (2001): Let's phrase it! – Focus, word order, and prosodic phrasing in German double object constructions. In **Müller, G. / W. Sternefeld** (eds.), *Competition in Syntax.* Berlin: de Gruyter Mouton, pp. 69–105.

Burzio, Luigi (1994): *Principles of English Stress.* Cambridge: Cambridge University Press.

Bybee, Joan / Östen Dahl (1989): The creation of tense and aspect systems in the languages of the world. *Studies in Language* 13(1), 51–103.

Carr, Philip (2015): *English Phonetics and Phonology: An Introduction.* 2nd edn. Chichester: Wiley-Blackwell.

Carstairs-McCarthy, Andrew (2009): *An Introduction to English Morphology: Words and their Structure.* Edinburgh: Edinburgh University Press.

Chomsky, Noam / Morris Halle (1968): *The Sound Patterns of English.* New York: Harper & Row.

Comrie, Bernard (1976): *Aspect.* Cambridge: Cambridge University Press.

Comrie, Bernard (1985): *Tense.* Cambridge: Cambridge University Press.

Comrie, Bernard (1989): *Language Universals and Linguistic Typology.* 2nd edn. Oxford: Blackwell.

Connor, Ulla (1996): *Contrastive Rhetoric: Cross-Cultural Aspects of Second-Language Writing.* Cambridge: Cambridge University Press.

Corbett, Greville (2010): Implicational hierarchies. In **Song, J. J.** (ed.), *The Oxford Handbook of Linguistic Typology.* Oxford: Oxford University Press, pp. 190–205.

Corder, Pit (1967): The significance of learners' errors. *International Review of Applied Linguistics* 5(4), 161–169.

Couper-Kuhlen, Elizabeth (1979): *The Prepositional Passive in English.* Tübingen: Niemeyer.

Croft, William (2003): *Typology and Universals.* 2nd edn. Cambridge: Cambridge University Press.

Cruttenden, Alan (2014): *Gimson's Pronunciation of English.* 8th edn. London: Routledge.

Crystal, David (1989): Why did he say it? *English Today* 5(1), 41–42.

Czepluch, Hartmut (2000): Deutsch als pragmatisierte Sprache: Zum Verhältnis von grammatischen und diskursfunktionalen Eigenschaften. In **Hess-Lüttich, E.W.B. / H.W. Schmitz** (eds.), *"Botschaften verstehen": Kommunikationstheorie und Zeichenpraxis. Festschrift für Helmut Richter.* Frankfurt: Lang, pp. 29–45.

Czulo, Oliver / Silvia Hansen-Schirra (eds.) (2017): *Crossroads Between Contrastive Linguistics, Translation Studies and Machine Translation.* Berlin: Language Science Press.

Davidse, Kristin / Liesbet Heyvaert (2007): On the middle voice: An interpersonal analysis of the English middle. *Linguistics* 45(1), 37–82.

Davis, John F. (2015): *Phonetics and Phonology.* 3rd edn. Stuttgart: Klett.

Davison, Alice (1980): Peculiar passives. *Language* 56, 42–66.

de Groot, Caspar (2000): The absentive. In **Dahl, Ö.** (ed.), *Tense and Aspect in the Languages of Europe*. Berlin: de Gruyter Mouton, pp. 693–719.

Declerck, Renaat (1991): *Tense in English: Its Structure and Use in Discourse*. London: Routledge.

Declerck, Renaat (2006): *The Grammar of the English Verb Phrase, Vol.1: The Grammar of the English Tense System*. In collaboration with Susan Reed and Bert Capelle. Topics in English Linguistics, No 60. Berlin: de Gruyter Mouton.

Demske-Neumann, Ulrike (1994): *Modales Passiv und Tough Movement. Zur strukturellen Kausalität syntaktischen Wandels im Deutschen und Englischen*. Tübingen: Niemeyer.

Depraetere, Ilse (2008): Source of modality: A reassessment. *English Language and Linguistics* 12(1), 1–25.

Diewald, Gabriele (1999): *Die Modalverben im Deutschen. Grammatikalisierung und Polyfunktionalität*. Tübingen: Niemeyer.

Dirven, René (1976): A redefinition of Contrastive Linguistics. *International Review of Applied Linguistics* 14, 1–14.

Dixon, Robert M.W. (1991): *A New Approach to English Grammar, on Semantic Principles*. Oxford: Clarendon.

Domahs, Ulrike / Ingo Plag / Rebecca Carroll (2014): Word stress assignment in German, English and Dutch: Quantity-sensitivity and extra-metricality revisited. *Journal of Comparative German Linguistics* 17, 59–96.

Don, Jan (2014): *Morphological Theory and the Morphology of English*. Edinburgh: Edinburgh University Press.

Donalies, Elke (2005): *Die Wortbildung des Deutschen: Ein Überblick*. Tübingen: Narr.

Dryer, Matthew S. / Martin Haspelmath (eds.) (2013): *WALS Online*. Leipzig: Max Planck Institute for Evolutionary Anthropology. http://wals.info/.

Ebert, Karin (1982): The definite article with inalienables in English and German. In **Lohnes, W. / E. A. Hopkins** (eds.), *The Contrastive Grammar of English and German*. Ann Arbor: Karoma, pp. 64–75.

Eckardt, Regine (2001): Reanalysing *selbst*. *Natural Language Semantics* 9(4), 371–412.

Edmondson, Jerold / Frans Plank (1978): Great expectations: An intensive self-analysis. *Linguistics and Philosophy* 2, 373–413.

Eisenberg, Peter (2006a): *Das Wort. Grundriss der Deutschen Grammatik*. 3rd edn. Stuttgart: Metzler.

Eisenberg, Peter (2006b): *Der Satz. Grundriss der Deutschen Grammatik*. 3rd edn. Stuttgart: Metzler.

Elsen, Hilke (2011): *Grundzüge der Morphologie des Deutschen*. Berlin: de Gruyter Mouton.

Emonds, Joseph Embley / Jan Terje Faarlund (2014): *English: The Language of the Vikings* Olomouc: Palacký University.

Engel, Ulrich (1988): *Deutsche Grammatik*. Heidelberg: Julius Groos.

Erben, Johannes (1992): *Einführung in die deutsche Wortbildungslehre*. Berlin: Erich Schmidt Verlag.

Ewen, Colin J. / Harry van der Hulst (2001): *The Phonological Structure of Words: An Introduction*. Cambridge: Cambridge University Press.

Fagan, Sarah M.B. (1992): *The Syntax and Semantics of Middle Constructions: A Study with Special Reference to German*. Cambridge: Cambridge University Press.

Faltz, Leonard (1985): *Reflexivity: A Study in Universal Syntax*. New York: Garland.

Fellbaum, Christiane (1989): On the 'reflexive middle' in English. In *Papers from the Parasession on Causatives and Agentivity at the 25th Annual Regional Meeting of the Chicago Linguistic Society*, pp. 123–132.

Fischer, Klaus (1997): *German-English Verb Valency. A Contrastive Analysis*. Tübingen: Narr.

Fischer, Klaus (1999): Englische und deutsche Satzstrukturen: Ein valenztheoretischer Vergleich mit statistischen Anmerkungen. *Sprachwissenschaft* 2, 221–255.

Fischer, Klaus (2013): *Satzstrukturen im Deutschen und Englischen: Typologie und Textrealisierung*. Berlin: Akademie-Verlag.

Fisiak, Jacek (ed.) (1981): *Contrastive Linguistics and the Language Teacher*. Oxford: Pergamon.

Fleischer, Wolfgang / Irmhild Barz (1992): *Wortbildung der deutschen Gegenwartssprache*. Tübingen: Niemeyer.

Fox, Barbara / Paul Hopper (eds.) (1994): *Voice: Form and Function*. Amsterdam: Benjamins.

Frey, Werner / Karin Pittner (1999): Adverbialpositionen im deutsch-englischen Vergleich. In **Doherty, M.** (ed.), *Sprachspezifische Aspekte der Informationsverteilung*. Berlin: Akademie Verlag, pp. 14–40.

Fries, Charles C. (1945): *Teaching and Learning English as a Foreign Language*. Ann Arbor: University of Michigan Press.

Fuhrhop, Nanna (1998): *Grenzfälle morphologischer Einheiten*. Tübingen: Stauffenburg.

Gast, Volker (2006a): The distribution of *also* and *too*. A preliminary corpus study. *Zeitschrift für Anglistik und Amerikanistik* 54(2), 163–176.

Gast, Volker (2006b): *The Grammar of Identity. Intensifiers and Reflexives in Germanic Languages*. London: Routledge.

Gast, Volker (2007): *I gave it him*. On the motivation of the 'Alternative Double Object Construction' in varieties of British English. *Functions of Language* 14, 14–56.

Gast, Volker (2008a): Modal particles and context updating - the functions of German *ja, doch, wohl* and *etwa*. In **Vater, H. / O. Letnes** (eds.), *Modalverben und Grammatikalisierung*. Wissenschaftlicher Verlag, pp. 153–177.

Gast, Volker (2008b): V-N compounds in English and German. *Zeitschrift für Anglistik und Amerikanistik* 56(3), 269–282.

Gast, Volker (2010): Contrastive topics and distributed foci as instances of subinformativity: A comparison of English and German. In **Breul, C. / E. Göbbel**

(eds.), *Comparative and Contrastive Studies of Information Structure.* Amsterdam: Benjamins, pp. 15–50.

Gast, Volker (2015): On the use of translation corpora in contrastive linguistics: A case study of impersonalization in English and German. *Languages in Contrast* 15(1), 4–33.

Gast, Volker (2017): The scalar operator *even* and its German equivalents: Pragmatic factors determining the use of *auch*, *selbst* and *sogar*. In De Cesare, A.-M. (ed.), *Focus on Additivity. Multifaceted Views on Focusing Modifiers.* Amsterdam: Benjamins, pp. 201–234.

Gast, Volker / Daniel Hole (2003): On paradigmatic (in)coherence in Romance and Germanic reflexives. In Gunkel, L. / G. Müller / G. Zifonun (eds.), *Arbeiten zur Reflexivierung.* Tübingen: Niemeyer, pp. 75–90.

Gast, Volker / Natalia Levshina (2013): Motivating w(h)-clefts in English and German. A hypothesis-driven parallel corpus study. In De Cesare, A.-M. (ed.), *Frequency, Forms and Functions of Cleft Constructions in Romance and Germanic. Contrastive, Corpus-Based Studies.* Berlin: de Gruyter Mouton, pp. 377–414.

Gast, Volker / Daniel Wiechmann (2012): W(h)-Clefts im Deutschen und Englischen. Eine quantitative Untersuchung auf Grundlage des Europarl-Korpus. In Gunkel, L. / G. Zifonun (eds.), *Jahrbuch des IDS 2011.* Berlin: de Gruyter Mouton, pp. 333–362.

Geniušienė, Emma (1987): *The Typology of Reflexives.* Berlin: de Gruyter Mouton.

Giegerich, Heinz J. (1992): *English Phonology. An Introduction.* Cambridge: Cambridge University Press.

Giegerich, Heinz J. (2015): *Lexical Structures. Compounding and the Modules of Grammar.* Edinburgh: Edinburgh University Press.

Gradman, Harry (1973): *The Contrastive Analysis Hypothesis. What it is, and what it isn't.* Ann Arbor: University of Michigan Press.

Granger, Sylviane (1996): From CA to CIA and back: An integrated approach to computerised bilingual and learner corpora. In Aijmer, K. / B. Altenberg / M. Johansson (eds.), *Language in Contrast.* Lund: Lund University Press, pp. 37–51.

Granger, Sylviane (2015): Contrastive interlanguage analysis: A reappraisal. *International Journal of Learner Corpus Research* 1(1), 7–24.

Granger, Sylviane / Jacques Lerot / Stephanie Petch-Tyson (eds.) (2003): *Corpus-Based Approaches to Contrastive Linguistics and Translation Studies.* Amsterdam: Rodopi.

Gunkel, Lutz / Adriano Murelli / Susan Schlotthauer / Bernd Wiese / Gisela Zifonun (2017a): *Grammatik des Deutschen im europäischen Vergleich: Das Nominal. Teilband 1: Funktionale Domänen, Wort und Wortklassen.* Berlin: de Gruyter Mouton.

Gunkel, Lutz / Adriano Murelli / Susan Schlotthauer / Bernd Wiese / Gisela Zifonun (2017b): *Grammatik des Deutschen im europäischen Vergleich: Das Nominal. Teilband 2: Nominalflexion, nominale Syntagmen.* Berlin: de Gruyter Mouton.

Gunkel, Lutz / Gisela Zifonun (2008): Constraints on relational-adjective noun constructions. A comparative view of English, German and French. *Zeitschrift für*

Anglistik und Amerikanistik 56, 9–22.

Haftka, Brigitte (ed.) (1994): *Was determiniert Wortstellungsvariation?* Opladen: Westdeutscher Verlag.

Haider, Hubert (2000): Adverb placement – convergence of structure and licensing. *Theoretical Linguistics* 26, 95–135.

Hall, Tracy (1992): *Syllable Structure and Syllable-Related Processes in German.* Tübingen: Niemeyer.

Hall, Tracy (2000): *Phonologie: Eine Einführung.* Berlin: de Gruyter Mouton.

Hartmann, Reinhard R.K. (1996): Contrastive textology and corpus linguistics: On the value of parallel texts. *Language Sciences* 18, 947–957.

Haspelmath, Martin (1999): External possession in a European areal perspective. In **Payne, D. / I. Barshi** (eds.), *External Possession.* Amsterdam: Benjamins, pp. 109–35.

Haspelmath, Martin (2010): Comparative concepts and descriptive categories in crosslinguistic studies. *Language* 86(3), 663–687.

Haspelmath, Martin / Ekkehard König (eds.) (1995): *Converbs in Cross-Linguistic Perspective.* Berlin: de Gruyter Mouton.

Hatav, Galia (1993): The aspect system in English: An attempt at a unified analysis. *Linguistics* 31, 209–237.

Havers, Wilhelm (1911): *Untersuchungen zur Kasussyntax der indogermanischen Sprachen.* Straßburg: Trübner.

Hawkins, John (1986): *A Comparative Typology of English and German. Unifying the Contrasts.* London: Croom Helm.

Hawkins, John (1992): A performance approach to English/German contrasts. In **Mair, Ch. / M. Markus** (eds.), *New Departures in Contrastive Linguistics.* Universität Innsbruck, pp. 115–136.

Hawkins, John (1994): *A Performance Theory of Order and Constituency.* Cambridge: Cambridge University Press.

Hawkins, John (1999): Processing complexity and filler-gap dependencies across grammars. *Language* 75, 244–285.

Hawkins, John (2004): *Efficiency and Complexity in Grammars.* Oxford: Oxford University Press.

Hawkins, John (2018): Word-external properties in a typology of Modern English: A Comparison with German. *English Language and Linguistics*, 1–27. Doi: 10.1017/S1360674318000060.

Heinold, Simone (2015): *Tempus, Modus und Aspekt im Deutschen. Ein Studienbuch.* Tübingen: Narr.

Hellinger, Marlis (1977): *Kontrastive Grammatik Deutsch/Englisch.* Tübingen: Niemeyer.

Hellinger, Marlis / Ulrich Ammon (1996): *Contrastive Sociolinguistics.* Berlin: de Gruyter Mouton.

Hentschel, Elke / Petra M. Vogel (eds.) (2009): *Deutsche Morphologie.* Berlin: de Gruyter Mouton.

References

Herbst, Thomas / Susen Schüller (2008): *Introduction to Syntactic Analysis. A Valency Approach*. Tübingen: Narr.

Heyvaert, Liesbeth (2003): *A Cognitive-Functional Approach to Nominalization in English*. Berlin: de Gruyter Mouton.

Hickey, Raymond (2012): Early English and the Celtic Hypothesis. In **Nevalainen, T. / E. C. Traugott** (eds.), *The Oxford Handbook of the History of English*. Oxford: Oxford University Press, pp. 497–507.

Hole, Daniel (2002): Agentive *selbst* in German. In **Katz, G. / S. Reinhard / P. Reuter** (eds.), *Sinn und Bedeutung VI – Proceedings of the 6th Annual Meeting of the Gesellschaft für Semantik*. Osnabrück: Institute of Cognitive Science, pp. 133–150.

Hole, Daniel (2014): *Dativ, Bindung und Diathese*. Berlin: de Gruyter Mouton.

Hole, Daniel (2015): Arguments and adjuncts. In **Kiss, T. / A. Alexiadou** (eds.), *Syntax. Theory and Analysis. An International Handbook*. Handbooks of Linguistics and Communication, No 42/2. Berlin, New York: de Gruyter Mouton, pp. 1285–1321.

Huddleston, Rodney (1984): *Introduction to the Grammar of English*. Cambridge: Cambridge University Press.

Huddleston, Rodney / Geoffrey Pullum (2002): *The Cambridge Grammar of the English Language*. Cambridge: Cambridge University Press.

Hudson, Richard (1995): Does English really have case? *Journal of Linguistics* 31, 375–392.

Hundt, Marianne (2001): What corpora tell us about the grammaticalisation of voice in *get*-constructions. *Studies in Language* 25(1), 49–87.

Hundt, Marianne (2007): *English Mediopassive Constructions. A Cognitive, Corpus-Based Study of their Origin, Spread and Current Status*. Amsterdam: Rodopi.

Ingham, Richard P. (ed.) (2010): *The Anglo-Norman Language and its Contexts*. York: York Medieval Press.

Ingham, Richard P. (2012): *The Transmission of Anglo-Norman. Language History and Language Acquisition*. Amsterdam: Benjamins.

James, Carl (1980): *Contrastive Analysis*. Harlow: Longman.

James, Carl (2005): Contrastive analysis and the language learner. In **Allerton, D.J. / C. Tschichold / J. Wieser** (eds.), *Linguistics, Language Teaching and Language Learning*. Basel: Schwabe, pp. 1–20.

Johansson, Stig (1998): On the role of corpora in cross-linguistic research. In **Johansson, S. / S. Oksefjell** (eds.), *Corpora and Cross-Linguistic Research: Theory, Method, and Case Studies*. Amsterdam / Atlanta: Rodopi, pp. 3–24.

Kamińska, Tatiana Ewa (1995): *Problems in Scottish English Phonology*. Linguistische Arbeiten, No 328. Tübingen: Niemeyer.

Kaufmann, Ingrid (2004): *Medium und Reflexiv – Eine Studie zur Verbsemantik*. Tübingen: Niemeyer.

Keenan, Edward (1976): Towards a universal definition of 'subject'. In **Li, C.** (ed.), *Subject and Topic*. New York: Academic Press, pp. 303–330.

Keenan, Edward (2002): Explaining the creation of reflexive pronouns in English. In **Minkova, D. / R. Stockwell** (eds.), *Studies in the History of the English Language: A Millenial Perspective*. Berlin & New York: de Gruyter Mouton, pp. 325–354.

Kemmer, Suzanne (1993): *The Middle Voice*. Amsterdam: Benjamins.

Klein, Wolfgang (1994): *Time in Language*. London: Routledge.

König, Ekkehard (1980): On the context dependence of the progressive in English. In **Rohrer, C.** (ed.), *Time, Tense and Quantifiers*. Tübingen: Niemeyer, pp. 269–91.

König, Ekkehard (1982): Scalar particles in German and their English equivalents. In **Lohnes, F.W. / E.A. Hopkins** (eds.), *The Contrastive Grammar of English and German*. Ann Arbor: Karoma Publishers, pp. 76–101.

König, Ekkehard (1987): Towards a typological characterization of English: Some traditional and some recent proposals. In **Böhm, R. / H. Wode** (eds.), *Anglistentag 1986. Kiel. Vorträge*. Gießen: Hoffmann Verlag, pp. 229–244.

König, Ekkehard (1990): Kontrastive Linguistik als Komplement zur Typologie. In **Gnutzmann, Claus** (ed.), *Kontrastive Linguistik*. Frankfurt am Main: Lang, pp. 117–131.

König, Ekkehard (1991): *The Meaning of Focus Particles. A Comparative Perspective*. London: Routledge.

König, Ekkehard (1995): He is being obscure: Non-verbal predication and the progressive. In **Bertinetto, P.-M. / V. Bianchi / J. Higginbotham / M. Squartini** (eds.), *Temporal Reference, Aspect and Actionality*. Torino: Rosenberg & Sellier, pp. 155–68.

König, Ekkehard (1996): Kontrastive Grammatik und Typologie. In **Lang, E. / G. Zifonun** (eds.), *Deutsch typologisch*. Berlin: de Gruyter Mouton, pp. 31–54.

König, Ekkehard (2001): Internal and external possessors. In **Haspelmath, M. / E. König / W. Raible / W. Oesterreicher** (eds.), *Language Typology and Language Universals – An International Handbook*. Berlin: de Gruyter Mouton, pp. 970–78.

König, Ekkehard (2012): Contrastive linguistics and language comparison. *Languages in Contrast* 12(1), 3–26.

König, Ekkehard / Volker Gast (2002): Reflexive pronouns and other uses of *self*-forms in English. In **König, E. / V. Gast** (eds.), *Intensifiers and Reflexives – the Use of Self-forms in English*. Special issue of the *Zeitschrift für Anglistik und Amerikanistik*, 50.3 Tübingen: Stauffenburg, pp. 225–38.

König, Ekkehard / Volker Gast (2006): Focused expressions of identity – a typology of intensifiers. *Linguistic Typology* 10(2), 223–276.

König, Ekkehard / Martin Haspelmath (1997): Les constructions à possesseur externe dans les langues de l'Europe. In **Feuillet, J.** (ed.), *Actance et Valence dans les langues de l'Europe*. Berlin: de Gruyter Mouton, pp. 525–606.

König, Ekkehard / Peter Siemund (1996): *Selbst*-Reflektionen. In **Harras, G.** (ed.), *Wenn die Semantik arbeitet – Festschrift für Klaus Baumgärtner*. Tübingen: Niemeyer, pp. 277–302.

König, Ekkehard / Peter Siemund (1999): Intensifikatoren und Topikalisierung: Kontrastive Beobachtungen zum Deutschen, Englischen und anderen germanischen

Sprachen. In **Wegener, Heide** (ed.), *Deutsch kontrastiv*. Tübingen: Stauffenburg, pp. 87–110.

König, Ekkehard / Peter Siemund (2000a): The development of complex reflexives and intensifiers in English. *Diachronica* XVII(1), 39–84.

König, Ekkehard / Peter Siemund (2000b): Intensifiers and reflexives – a typological perspective. In **Frajzyngier, Z. / T. Curl** (eds.), *Reflexives – Forms and Functions*. Amsterdam: Benjamins, pp. 41–74.

König, Ekkehard / Peter Siemund (2000c): Locally free *self*-forms, logophoricity and intensification in English. *English Language and Linguistics* 4(2), 183–204.

König, Ekkehard / Detlev Stark / Susanne Requardt (1990): *Adverbien und Partikeln. Ein deutsch-englisches Wörterbuch*. Heidelberg: Julius Groos.

König, Ekkehard / Letizia Vezzosi (2004): The role of predicate meaning in the development of reflexivity. In **Bisang, W. / N. Himmelmann / B. Wiemer** (eds.), *What Makes Grammaticalization? A Look from its Fringes and its Components*. Berlin: de Gruyter Mouton, pp. 214–244.

Köpcke, Klaus-Michael (1982): *Untersuchungen zum Genussystem der deutschen Gegenwartssprache*. Tübingen: Niemeyer.

Kortmann, Bernd (1991): *Free Adjuncts and Absolutes in English*. London: Routledge.

Kortmann, Bernd (1988): Freie Adjunkte und absolute Konstruktionen im Englischen und Deutschen. *Papiere zur Linguistik* 38(1), 61–89.

Kortmann, Bernd (1996): Kontrastive Linguistik und Fremdsprachenunterricht. In **Börner, W. / K. Vogel** (eds.), *Kontrast und Äquivalenz. Beiträge zu Sprachvergleich und Übersetzung*. Tübingen: Narr, pp. 136–167.

Kortmann, Bernd / Ekkehard König (1992): Categorial reanalysis: The case of deverbal prepositions. *Linguistics* 30, 671–697.

Kortmann, Bernd / Paul Georg Meyer (1992): Is English grammar more explicit than German grammar, after all? In **Mair, C. / M. Markus** (eds.), *New Departures in Contrastive Linguistics/Neue Ansätze in der kontrastiven Linguistik*. Innsbruck: Institut für Anglistik, pp. 155–165.

Kortmann, Bernd / Edgar Schneider / Kate Burridge / Rajend Mesthrie / Clive Upton (2004): *A Handbook of Varieties of English*. 2 Vols. Berlin: de Gruyter Mouton.

Koster, Jan (1999): The word orders of English and Dutch: Collective vs. individual checking. In **Abraham, W.** (ed.), *Groninger Arbeiten zur Germanistischen Linguistik*. University of Groningen, pp. 1–42.

Koster, Jan (2000): Pied piping and the word orders of English and Dutch. In **M. Hirotani, N. Hall, A. Coetzee / J.-Y. Kim** (eds.), *Proceedings of the North East Linguistic Society*. GLSA, Amherst, Massachusetts, pp. 415–26.

Krause, Olaf (2002): *Progressiv im Deutschen. Eine empirische Untersuchung im Kontrast mit Niederländisch und Englisch*. Tübingen: Niemeyer.

Kreidler, Charles W. (1997): *Describing Spoken English: An Introduction*. London: Routledge.

Kreidler, Charles W. (2004): *The Pronunciation of English: A Course Book*. 2nd edn. Malden: Blackwell.

Krohn, Dieter (1980): *Dativ und Pertinenzrelation*. Gothenburg: Acta Universitatis Gothenburgensis.

Krug, Manfred (1998): Englisch-deutsche Korpusanalysen: Kontrastive und diachrone Aspekte und ihre Relevanz im universitären Sprachunterricht. In **Börner, W.** / **K. Vogel** (eds.), *Kontrast und Äquivalenz. Beiträge zu Sprachvergleich und Übersetzung*. Tübingen: Narr, pp. 168–193.

Kufner, Herbert L. (1962): *The Grammatical Structures of English and German*. Chicago: University of Chicago Press.

Kufner, Herbert L. (1971): *Kontrastive Phonologie Deutsch-Englisch*. Stuttgart: Klett.

Kunz, Kerstin (2010): *English and German Nominal Co-Reference. A Study of Political Essays*. Frankfurt: Lang.

Kunz, Kerstin (2015): *Cohesion in English and German. A Corpus-Based Approach to Language Contrast, Register Variation and Translation*. Habilitationsschrift, Universität des Saarlandes.

Kunze, Jürgen (1996): Plain middles and *lassen*-middles in German: Reflexive constructions and sentence perspective. *Linguistics* 34, 645–95.

Lado, Robert (1957): *Linguistics across Cultures*. Ann Arbor: University of Michigan Press.

Ladusaw, William (1979): Polarity Sensitivity as Inherent Scope Relations. Ph.D. thesis, University of Texas at Austin.

Laffut, An (2006): *Three-participant Constructions in English*. Amsterdam: Benjamins.

Lang, Ewald / Gisela Zifonun (eds.) (1996): *Deutsch typologisch*. Berlin: de Gruyter Mouton.

Larsson, Richard (1988): On the double object construction. *Linguistic Inquiry* 19, 335–391.

Leech, Geoffrey (1971): *Meaning and the English Verb*. London: Longman.

Lehmann, Christian (2008): Roots, stems and word classes. *Studies in Language* 32, 546–567.

Leirbukt, Oddleif (1997): *Untersuchungen zum bekommen-Passiv im heutigen Deutsch*. Tübingen: Niemeyer.

Leisi, Ernst (1975): *Der Wortinhalt. Seine Struktur im Deutschen und Englischen*. 5th edn. Heidelberg: Quelle & Meyer.

Lenerz, Jürgen (1977): *Zur Abfolge nominaler Satzglieder im Deutschen*. Tübingen: Narr.

Levin, Beth (1993): *English Verb Classes and Alternations*. Chicago: University of Chicago Press.

Ljung, Magnus (1980): *Reflections on the English Progressive*. Göteborg: Acta Universitatis Gothoburgensis.

Lohnes, Walter / Edwin Hopkins (eds.) (1982): *The Contrastive Grammar of English and German*. Ann Arbor: Karoma.

Maché, Jakob (forthcoming): *On Black Magic. How Epistemic Modifiers Emerge*. Berlin: de Gruyter Mouton.

References

Mair, Christian (1992): A contrastive analysis of object control in English and German. *Papers and Studies in Contrastive Linguistics* 25, 85–101.

Mair, Christian (2005): Recent advances in contrastive linguistics and language typology: The spin-off for language teachers. In **Allerton, D.J.** / **C. Tschichold** / **J. Wieser** (eds.), *Linguistics, Language Teaching and Language Learning*. Basel: Schwabe, pp. 21–39.

Mair, Christian / **Manfred Markus** (eds.) (1992): *New Departures in Contrastive Linguistics/Neue Ansätze in der kontrastiven Linguistik*. Proceedings of a conference held at the Leopold-Franzens-University of Innsbruck, Austria, 10-12 May 1991. 2 Volumes. Innsbruck: Institut für Anglistik.

Marchand, Hans (1969): *The Categories and Types of Present-Day English Word Formation*. München: Beck'sche Verlagsbuchhandlung.

McCawley, James (1971): Tense and time reference in English. In **Fillmore, C.** / **T. Langendoen** (eds.), *Studies in Linguistic Semantics*. New York: Holt, pp. 97–113.

Meillet, Antoine (1903): *Introduction à l'étude comparative des langues indo-européennes*. Paris: Hachette.

Miller, Jim (2004): Scotish English: Morphology and Syntax. In **Kortmann, B.** / **E. Schneider** (eds.), *A Handbook of Varieties of English*. Berlin: de Gruyter Mouton, pp. 47–72.

Mondorf, Britta (2007): Recalcitrant problems of comparative alternation and new insights emerging from internet data. In **Hundt, M.** / **N. Nesselhauf** / **C. Biewer** (eds.), *Corpus Linguistics and the Web*. Amsterdam: Rodopi, pp. 211–232.

Mondorf, Britta (2009): *More Support for More-Support: The Role of Processing Constraints on the Choice between Synthetic and Analytic Forms*. Amsterdam: Benjamins.

Moravcsik, Edith (2013): *Introducing Language Typology*. Cambridge: Cambridge University Press.

Moulton, William G. (1962): *The Sounds of English and German*. Chicago: University of Chicago Press.

Müller, Stefan (2002): *Complex Predicates: Verbal Complexes, Resultative Constructions, and Particle Verbs in German*. Studies in Constraint-based Lexicalism, Vol. 13. Stanford: CSLI Publications.

Müller, Stefan (2005): Zur Analyse der scheinbar mehrfachen Vorfeldbesetzung. *Linguistische Berichte* 203, 29–62.

Nemser, William (1971): *An Experimental Study of Phonological Interference in the English of Hungarians*. Bloomington: Indiana University Press.

Neumann, Stella (2013): *Contrastive Register Variation: A Quantitative Approach to the Comparison of English and German*. Berlin: de Gruyter Mouton.

Newmark, Leonard / **David Reibel** (1968): Necessity and sufficiency in language learning. *IRAL* 6(2), 145–64.

Nickel, Gerhard (ed.) (1971): *Papers in Contrastive Linguistics*. Cambridge: Cambridge University Press.

Öhlschläger, Günther (1989): *Zur Syntax und Semantik der Modalverben des Deutschen*. Tübingen: Niemeyer.

Oleksy, Wieslaw (ed.) (1989): *Contrastive Pragmatics*. Amsterdam: Benjamins.

Palmer, Frank (1990): *Modality and the English Modals*. 2nd edn. London: Longman.

Palmer, Frank (2001): *Mood and Modality*. 2nd edn. Cambridge: Cambridge University Press.

Panther, Klaus-Uwe / Klaus-Michael Köpcke (1991): Kontrolle und Kontrollwechsel im Deutschen. *Zeitschrift für Phonetik, Sprachwissenschaft und Kommunikationsforschung* 44, 143–66.

Panther, Klaus-Uwe / Klaus-Michael Köpcke (1993): A cognitive approach to obligatory control phenomena in English and German. *Folia Linguistica* 27, 57–105.

Payne, Doris / Immanuel Barshi (eds.) (1999): *The Grammar of External Possession*. Amsterdam: Benjamins.

Plag, Ingo (2003): *Word Formation in English*. Cambridge: Cambridge University Press.

Plank, Frans (1979a): Exklusivierung, Reflexivierung, Identifizierung, relationale Auszeichnung. Variationen zu einem semantisch-pragmatischen Thema. In **Rosengren, I.** (ed.), *Sprache und Pragmatik. Lunder Symposium 1978*. Malmö: Gleerup, pp. 330–54.

Plank, Frans (1979b): Zur Affinität von *selbst* und *auch*. In **Weydt, H.** (ed.), *Die Partikeln der deutschen Sprache*. Berlin: de Gruyter, pp. 269–284.

Plank, Frans (1984): Verbs and objects in semantic agreement: Minor differences between English and German that might suggest a major one. *Journal of Semantics* 3, 305–60.

Plank, Frans (1987): Direkte indirekte Objekte, oder: Was uns *lehren* lehrt. *Leuvense Bijdragen* 76, 37–61.

Poussa, Patricia (1982): The evolution of Early Standard English: The Creolization Hypothesis. *Studia Anglia Posnaniensia* 14, 69–85.

Purves, Alan C. (ed.) (1988): *Writing across Languages and Cultures: Issues in Contrastive Rhetoric*. Newbury Park: Sage Publications.

Quirk, Randolph / Sidney Greenbaum / Geoffrey Leech / Jan Svartvik (1985): *A Comprehensive Grammar of the English Language*. London: Longman.

Reichenbach, Hans (1947): *Elements of Symbolic Logic*. New York: Macmillan.

Rein, Kurt (1983): *Einführung in die kontrastive Linguistik*. Darmstadt: Wissenschaftliche Buchgesellschaft.

Reinhart, Tanya / Eric Reuland (1993): Reflexivity. *Linguistic Inquiry* 24, 657–720.

Reis, Marga (ed.) (1993): *Wortstellung und Informationsstruktur*. Tübingen: Niemeyer.

Rinas, Karsten (2006): *Die Abtönungspartikeln* doch *und* ja. *Semantik, Idiomatisierung, Kombinationen, tschechische Äquivalente*. Frankfurt: Lang.

Roach, Peter (2010): *English Phonetics and Phonology: A Practical Course*. 4th edn. Cambridge: Cambridge University Press.

Rohdenburg, Günter (1974): *Sekundäre Subjektivierungen im Englischen und Deutschen. Vergleichende Untersuchungen zur Verb- und Adjektivsyntax*. Bielefeld: Cornelsen-Velhaben & Klasing.

Rohdenburg, Günter (1990): Aspekte einer vergleichenden Typologie des Englischen und Deutschen. Kritische Anmerkungen zu einem Buch von John A. Hawkins. In **Gnutzmann, C.** (ed.), *Kontrastive Linguistik*. Frankfurt: Lang, pp. 133–152.

Rohdenburg, Günter (1992): Bemerkungen zu infiniten Konstruktionen im Englischen und Deutschen. In **Mair, Ch. / M. Markus** (eds.), *New Departures in Contrastive Linguistics*. Universität Innsbruck, pp. 187–207.

Rohdenburg, Günter (1996): Cognitive complexity and increased grammatical explicitness in English. *Cognitive Linguistics* 7, 149–182.

Rohdenburg, Günter (2000): The complexity principle as a factor determining grammatical variation and change in English. In **Plag, I. / K. P. Schneider** (eds.), *Language Use, Language Acquisition and Language History: (Mostly) Empirical Studies in Honour of Rüdiger Zimmermann*. Trier: Wissenschaftlicher Verlag, pp. 25–44.

Rohdenburg, Günter (2008): Measure phrases in English and German. *Zeitschrift für Anglistik und Amerikanistik* 56(3), 215–236.

Rohdenburg, Günther (2016): Testing two processing principles with respect to the extraction of elements out of complement clauses in English. *English Language and Linguistics* 20(3), 463–486.

Rohdenburg, Günter / Julia Schlüter (2009): New departures in the contrastive study of British and American English grammar. In **Rohdenburg, G. / J. Schlüter** (eds.), *One Language, Two Grammars? Differences between British and American English*. Cambridge: Cambridge University Press, pp. 364–423.

Schäfer, Roland (2016): *Einführung in die grammatische Beschreibung des Deutschen*. 2nd edn. Language Science Press.

Scheffer, Johannes (1975): *The Progressive in English*. Amsterdam: North-Holland.

Schlüter, Julia (2009): The conditional subjunctive. In **Rohdenburg, G / J. Schlüter** (eds.), *One Language – Two Grammars? Differences between British and American English*. Cambridge: Cambridge University Press, pp. 277–305.

Schmid, Hans-Jörg (2011): *English Morphology and Word Formation: An Introduction*. 2nd edn. Berlin: Erich Schmidt Verlag.

Schopf, Alfred (ed.) (1974): *Der englische Aspekt*. Darmstadt: Wissenschaftliche Buchgesellschaft.

Scollon, Ron / Suzanne Wong Scollon (1995): *Intercultural Communication: A Discourse Approach*. Oxford: Blackwell.

Selinker, Larry (1972): Interlanguage. *International Review of Applied Linguistics* 10, 209–231.

Shibatani, Masayoshi (1985): Passives and related constructions. *Language* 61, 821–48.

Siemund, Peter (1998): Reflexivität und Intensivierung: Ein deutsch-englischer Vergleich. In **Börner, W. / K. Vogel** (eds.), *Kontrast und Äquivalenz. Beiträge zu Sprachvergleich und Übersetzung*. Tübingen: Narr, pp. 281–302.

Siemund, Peter (2000): *Intensifiers in English and German – A Comparison*. London: Routledge.

Siemund, Peter (2004): Analytische und synthetische Tendenzen in der Entwicklung des Englischen. In Hinrichs, U. (ed.), *Die europäischen Sprachen auf dem Wege zum analytischen Sprachtyp*. Wiesbaden: Harrassowitz, pp. 169–96.

Siemund, Peter (2008): *Pronominal Gender in English: A Study of English Varieties from a Cross-Linguistic Perspective*. London: Routledge.

Siemund, Peter (2013): *Varieties of English: A Typological Approach*. Cambridge: Cambridge University Press.

Siewierska, Anna (1984): *The Passive: A Comparative Linguistic Analysis*. London: Croom Helm.

Sinclair, John / Jonathan Payne / Chantal Pérez Hernández (1996): Corpus to corpus: A study of translation equivalence. *International Journal of Lexicography* 9(3), 171–178.

Song, Jae Jung (ed.) (2010): *The Oxford Handbook of Linguistic Typology*. Oxford: Oxford University Press.

Steinbach, Markus (2002): *Middle Voice. A Comparative Study in the Syntax-Semantics Interface of German*. Amsterdam: Benjamins.

Steiner, Erich (2017): Methodological cross-fertilization: Empirical methodologies in (computational) linguistics and translation studies. In Czulo, O. / S. Hansen-Schirra (eds.), *Crossroads Between Contrastive Linguistics, Translation Studies and Machine Translation*. Berlin: Language Science Press, pp. 65–90.

Storrer, Angelika (2003): Ergänzungen und Angaben. In Ágel, V. / L.M. Eichinger / H.-W. Eroms / P. Hellwig / H.J. Heringer / H. Lobin (eds.), *Dependenz und Valenz. Ein internationales Handbuch der zeitgenössischen Forschung*, Vol. 1. Berlin: de Gruyter Mouton, pp. 764–780.

Svartvik, Jan (ed.) (1966): *On Voice in the English Verb*. The Hague: Mouton.

Szigeti, Imre (2017): *Derivation*. Heidelberg: Universitätsverlag Winter.

Tagliamonte, Sali A. / Rika Ito (2002): Think "really different": Continuity and specialization in the English dual form adverbs. *Journal of Sociolinguistics* 6, 236–267.

Takami, Ken-Ichi (1992): *Preposition Stranding: From Syntactics to Functional Analyses*. Berlin: de Gruyter Mouton.

Talmy, Leonard (1975): Semantics and syntax of motion. In Kimball, J.P. (ed.), *Syntax and Semantics*, Vol. 4. New York: Academic Press, pp. 181–238.

Talmy, Leonard (1985): Lexicalization patterns: Semantic structure in lexical forms. In Shopen, T. (ed.), *Language Typology and Syntactic Description 3: Grammatical Categories and the Lexicon*. Cambridge: Cambridge University Press, pp. 57–149.

Thieroff, Rolf (1992): *Das finite Verb im Deutschen: Tempus, Modus, Distanz*. Tübingen: Narr.

Uhrig, Peter (2018): *Subjects in English*. Berlin: de Gruyter Mouton.

van der Auwera, Johan (2012): From contrastive linguistics to linguistic typology. *Languages in Contrast* 12(1), 69–86.

References

van der Auwera, Johan / Volker Gast / Jeroen Vanderbiesen (2012): Human impersonal pronouns in English, Dutch and German. *Leuvense Bijdragen* 98(1), 27–64.

van Gelderen, Elly (2000): *A History of English Reflexive Pronouns – Person, Self, and Interpretability.* Amsterdam: Benjamins.

Vendler, Zeno (1967): *Linguistics in Philosophy.* Ithaca: Cornell University Press.

von der Gabelentz, Georg (1901): *Die Sprachwissenschaft: Ihre Aufgaben, Methoden, und bisherigen Ergebnisse.* Leipzig: Weigel.

Wagner, Susanne (2003): Gendered Pronouns in English Dialects – Myth and Reality. Ph.D. thesis, University of Freiburg.

Wagner, Susanne (2004): 'Gendered' pronouns in English dialects – a typological perspective. In Kortmann, B. (ed.), *Dialectology meets Typology.* Berlin: de Gruyter Mouton, pp. 479–496.

Wardhaugh, Ronald (1970): The contrastive analysis hypothesis. *TESOL Quarterly* 4(2), 123–130.

Wegener, Heide (1985): *Der Dativ im heutigen Deutsch.* Tübingen: Narr.

Wegener, Heide (1995): *Die Nominalflexion des Deutschen – verstanden als Lerngegenstand.* Tübingen: Niemeyer.

Wegener, Heide (1999): Die Pluralbildung im Deutschen – ein Versuch im Rahmen der Optimalitätstheorie. *Linguistik Online* 4.

Wegener, Heide (2006): Das Hühnerei vor der Hundehütte: Von der Notwendigkeit historischen Wissens in der Grammatikographie des Deutschen. In Berner, E. / M. Böhm / A. Voeste (eds.), *Ein gross und narhafft haffen. Festschrift für Joachim Gessinger.* Potsdam: Universitätsverlag, pp. 175–187.

Weinreich, Uriel (1953): *Languages in Contact. Findings and Problems.* New York: Linguistic Circle of New York.

Welke, Klaus (2005): *Tempus im Deutschen. Eine Rekonstruktion eines semantischen Systems.* Berlin: Walter de Gruyter.

Wienold, Götz (1973): *Die Erlernbarkeit der Sprachen.* München: Kösel.

Wierzbicka, Anna (1985): Different cultures, different languages, different speech acts. *Journal of Pragmatics* 9(2/3), 145–178.

Wierzbicka, Anna (1992): *Cross-Cultural Pragmatics: The Semantics of Human Interaction.* Berlin: de Gruyter Mouton.

Wiese, Richard (1996): *The Phonology of German.* Oxford: Clarendon Press.

Wittgenstein, Ludwig (1953): *Philosophische Untersuchungen.* Frankfurt am Main: Suhrkamp.

Xiao, Richard (2010): *Using Corpora in Contrastive and Translation Studies.* Cambridge: Cambridge Scholars.

Zifonun, Gisela / Ludger Hoffman / Bruno Strecker (1997): *Grammatik der deutschen Sprache. 3 Vols.* Berlin/New York: de Gruyter Mouton.

Zribi-Hertz, Anne (1989): Anaphor binding and narrative point of view: English reflexive pronouns in sentence and discourse. *Language* 65, 695–727.

Zubin, David / Klaus-Michael Köpcke (1989): Affect classification in the German gender system. *Lingua* 63, 41–96.

Sources

BNC   British National Corpus.

LH   Virginia Woolf, *Lighthouse*. Oxford: Oxford UP, 1992.

LLELC Longman/Lancaster English Language Corpus.

PFA   Elizabeth George, *Playing for the Ashes*. London: Bantam, 1992.

PN   David Lodge, *Paradise News*. London: Penguin, 1992.

WSM   Elizabeth George, *Well-Schooled in Murder*. London: Bantam, 1992.

Author index

Subject index